IN FROM THE COLD

REFLECTIONS ON AUSTRALIA'S KOREAN WAR

IN FROM THE COLD

REFLECTIONS ON AUSTRALIA'S KOREAN WAR

EDITED BY JOHN BLAXLAND,
MICHAEL KELLY AND
LIAM BREWIN HIGGINS

Published by ANU Press
The Australian National University
Acton ACT 2601, Australia
Email: anupress@anu.edu.au

Available to download for free at press.anu.edu.au

ISBN (print): 9781760462727
ISBN (online): 9781760462734

WorldCat (print): 1140933889
WorldCat (online): 1140933931

DOI: 10.22459/IFTC.2019

This title is published under a Creative Commons Attribution-NonCommercial-NoDerivatives 4.0 International (CC BY-NC-ND 4.0).

The full licence terms are available at creativecommons.org/licenses/by-nc-nd/4.0/legalcode

Cover design and layout by ANU Press.

Cover photograph: The story of a patrol 15 miles into enemy territory, c. 1951. Photographer: A. Gulliver. Source: Argus Newspaper Collection of Photographs, State Library of Victoria.

This edition © 2020 ANU Press

CONTENTS

Acknowledgements vii
List of maps and figures ix
Maps xiii
Chronology. xix
Contributors xxvii
Glossary. xxxiii
Introduction 1
John Blaxland

Part 1. Politics by other means: Strategic aims and responses

1. Setting a new paradigm in world order: The United Nations action in Korea 29
   Robert O'Neill
2. The Korean War: Which one? When? 49
   Allan Millett
3. China's war for Korea: Geostrategic decisions, war-fighting experience and high-priced benefits from intervention, 1950–53. 61
   Xiaobing Li
4. Fighting in the giants' playground: Australians in the Korean War 87
   Cameron Forbes
5. The transformation of the Republic of Korea Army: Wartime expansion and doctrine changes, 1951–53 97
   Jongnam Na

Part 2. Korean skies and Korean waters

6. The air war in Korea: Coalition air power in the context of limited war 121
   Richard Hallion

7. Offensive air operations over Korea: The first challenge for Australian naval aviation 143
Jack McAffrie

Part 3. From generals to lieutenants: Command in the war

8. Australian higher command in the Korean War: The experience of Brigadier John Wilton. 165
David Horner

9. The reliving of minor tactics: Reflections of a platoon commander's war in Korea. 183
Colin Kahn

Part 4. The war on the ground

10. The Battle of Maryang San: Australia's finest feat of arms in the Korean War?. 205
Bob Breen

11. Conquering Kowang San, Assaulting United: Myth and misunderstanding in the shade of Maryang San, October 1951. 217
Nigel Steel

12. The Battle for Hill 317 (Maryang San): One man's account 235
William Purves

13. The Samichon: A final barb in the Hook, 24–27 July 1953 245
Michael Kelly

14. Continuing the legacy and beginning a new era: Australian nursing in the Korean War 259
Rebecca Fleming

Part 5. Legacies

15. From Korea to Vietnam: Australian strategic policy after the Korean War 279
Peter Edwards

16. China and the Koreas: An Australian perspective 289
Rowan Callick

Conclusion: Korea armistice and reflections for the twenty-first century. 301
John Blaxland

Appendix 311

Index 313

ACKNOWLEDGEMENTS

This publication is the result of a close collaboration between the Australian War Memorial (AWM), and the Strategic and Defence Studies Centre (SDSC) within the Coral Bell School of Asia Pacific Affairs as part of the College of Asia and the Pacific at The Australian National University (ANU). *In from the Cold: Reflections on Australia's Korean War* is based largely on the papers presented at the 'Korea: In from the cold', international military history conference that took place between 6 and 7 October 2011 at the AWM. We would like to thank Dr Peter Pedersen, whose singular vision in bringing together an international cast of veterans and academics delivered a conference that was truly unique.

The success of a book like this hinges on the quality of its contributors. We would like to sincerely thank the Australian and international presenters whose papers covered the Korean War from both sides of the wire and viewed the war from the land, air and sea: Professor Robert O'Neill AO, Professor Allan Millett, Professor Xiaobing Li, Cameron Forbes, Dr Jongnam Na, Dr Richard P. Hallion, Commodore Jack McCaffrie RAN (retd), Rowan Callick, Professor David Horner, Brigadier Colin Kahn DSO AO, Dr Bob Breen, Sir William Purves CBE DSO GBM, Nigel Steel, Brigadier Jim Shelton DSO MC, Lieutenant Colonel Maurie Pears MC, Lieutenant Colonel Alf Argent, Dr Rebecca Fleming and Dr Peter Edwards. The book is a reflection of the diverse gathering of veterans, scholars and journalists whose perspectives have been at all times informative and engaging.

We would like to sincerely thank all the staff at the AWM and ANU College of Asia and the Pacific who assisted and contributed to the book for their support. In particular, we would like to thank the wonderfully talented Kay Dancey and Jenny Sheehan at CartoGIS services at the ANU College of Asia and the Pacific for their efforts in creating the maps. The publication has also benefited greatly from the extensive work done by the Military History section at the AWM. In particular, we would like to acknowledge Duncan Beard, Emma Campbell, Ashley Ekins, Lachlan Grant, Meleah Hampton, Karl James, Aaron Pegram, Thomas Rogers, David Sutton and Christina Zizzis. Andrew McDonald also cannot be thanked enough for his work transcribing, editing and liaising with authors and for his unfailing support and advice throughout. We also acknowledge the extensive assistance of Ron Schroer throughout the publication process. Special thanks are also due to our copy-editor, Cathryn Game. The Military History Section would also like to acknowledge Steve and Ruth Lambert, and thank them for their ongoing support of the AWM.

The book draws on the seminal research and findings of the Australian official historian of the Korean War Professor Robert O'Neill, and we thank him for his ongoing support and enthusiasm for the project. In addition, this book would not have been possible without the generous support and publishing guidance from Emily Tinker, Dr Greg Raymond and the publishing team at ANU Press.

We would like to acknowledge and thank our families for their ongoing support, without which this book would not have happened.

John Blaxland
Michael Kelly
Liam Brewin Higgins

LIST OF MAPS AND FIGURES

Map 1. The United Nations Command counter-offensive, September–November 1950. xiv

Map 2. Korean Peninsula highlighting major actions fought by Australians, 1950–53. xv

Map 3. Positions held by the United States Eighth Army, 15 March 1952 xvi

Map 4. Brigade dispositions of the 1st Commonwealth Division during the final weeks of the war, June–July 1953 xvii

Squadron Leader Ronald Rankin (second left) and Major Stuart Peach (right) travelled to the 38th parallel in June 1950. Their report assisted the United Nations Security Council's decision to aid the Republic of Korea. 25

General Douglas MacArthur was the driving force behind the initial UN response to North Korea. His decision to invade North Korea would have fateful consequences for the outcome of the war. 26

China's entry into the Korean War caught the United Nations Command by surprise and forced the UN and South Korean troops to withdraw from near the Chinese border back beyond Seoul 26

The Republic of Korea Army recovered quickly from its mauling by North Korea and became a battle-hardened and effective force . . . 27

ANZUS saw Australia, New Zealand and the United States form a defence pact for the Pacific region. For Australia, the treaty offered some protection against any future Chinese or Soviet aggression 27

Australian soldiers were initially not equipped to deal with the onset of the Korean winter. The deficit was made up from US and British stores. Private Ian 'Robbie' Robertson, a member of 3RAR's sniper section, wears a mixture of British and US winter kit, c. November 1950 28

The RAAF transitioned to jet fighters during the Korean War. The Meteor F.8 was outclassed by the MiG-15 in dogfights, but it was an excellent ground attack platform 119

The RAN Fleet Air Arm's 21st Carrier Air Group, flying Sea Fury and Firefly aircraft off the deck of HMAS *Sydney* (III), conducted 2,366 sorties over a period of 64 days during the latter months of 1951............................. 120

HMAS *Sydney* (III)'s deployment to Korean waters was the first time a dominion carrier had been deployed on active service. It was the only time *Sydney* saw active service as an aircraft carrier 120

Senior Australian army officers in Korea, c. April 1953........... 163

The dogged defence by Australians, Canadians and New Zealanders at Kapyong was instrumental in blunting the Chinese drive on Seoul, and helped to save the city from falling into communist hands again 164

New Zealand artillerymen provided accurate and devastating firepower in attack and defence to various nationalities of the United Nations Command 197

Lieutenant Colonel Frank Hassett (centre) took over 3RAR during a period of change and, with support of his junior officers, welded the battalion into a fine fighting unit 198

In the early hours of 3 October 1951, the start of Operation Commando, A and B Companies, 3RAR, crossed this valley floor and captured Hill 199 198

British units in Korea were brought up to strength with national servicemen and men from other battalions. Private Bill Speakman of the Argyll and Sutherland Highlanders served with the King's Own Scottish Borderers and was awarded the Victoria Cross 199

Wounded soldiers were often sent to Japan for further treatment and convalescence. Pictured is Second Lieutenant William Purves of the King's Own Scottish Borderers, resting at the Commonwealth Forces Convalescent Depot in Kure, Japan... 200

Captain Perditta 'Dita' McCarthy, of the Royal Australian Army Nursing Service, served at the British Commonwealth General Hospital at Kure during the Korean War and took part in aeromedical evacuation flights to Korea 201

Sister Betty Washington, of the Royal Australian Air Force Nursing Service, had over a period of 10 months amassed 259 hours on casualty evacuation flights between Kimpo and Japan 202

The morning after the armistice came into effect, Australian soldiers stand above their front-line trenches at the Hook. For the first time in more than three years the front line was silent 202

Defence in depth was vital in case of a Chinese breakthrough. Here men from 2RAR unload timber baulks to construct bunkers, most likely on the Hook 203

A Chinese officer, Hshwang Shon Kwang, presents a red 'peace' flag to Douglas Bushby, an Australian war correspondent, in no man's land, the day after the ceasefire in Korea took effect. Jamestown Line, the Hook, 28 July 1953................. 275

A Republic of Korea military policeman stands guard at Panmunjom in 2001. South Korean and North Korean guards still continue to face off, only metres apart, at Panmunjom 276

The Korean War remains unfinished. As yet, no peace treaty exists between the West and North Korea. This propaganda poster, produced after the armistice in July 1953, remains relevant today. c. 1953 277

The long-lasting individual and social influences of the Korean War on Australia are remembered and recognised at the Australian National Korean War Memorial in Canberra, Australia 277

MAPS

IN FROM THE COLD

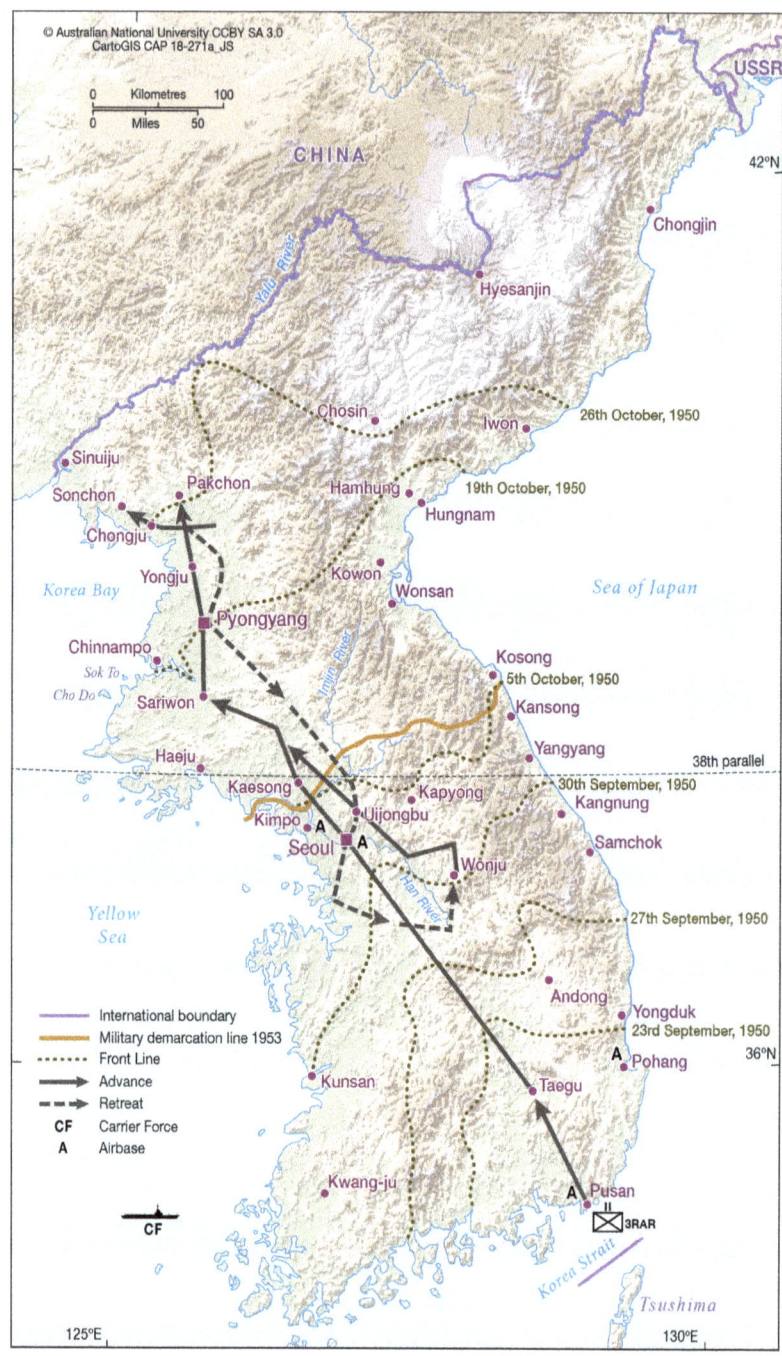

Map 1. The United Nations Command counter-offensive, September–November 1950

MAPS

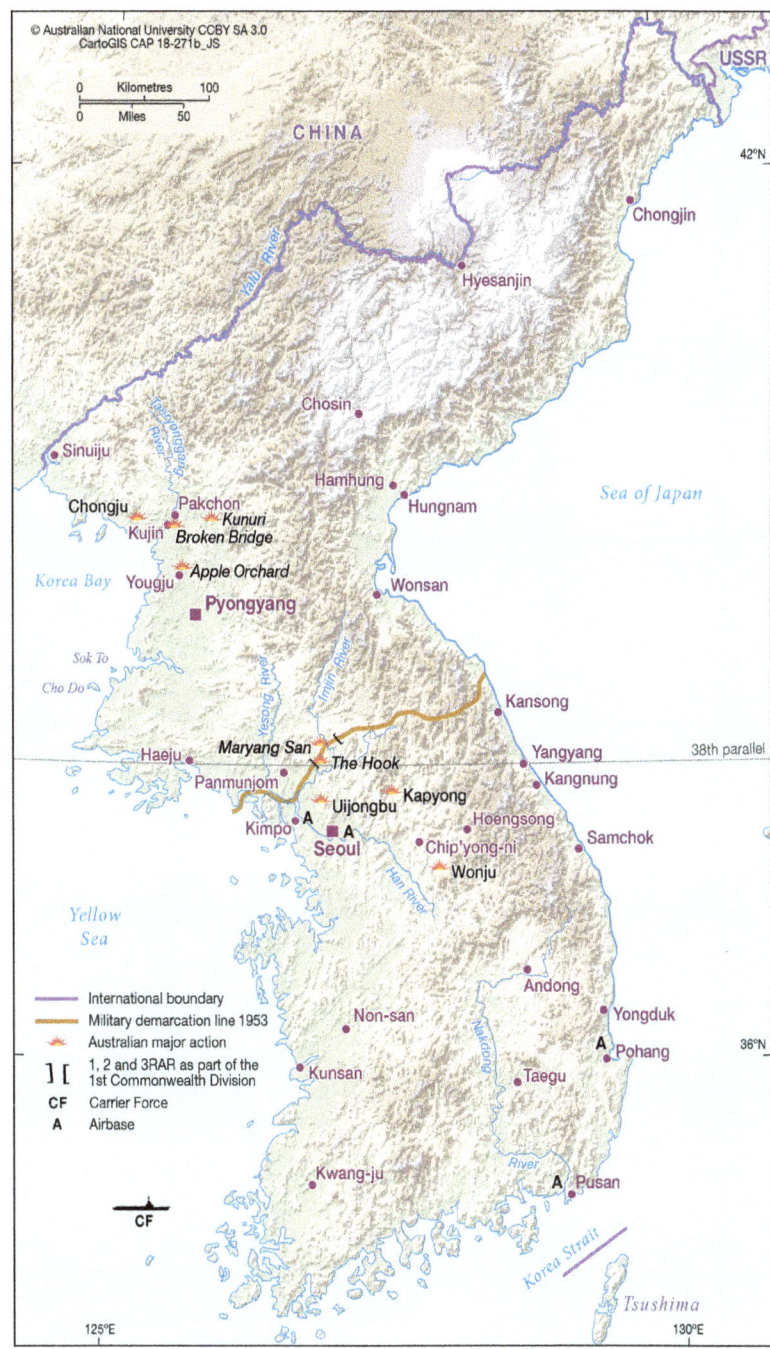

Map 2. Korean Peninsula highlighting major actions fought by Australians, 1950–53

xv

IN FROM THE COLD

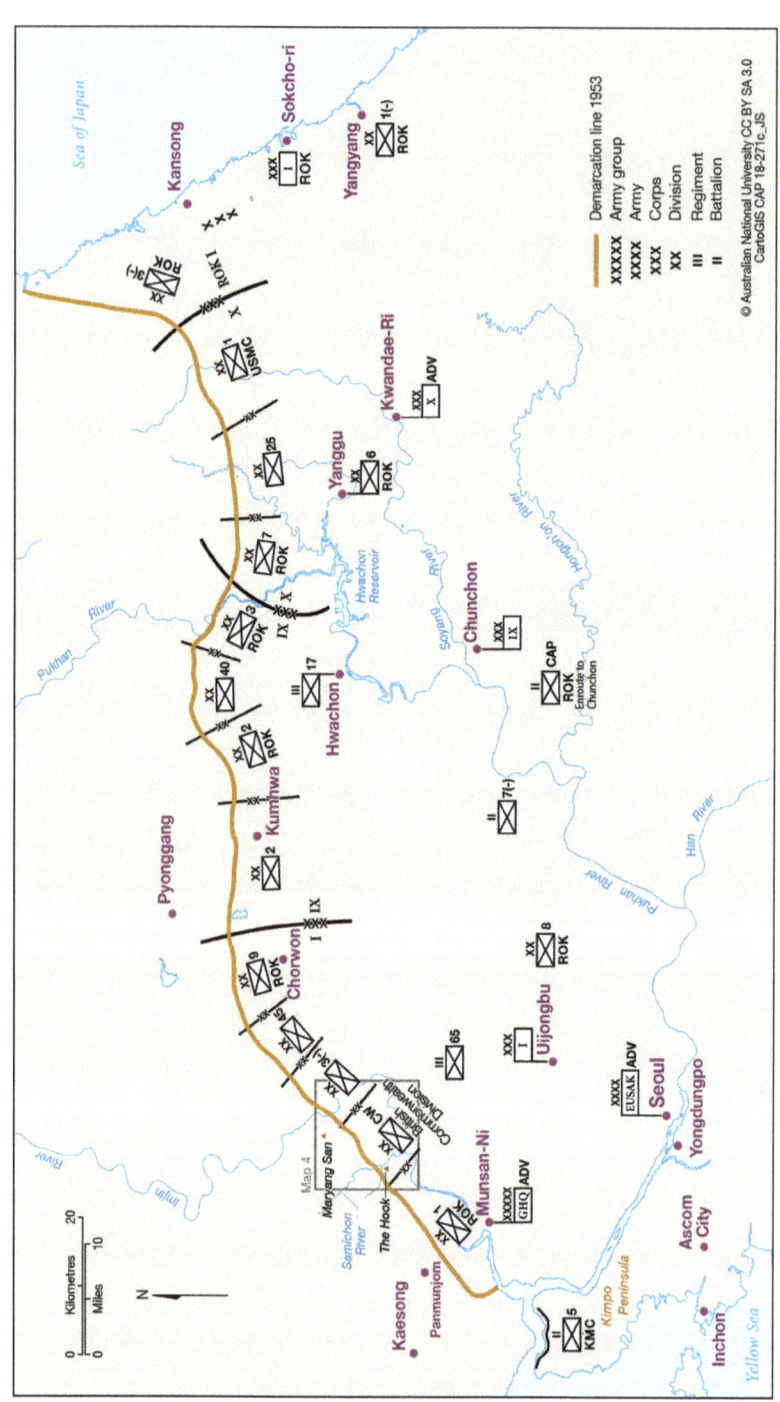

Map 3. Positions held by the United States Eighth Army, 15 March 1952

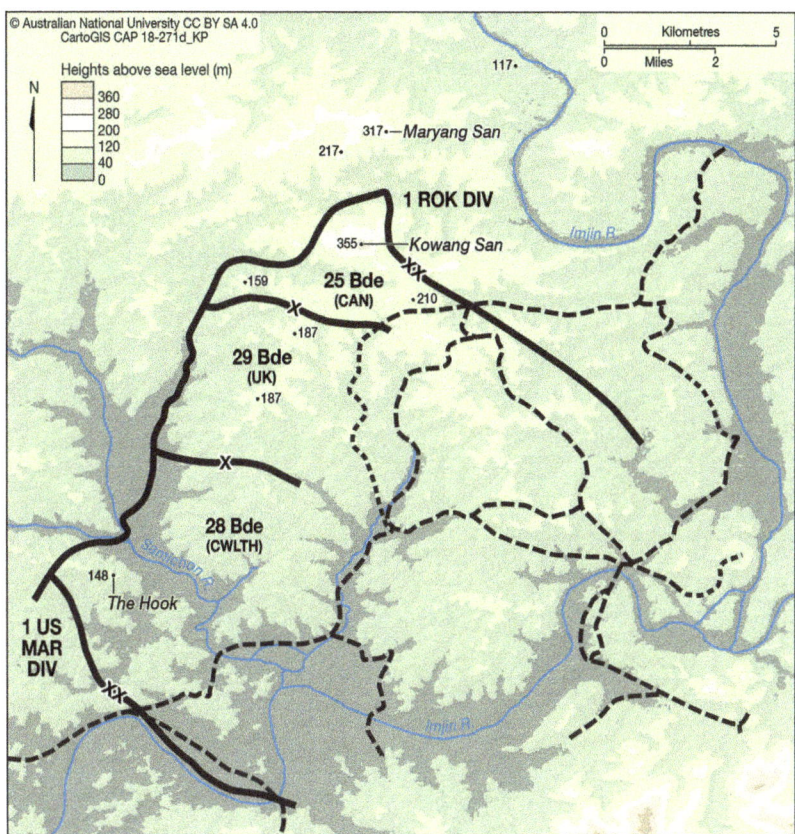

Map 4. Brigade dispositions of the 1st Commonwealth Division during the final weeks of the war, June–July 1953

CHRONOLOGY

1950

25 June – The North Korean People's Army (NKPA) crosses the 38th parallel into South Korea, starting the Korean War.

25 June – The United Nations drafts UN Security Council Resolution 82 calling for the cessation of hostilities and withdrawal of North Korean forces from the Republic of Korea (ROK). Australia endorses the resolution and offers military assistance.

27 June – UN Security Council passes Resolution 83, which allows the United Nations to act militarily to support the ROK.

29 June – Royal Australian Navy frigate HMAS *Shoalhaven*, stationed in Japan, and destroyer HMAS *Bataan*, which had been sent to replace *Shoalhaven,* are committed to UN maritime operations.

1 July – HMAS *Shoalhaven* and HMAS *Bataan* leave Japan as part of a naval escort for Korea-bound US troops.

2 July – No. 77 Squadron, Royal Australian Air Force, flying P-51D Mustang fighters, begin their first ground attack operations in Korea.

15 September – UN forces land at Inchon as part of operations to recapture Seoul and restore South Korea. HMAS *Warramunga* (which had replaced HMAS *Shoalhaven*) and HMAS *Bataan* are part of the naval covering force.

17 September – UN forces begin their breakout from the Pusan Perimeter and drive towards Seoul. No. 77 Squadron flies supporting operations to harass retreating NKPA forces.

28 September – The 3rd Battalion, Royal Australian Regiment (3RAR), arrives at Pusan, South Korea. The battalion was attached to the British 27th Brigade, which at that point consisted of the 1st Battalion, Argyll and Sutherland Highlanders, and 1st Battalion, Middlesex Regiment. The brigade was renamed 27th British Commonwealth Brigade to reflect its new antipodean element.

1 October – ROK forces pursue NKPA forces across the 38th parallel and into North Korea.

7 October – UN troops cross the 38th parallel and drive towards the North Korean capital, Pyongyang.

15 October – HMAS *Warramunga* provides gunfire support during the landing of the US X Corps at Wonsan on the north-east coast of Korea.

17 October – During the advance into North Korea, 3RAR encounter an NKPA regiment at Sariwon. In the ensuing encounter, 1,982 North Koreans are taken prisoner, the largest capture of enemy troops during the war.

19 October – Pyongyang falls to the US 1st Cavalry Division, whose commander had sidelined the 27th Brigade, enabling his division to be the first UN unit into the capital.

19 October – Units of the Chinese People's Volunteer Army (PVA) begin moving across the Yalu River and infiltrating North Korea. They are undetected by UN air observers or ground troops.

22 October – 3RAR fights its first battle (the first time a unit of the Royal Australian Regiment engaged in combat) against North Korean forces, north-west of Yongju, at a place known as the Apple Orchard. It was a decisive Australian victory.

25 October – 3RAR fights its second battle, the battle of the Broken Bridge, near Kujin on 25–26 October during the UN drive north.

25 October – ROK troops encounter Chinese forces at Onjong, North Korea, the ROK II Corps being defeated in a four-day battle. As the remnants of the corps retreat, the US 8th Cavalry Regiment flank is exposed.

29–30 October – After an advance of 80 kilometres to Chongju, 3RAR fights its third successful battle in a week. On the evening of 30 October, the battalion's commanding officer Lieutenant Colonel Charles Green is mortally wounded, dying at a nearby hospital on 1 November.

1 November – US troops encounter Chinese forces at Unsan. US forces retreat, but food and ammunition shortages force a temporary halt to the Chinese offensive, prompting UN commanders to believe that China had not committed further to the war in Korea.

5 November – Under its new CO, Lieutenant Colonel Floyd Walsh (who had commanded 3RAR in Japan before the war), 3RAR encounters the Chinese at the battle of Pakchon, marking the first instance of No. 77 Squadron flying support operations for 3RAR. 3RAR suffered 12 men killed and 64 wounded. Walsh's precipitous withdrawal temporarily cedes high ground to the Chinese and causes the bulk of casualties. After Walsh is relieved of command by Brigadier Aubrey Coad, Major Bruce Ferguson is promoted and takes command of the battalion.

November – The US Eighth Army renews its drive to the Yalu. The Chinese respond with their second-phase offensive, forcing the withdrawal of UN forces.

26 November – 13 December – Marines of the US 1st Marine Division and the British 41 Royal Marine Commando fight the battle of the Chosin Reservoir, resulting in US and British forces conducting a fighting withdrawal to the ports of Hungnam and Wonsan where UN navy vessels, including HMAS *Warramunga*, wait to take them off the Korean Peninsula.

4 December – As part of a UN destroyer group, HMAS *Bataan* and HMAS *Warramunga* sail up the Taedong River to Chinnampo, North Korea, to assist in evacuating UN soldiers and refugees.

December – By year's end, the 27th Brigade had withdrawn some 320 kilometres over nine days.

1951

1–4 January – The 27th Brigade fights a series of holding actions and fighting withdrawals at Uijonbu, allowing the US Eighth Army to withdraw and move back beyond Seoul. 3RAR is the last UN unit to cross the Han River south of Seoul before the bridge is blown up. The brigade's withdrawal ends on 4 January at Toda-Nae, 160 kilometres south of Seoul.

11 January – Terms for a ceasefire put forward by the United Nations to China and North Korea are rejected.

20–22 January – The 16th Field Regiment, Royal New Zealand Artillery, joins the 27th Brigade, providing a vital fire support element.

5 February – HMAS *Warramunga* participates in the naval blockade of Wonsan, North Korea.

18 February – 2nd Battalion, Princess Patricia's Canadian Light Infantry (2PPCLI), joins the 27th Brigade, replacing the 1st Battalion, Argyll and Sutherland Highlanders, who are rotated out of Korea.

6 April – No. 77 Squadron fly their last operations in Mustangs before withdrawing to Japan to undertake conversion training to Meteor F.8 jets.

11 April – US President Harry Truman appoints General Matthew Ridgway as head of United Nations Command, replacing General Douglas MacArthur.

23–24 April – The Battle of Kapyong takes place, with heavy involvement from 3RAR. During two days of fighting against large-scale Chinese infantry attacks, 3RAR suffers 32 killed, 59 wounded and three captured. With assistance from other units of the 27th Brigade, notably 2PPCLI, the Chinese attack is halted. The 27th Brigade leaves Korea soon after as fresh British and Canadian units begin to arrive.

26 April – 3RAR is taken on strength of the 28th British Commonwealth Brigade.

6 July – Lieutenant Colonel Frank Hassett replaces Lieutenant Colonel Bruce Ferguson as CO of 3RAR. Around this time the bulk of 3RAR are replaced with new troops and original members are rotated home.

CHRONOLOGY

28 July – The 1st Commonwealth Division, including British, Canadian and combined Commonwealth brigades, is formed.

29 July – No. 77 Squadron returns to the skies over Korea, flying sorties from Kimpo airfield, and marking the first clash between the squadron's Meteors and Chinese MiGs flown by veteran Russian pilots.

3–8 October – As part of Operation Commando, 3RAR, supported by New Zealand artillery and British tanks, attacks and captures the strategically important hill known as Maryang San.

5 October – HMAS *Sydney* (III) begins operations in Korean waters. Aboard *Sydney* are three squadrons of the RAN Fleet Air Arm: No. 805 and No. 808 Squadrons, flying Sea Fury fighters, and No. 817 Squadron, flying Fairey Firefly aircraft. Over four months *Sydney*'s aircraft flew 2,366 sorties for the loss of 11 aircraft and three pilots killed.

25 October – Truce talks resume, taking place at Panmunjom.

4 November – A Chinese attack drives British troops from Maryang San.

12 November – The UN offensive is called off by General Matthew Ridgway. The static phase of the Korean War begins.

1 December – Fourteen Meteors of No. 77 Squadron are involved in a dogfight with 50 MiGs. Three Meteors are shot down, and one pilot is killed for the loss of one MiG. The following day, the squadron is prevented from flying fighter sweeps to the border of North Korea and China. No. 77 Squadron returns to their original ground-attack role.

1952

6 April – 1st Battalion, Royal Australian Regiment (1RAR), arrives in Korea, joining 3RAR in the 28th Brigade.

12 May – General Mark Clark takes over command of UN forces from General Matthew Ridgway.

2 July – As part of Operation Blaze, A Company, 1RAR, led by Major David Thompson, raids Chinese positions on Hill 227. The Chinese positions are largely destroyed, but the Australians are forced to withdraw under heavy Chinese artillery fire and infantry counter-attacks.

A Company suffers three men killed and 34 wounded, one of whom died the following day. Thompson is later awarded the Military Cross for his leadership and courage.

July–September – As part of a wider naval blockade action, HMAS *Murchison* undertakes Operation Han, engaging North Korean targets along the Han River near Kaesong. *Murchison*'s actions during this operation were highly commended by the commander of the force.

13–14 August – B Company, 3RAR, is tasked with Operation Buffalo, raiding a Chinese position known as Hill 75. The raiding party quickly captures Chinese positions, but owing to the ferocity of the fighting is unable to secure a prisoner. The company is withdrawn in the early hours of the following morning. Australian casualties for the operation are two killed, 22 wounded and one missing.

10–11 December – 1RAR launches Operation Fauna, a raid on Chinese positions on Hill 355, in an attempt to capture a prisoner and identify the Chinese unit facing the Australians. The attack proceeds in icy weather and, after an initial surprise, the Chinese fight back, forcing 1RAR to withdraw. The Australians suffer 22 men wounded and three missing.

1953

31 January – The 1st Commonwealth Division is withdrawn from front-line operations for rest, having been involved in extensive combat operations since its inception.

16 March – No. 77 Squadron destroys more than 90 North Korean and Chinese trucks during ground-attack operations.

21 March – 1RAR is replaced by the 2nd Battalion, Royal Australian Regiment (2RAR).

27 March – The last air-to-air combat between No. 77 Squadron's Meteors and Chinese MiGs occurs. No losses are reported on either side.

8 April – The 1st Commonwealth Division returns to the front line.

9–10 July – The 28th Brigade is sent to the position known as 'the Hook' to replace the British 29th Brigade. 2RAR and 3RAR are made the forward battalions on the Hook.

19 July – Terms for the armistice in Korea are agreed by UN, Chinese and North Korean delegates at Panmunjom.

24–27 July – Chinese forces launch a last offensive against the Australians at the Hook and nearby US Marines in order to capture strategic high ground, suffering heavy casualties for no gain. 2RAR suffer six men killed or dead from wounds, and 24 wounded.

27 July – The armistice is signed at 10 am at Panmunjom while fighting is still going on near the Hook. The armistice takes effect at 10 pm.

CONTRIBUTORS

John C. Blaxland is Professor of International Security and Intelligence Studies, Senior Fellow of the Higher Education Academy and formerly Head of the Strategic and Defence Studies Centre (SDSC) at The Australian National University (ANU). He holds a PhD in war studies from the Royal Military College of Canada, an MA in History from ANU, a BA (Hons) from the University of New South Wales, and is a graduate of the Royal Thai Army Command and Staff College and the Royal Military College, Duntroon (Blamey Scholar, 1986). He is a former director Joint Intelligence Operations (J2) at Headquarters Joint Operations Command and was Australia's Defence Attaché to Thailand and Burma/Myanmar. He is a member of the editorial board of the *Australian Army Journal* and an occasional media commentator. His published works include *The Secret Cold War* (co-authored with Dr Rhys Crawley; 2016), *East Timor Intervention* (2015), *The Protest Years* (2015), *The Australian Army from Whitlam to Howard* (2014), *Strategic Cousins* (2006) and *Signals: Swift and Sure* (1998).

Bob Breen is an associate professor of Strategic Studies at Deakin University, and was formerly on staff at SDSC. Professor Breen graduated from the Royal Military College, Duntroon, in 1973. His first assignment to peace support operations came in 1993 in Somalia; he then continued in Rwanda, the Middle East and East Timor. He is the author of *First to Fight*, about Australia's role in the Vietnam War, and a number of books on peacekeeping. Dr Breen is joint author of the fourth volume of the Official History of Australian Peacekeeping, Humanitarian and Post–Cold War Operations, *The Limits of Peacekeeping: Australian Peacekeeping in Internal Conflicts, 1993–2006* (2018), and sole author of the fifth volume, *The Good Neighbour: Australian Peace Support Operations in the Pacific Islands, 1980–2006* (2016).

Liam P. Brewin Higgins is a research assistant at SDSC. *In from the Cold: Reflections on Australia's Korean War* is his first publication as an editor. Liam tutors in international security studies and history courses at the Tjabal Indigenous Higher Education Centre, ANU. He has received a number of scholarships for pursuing studies abroad, including a Department of Foreign Affairs and Trade New Colombo Plan Short Term Mobility Grant (2017). He is in his final year of a Bachelor of Arts and a Bachelor of International Security Studies, majoring in international security and history at ANU.

Rowan Callick OBE graduated with BA (Hons) from Exeter University, England. He worked as a journalist and publisher in Papua New Guinea for 10 years, then for 20 years for the *Australian Financial Review*, including as a China correspondent based in Hong Kong from 1996 to 2000, then Asia-Pacific editor. He joined the *Australian* as China correspondent from 2006 to 2009 in Beijing, before becoming a Melbourne-based Asia-Pacific editor, then returning to Beijing as China correspondent from 2016 to 2018. On his return he became an Industry Fellow at Griffith University's Asia Institute while remaining a regular columnist for the *Australian*. He has been a member of the Foreign Minister's Foreign Affairs Council, and is a fellow of the Australian Institute of International Affairs. He was appointed OBE on the recommendation of the Papua New Guinea Government in 2015. His publications include *Comrades and Capitalists: Hong Kong Since the Handover* (1998), *Channar: A Landmark Venture in Iron Ore* (2012), and *Party Time: Who Runs China and How* (2013). He has won the Graham Perkin Award for Australian journalist of the year, and two Walkley Awards for coverage of Hong Kong and China.

Peter Edwards AM is Official Historian for the Official History of Australia's Involvement in Southeast Asian Conflicts, 1948–1975, and has a major research interest in the development of Australia's alliances in this period. He is a graduate of the universities of Western Australia and Oxford, and was a Rhodes Scholar. He is an honorary professor at Deakin University, Melbourne, and a visiting professor at the Australian Defence Force Academy, University of New South Wales. In 2009, he was made a Fellow of the Australian Institute for International Affairs.

Rebecca Fleming specialises in researching the role of women in war. Her PhD thesis was the first major study to examine the experiences of Australian army and air force nurses in the Korean War. She completed her PhD, 'Forgotten women of the forgotten war: Australian nurses in the

Korean War, 1950–1956', at the University of New England in 2011, and has since become a historian in the Australian Public Service. Dr Fleming's research interests include social and cultural history, with a focus on the experiences of Australian women during periods of conflict. Her publications include *The First of Its Kind: A History of the New South Wales Institute of Educational Research* (2008) and 'Making the invisible link visible: The symbiotic relationship between the paid and voluntary labour of women in the NSW Institute for Educational Research' (*Australian Journal on Volunteering*, 2007). In 2017, she wrote the six-episode series *Total War* for Wildbear Entertainment, and is working on a new series.

Cameron Forbes has worked as a European, Asian and US correspondent for the *Age* and the *Australian*. He has reported from a number of conflict areas, including the Middle East, Rwanda, Afghanistan and Bougainville, and in 2010 received a Walkley Award for most outstanding contribution to journalism. He is the author of several books, including *The Korean War: Australia in the Giants' Playground* (2011) and *Australia on Horseback: The Story of the Horse and the Making of a Nation* (2014).

Richard P. Hallion is a former historian of the United States Air Force, was a founding museum curator at the National Air and Space Museum of the Smithsonian Institution, held the General Harold Keith Johnson Chair of Military History at the US Army War College, and has served as a senior adviser on aerospace technology and policy for the Secretary of the Air Force. Dr Hallion serves as an adviser to the Royal Air Force Centre for Air Power Studies and as a trustee of the Florida Polytechnic University; he is also a consultant to various organisations including the Mitchell Institute of the Air Force Association. He is a Fellow of the American Institute of Aeronautics and Astronautics, the Royal Aeronautical Society and the Royal Historical Society. His books include *The Naval Air War in Korea* (1986).

David Horner AM served as an infantry platoon commander in Vietnam in 1971, and is Emeritus Professor of Australian Defence History at SDSC and a Fellow of the Academy of Social Sciences in Australia. As well as being the author or editor of more than 30 books, he is the Official Historian of Australian Peacekeeping, Humanitarian and Post–Cold War Operations and wrote two of the six volumes: *Australia and the 'New World Order'* (2011) and *The Good International Citizen: Australian Peacekeeping in Asia, Africa and Europe, 1991–1993* (with John Connor; 2014). He was jointly awarded the 2015 Prime Minister's Literary Award for Australian History for his book, *The Spy Catchers: The Official History of ASIO, 1949–1963*. In 2016, he received the ANU Chancellor's Award for distinguished contributions to ANU.

Michael Kelly served as a rifleman in the 8th/9th Battalion, Royal Australian Regiment, and is a historian in the Military History Section at the Australian War Memorial. He has a special interest in Australia's role in the Korean War, and is writing a book on combat operations for Cambridge University Press. He has led a number of Australian battlefield tours, and is working towards completing his undergraduate degree at the University of New England, majoring in history.

Colin Khan DSO AM is a retired brigadier who was a commander during the static phase of the Korean War, during which he led numerous fighting and reconnaissance patrols until seriously wounded on Hill 355 during a night patrol. He was mentioned in dispatches for his Korean War service, and commanded the 5th Battalion, Royal Australian Regiment, in Vietnam between 1969 and 1970, for which he was awarded the Distinguished Service Order.

Xiaobing Li is Professor and Chairman of the Department of History and Geography, Director of the Western Pacific Institute at the University of Central Oklahoma, and executive editor of *The Chinese Historical Review*. His research interests include the Cold War, Sino-US relations and Chinese military history. Among his recent books are *East Asia and the West* (2019), *The Cold War in East Asia* (2018), *Power vs Law in Modern China* (co-author with Qiang Fang; 2017), *Urbanization and Party Survival in China* (co-editor with Xiansheng Tian; 2017), *Modern China* (2016), *Ethnic China* (co-editor with Patrick Fuliang Shan; 2015), *Oil* (co-editor with Michael Molina; 2014), *Evolution of Power* (co-editor with Xiansheng Tian; 2014), *China's War for Korea* (2014), *Legal Reforms in China* (co-editor with Qiang Fang; 2013), *China at War* (2011), *Voices from the Vietnam War* (2010), *Civil Liberties in China* (2010), *A History of the Modern Chinese Army* (2007), *Voices from the Korean War* (co-author with Richard Peters; 2003) and *Mao's Generals Remember Korea* (co-editor with Allan R. Millett and Bin Yu; 2001).

Jack McCaffrie served with the Royal Australian Navy until he retired as a commodore in 2003. He is the author of many papers on sea power issues, and is a Visiting Fellow at the RAN's Sea Power Centre and at the Australian National Centre for Ocean Resources and Security,

University of Wollongong. McCaffrie recently received his PhD from the University of Wollongong. His current research projects include a history of the Pacific Patrol Boat Program and the development of the Royal Australian Navy between 1955 and 1983.

Allan R. Millett is a retired colonel in the US Marine Corps Reserve, Ambrose Professor of History at the University of New Orleans, and senior military adviser to the National World War II Museum. He was previously Associate Director of the Mershon Center for International Security Studies at Ohio State University. Since 1995 he has published five books on the Korean War, including two volumes of a projected three-volume history of the war, *The War for Korea: A House Burning, 1945–1950* (2005) and *The War for Korea: They Came from the North, 1950–1951* (2010). Five of his books have been translated into Mandarin. He is the co-author of a military history of the United States and the Second World War, a Fulbright Distinguished Visiting Professor in Korea and a senior fellow of the Korea Foundation.

Jongnam Na is a professor of the Department of Military History, Korea Military Academy at Seoul. He graduated from the Korea Military Academy in 1993 and received his MA in history from Segang University in 1997 and his PhD in history from the University of North Carolina in 2006. He is an active duty infantry officer and lieutenant colonel of the ROK Army. His main research interests are military history, the history of the Cold War, wars in Asia, the Korean War, the US–South Korea military relationship and the military cultures of Asian countries. Dr Na's recent publications include *Sixty Key Battles of the Korean War* (2010), *The Stories of Student Soldiers during the Korean War* (with the ROK Military History Compilation Committee; 2012) and *The Military Operations of the Korean War* (2018). He is working on a project on military decorations and awards during the Korean War.

Robert O'Neill AO chairs the International Academy Advisory Committee for the United States Studies Centre at the University of Sydney. He graduated from Duntroon in 1958 and served in the Australian Army as an officer during the Vietnam War before completing his doctorate at Oxford University. Professor O'Neill has been the head of SDSC, Director of the International Institute for Strategic Studies in London and Chichele Professor of the History of War at the University of Oxford, and has chaired the Council of the Australian Strategic Policy Institute and the Council of Trustees of the Imperial War Museum. As Australia's official historian of the Korean War, he has published two volumes of the history: *Strategy and Diplomacy* (1981) and *Combat Operations* (1985). He was series editor of *The Official History of Australia in the War of 1914–1918* (1981–89).

William Purves CBE DSO GBM was called for national service at the age of 18 and was later commissioned into the King's Own Scottish Borderers serving the majority of his national service during the Korean War. Sir William received his Distinguished Service Order after experiencing considerable front-line action during the Korean War. After the war, Purves moved on to work for the Hong Kong and Shanghai Banking Corporation, rising to become chief executive and later chairman. He has served on a number of boards of small and large companies, including the Shell Transport and Trading Company Limited. Sir William is a trustee of the National Museums of Scotland and the Imperial War Museum.

Nigel Steel is Principal Historian at the Imperial War Museum (IWM), London, where he has worked since 1988. He was Head of the Research and Information Department from 1999 to 2006, and spent a two-year period at the Australian War Memorial, where he completed the Korean War Gallery. Upon returning to the United Kingdom, Steel became Principal Historian for the IWM's First World War Centenary Programme. His research interests include First World War military operations, military awards for bravery, the 1st Commonwealth Division in the Korean War, and Second World War prisoners of war. His publications include *The Battlefields of Gallipoli: Then and Now* (1990), *Gallipoli* (1999) within the Battleground Europe series, and a number of works co-authored with Peter Hart, such as *Defeat at Gallipoli* (1994), *Passchendaele: The Sacrificial Ground* (2000) and *Jutland 1916: Death in the Grey Wastes* (2003).

GLOSSARY

AANS	Australian Army Nursing Service
ADFA	Australian Defence Force Academy
AGPS	Australian Government Publishing Service
AHQ	Army Headquarters
AIF	Australian Imperial Force
AM	Member of the Order of Australia
ANAG	Australian Naval Aviation Group
ANU	The Australian National University
ANZAC	Australia and New Zealand Army Corps
ANZUS	Australia, New Zealand, United States Security Treaty
AO	Officer of the Order of Australia
ASW	Anti-Submarine Warfare
AWM	Australian War Memorial
BAI	battlefield air interdiction
BBC	British Broadcasting Corporation
BCCZMU	British Commonwealth Communications Zone Medical Unit
BCGH	British Commonwealth General Hospital
BCOF	British Commonwealth Occupation Force
Bdr	Bombadier
Brig	Brigadier
Capt	Captain
CAS	close air support
CBALO	Carrier Borne Army Liaison Officer

CBE	Commander of the Order of the British Empire
CCP	Chinese Communist Party
CGS	Chief of the General Staff
CMC	Central Military Commission
CO	Commanding Officer
Cpl	Corporal
CPVF	Chinese People's Volunteer Force
CSM	Company Sergeant Major (Warrant Officer Class 2)
DA	Department of the Army (United States)
DLI	Durham Light Infantry
DMZ	Demilitarised Zone
DOS	Department of State (United States)
DPRK	Democratic People's Republic of Korea (North Korea)
DSM	Distinguished Service Medal
DSO	Distinguished Service Order
FEAF	Far East Air Forces
GBM	Grand Bauhinia Medal
GMD	Guomindang (aka KMT)
GOC	General Officer Commanding
HMAS	Her Majesty's Australian Ship
HMNZS	Her Majesty's New Zealand Ship
HMS	Her Majesty's Ship (UK)
HQ	Headquarters
IDA	Institute for Defence Affairs
IWM	Imperial War Museum
KAFTA	Korea–Australia Free Trade Agreement
KATCOM	Koreans Attached Commonwealth Division
KIA	Killed in Action
KMAG	Korean Military Advisory Group
KMT	Kuomintang (aka GMD)
KOSB	King's Own Scottish Borderers
KPG	Korean Provisional Government

KSLI	King's Shropshire Light Infantry
Lt Col	Lieutenant Colonel
Lt	Lieutenant
Maj	Major
MC	Military Cross
MLR	Main Line of Resistance
MM	Military Medal
NATO	North Atlantic Treaty Organization
NCO	non-commissioned officer
NEBDA	North-East Border Defence Army
NKPA	North Korean People's Army
NKPAAF	North Korean People's Army Air Force
OBE	Order of the British Empire
PLA	People's Liberation Army (China)
PLAAF	People's Liberation Army Air Force (China)
PNF	Permanent Naval Forces
PPCLI	Princess Patricia's Canadian Light Infantry
PRC	People's Republic of China
RAAF	Royal Australian Air Force
RAAFNS	Royal Australian Air Force Nursing Service
RAANC	Royal Australian Army Nursing Corps
RAF CAPS	Royal Air Force Centre for Air Power Studies Institute for Defence Analysis
RAF	Royal Air Force (UK)
RAN	Royal Australian Navy
RAR	Royal Australian Regiment
RF	Royal Fusiliers
RN	Royal Navy (UK)
RNF	Royal Northumberland Fusiliers
ROC	Republic of China (Taiwan)
ROK	Republic of Korea (South Korea)
RSM	Regimental Sergeant Major (Warrant Officer Class 1)

RTSC	Replacement Training and School Command (ROK Army)
RUF	Royal Ulster Fusiliers
SDSC	Strategic and Defence Studies Centre
SEATO	Southeast Asia Treaty Organization
Sgt	Sergeant
TACP	Tactical Air Control Party
UN	United Nations
UNC	United Nations Command
UNCOK	United Nations Commission on Korea
UNCURK	United Nations Commission for the Unification and Rehabilitation of Korea
UNSC	United Nations Security Council
UNSCR	United Nations Security Council Resolution
US	United States
USAF	United States Air Force
USMC	United States Marine Corps
USN	United States Navy
USS	United States Ship
USSR	Union of Soviet Socialist Republics
VC	Victoria Cross
VVS	Voenno-Vozdushnye Sily (Soviet air force)
WIA	Wounded in Action
WO	Warrant Officer (see RSM and CSM)

INTRODUCTION

John Blaxland

The Korean Peninsula and the Korean people have survived and struggled through more than their fair share of great conflicts, invasions and power struggles, dating back to the Mongol invasions in the thirteenth century. The Korean War (1950–53) continues to be remembered on both sides of the Korean Demilitarised Zone (DMZ) and with increasing significance, as relations between the Republic of Korea (ROK), commonly known as South Korea, and the Democratic People's Republic of Korea (DPRK), or North Korea, are subject to volatile oscillating changes. In Australia, the details of the Korean War and Australia's involvement in it are less widely known in comparison with the first and second world wars. Unlike the previous global conflicts of 1914–18 and 1939–45, the Korean War concluded with an armistice and without a signed peace treaty. Without a clear victor, and with subsequent Australian military commitments in other Cold War conflicts having high public profiles, the Korean War has been understandably less well known.

On 8 November 2017, US President Donald Trump's inaugural visit to the Korean DMZ was halted because of the familiar onset of a cold and thick fog over one of the most contested and heavily militarised borders in the world. The cold and the fog is a physical reality of the weather patterns common to the Korean Peninsula, but the fog of war is also a military and political reality. Deception, covert action, subversion and nuclear brinksmanship have long been hallmarks of the relationship between North and South Korea. In the past North Korea has utilised conciliatory statements about further dialogue with the South while threatening nuclear and conventional attacks against the ROK, Japan and the United States.

The significant degree of uncertainty in decision-making during such conflicts as the Korean War was summed up by former US Defence Secretary Robert S. McNamara when he declared that 'war is so complex, it is beyond the ability of the human mind to comprehend the variables'.[1] To paraphrase the renowned German military philosopher Carl von Clausewitz, it is important to note the friction that exists between what each side expects a war to be like and what the nature of combat turns out to be.[2] At present, the fog of war continues to hover over the Korean Peninsula because comparatively little of what is known and understood about North Korea is ever put in the context of its strategic decisions and ambitions. The ancient Chinese strategist Sun Tzu is said to have declared that 'he who knows the enemy and himself will never in a hundred battles be at risk'.[3] The fog of war hung over the heads of military commanders on both sides during land battles such as the Battle of Maryang San, and the deception and uncertainty associated with the fog of war continues to this day through the brinkmanship and military posturing associated with deliberations between the United States, China and North Korea, among others.

This edited compilation of papers on the history of Australia's involvement in the Korean War is based on the 2011 Australian War Memorial international conference, 'Korea: In from the Cold', which marked the sixtieth anniversary of the Battles of Kapyong and Maryang San, landmark events in which Australian troops were involved. This volume closely explores some widely forgotten aspects of the Korean War with historical analysis, and with a focus on bringing to light perspectives of the digger, the nurse, the ally, the strategist, the historian and the adversary. Since 2011, the introduction, conclusion and some of the chapters—particularly chapters 12 and 16—have been updated and revised to ensure that the publication is relevant.

This edited collection draws upon the experiences and expertise of senior military figures and scholars to assess the extent and scope of the Korean War's ongoing relevance for the future of Australia and the globe in the twenty-first century. It is more than just an anecdotal account

---

1 E. Morris, *Fog of War: Eleven Lessons from the Life of Robert S. Mcnamara*, documentary, Sony Pictures Classic, United States, 2003.
2 S.J. Cimbala, *Clausewitz and Chaos: Friction in War and Military Policy*, Praeger, Westport, CT, 2001, p. 197.
3 S. and R.T. Ames, *Sun-Tzu: The Art of Warfare: The First English Translation Incorporating the Recently Discovered Yin-Ch'üeh-Shan Texts*, 1st edn, Ballantine Books, New York, 1993, p. 113.

of participant figures. It is a reflection that has considerable resonance for military practitioners, policy-makers and strategists considering possible futures. The purpose of this book is to draw upon this expertise, knowledge and experience of Australia's role and the roles of others in the Korean War and reiterate the ongoing relevance and significance of the Korean War because, ultimately, the conflict remains unresolved to this day. Indeed, with security challenges on the Korean Peninsula often dominating headlines, a detailed understanding of Australia's military role 70 years ago is particularly pertinent; even more so as contingencies that could see Australian troops deployed once more on operations in northeast Asia are not far-fetched.

The Korean War began in June 1950, when communist North Korea invaded US-aligned but independent South Korea. With a rare UN Security Council mandate authorised after the Soviet Union walked out, a US-led UN coalition promptly drove the North Koreans back, but an optimistic pursuit of North Korean forces right up to the Yalu River, bordering communist China, should have raised real questions about how the People's Republic of China (PRC) would react. The Soviet delegate was absent from the vote on Korea because the Union of Soviet Socialist Republics (USSR) was boycotting the UN Security Council over the US refusal to replace Nationalist China (Taiwan) with the PRC. The UN high command should have considered Chairman Mao Zedong's imperative to prevent the collapse of the DPRK and secure China's border with the Korean Peninsula. The confidence of the UN commander, General Douglas MacArthur, lay at least in part on his belief that he could once again employ nuclear weapons to tip the balance. US President Truman's refusal and subsequent dismissal of MacArthur set a precedent that has lasted to the time of writing; nuclear weapons remain off limits for limited military contingencies such as the Korean War. When an armistice was signed in July 1953, the border between the two Koreas remained close to where it had been at the start of the war. A state of suspended hostilities has existed between the two states ever since. We are reminded periodically by exchanges of fire over the Korean border, blusterous provocations, nuclear brinksmanship and high-stakes 'peace talk' negotiations that the Korean War, long dormant, has never quite ended.

The inconclusive outcome of the Korean War is in distinct contrast to the total defeat of the Axis powers at the end of the Second World War. That had been a total war, fought by mass armies that required the mobilisation of resources on a global scale and which culminated with the dropping of atomic bombs. In the shadow of the nuclear age and with Korea being only one of a number of US security problems, the Korean War was conducted as a geographically and politically limited conflict—a conflict that the communists and the UN forces wanted to confine to the peninsula and surrounding areas for fear of escalating to global proportions. Dwarfed by the enormity of the Second World War and coming so soon after it, the Korean conflict took place, to all intents and purposes, under the vast and lingering shadow cast by the Second World War.

For all these reasons, the Korean War has only occasionally engaged the popular imagination and collective memory. Indeed, it was initially described as a 'police action' of the United Nations, reflecting the lack of a formal declaration of war. For the most part, it is known simply as the forgotten war. These appellations could not be more wide of the mark; the Korean conflict was, and remains, extremely significant on any number of grounds. It was the first war fought under the aegis of the United Nations (the next coming 40 years later with the Gulf War of 1991). The entry of the PRC into the war against the UN coalition put the PRC under the leadership of Chairman Mao Zedong on the world stage for the first time. Incidentally, the entry of the PRC indirectly into the conflict took place barely a year after their defeat of Chiang Kai-shek's Kuomintang (KMT) forces in 1949, the culmination of a long Chinese civil war. The PRC continues to view the sustained US Army presence and the Terminal High-Altitude Area Defence (THAAD) air defence system in South Korea with considerable suspicion and as a threat to its core security interests on the Korean Peninsula.

As the conflict took place at a time of acute Cold War tensions, and when the United States no longer had a nuclear monopoly, a key concern was to prevent escalation. A policy of conflict containment rather than decisive victory ensued, which resulted in the Korean War being the first 'limited war'. Neither side wanted to see the conflict in Korea escalate to open warfare beyond the Korean Peninsula for fear of a nuclear conflagration. Not surprisingly, the political context was uncertain and a clear-cut plan for military victory was absent, which meant that, over time, and in the absence of a clear path to victory, popular support for the Korean conflict waned among the major UN coalition partners. This pattern has since been repeated in such conflicts as Vietnam and Afghanistan. During the three years that the conflict lasted, and particularly in the first year, the fighting was frequently on an epic scale. It involved new technologies, such as jet aircraft, and took place over very hilly terrain and in climatic extremes, among which the harsh Korean winter imposed the severest trial.

The casualties of the conflict were appalling. South Korea and the 21-member UN coalition that supported it suffered almost 800,000 military casualties—dead, wounded and missing. The vast majority—well over 600,000—came from South Korea, whose critical role in bearing the brunt of the war often goes unsung. Above this, almost a million ROK civilians died. Some estimates put North Korean and Chinese losses as high as 1.5 million. The United States lost 36,574 dead.[4] The Korean Peninsula was devastated. All this goes to show that, far from being a mere police action, the Korean conflict was a devastating war and one of the most important conflicts, politically and militarily, of the twentieth century. Indeed, the conflict has shaped the geopolitics of north-east Asia for the last 70 years and continues to be of acute geopolitical significance today.

Australia played its part in the war. It was among the first nations to answer the United Nations' call, with its Korean Force, or 'K Force'. Royal Australian Air Force (RAAF) fighter and transport aircraft flew in Korean skies, and Royal Australian Navy (RAN) frigates, destroyers and the aircraft carrier HMAS *Sydney* operated in Korean waters. As Korea was principally a ground war, the main Australian combat elements came from the army. The three battalions of the new Royal Australian Regiment (RAR) fought in Korea as part of a Commonwealth formation alongside British, Canadian, New Zealand and other Commonwealth units. This was also the last time a volunteer force was raised by Australia to fight overseas. The scheme required men to serve in the Australian Army for a period of three years, which included a year in Korea. Recruiting centres opened in August 1950, and the initial quota of a thousand men was swiftly reached. Direct entry was also accepted from the United Kingdom. Volunteers continued to be accepted, and so successful was the K Force scheme that all three Australian infantry battalions were able to be brought up to full strength over time.[5] More than 17,000 Australians served in Korea during the war. Almost 100,000 British servicemen served in Korea; 1,078 lost their lives

---

4 Office of Public Affairs, Washington, DC, 'America's Wars Fact Sheet', US Department of Veterans Affairs, May 2017, www.va.gov/opa/publications/factsheets/fs_americas_wars.pdf.
5 R. O'Neill, *Australia in the Korean War 1950–1953*, vol. 2: *Combat Operations*, AWM & AGPS, Canberra, 1981, p. 8.

fighting on the peninsula while Australia suffered 1,500 casualties, of whom 340 were killed.[6] The Canadians suffered 1,558 casualties of whom 516 were killed, and New Zealand suffered 33 servicemen killed in action during the war.[7] Some Australian and New Zealand elements remained in Korea until 1957 as part of the UN peace monitoring group.

The Korean War was also important for Australia because it was an opportunity to strengthen ties forged with the United States during the Second World War and to deepen various aspects of the bilateral relationship. Contrary to popular historical narratives, Australia looked both to the United Kingdom and to the United States after the Second World War for military support and protection, at least until the British virtually withdrew from the region in the late 1960s. Australia was particularly willing to commit forces so promptly in 1951 in part because it hoped to cement support in Washington for the Australia, New Zealand, United States Security Treaty (ANZUS), which has subsequently been widely regarded as the linchpin of Australia's security infrastructure and policy. Australia was also willing to make a limited commitment to the Korean War because of the fear that the apparent communist monolith would extend its 'red tentacles' across the Asia-Pacific region, and take over countries on Australia's periphery, threatening Australia's security. The Menzies government was also persuaded to support the UN force in Korea because it was a multinational effort that included smaller powers such as South Africa and Ethiopia, and newly independent powers such as India, as well as Australia's traditional allies, the United States and the United Kingdom.

Literature review

This work provides a fresh take on a war that has receded from mainstream consciousness, but that does not mean that the war has not been examined in detail by others. Indeed, there is a considerable body of literature that covers many aspects of the Korean War. What follows is by no means a comprehensive review of the literature, but it emphasises the different

---

6   BBC, 'Britain's Forgotten War', 20 April 2001, news.bbc.co.uk/2/hi/uk_news/1285708.stm.
7   'Canadians in Korea', www.kvacanada.com/canadians_in_the_korean_war.htm; 'New Zealand in the Korean War', Ministry for Culture and Heritage, nzhistory.govt.nz/war/korean-war.

national and military perspectives on the Korean War and the different historical approaches and ways in which scholars and military practitioners have analysed the conflict.

For Australia, the most significant and authoritative voice is Robert O'Neill's two-volume official history of Australia in the Korean War. O'Neill has written a detailed, comprehensive and seminal history of Australian air, sea and land operations on the peninsula between 1950 and 1953. O'Neill's first volume, *Strategy and Diplomacy*, adopts a broad perspective on why and how Australia chose to contribute to the Korean War, noting that while the Korean War 'did not create the ANZUS alliance', the Australian Government did see the war as an opportunity to strengthen its security ties with the United States.[8] O'Neill's *Strategy and Diplomacy* argues that the Korean War was caused by the combination of 'local issues and tensions amongst great powers'.[9] O'Neill explains that in the immediate post–Second World War environment, the Australian Government was rebuilding its security relationship with the United Kingdom while attempting to build a stronger security relationship with the United States. He states that if 'the war had not occurred in 1950, Australia might have become so closely involved with British security arrangements ... that the strategic nexus across the Pacific with the United States might have been weakened further'.[10] O'Neill highlights that the Australian Government often shared some of the concerns of other Commonwealth nations, like India, Canada and the United Kingdom, particularly their desire 'to restrain the United States from precipitate action in response to a sudden crisis'.[11] However, the Australian Government was also reluctant 'to be a British appendage' in the Korean War, but it often worked within the context of cooperation with other Commonwealth nations to ensure that Australian forces were utilised appropriately.[12]

O'Neill's second volume, *Combat Operations*, presents a thorough account of the ground operations conducted by the three battalions of the Royal Australian Regiment deployed to the peninsula during the war. This volume includes analysis of key land battles involving these battalions such as the Battles of Kapyong and Maryang San. It also provides a substantial

---

8   R. O'Neill, *Australia in the Korean War 1950–1953*, vol. 1: *Strategy and Diplomacy*, AWM & AGPS, Canberra, 1981, p. 200.
9   Ibid., p. 1.
10 Ibid., p. 406.
11 Ibid., p. 407.
12 Ibid., p. 404.

amount of analysis and detail on the contribution of Australia's Fleet Air Arm, the maritime operations conducted by the RAN and the missions flown by the RAAF. Of particular significance were the operations of the Australian light air aircraft carrier, HMAS *Sydney*, the missions flown by No. 77 Fighter Squadron RAAF, and the deployment of HMAS *Shoalhaven* and HMAS *Bataan* shortly after commencement of hostilities in 1950.

In the official British history of the Korean War, *The British Part in the Korean War*, Sir Anthony Farrar-Hockley argues that in 1950 the British Government saw little to gain from contributing to the UN force in Korea because of the perceived lack of substantial British interests. Farrar-Hockley explores how the United Kingdom was also dealing with lingering wartime debts, worldwide imperial commitments and the decolonisation of parts of the British Empire.[13] In the end, Britain contributed to the UN force at the request of the United States and because the spread of communism in 1950 in 'Korea could not be ignored'.[14]

In the official history *New Zealand and the Korean War*, Ian McGibbon emphasises that Wellington's decision to send a ground force, as well as offering to commit HMNZS *Pukaki* and HMNZS *Tutira* to the war, resulted in a 'conflict between New Zealand's ... Commonwealth-oriented approach to international affairs and the long-term strategic requirements of its Pacific location'.[15] The New Zealand official historian argues that Wellington's decision to contribute forces to the Korean War was founded in historical precedent, emotional bonds to the United States and the Commonwealth, and New Zealand's national self-interest.

In *Canada's Army: Waging War and Keeping the Peace*, Jack Granatstein presents a uniquely Canadian perspective on the Korean War, arguing that, although there were significant areas of commonality within the armed forces of the Commonwealth countries and the United States, there were also differences, for example in command style and equipment. Noting the composition of the Canadian ground forces, Granatstein argues that the formation of the 25th Canadian Infantry Brigade was chaotic and involved the recruitment of large numbers of Second World War veterans.

---

13   A.H. Farrar-Hockley, *The British Part in the Korean War*, vol. 1: *A Distant Obligation*, HMSO, London, 1990, p. 1.
14   Ibid., p. 4.
15   I.C. McGibbon, *New Zealand and the Korean War*, Oxford University Press, Melbourne, in association with Historical Branch, Department of Internal Affairs, Wellington, 1992, pp. 15, 101.

He also notes that, whereas senior American commanders would give very detailed instructions to their subordinates, British Commonwealth officers often allowed for more discretion on the part of their subordinates. The book also explores how Canada's forces increasingly preferred US equipment over British equipment, but at the same time resisted 'every suggestion that they draw on British or Australian supply lines'.[16] This Canadian perspective reaffirms the fact that coordinating and managing the Commonwealth force in Korea—and indeed the wider UN force—took an immense effort. In the Official Canadian Army History of the Korean War, *Strange Battleground*, Herbert Fairlie Wood states that the Canadian Government was keen to stop the spread of communism in north-east Asia but also recognised that Canada had national interests to protect on the Korean Peninsula.[17]

The US Army in the Korean War by Schnabel, Appleman, Hermes and Mossman offers an authoritative insight into the operations and experiences of US ground forces during the war. Beyond these works, there has been a substantial amount of scholarship on the Korean War from the United States covering a wide range of topics. Some of the subjects covered include biographies of General Douglas McArthur, including that by Weintraub, and Millett's three-volume history of the war in which he argues that the Korean War was first and foremost a conflict between the ROK and the DPRK.[18] James Field Jr's *History of United States Naval Operations: Korea* states that free access to the sea is essential for the United States to 'wield influence upon this distant peninsula' and argues that the US Navy's presence in the Far East is the 'alpha and omega of Korean–American relations'.[19] Malcom Cagle and Frank Manson's *Sea War in Korea* reaffirms the important role played by naval forces in the Korean War, stating that 'without command of the seas between the Free World and Korea … the Korean War, as fought, most certainly would have been lost both militarily and politically'.[20] Robert Futrell in *The United States*

---

16 J.L. Granatstein, *Canada's Army: Waging War and Keeping the Peace*, University of Toronto Press, Buffalo, 2002, p. 323.
17 H.F. Wood, *Strange Battle Ground: Official History of the Canadian Army in Korea*, Queen's Printer and Controller of Stationery, Ottawa, 1966, p. 12.
18 A. Millett, *The War for Korea, 1945–1950: A House Burning*, University Press of Kansas, Lawrence, KS, 2005; A. Millett, *The War for Korea, 1950–1951: They Came from the North*, University Press of Kansas, Lawrence, KS, 2010.
19 J.A. Field, *History of United States Naval Operations: Korea*, Department of the Navy, Washington, DC, 1962, p. 1.
20 M.W. Cagle and F.A. Manson, *The Sea War in Korea*, United States Naval Institute, Annapolis, MD, 1957, p. 491.

Air Force in Korea 1950–1953 writes that the 'shooting war in Korea' and Russia's growing nuclear air power meant that the United States Air Force (USAF) had to be rebuilt, as it had been reduced in size after 1945.[21] The USAF grew to such an extent that its forces on the Korean Peninsula grew from 48 air wings at the start of the war to 93 active air wings at the war's conclusion.[22] *US Marines in the Korean War*, edited by Charles Smith, contends that the war on the Korean Peninsula was probably the last time that the United States Marine Corps (USMC) would undertake a Second World War–style amphibious landing.[23] Smith's history also makes the point that the 'political twists and turns' of the Korean War made it difficult for the USMC to do its job.[24]

The Korea Institute of Military History has produced an extensive three-volume history of the Korean War, which includes an introduction by Allan Millett that provides valuable insight into South Korean perspectives on the conflict. This work explores ROK strategic and operational perspectives as well as the views of ROK veterans translated into English from Korean.[25]

Albert Palazzo in *The Australian Army: A History of its Organisation 1901–2001* argues that, compared with the Second World War in which Australia raised the equivalent of 14 divisions, Australia's contribution to the Korean War was numerically smaller and part of a much more limited commitment to the war on the peninsula.[26] Palazzo also states that the Korean War identified 'continuing deficiencies' within the Australian Army that had developed after the Second World War.[27]

David Horner in *The Commanders* and his more detailed biography of General Sir John Wilton, *Strategic Command*, provides a close analysis of Wilton's role as Commander of the 28th British Commonwealth Brigade from April 1953. Horner argues that Wilton gained valuable experience and training after the Second World War, unlike many of his

---

21   R.F. Futrell, *The United States Air Force in Korea 1950–1953*, 2nd edn, Office of Air Force History, United States Air Force, Washington, DC, 1983, p. 709.
22   Ibid.
23   C.R. Smith (ed.), *US Marines in the Korean War*, History Division, US Marine Corps, Washington, DC, 2007, p. 3.
24   Ibid.
25   Korea Institute of Military History, *The Korean War*, 3 vols, University of Nebraska Press, Lincoln, 2000.
26   A. Palazzo, *The Australian Army: A History of Its Organisation 1901–2001*, Oxford University Press, Melbourne, 2001, pp. 217–18.
27   Ibid., p. 217.

INTRODUCTION

Australian Army officer colleagues, because of defence budget cuts, and that many of Wilton's 'ideas of military organisation on the grand scale' were influenced by the conduct of warfare in the European theatre of the Second World War.[28] Given the strong coalition flavour of the force that Australia found itself fighting alongside on the Korean Peninsula, Horner argues that Wilton 'had become well versed in joint operations and had witnessed decision-making between allies on questions of grand strategy'.[29] While *The Commanders* provides important biographical sketches of Wilton and other significant military figures, *Strategic Command* is the more significant text for understanding how Wilton performed his duties as head of the 28th Brigade towards the end of the war.

David Wilson's *Lion over Korea: 77 Fighter Squadron RAAF 1950–1953* demonstrates that the Korean War not only exposed weaknesses in the training of RAAF personnel but also was an important experience for the future leaders of the RAAF. Wilson describes in detail the difficulties that No. 77 Squadron faced in the transition from piston-powered aircraft to the jet-powered Meteor, particularly the lack of planning and doctrine that inhibited the use of the new aircraft.

David Horner and Jean Bou's *Duty First: A History of the Royal Australian Regiment* provides a regimental-level perspective on the operations and tactics of the Royal Australian Regiment during the Korean War. It is significant, in the context of understanding Australia's involvement, that the RAR was reliant, to a large extent, on its UN partners for artillery support, medical services, intelligence, logistics and air cooperation administration.[30] Importantly, this book likens the Korean War during the static period to the fighting conditions on the Western Front between 1915 and 1917, arguing that it was 'no less bloody' than earlier phases.[31] The harsh climatic and terrain extremes are highlighted as another challenge that had to be overcome by the RAR, especially by those soldiers who had been wounded.[32]

---

28 D. Horner, *The Commanders: Australian Military Leadership in the Twentieth Century*, George Allen & Unwin, Sydney, 1984, p. 320.
29 Ibid., p. 321.
30 D. Horner and J. Bou, *Duty First: A History of the Royal Australian Regiment*, Allen & Unwin, Sydney, 2008, p. 57.
31 Ibid., p. 73.
32 Ibid., p. 63.

A number of corps or regimental histories have explored various aspects of the Korean War from the perspective of other combat, combat support and service support elements of the Australian Army. John Blaxland's *Signals: Swift and Sure: A History of the Royal Australian Army Corps of Signals 1947–1972* examines the significance of a technical corps in the conduct of operations of this type. This work shows us that close working relationships developed between signallers from the United States and participating Commonwealth countries because signalling equipment and procedures had become standardised during the static period of the war.[33] While no complete Australian signals unit was deployed to the Korean War, Australian signallers did serve at the battalion and regimental levels in Korea, as well as with other Commonwealth and US units.[34]

Cameron Forbes's *Korean War: Australia in the Giant's Playground* focuses specifically on the experiences of individual Australian soldiers. In the context of the Cold War and the atomic age, Forbes explains how the 'stunning hills and mountains' of the Korean Peninsula 'were turned into contour lines on two-dimensional military maps'.[35] Gallaway's *Last Call of the Bugle: The Long Road to Kapyong* also places considerable emphasis on exploring the everyday experiences and thoughts of Australian servicemen and servicewomen during the Korean War.

Despite much being forgotten amid the cold, the fog and the friction of war, a considerable body of work on the Korean War pre-dates the efforts made in this volume. Recognising the breadth and depth of scholarship in this realm is important as a point of departure for the matters discussed in the following chapters. This work not only recognises the significance of these earlier works but also relies on them as points of reference, not the least of which is the extensive work by Robert O'Neill.

Chapter outline

Australia's official historian of the Korean War, Robert O'Neill, presents Chapter 1, 'Setting a new paradigm in world order', which explores how the intervention of UN forces in defence of South Korea against the

---

33 J. Blaxland, *Signals: Swift and Sure: A History of the Royal Australian Army Corps of Signals 1947–1972*, Royal Australian Corps of Signals Association, Melbourne, 1999, p. 64.
34 Ibid., pp. 68, 69.
35 C. Forbes, *The Korean War: Australia in the Giant's Playground*, Pan Macmillan, Sydney, 2010, p. 21.

invasion of the DPRK demonstrates the willingness of the international community to act effectively to curb interstate aggression in a post–Second World War context. Importantly, O'Neill states that there have been no other wars like the Korean War (after the Russians abstained from UN voting on the Korean War) because the permanent five members of the UN Security Council have since recognised their ability to veto and safeguard their interests. The UN Security Council veto power remains an enduring feature of geopolitics. It is clear from this chapter's analysis that British Commonwealth countries, such as Australia and Canada, sought to work especially closely and maximise the use of their fairly limited resources and manpower to full effect. Despite being geographically remote, these 'strategic cousins' have since found cause to work collaboratively in a low key manner on a range of security challenges.[36]

Chapter 2 by Allan Millett, 'The Korean War: Which One? When?', suggests that the Korean War was a conflict that arguably began much earlier than 1950. Exploring the often overlooked period between the end of the Second World War and the beginning of the Korean War, Millett focuses on the strong sense of Korean nationalism evident on both sides of the DMZ that had emerged through hundreds of years of struggle against foreign invasions and Japan's brutal occupation between 1910 and 1945. This chapter also details Kim Il-Sung's sponsorship of a South Korean communist insurgency before the outbreak of the Korean War. It explains that a great number of North Koreans moved to the ROK because they were Christian and/or a member of the professional class, and were fearful for their lives under communist rule. Millett states that in 1950 the Soviets and the North Koreans hoped that if they conquered Seoul the ROK government would capitulate and the whole peninsula would swiftly be brought under communist control. Controversially, he argues that General McArthur's famous amphibious landing at Inchon was a strategic error because it meant that China was forced to intervene. He goes on to demonstrate that the Soviets and the Chinese gave the North Koreans competing advice as to where they believed the amphibious landing would take place. Millett's final point—that both Koreas sought greater independence and self-reliance—is particularly poignant now as the DPRK and ROK entertain possibilities of rule without the military presence of the great powers on the peninsula.

---

36   For more on the strategic and military partnerships between Australia, the United States, the United Kingdom and Canada, see J.C. Blaxland, *Strategic Cousins: Australian and Canadian Expeditionary Forces and the British and American Empires*, McGill-Queen's University Press, Montreal, 2006.

The Korean War is not forgotten in the PRC. Xiaobing Li's 'China's war for Korea' (Chapter 3) argues that the military setbacks experienced by Chinese communist forces between 1950 and 1953 are still very much remembered and analysed by commanders of the People's Liberation Army (PLA) and leaders of the Chinese Communist Party (CCP). The chapter goes on to describe how Mao's intervention in the Korean War was a manifestation of the strategy of 'active defence' in which China would intervene on the peninsula to prevent the fall of the Kim dynasty, a move that he believed would destabilise China's northern provinces. Li makes an important observation when he notes that the disparity between the technological capabilities, military strength and experience of China and the United States was considerably greater in 1950. This raises some interesting concerns about the strength and resolve of China to safeguard its own territories and seek to influence those of its immediate neighbours.

In 'Fighting in the Giant's Playground' (Chapter 4), Cameron Forbes explains that Australia's contribution to the US-led UN force was used as a lever to assist Australia in securing the support of the United States in signing the ANZUS Treaty. Forbes paints a vivid image of the human cost of war and the lack of attention given to the hardships of Australian soldiers in the Korean War. The chapter states that the British and Commonwealth Forces were able to veto orders and operations given by US military leaders if they deemed them to be potentially too costly or wasteful in human lives and resources. This point reflects contrasting approaches to the use of force in a limited war.

The rapid advance of the Korean People's Army (KPA) in 1950 left the ROK Army demoralised and in complete disarray. In Chapter 5, 'The transformation of the Republic of Korea Army', Jongnam Na argues that this series of military defeats convinced the US high command that the ROK Army needed considerable reform. In particular, Na argues that the United States sought to increase the effectiveness and self-sufficiency of the ROK Army by replicating US military training academies in the ROK, emphasising the importance of a better trained and better educated officer corps. US General James Van Fleet argued that the US Korea Military Advisory Group (KMAG) was essential not only in training the ROK Army but also in building stronger bonds of comradeship and closer interpersonal relationships between US troops and their South Korean counterparts. Na states that a considerable proportion of the political establishment in Washington preferred diverting US military resources and manpower to the Middle East because they feared that the next world war would erupt there. The US political impetus behind the move to enhance the military training of the ROK Army, Na argues, was Washington's desire to relieve the political and economic pressure that the Korean War had generated on the home front.

After the intervention of the United Nations, US air power was initially forced to deploy mainly from naval air assets stationed in the Yellow Sea, the Korea Strait and the Sea of Japan because the few remaining airfields on the peninsula were vulnerable to DPRK attack. In 'The air war in Korea' (Chapter 6), Richard Hallion argues that the contributing UN air forces, led by the combined air forces of the United States, did not sustain total air superiority over the peninsula but did exercise considerable control over the skies. UN air forces exercised dominance in the air until the unofficial intervention of the Soviet air force, Voyenno-Vozdushnye Sily (VVS), concentrated on an area known as 'MiG Alley'. Hallion argues that despite the popular narrative of fierce aerial dog fights between communist and UN fighter aircraft, 29.67 per cent of missions flown by UN aircraft were classified as air interdiction missions that targeted important ground objectives, such as bridges and supply dumps. Air interdiction is an aerial strategy that was utilised extensively during the Korean War to delay and hinder the vital military components by which communist forces could launch an attack or repel an advance from UN forces. Hallion explains that, after a virtual stalemate descended on the Korean Peninsula after the beginning of negotiations, the importance of the air war became even greater as holding territory already gained became the key objective for both sides on the ground.

In Chapter 7, 'Korea: The first challenge for Australian naval aviation', Jack McCaffrie explores how the Australian Navy Aviation Group (ANAG) was able to deploy on HMAS *Sydney* to the Korean Peninsula in 1951. McCaffrie argues that Australia, as one of three countries in the Asia-Pacific region that had aircraft carriers, played an important role early in the Korean conflict, especially when South Korean and UN forces were forced onto the back foot at the southern tip of the peninsula. The ANAG initially deployed with fixed-wing propeller aircraft and later acquired a helicopter squadron. Of particular significance for interforce communication, the Australian Army posted a carrier-borne army liaison section to provide machine gun instruction and training on evading the enemy for pilots who were shot down. The section provided the Navy air wing with anti-aircraft flak maps that would allow pilots to avoid heavy concentrations of North Korean anti-aircraft fire. This chapter explains that British Commonwealth countries such as Australia and Canada could ill-afford to lose naval assets, which helps explain their reluctance to follow unquestioningly the orders of US officers.

In Chapter 8, 'Australian higher command in the Korean War', David Horner argues that governments and military leaders are forced to assess the effectiveness and suitability of their training, equipment, technology and tactics more intensely during periods of conflict than in peacetime. The Australian Army's experienced officers and non-commissioned officers utilised much of their experience and training from the Second World War in the fighting on the Korean Peninsula. Horner explores how the Australian military gained more command independence during the two world wars and how the Australian Government developed a greater ability to control the use of its assets in wartime. By 1950 the Australian military had fought in a series of conflicts alongside Commonwealth allies and the United States. These close military ties were essential in creating effective communication between contributors to the UN multinational force. In many respects, Australia's ability to shape the plans and objectives of the UN High Command was in proportion to its modest contribution of personnel and military assets. Operating as part of British and Commonwealth formations, however, saw countries working together in the face of US command dominance, and Australia achieved a high level of interoperability as a result.

Chapter 9 presents Colin Kahn's vivid front-line account of the Korean War, 'The reliving of minor tactics'. Kahn crystallises the sharp distinctions between the experiences of rank-and-file infantry men and high-ranking officers. He provides a detailed illustration of the hardships endured by soldiers on both sides, including the sheer brutality of the conflict, the difficult terrain and the bitterly cold winters on the peninsula. The chapter points out that the Australian Army's force in Korea utilised an effective combination of experienced Second World War veterans and fresh recruits eager to prove their worth after 'missing out' on fighting in the Second World War. Kahn observes that during armistice talks, Australian Army units were tasked with adopting a policy of aggressive defence, in which the primary objective was to hold on to territory already gained and to attempt to occupy more advantageous positions. He notes that Australian units were engaged in combat patrols against communist forces, as well as trench warfare during the static period of the war, concentrated around the 38th parallel and the current DMZ. Kahn considers the cold to be the only major factor that meant Australian troops had to fight in a different fashion from the Second World War. In this context, it is noteworthy that the Australian Army fought in the Korean War with virtually the same armoury of weapons that it used during the Second World War. Skilled artillery units on both sides were essential in providing cover for combat patrols and to secure defensive positions. Kahn asserts that at a small-unit level, courage, resourcefulness and determination were essential in maintaining discipline and military effectiveness.

In Chapter 10, 'The Battle of Maryang San', Bob Breen asserts the primary importance of this 1951 engagement near the Imjin River. Breen agrees with Robert O'Neill that 3RAR and other British Commonwealth forces securing vital high ground before the beginning of ceasefire talks won an impressive but fleeting victory over numerically superior communist forces. According to Breen, the defence of Seoul and other key cities in South Korea overshadows smaller and less emotionally charged battles such as Maryang San because 'saving Seoul from advancing Chinese troops' has been perceived as more historically significant. This highly detailed analysis of the Battle of Maryang San includes a blow-by-blow tactical account of the battle, with primary source testimony from a range of ranks revealing the difficulties experienced during the operation. Breen explores the battle's legacy by highlighting that British and US forces had previously attempted to take the high ground at Maryang San and failed whereas 3RAR achieved short-term success. He attributes this success to the expertise, training and experience of individuals in the regiments rather than 'unit cohesion'. Going into the battle, 3RAR's companies were not all at full strength, and had spent the previous three months dug into defensive positions repelling attacks from communist forces and fighting a relatively static war. Breen argues that the Battle of Maryang San demonstrated the fighting tenacity of Australian troops in the Korean War and that, quoting O'Neill, it can be considered 'the greatest single feat of the Australian Army during the Korean War'.[37]

In Chapter 11, 'Conquering Kowang San', Nigel Steel explores how the wartime experiences of soldiers and the emergence of narratives of battle can form part of a country's national identity or national story. Steel highlights how national narratives and official national histories can differ, even between close allies. This chapter demonstrates an important

---

37   O'Neill, *Combat Operations*, p. 200.

and often overlooked point: that there is not a single definitive or uniform version of a battle, a war or, indeed, of history. Steel examines command rivalry within the Commonwealth force during the Korean War, in particularly between the Australian and UK contingents, with both sides disagreeing over which contingent should be acknowledged more than the others. The recognition of a military unit in a particular battle can be contentious because multiple units might claim the right to be recognised and acknowledged for an achievement in an action. In any conflict each state actor seeks to cast their own forces in a positive and important light by awarding praise and acknowledgement to their own forces even when this might be at the expense of allies. A recurring theme in this volume is expanded upon in this chapter: the significant reliance that UN troops placed on supporting artillery bombardments and close air support (CAS) to level the playing field because of communist numerical superiority on the ground.

In Chapter 12, 'The Battle for Hill 317: One man's account', William Purves provides a personal reflection on his service as a young national serviceman in the British contingent serving during the Korean War. In so doing, he provides an important glimpse into the hardships and difficulties experienced by front-line soldiers. He acknowledges that communication and coordination between ground units and air assets was often difficult because of the unreliability of some of the communication equipment, and highlights the significant roles played by other Commonwealth troops in defending territory occupied by British and Commonwealth troops. The development of bonds of comradeship and trust because of the shared fighting experience in adverse conditions provides a strong emotional theme that ties Purves's highly personal account together. This chapter provides an excellent contrast in national perspective because, unlike the United Kingdom, Australia did not have compulsory national service during the Korean War; the composition of British forces on the Korean Peninsula was a mixture of professional soldiers and reservists with Second World War experience, as well as national servicemen. Purves's observation that the Chinese 'volunteers' were creative in camouflaging their positions and weaponry highlights that the PLA employed its guerrilla and conventional tactics drawn from their experiences in fighting in the Chinese Civil War to good effect during the Korean War.

In Chapter 13, 'The Samichon', Michael Kelly argues that units of the US Marine Corps, together with 2RAR and 3RAR, played a pivotal role on the Korean Peninsula through their resolute defence of the Samichon

Valley in July 1953, just days before the ceasefire. By consistently repelling Chinese forces from the defensive positions around Height 146, known by the United Nations Command as 'the Hook', UN forces prevented the communists from gaining a vital piece of territory that could have been used as diplomatic leverage or resulted in a more prolonged conflict. Kelly notes that the Hook had been highly contested before the final days of the conflict. The chapter makes the important point that, despite the war having gone into a period of little territorial movement, the visceral intensity of the military exchanges had by no means diminished. Both sides demonstrated significant tenacity in preventing their opponents from gaining ground towards the end of the conflict, despite peace negotiations having demonstrably reached the final stages before the signing of the armistice agreement. Effective artillery units were essential for both sides not only for defending key positions but also to provide cover for units on patrol forward of defended positions. Kelly highlights the key role played by New Zealand artillery units in providing effective and targeted support to UN positions in the Samichon Valley, which were under sustained attacks from Chinese artillery and infantry units. Finally, Kelly argues that there was more at stake in the Samichon Valley in July 1953 than in previous battles because the capital, Seoul, could have been threatened by a Chinese territorial victory near the current DMZ. US and Commonwealth troops overcame the Chinese offensive advances, he argues, because of better 'coordination and support between allied nations', resulting in a more effective defence of the Samichon Valley.

The Korean War marked a turning point in Australian military nursing, argues Rebecca Fleming in 'Continuing the legacy' (Chapter 14), as military nursing became increasingly professionalised and incorporated within more traditionally masculine aspects of Australian military life. This professionalisation encompassed the creation of a permanent nursing unit, as well as increased expectations within the Australian military that nurses would adhere closely to military protocols. Changes also included skills-based initiatives to allow nurses to gain more experience and have access to medical training initiatives. Fleming argues that the Korean War was the catalyst for a conflict between the established nursing focus on maintaining procedures that promoted practicality, and a wider command focus upon militarising the culture of Australian military nurses.

Peter Edwards's 'From Korea to Vietnam' (Chapter 15) provides a broader strategic perspective on the Korean conflict, contextualising it within four periods of Australian strategic policy. Edwards argues that Australia, like other rational state actors, must consider its own national interests when they diverge from the interests of allied countries. This chapter puts into perspective the Menzies government's decision to contribute to the UN mission in Korea by exploring the tension between the globalist and regionalist approaches in Australian strategic history. Edwards argues that Australia has 'generally succeeded' in navigating the changes in the political landscape and the different security challenges that have arisen in the Asia-Pacific region. The Menzies government sought to utilise Australia's involvement in the Korean War to consolidate US support for the ANZUS alliance with Australia and New Zealand. Edwards explains that in the 1950s Australia was part of a number of different strategic triangles, which included Australia's newer Anglosphere ally, the United States, as well as the United Kingdom. Australia's alliance policy and close relationships with the United Kingdom and the United States were closely linked to fear of communism and the potential for regional conflicts to destabilise security. As a relatively minor power in the broader context of the Asia-Pacific region, Australia preferred to support multilateral military actions with other Commonwealth countries during this period. After the end of the Second World War, Australia increasingly sought to maintain the support and protection of both the United Kingdom and the United States. It was not until 1957 that Australian weapons systems would be realigned more closely with those of the United States.

Chapter 16, 'China and the Koreas', by Rowan Callick emphasises the ongoing importance of understanding the Korean War; however much the leaders have changed on both sides, many of today's tensions remain the same. Callick examines Australia's involvement on the peninsula since the war and the likelihood of Australia being embroiled in another regional conflict. He states that, while Australia has no direct territorial interest in the Korean Peninsula, the ongoing provocations between the DPRK and the ROK, and growing tensions between the PRC and the United States, form part of a wider Australian strategic concern for Australia's alliance with the United States. The chapter explores Australian political responses to the periodic sabre-rattling of the Kim dynasty, in particular Australia's close relationship with South Korea and the finalisation of the Australia–South Korea trade deal in 2014. Callick cites data from the Lowy Institute that demonstrates that the Australian public are generally aware of the Korean War but are mostly unaware of the details of the conflict, generally perceiving tensions on the Korean Peninsula in the wider context of Australia's relationship with the PRC.

Callick reinforces the idea that Australia continues to prefer working with other Anglosphere countries because of a sense of cultural familiarity and shared historical experience. His work concludes the volume by highlighting how some of the experiences and lessons of the Korean War might resonate for contemporary Australian military strategists, planners and politicians.

***

Reflecting on this book as a whole, it is clear that the participation of leading Korean War experts from the United States and Britain provided an appropriate coalition flavour to the original conference, and the book now provides important contrasts in perspective and experience. Chinese and Korean contributions provide views 'from the other side of the hill', which are essential in understanding the ongoing significance and lingering effects of the Korean War in north-east Asia, while the contributions of war veterans provide their personal views from the actual hills they attacked and occupied. Fleming's contribution in particular provides an informative and detailed perspective on the essential but underacknowledged role of Australian nurses in the Korean War.

As part of the UN coalition, Australia contributed to the preservation of the independence of the Republic of Korea. This contribution gave the South Korean people the ability to develop their own democratic institutions over time, enabling the country to emerge as a global economic powerhouse and an important actor in the Asia-Pacific region. While it is important not to overestimate the extent to which the Australian contribution to the UN force secured a prosperous Republic of Korea, how worthwhile this defence of the ROK is today is evident in its contrast with North Korea, which has been economically crippled by one of the harshest totalitarian regimes in history. During the Soviet era, considerable economic assistance from the USSR was essential in propping up the Kim dynasty. The DPRK today relies heavily on cross-border trade and economic aid from China and upon a vast network of covert businesses bypassing UN sanctions and restrictions. As dynamics shift and pressure mounts for a dramatic shift in relations on the Korean Peninsula, it is imperative to be aware of why Australia fought in the Korean War and consider the implications for Australia's engagement on matters concerning the Korean Peninsula today.

Considerable uncertainty remains over the prospects of a peaceful denuclearisation of the Korean Peninsula. Pundits observe a fine line between crisis and opportunity, not least concerning the fate of the two Koreas. Looking back over three-quarters of a century, much has changed since the Korean War, but much remains unchanged. The military technology used by both sides today has altered immensely since the DPRK invaded the ROK in 1950. However, the difficult terrain of the Korean Peninsula and its precarious geographical position as the fulcrum of north-east Asia between Russia, China and Japan has certainly not changed. In the event of a military confrontation or crisis of some kind, Washington would expect the military support of Canberra as a major non–North Atlantic Treaty Organization member. Given Australia's contemporary and historic close military, political and institutional alliance with the United States, it is highly likely that, should conflict erupt, Australia could become embroiled in developments on the peninsula. Australia must then seriously consider whether and in what manner it would be prepared to fight in support of allies in a regional war in north-east Asia. Understanding how Australia has done so in the past and learning the lessons from that experience is an important starting point.

PART 1
POLITICS BY OTHER MEANS
Strategic aims and responses

Squadron Leader Ronald Rankin (second left) and Major Stuart Peach (right) travelled to the 38th parallel in June 1950. Their report assisted the United Nations Security Council's decision to aid the Republic of Korea.
Source: AWM P00716.051.

General Douglas MacArthur was the driving force behind the initial UN response to North Korea. His decision to invade North Korea would have fateful consequences for the outcome of the war.
Source: AWM P00716.077.

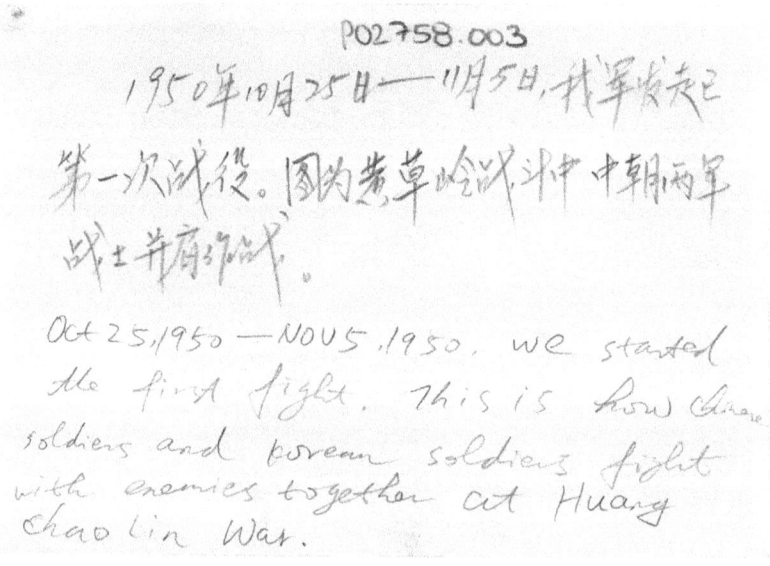

China's entry into the Korean War caught the United Nations Command by surprise and forced the UN and South Korean troops to withdraw from near the Chinese border back beyond Seoul.
Source: AWM P02758.003.

The Republic of Korea Army recovered quickly from its mauling by North Korea and became a battle-hardened and effective force.
Source: AWM HOBJ1545.

ANZUS saw Australia, New Zealand and the United States form a defence pact for the Pacific region. For Australia, the treaty offered some protection against any future Chinese or Soviet aggression.
Source: AWM P00474.019.

Australian soldiers were initially not equipped to deal with the onset of the Korean winter. The deficit was made up from US and British stores. Private Ian 'Robbie' Robertson, a member of 3RAR's sniper section, wears a mixture of British and US winter kit, c. November 1950.
Source: AWM P03732.001.

1

SETTING A NEW PARADIGM IN WORLD ORDER
The United Nations action in Korea

Robert O'Neill

In June 1950, the Republic of Korea (ROK) was essentially occupied by the Democratic People's Republic of Korea's (DPRK) Korean People's Army (KPA).[1] Its people were dying or being slaughtered in the thousands. Its army was shattered, and all that remained under its control was the tiny area within the Pusan Perimeter in the south-east corner of the peninsula. Today the ROK is a powerful, thriving state, recently rated as the most wired via the Internet of all countries in the world. Its science and maths students are winning global awards for their outstanding intellectual performance. It is a marked difference, and a tribute both to the Korean people themselves and to those who placed their lives on the line to help them recover: first by repelling the invaders; second by fighting their more powerful allies to a standstill; and third by imparting the lessons that have enabled the South Koreans to be largely self-sufficient in security while creating a strong economy and a progressive, democratic society since the ceasefire in 1953.

---

1 This chapter is based on Robert O'Neill's presentation at the international military history conference 'Korea: In from the Cold', Australian War Memorial, Canberra, 2011.

The Korean War was a severe test for Western leaders, political and military, and for the soldiers, sailors and airmen under their command. It was a long, frustrating and bloody conflict. The Korean War achieved its aims and laid the basis for those successful developments in South Korea. The war has also had wider consequences for the state of international order since 1950. It raised the standing of the United Nations and initiated an era in which political leaders have had to think much harder about taking unilateral action. How did this happen? Let me offer some thoughts from the strategic level.

Building collective interest in world order after 1945

For most of human history, since tribes and communities coalesced into nation states, security has been determined by one state's capacity to go to war with another. If a more powerful state wanted to take over the territory, people or resources of a less powerful state next door, it was free to try. Smaller states preserved their security by being tough nuts to crack and by allying themselves with larger powers that could threaten retaliatory action against any aggressive third party.

By the end of the First World War, the world generally was so nauseated by the scale of slaughter inflicted by war on military and civilians alike that the League of Nations was formed as a kind of higher level of global governance, to hold belligerence in check. The league's authority was made credible by an international legal structure backed by sanctions, including the use of force. Otherwise force was outlawed as an instrument of national policy. Economic depression, lack of political will and the refusal of the United States to join the league undermined this grand design in the 1930s, and the Second World War resulted. By 1945, it was clear to most national leaders that the world needed more governance, not less, especially in view of the development of the atomic bomb.

The United Nations, formed in 1945, was intended by its founders to do better than the League of Nations. Certainly it had a more impressive membership than the league, for it included the United States and the Soviet Union. Yet any one of the five permanent UN Security Council members could paralyse the world body by use of its veto powers. Both sides in the Cold War sought to circumvent this deficiency by forming military alliances on traditional lines. But, for different reasons, neither East nor West could afford to assume that the United Nations had no teeth.

Security in Asia: Collective action by concerned powers

Curiously, the Soviet Union appeared to do just that when Stalin suspended Soviet participation in the work of the Security Council in January 1950. His aim was to force a change in China's representation, so that Mao Zedong's newly founded People's Republic of China (PRC) would replace Chiang Kai-shek's Republic of China (ROC), now confined to Taiwan. This was a foolish policy for Stalin to adopt when one of the world's major trouble-spots, north-east Asia, was about to erupt.

The Korean Peninsula and the Yellow Sea, sadly for the doughty Korean people, have provided the battlegrounds for great powers, especially China and Japan, to strive for control of north-east Asia for centuries. Once Russia had expanded eastwards to the Pacific seaboard of Siberia, the situation became more complex and more dangerous for those who lived in north-east Asia. In 1898 a group of young nationalist Chinese launched an uprising to protest the humiliations imposed by the demands of foreigners on China. The young Chinese dissidents formed the Society of Harmonious Fists, so foreigners termed them the 'Boxers'. They besieged foreign embassies in Peking, which led eight of the affected powers to form a joint force in order to break the siege, smash the power of the Boxers and restore order. It was a remarkable effort because it was an early example of nations coming together under joint command arrangements, not for the sake of conquest but to restore order, hand power back to a legitimate government, then depart from the scene of conflict. This was largely achieved in the space of two years by a force of 49,000 soldiers, 5,000 marines and 54 warships.

My paternal grandfather was a member of the Australian naval contingent to that conflict, so the Boxer Rebellion of 1900–01 is part of my family history. Because he was a good horseman, Grandfather was chosen to serve with the British Royal Horse Artillery on their ride to Peking, so he had unusually broad experience in his first war—one in which the Japanese, the Germans, the Austrians, the Italians and the Russians were his allies, together with the Americans, the British and the French. How radically and how swiftly alignments can change in international politics. But at least the example of a joint action to restore order and then withdraw had been set. Great powers acted as policemen, not conquerors.

Only three years later the Russo-Japanese War broke out—a huge conflagration in which the Japanese emerged so triumphantly that the Americans felt they had to take them seriously as potential enemies and so sought to contain them and develop war plans—Plan Orange in particular—to deal with them if containment did not work.

The Japanese formally incorporated Korea into their empire in 1910 and ruled it harshly for the next 35 years.

The region stayed fairly quiet under Japanese domination during the First World War, but as the Japanese became more assertive in the early 1930s and invaded Manchuria, international will to intervene, especially that of the League of Nations, was sorely tested. It failed. All the league could agree to do was to send a commission, chaired by Lord Lytton, to investigate the scene. The commission's report, a masterpiece of weasel-wording, avoided accusing the Japanese of aggression. Despite strongly critical international opinion, the Japanese got away with their use of force and added Manchuria (later renamed Manchukuo) to their domains. They then withdrew from the league, to the widespread dismay of the international community at the time.

The United Nations and Korea, 1945–50

While the great powers fought for influence during the Second World War, the poor Korean people were the grass under the elephant's feet. Their culture and sense of national identity were suppressed until the defeat of the Japanese in 1945. Then the Koreans might have had a chance to rule themselves. They asked for it, but their hopes were frustrated by great power rivalry and politics once again. The United States and the Soviets divided the Korean Peninsula at the 38th parallel in late 1945, and each side installed nationalist leaders of their own stripe: Kim Il Sung, a communist in the north, and Syngman Rhee, of Western orientation, in the south. The two Korean governments detested each other, and each threatened to take over the other's domain by force. This problem became particularly serious when the Soviet Union and the United States withdrew their forces in 1948–49. Syngman Rhee continued to offer belligerent rhetoric to the north, and this was returned with interest by Kim Il Sung—indeed, to the level of a military invasion commencing on 25 June 1950.

The North proved to be much stronger than the South militarily, and the world was presented with the spectacle of a rapid advance, first to take Seoul on 28 June, then to occupy most of South Korea in the following month. US President Harry S. Truman chose to react with firmness lest the Cold War escalate out of control through the West giving the appearance of weakness. The lessons of the 1930s had certainly been learned. After the tensions aroused in 1948–49 by the Soviet attempt to deny British, French and US access to West Berlin by land, and the foundation of the North Atlantic Treaty Organization (NATO) in 1949, President Truman was not prepared to stand idly by while South Korea was absorbed into Kim Il Sung's domain and the increasing Sino-Russo communist monolith. He responded in two ways: by immediately deploying what US forces were available in Japan to help stem the North Korean advance, and by appealing to the UN Security Council to condemn Kim Il Sung's aggression and to authorise retaliatory action under the aegis of the United Nations.

The Soviets were absent from the UN Security Council at this time, and President Truman's desires could not be thwarted by Stalin's veto. So the United States was invited to name a commander-in-chief to drive the invaders out of South Korea on behalf of the United Nations, with forces contributed by a wide range of UN members. Britain immediately placed most of its naval forces in the Far East under General Douglas MacArthur's command, and Australia did likewise. Next day Australia also committed its fighter squadron based in Japan, No. 77 Squadron, Royal Australian Air Force (RAAF). The greatest need, however, was for ground forces, and these were indeed in short supply throughout the manpower-conscious West. The Middle East had looked to be the most likely theatre of war in 1949–50, and Britain required some convincing that it should spare even a single infantry brigade for Korea in 1950. It did so in late July, and Australia offered an infantry battalion, also based in Japan. Altogether, 15 UN members, plus the ROK, placed forces under MacArthur's command. For the first time, a global security organisation had agreed to meet force with force.

A dilemma for Australia: The Middle East or East Asia?

Australia, like Britain, had been more focused on the Middle East than on north-east Asia as a likely force deployment area. The Commonwealth was Australia's principal source of friends and allies in 1950, with Britain remaining its principal trading partner and with much of that trade passing through the Suez Canal. It was not a simple matter for the Menzies government to relinquish its obligations to assist Britain in the Middle East and switch its commitments to the United States in Korea. But much was at stake here for Australia. Securing an alliance with the United States was seen by the Minister for External Affairs Percy Spender as a major prize. Menzies doubted Spender's ability to win it, but Spender proved equal to the challenge. He chose his moment well, and in 1951 the terms of the Australia, New Zealand and United States security alliance between Canberra, Wellington and Washington, DC was worked out between the three capitals.

The British Government was not pleased by Australia's formal realignment as an ally of the United States, and quietly tried to discourage the Americans from going this far. But Truman felt obliged to Australia for its support in Korea, and he also recalled the stout performance of the Australian Army when he was in France in 1918 as a captain of artillery. He silenced US Secretary of State Dean Acheson's doubts about the wisdom of yet another alliance by telling him that in a crisis, Australians were good people to have alongside the United States.[2]

This new arrangement did not mean, of course, that Australia ceased to work closely with Britain in security matters. Australia was becoming increasingly involved in the Malayan Emergency, and continued to work with British forces until Harold Wilson's government withdrew its forces from South-East Asia in the late 1960s. But the Korean War did mark a clear divergence of their respective paths.

---

2   R. O'Neill, *Australia in the Korean War 1950–1953*, vol. 1: *Strategy and Diplomacy*, AWM & AGPS, Canberra, 1981, p. 191.

The United Nations Command alliance at work: Political control and military reality, 1950

In the first few months of the war, several NATO governments, including Canada, France, the Netherlands, Belgium, Luxembourg, Greece and Turkey—and other friends of the United States, such as Colombia, Ethiopia, the Philippines, Thailand, South Africa and New Zealand—provided force contingents for Korea. Denmark, Norway, Sweden, Italy and India provided medical units to support the UN Command (UNC). It was indeed an impressive array of national flags to put beneath that of the United Nations, but most of the forces under General MacArthur's command were American and South Korean. It was also quite a handful for the United States to manage, not least because all these allied contingents had their own organisations, operational methods, logistical requirements and political sensitivities. Language was frequently a barrier. A lot of useful lessons were learned all round.

We should now look briefly at the effectiveness of American leadership. The UNC did not have an elaborate structure. Militarily, the land, sea and air forces were commanded by General MacArthur in Japan, with subordinates in South Korea. Politically, control was essentially in the hands of the Truman administration, although it had to run the gauntlet of debate in the United Nations, both in the Security Council and in the General Assembly.

Within that framework, the six Commonwealth nations (the United Kingdom, Canada, Australia, New Zealand, India and South Africa) made a very important subgroup, representing among them many viewpoints, including some that were inclined to be critical of the United States. Debates among the Commonwealth nations tended to mirror those within the UN General Assembly. India's continued approval of key policy decisions was seen as very important, particularly by the United States. If India had gone into open opposition, siding with the Soviet Union and the as yet unrepresented People's Republic of China, the United States would have been in danger of losing its precious UN mandate for intervention in Korea. Thus India's Commonwealth partners had enhanced leverage in both Washington and New Delhi.

For the 'old dominions' (Australia, Canada, New Zealand and South Africa), the Commonwealth grouping was extremely important throughout the Korean War. Old habits and conveniences proved durable and indeed warm and welcoming in a tough Cold War world. The nexus between these four and Britain was strong. The flow of information between them, and their pattern of consultation, was both extensive and intensive.

In the opening months of the war, when the UNC was struggling desperately to save South Korea from being incorporated into an all-communist Korea, policy differences were few. But once MacArthur's brilliant stroke of landing forces at Inchon had been successfully made, Seoul recaptured and the North Koreans pushed back to the 38th parallel, the nature of the conflict changed. The question now before UNC leaders was not whether South Korea could be saved but whether North Korea should be smashed and conquered.

On this issue many allies were apprehensive. To be fair to the Truman administration, there were major differences between their commander in the field and the government in Washington. MacArthur wanted to invade North Korea up to the Yalu River frontier with China, to remove Kim Il Sung and company from the government and, in effect, hand it all over to Syngman Rhee—the ironic mirror image of what the North had intended to do to the South. The political climate in the United States was not right for Truman to halt MacArthur on the 38th parallel, and indeed there was military logic in attempting to destroy the North Korean armed forces so that they could not repeat their aggression. There was, however, no clear agreement among the UNC allies as to how far this goal should be pursued. Nonetheless, the 27th British Commonwealth Brigade, under MacArthur's command and including the 3rd Battalion, Royal Australian Regiment (3RAR), set off across the parallel and headed towards the Yalu River.

Keeping the war limited, 1950–51

The most apparent danger in October 1950 was a widening of the war to include China, and the Chinese were explicit about their intentions as MacArthur's forces advanced ever more deeply into North Korea. Britain, Australia, Canada, India, New Zealand and others all had reservations about MacArthur's plans. Diplomatic channels were humming with traffic on this theme in October and early November 1950. When President Truman stated, in response to a journalist's question on 30 November, that the use of nuclear weapons against China was under consideration, alarm bells rang loudly in allied capitals. He faced strong criticism from the British and French prime ministers when he met them in Washington on 4 December. The three leaders agreed to establish a consultative system for any decisions on the use of nuclear weapons in the conflict. Truman managed to restore Attlee's confidence that he, Truman, was in charge of US policy, politically and militarily, and that he was not seeking to escalate the war into a nuclear confrontation—which was particularly important because the Soviet Union had demonstrated its own nuclear capability in a test firing in 1949.

The episode revealed major tensions between Truman and MacArthur, and when, in early 1951, MacArthur attempted to thwart his president by rallying Republicans to the cause of an expanded war, Truman recalled him. The recall came too late to prevent serious damage, because by November 1950 not only were the Chinese powerfully committed militarily in Korea but also, more importantly, MacArthur had divided his forces, leaving them open to defeat in detail. He had sent them forward on offensive missions without the capacity to sustain themselves against the Chinese. The result was a series of Chinese victories on the ground and, by 4 January 1951, Seoul was back in communist hands. The UNC allies were worrying about whether they might not be forced to evacuate Korea altogether.

MacArthur's successor, General Matthew Ridgway, thought in much more appropriate terms than his predecessor. He judged that with the existing balance of forces, the UNC could not only hold its ground without resorting to nuclear weapons but also could begin to grind down the Chinese and North Koreans so effectively that they would want to negotiate an end to their unsuccessful efforts. He let the Chinese Fifth Phase Offensive beat itself out against the UNC's defences across Korea in April and May 1951, as part of which the Battle of Kapyong was fought. He then prepared to drive the communists back and seize the favourable high ground that his forces were to hold while both sides negotiated their way towards an armistice. These talks began on 10 July 1951 at Kaesong and continued at Panmunjom for the following two years. Ridgway's strategy was exactly right for this war. He was fortunate to have available forces that could carry it through without being minced up themselves by the Chinese.

Sea and air power in a peninsular war

While we tend to think of the Korean War as having been mainly a contest between the armies of both sides—and that indeed is where the great bulk of the casualties occurred—there were also important naval and air dimensions to the war.

One key strategic factor that seemed to have escaped Kim Il Sung when he launched his attack in mid-1950 was that Korea is a peninsula. The further south a northern aggressor came, the longer were the flanks he had to defend against seaward attack. All his ports were open to bombardment, as were his coastal railway lines, roads and bridges, and any vital facility could be raided by marines coming ashore. The rugged geography of Korea means that most of the communications arteries run along the coast, making sea power all the more influential in a conflict there. Similarly, the further south an invader came, the more he was open to attack by air, both tactical against his ground forces and strategic against his logistics, war industry and sources of food. It took some little time for the United States to marshal, train and equip naval and air forces to perform these missions around and over the Korean Peninsula, but by late 1950 the Korean War had become a land, sea and air conflict in which the UNC had dominance in two of these three elements.

Let us now look at the contributions that the British Commonwealth group of nations made to the effectiveness of UNC operations.

Naval operations

Because Britain in 1950 still deployed a Far Eastern fleet based in Hong Kong, it was well placed to command the Australian, Canadian and New Zealand naval contingents during the Korean War. This fleet included an aircraft carrier as well as several cruisers, destroyers and frigates, and was able to take responsibility for exerting control over the Yellow Sea and the west coast of the Korean Peninsula. Looking back on three years of deployments of Commonwealth warships in Korean waters, two elements stand out: the navigation, seamanship and hitting power of the smaller ships, especially the frigates; and the strategic role played by the fleet's aircraft.

For Australia, the Korean War offered the opportunity of deploying its new aircraft carrier, HMAS *Sydney*. Australia maintained one destroyer and one frigate in Korean waters throughout the war. *Sydney* replaced the usual British aircraft carrier on the west coast of Korea (one had been stationed in the Far East since 1945) from October 1951 to late January 1952—122 days of continuous service. There is no more complex instrument of war to operate than an aircraft carrier. Australia had acquired *Sydney* after the Second World War, and was about to acquire a second carrier, HMAS *Melbourne*, when the Korean War began.

Despite their lack of experience, the ship's company of HMAS *Sydney* achieved a good record. Her pilots destroyed 66 bridges, seven tunnels, seven railway sidings, 159 railway wagons, two locomotives, 495 junks and other fishing vessels, 15 artillery pieces and more than 2,000 houses. *Sydney*'s aircraft sustained 99 hits by enemy flak, and nine of her aircraft were shot down. Several pilots were killed, and others were rescued by daring action while under enemy fire, on land or in shallow coastal waters. On some patrols, *Sydney*'s pilots and support crew achieved two sorties per day for all aircraft. Given that 38 per cent of *Sydney*'s aircraft returned to the ship in unserviceable condition, this was a notable achievement. (For more on Australia's carrier operations, see Chapter 7.)

As for inshore patrolling and bombardment, it is invidious to pick out a single frigate, but HMAS *Murchison*'s performance was remarkable. The ship, and especially her commanding officer, Commander A.N. Dollard, performed some remarkable feats of navigation—often while under fire between mud banks and along narrow estuarine channels—to attack shore targets or make attempted rescues. *Murchison* was often a sitting duck for North Korean artillery batteries on shore, only a few hundred yards away, and the vessel frequently took enemy rounds in the hull. When these were armour-piercing shells, they went straight through and out the other side without doing much damage, but a 75mm high-explosive shell in the engine room was a different matter. When it happened on 30 September 1951, *Murchison* was lucky not to have had a high-pressure steam line cut. The ship would have lost the power of one of its two turbines, run aground and been pounded to pieces.

The proficiency of the companies of these two Australian warships demonstrated that in the early 1950s the Royal Australian Navy (RAN) could claim to be taken seriously as a regional force; as such, its effectiveness was magnified by its ability to operate within a larger Commonwealth force under British command and as part of a US-led coalition. Australia was one of three countries then operating an aircraft carrier in the Pacific.

Land operations

It was on land that the Commonwealth, including Australia, made its greatest military contribution in Korea. The war was fought primarily by ground forces, and the other side had clear numerical superiority. The essence of a successful ground strategy for the UNC was threefold: to reclaim the territory of South Korea, to inflict such a level of casualties on enemy forces that they would negotiate a ceasefire, and to avoid precipitating a much larger war by taking action directly against China or the Soviet Union.

This strategy called for well-trained and well-equipped soldiers who could work together in a carefully controlled way and successfully wear down a numerically superior enemy fighting close to his home bases—all this without suffering heavy losses themselves. These three objectives called for British force commanders who understood their guidelines and could produce a satisfactory result. Generals Cassells and West, the two Commonwealth Division commanders, and Brigadiers Coad and MacDonald, commanding the 27th and 28th British Commonwealth Brigades, were all equipped by the British Government with a directive that, as well as requiring them to obey the orders of senior (and therefore American) commanders, also required them to make representations directly to the British Government if they thought that their forces were being exposed to undue risk. The American commanders knew about this directive and therefore did not wish it to be put into effect against themselves. If either of the British generals thought there was a possibility of their forces being committed unwisely, all they had to do was go to their US Corps commander and 'wave the paper', as General Cassells termed it. He did not have to do it often, and when he did, it was effective. The two Australian commanders of the 28th Brigade, Brigadiers Daly and Wilton, were also glad to have been under the protection of this directive.

Australia's role in the broad panoply of land forces was modest, being initially limited to one, then two infantry battalions. Nonetheless, they received acclaim for their efforts. The successes of 3RAR, in the defensive Battle of Kapyong then in the attack on Maryang San, are well known, and the latter is the subject of detailed analysis in later chapters of this volume. Let me therefore focus on another aspect of the ground campaign that was important right through the three years for which Australian soldiers were committed to the war: patrolling.

Patrolling is a largely unsung art because it is performed by small groups of soldiers, typically 10 to 30 strong. It does not make the headlines, so journalists and the public tend to overlook the powerful contribution that well-conducted patrolling can make. Without a successful patrol program, the enemy will come to dominate no man's land; that makes it easier for him 'to lean on our wire' by conducting offensive operations, thereby keeping the defenders confined, unable to take their own initiatives, and deprived of all the vital intelligence that can be gained from going out and having a close look at the enemy and what he is doing.

When in the early 1970s I interviewed the British commanders of the Commonwealth Division and 27th Brigade, they all emphasised how splendidly the three Australian battalions had performed in the patrolling role. They kept the Chinese well back from their own positions, and they intercepted large parties of Chinese at night as the enemy fought vainly for dominance in no man's land. Australian patrols were aggressive, and at last light the first patrols to go out from the Australian lines could be seen running down through the minefield and barbed-wire gaps to get into no man's land before darkness fell completely. They would go out on a variety of missions: reconnaissance, ambushing, direct combat against enemy patrols where possible and prisoner-snatching from enemy lines. Typically they were led by a platoon commander in his early twenties, or a non-commissioned officer (NCO). They were lonely missions—out there where they could bump into a larger group of Chinese all too easily. They had to depend for their survival on the weapons and ammunition they carried with them. Some patrols could call in artillery fire for protection, but as a patrol commander, you had to know exactly where you were before calling in fire support. Good navigation was essential, and often it was impossible to read a map accurately in the dark. Radio communications were desirable but not always available. Minefields, both enemy and our own, were a problem. And if a member of the patrol was wounded it could be very difficult to get him home again, with four men being required to carry an improvised stretcher. Often the wounded had to struggle along as best they could, even on all fours, because there was no other way to get home. That is how Captain John Salmon made it up the icy slopes of Hill 355 on the night of 10/11 December 1952—and he sets off the metal detectors as he goes through airport security nearly 60 years after being hit.

I carried out research on the Korean War in many countries where I could talk to allied veterans. Those who knew anything about the ground war marked out the Australian infantrymen as outstanding patrollers. 'Second to none' is an appropriate characterisation. And given that for nearly two years the ground war was largely static, good patrolling made a vital contribution to the war objective: keeping pressure on the enemy to negotiate without incurring such heavy losses to our own forces that public opinion would cease to support the war effort.

The war in the air

The air war was extremely important from a UNC perspective because it was a means of offsetting the enemy's superiority in numbers of troops on the ground. Given the context of the war and the need to avoid escalation, the most essential element of UNC air power was the tactical. There was a limited role available for the United States' greatest strength in the air, namely strategic bombing, and all the important strategic targets in North Korea were soon taken out. Australia provided one of only three national air force contingents to operate under the UNC, with the United States and South Africa.

The unit chosen to represent the RAAF was 77 Squadron, which was equipped with Mustangs. They put up a fine performance from the outset and received international acclaim. When the Australian Minister for External Affairs Percy Spender launched his campaign for an alliance with the United States in the Oval Office on 13 September 1950, the one key fact that President Truman knew about Australia's participation in the Korean War to that date was that No. 77 Squadron had done brilliantly. Buoyed by that evidence, Truman was confident in talking down the opposition of his Secretary of State and Joint Chiefs of Staff to taking on yet one more ally. Three weeks before Spender's meeting with Truman, on 22 August 1950, No. 77 Squadron's commanding officer, Wing Commander Lou Spence, had been invested as a member of the Legion of Merit by United States Air Force (USAF) Commander General George Stratemeyer for his outstanding leadership and the squadron's bravery in combat. Truman knew that Spence had been awarded this honour, but what he might not have known, when Spender came to the White House, was that Spence had been killed in Korea four days previously.

US and Australian aircrew soon received a sharp reminder that they had entered the jet era. The Soviets, utilising captured German jet fighter swept-wing designs and the British Rolls Royce Nene jet engine, produced under licence from the Attlee government in the USSR, had developed the MiG-15 fighter. This aircraft had excellent high-altitude performance that clearly outclassed that of the propeller-driven Mustangs. The Soviets had passed the MiGs on to the Chinese in mid-1950, and by late that year the danger arose that the Chinese would achieve dominance in the airspace over North Korea sufficient to permit the use of their own ground-attack, reconnaissance and transport aircraft. The Chinese were augmented by highly capable Soviet MiG-15 pilots.

This challenge had to be met and defeated quickly. The United States began to deploy Sabre jet fighters, but it was not so easy for Australia to find a source of supply for jet fighters. The Americans needed every aircraft then rolling off their assembly lines, and the only available option was the British-produced Gloucester Meteor. It was ordered and came into service with No. 77 Squadron on 29 July 1951. It soon became clear that the Meteor could not meet the MiG-15 on anything like equal terms, and it was relegated to the ground-attack role for which it was poorly suited. So the brave and able pilots of No. 77 Squadron put their lives at risk for the last two years of the war with little prospect of achieving much. The squadron lost 37 pilots killed and seven captured. So, despite a good beginning in 1950, No. 77 Squadron had a frustrating period of service for the greater part of the war. The RAAF moved to acquire Sabres as soon as US authorities cleared them for sale, but No. 77 Squadron had to persevere with the Meteors for the remainder of the war.

Diplomacy in the Korean War

In parallel with the military operations of the war ran intense diplomatic activity. The members of the newly established NATO busily tried to persuade the United States not to leave Europe open to a possible Soviet attack. Countries with interests in the Middle East (particularly Britain and France) sought to come to terms with the problems of resurgent

Arab nationalism, especially in Egypt, and the challenges of the Israeli–Palestinian relationship. These issues impinged on their relations with the United States.

For Australia, the Korean War represented a call to focus on the security of its own region. Although Britain was still heavily committed to military operations in Malaya, it seemed to most Australians on both sides of politics that they must choose the United States as a principal security partner in the Pacific. While seeking to minimise damage to the British–Australian relationship, the Menzies government now had to forge a partnership with the United States in which Australia would have a significant voice. In essence this meant continuing to impress Washington with Australia's usefulness as an ally and partner. It meant trying to play a stronger part in the Korean War and a major commitment of resources and manpower to a defence build-up in Australia, backed by a near-universal national service training scheme for Australia's young men. Public opinion supported the government and a major reorientation towards the United States was set in motion, which was largely unquestioned until Australia became heavily committed to the Vietnam War.

Australian diplomats also made a direct contribution in Korea. James Plimsoll, the Australian representative on the United Nations Commission on Korea, later the United Nations Commission for the Unification and Rehabilitation of Korea, achieved unusual prominence in Korean affairs. Plimsoll showed the talents that were to take him to the most senior appointments that his department had to offer. He was active in Seoul for much of the period 1950–52 and played a valuable role through developing an effective but not subservient relationship with President Syngman Rhee. The South Korean president was no liberal democrat, and it was all too easy for friction to arise between his government and the Truman administration, not to mention the United Nations itself. Plimsoll showed good judgement in choosing when and how to intervene in these disputes, often succeeding in finding a compromise that kept all parties together on the road to a negotiated truce. Without Plimsoll's mediation it would have been harder to keep the UN coalition together and to limit Rhee's propensity for dictatorial rule. Senior State Department officers praised him warmly when I interviewed them.

The contributions of the Republic of Korea

UNC strategy in Korea could not have worked well without a major contribution from the people and leaders of the ROK. Space does not permit more than a brief mention of this factor, but after the first year of the war, during which South Korea was struggling desperately to function as a state, it made a huge contribution to its own deliverance. Two-thirds of the troops in the main defensive lines across the peninsula were South Korean. They took their responsibilities seriously and performed well. The South Korean Government, while far from perfect, also made an important contribution by effectively organising its national resources in support of the UNC. This support ran from the unloading at wharves on the coast to the Korean porterage and support personnel attached to forward allied forces, known, in the case of the Commonwealth Division, as KATCOMs (Koreans Attached Commonwealth Division).

This aspect of the war is notable particularly because it was in marked contrast to allied experience in the Vietnam War, where one of the continually recurring questions was: why aren't our Vietnamese as good as their Vietnamese? In Korea that question had a very short lifetime.

Winding the war down

Let us return to the theme of this chapter: the setting of a new paradigm in maintaining world order. By the middle of 1951, it was fairly clear to both sides that neither was likely to be able to push the other out of the Korean Peninsula. The balance of forces appeared reasonably stable and robust, and the consequences of escalating the war—into China or Russia for the West, or into Indo-China or Taiwan for the communists—appeared negative, especially in the era of nuclear weapons.

So, in this unusual conflict, both sides agreed in July 1951 to sit down and negotiate a ceasefire that would lead, hopefully, to a peace treaty based on a divided Korean Peninsula. The war continued for a further two years. Many lives, civilian and military, were lost in the process. The soldiers, sailors and airmen at war had to face further hardships and tests of their courage and endurance so that their own side was not seen to be clearly losing on the battlefield, thereby undermining their negotiators or possibly creating an incentive for the other side to escalate. And for their valour and commitment in this period, these same soldiers, sailors and airmen deserve praise for persevering when at times the well-known Republican challenge to Truman's policy—'why die for a tie?'—seemed to have some point to it.

Incentives for concluding an armistice were strengthened by political factors on both sides: the war was becoming increasingly unpopular in the Western states most heavily involved in it, and the Chinese had other priorities on which to focus their limited resources.

By 26 July 1953, everyone had finally had enough, and the armistice was signed. The next day China was given a warning statement—which had been composed by Western powers over several rounds of intense diplomacy during the preceding 21 months—to the effect that if they renewed aggressive activity on the Korean Peninsula, or anywhere else such as Indo-China or Taiwan, the allied response would be swift and powerful. The resulting war would not necessarily be limited, leaving open the interpretation that the United States might use nuclear weapons in responding even to a non-nuclear provocation. President Eisenhower in mid-1953 made sure that the Chinese saw the warning as a serious threat.

This declaration probably had scant effect on Chinese policies in the region, but it offered a smokescreen of menace behind which the West was able to withdraw its forces from the Korean Peninsula. And the Chinese accepted that they needed to devote their efforts more to reconstruction at home than to supporting Kim Il Sung.

Living without a peace settlement since 1953

The armistice has continued in effect for the past 65 years. North and South Korea, and their respective allies, are still technically at war. And, as we have seen in recent times, the North occasionally commits hostile acts to which the South responds calmly and judiciously. But, despite ostentatious presidential summits, the possibility of a return to serious military operations remains a concern for both sides, and deterrence remains an important justification for continuing high levels of militarisation on both sides of the armistice line. Despite overtures for peace, given the North's development of nuclear weapons, many are still concerned that the people on the Korean Peninsula will not be fully at peace with each other for many a long year. But at least those who live in the South are able to continue their development towards a stronger and more prosperous democracy. Sadly, the pitiful condition of those in the North seems likely to persist for many years to come.

There has not been another war of this kind since 1953. The United Nations has sponsored many interventions but not on the scale of the Korean War, and perhaps that is a result of the learning process that occurred on both sides in 1950–51. The United Nations was able to show itself—at least when Stalin was looking the other way—to have teeth and to be capable of using them. That was an improvement over the League of Nations, and a huge improvement over the days preceding the foundation of international organisations dedicated to preserving the peace.

Since 1953, the United Nations has continued to exert itself in the cause of peace and international order, not always successfully, but it has made a powerful difference to outcomes in Africa, the Middle East and South-East Asia. The world of the twenty-first century is a very different place from that of the early twentieth century. We owe this change in part to the many men and women of the UN alliance who fought in Korea between 1950 and 1953, and made the point that aggression does not pay.

2

THE KOREAN WAR
Which one? When?

Allan Millett

To really understand the nature of the Korean War and to put a human face to the mountains of statistical analysis, it is imperative, as a scholar, to engage with Korean War veterans and other survivors of the conflict and listen to their stories.[1] I am often asked what I have learned about the Korean War, given all the time and energy I have exerted, even taking Korean language lessons. I have even been forgotten by the Korean Language Institute at Yonsei University because I was so miserable at *hangukmal* (Korean Language). From my American perspective, the most important thing is understanding the suffering of the Korean people during the Korean War in the geopolitical context of the interwar period of 1945–50 in north-east Asia. It is also essential that we account for the composition of weapons capabilities on both sides and for the influence of the Korean climate and terrain on the conflict.

First of all, the Korean War did not begin in 1950. It began at least in 1948. One could argue that it started in 1947 or the year before with what is known as the Autumn Harvest Rebellion. Indeed, one could talk

---

1   This chapter is based on Allan Millett's presentation at the international military history conference 'Korea: In from the Cold', Australian War Memorial, Canberra, 2011. Millett's remarks reflect his views and expertise outlined in his publications, including *The War for Korea, 1945–1950: A House Burning*, University Press of Kansas, Lawrence, KS, 2005, and *The War for Korea, 1950–1951: They Came from the North*, University Press of Kansas, Lawrence, KS, 2010.

about a 'Korean war in the making' by going all the way back to 1 March 1919—the period of a great Korean nationalist protest against the Japanese annexation of 1910. After this unsuccessful protest movement—which was suppressed with a loss of life numbering in the thousands—two kinds of Korean revolutionary movements emerged. It is very difficult to categorise them. Bruce Cumings at the University of Chicago divides the instigators of the rebellion between the good guys—who are almost always socialists—and the bad guys, who are everybody else. This clear-cut differentiation allows for a limited description of the nuances of resistance to the Japanese occupation of Korea. The leaders of the 1919 movement were not communists at all. The Korean Communist Party had not yet been formed: these revolutionaries were involved in lobbying for support at the peace conference in Versailles. The leaders of the 1919 movement produced the nationalistic resistance generation, which continued to be represented by Syngman Rhee, for example, well into the 1950s. And it was a movement that in essence was forced into exile, either in the United States or, more specifically, Hawaii, where Syngman Rhee based himself, or in China, led by Kim Ku, who was the president of the Korean Provisional Government (KPG) in exile. The KPG was closely associated with the Chinese Kuomintang.

Some authors assert that the Americans responsible for interwar and wartime policy of the 1930s and 1940s concerning the Korean peninsula did not know anything about Korean politics. This is simply not true. The problem was that what they knew led them to believe that there was no legitimate exile movement that was worthy of support whenever liberation came. Kim Ku and the provisional government were much too close to the Chinese Nationalists; they seemed to represent the most autocratic and corrupt part of Chinese politics. The United States Department of State had already begun distancing itself from the Chinese Nationalist Party, so anyone associated with it was going to be stained by that association. The State Department was not in love with Syngman Rhee either, whom it had known since the 1920s. He had come in exile to Hawaii and become a lobbyist for Korean nationalism in New York and Washington.

The United States has a habit of picking strange people to back, but Syngman Rhee was not one of them, nor was Kim Ku. If the United States had had a choice, the leadership of liberated Korea would have fallen into the hands of a man named Yo Hon-yong and another named Kim Kyu-sik. They were coffee-house liberals, inept when it came to governing in a post-colonial environment. It is often said the United States had no plan for Korea. That is true, but not because no one had thought about it. The State Department just did not have anybody whom it thought was worth American support. The one goal the United States had in 1945 was to free Allied prisoners of war, wherever they were, and to repatriate Japanese prisoners as rapidly as it could. The repatriation of the Japanese army and civilians (more than 5 million people abroad) was critical to the restoration and reform of Japan. That is why the United States went to Korea in 1945, a mission accomplished with considerable deftness by December 1945. Then the question facing Lieutenant General John R. Hodge was: what do I do now? It was a good question because nobody had yet told him.

The foreign ministers met in Moscow in early December 1945, and the great powers told General Hodge to prepare for Korean independence. This instruction came without his being offered some plan for how this should be accomplished, particularly now that the Russians were very much in control above the 38th parallel. They had brought with them a number of Korean communists, led by Kim Il Sung. That was not really his name. He called himself that because it was the name of a local hero, like Robin Hood or Jesse James or Ned Kelly. General Paik Sun-yup, very much a hero of mine as he is to many people in Korea, was at a meeting to which the Russians brought Kim Il Sung to meet Cho Man-sik, a prominent Christian liberationist leader in North Korea. A funny little man came in with the Russians and was introduced as Kim Il Sung. And everybody says, 'Who? That's not him'. Cho Man-sik turned to the Paik brothers—both later generals in the Republic of Korea (ROK) Army— and said, 'I think we've got trouble. I think you guys better get out of here. It's obvious that the Russians have chosen him [Kim] and they're going to get us'. And, in fact, Cho died in prison, basically neglected, ignored and killed by the Soviets.

There was an irreconcilable difference between two very broad liberation movements. One was a coalition of communists, some based in China, some based in Russia, and members of the Kapsan faction with Kim Il Sung as their champion. The other was an indigenous communist party, led by Pak Hon-yong. If you are looking for a hero of Korean nationalism and resistance to Japan, and the formation of an indigenous radical movement within Korea, Pak Hon-yong is the man. He did not survive the Korean

War. He was foreign minister and deputy premier of North Korea. He was later accused of working for the Central Intelligence Agency (CIA) and was executed by Kim Il Sung.

After a series of tortuous negotiations, it was clear that there would be no unification between the northern occupied zone and the southern occupied zone. There were, in fact, meetings and negotiations that went on for about a year and a half, but fundamentally there was no way to patch together the two Koreas. One proposal was for up to five years of trusteeship by the Soviet Union, the United States, China and Britain, which many Koreans opposed. To a large degree the Soviets made it unworkable, because their condition—even for negotiations on unifying Korea—was that every party that opposed trusteeship was illegitimate and should not be allowed to participate in the process. That ban included every party except the communist party, which had flip-flopped in January 1946. The South Korean Labor Party, which was the communist party of South Korea, had big signs in English: 'We're against trusteeship, no trusteeship'. It was in a coalition against trusteeship. Forty-eight hours later the communists had to get rid of their signs and put up new signs that said, 'We love trusteeship'. They had got the word from the Soviet legation in Seoul, and the word was that the Soviets thought trusteeship was a good deal. Everybody who opposed trusteeship should be disallowed as a participant in those negotiations.

After some rather considerable discussions within the State Department, the diplomats concluded that this mess should be turned over to the United Nations for solution. In fact, Australian representatives played an important role in what was first known as the UN Temporary Commission on Korea, which then evolved into several other iterations. The United States passed the Korean unification problem to the United Nations in the fall of 1947, and the elections that created the ROK in 1948 were supervised by the United Nations, which could not go north and hold similar elections there.

From a theoretical perspective of people's wars of national liberation, Korea begins to fit a Maoist Phase 2 uprising, in which one begins to see violent insurgency. The tax protest in the fall of 1946 does not appear to be communist-encouraged, but killed about a thousand people. American soldiers actually shot Koreans at a place called Nowon. The fall of 1946 was a very unpleasant time; there were some very serious divisions in Korea over the nation's future. In the general strike of 1947, the South

Korean Labour Party went underground and began to organise the foundation for some future insurgency, which was largely pre-empted in the spring of 1948 on the island of Cheju-do (today's Jeju). In any event, a direct conflict broke out there between the South Korean Labour Party and the government, represented by the Korean National Police and Constabulary and American military government advisers.

The war that started on Cheju-do spread to the mainland throughout the summer and fall of 1948. Before 25 June 1950, the casualty estimates run between 30,000 and 100,000 dead. These figures are wildly exaggerated. Counting the dead is a bad business. I was involved in having the figures revised for the American war dead in the Korean War, and we finally persuaded the US Defense Department to admit that it had made an error: 54,000 was not the right number. It was more like 37,000.[2] The South Korean security forces lost more than 7,200 dead during the insurgency of 1948–50. Their names are on the plaques at the Korean War Memorial in Seoul. How many other people died is difficult to know. I argue it would be 20,000 perhaps. It is a serious number, and it was a horrible conflict. The ROK government, established on 15 August 1948, won that war. By the spring of 1950, the South Korean communist-led insurgency in the south had been largely suppressed.

The nature of the relationship between Pyongyang and the communist insurgency is unknown. We do know that Kim Il Sung and his supporters joined in late 1948–49, because they took South Korean communist exiles who had crossed into North Korea, armed them, trained them, and sent them back. Eleven different efforts were made to return South Korean communists to South Korea to support this insurgency. There is definitely a comparison to be made here with the Vietnam War. Pak Hon-yong had gone north and was helping to direct this civil war by 1949–50. Whether there had been an invasion or not, there would have been a South Korean civil war of some kind. How it would have turned out and how bloody it would have been is subject to historical speculation.

During these years the ROK had become home to a large number of northern Koreans. These northern Koreans were often Christians, landholders, businessmen or other enemies of North Korean communism. Exiles from North Korea became a rock-hard anti-communist foundation within the politics of South Korea. The staunch Christian anti-communist

---

2   A. Millett, 'Korean War', *Encyclopaedia Britannica*, www.britannica.com/event/Korean-War.

society in South Korea was largely concentrated in the northern areas of the ROK: Kangwon province in the north-east and Kyonggi in the north-west. The radicals were concentrated in the south of the ROK. If this distribution had been reversed, it would have been a really serious problem for the anti-communists. This is because the infiltrators from the north—in order to marry up with the insurgents, who were largely concentrated in the south—had to go all the way down the Taebaeks, the mountain range that runs the length of the east coast. Then they had to find insurgent groups in the Chiri-sans in the lower part of the Taebaek range. That trek was a serious problem for the infiltration effort from the north.

When do the North Koreans enter this war? Pak Hon-yong had joined the government of the Democratic People's Republic of Korea (DPRK), officially founded in September 1948. He argued that there was still enough of a political base within South Korea for there to be a great uprising if the North Koreans invaded; between the uprising and the invasion, the communist cause would win. Kim Il Sung was convinced of this in 1949 and had drawn up plans to intervene in the civil war in the south. He went to Moscow for aid.

Traditional wisdom has it that this was Kim Il Sung's first trip to Moscow. Once we began to look at Russian documents, made possible through the Woodrow Wilson Center, it was clear that he had been to Russia before. A transcript of his meeting with Stalin in the spring of 1949 contains this event: Stalin looks at him and says, 'I believe you've put on weight. You look a lot fatter than the last time I saw you'. Then the question was: when was that? And it turned out that Kim Il Sung had been to Moscow in 1947, largely because he was lobbying to have printing presses replaced. The printing presses belonged to three communist newspapers in Seoul. They printed newspapers, to be sure, but at the same time were counterfeiting South Korean currency. The military government went in and grabbed the presses. The communists were distressed, so they went off to get more presses. That is why Kim Il Sung and Pak Hon-yong had gone to Moscow. We know they made contact with Stalin. How much happened between that time and 1949 we still do not know.

But in any event, Stalin talked with Kim Il Sung about an invasion, and he said, 'No, not yet'. But Stalin also said: 'Try me again later—but here are the preconditions for my giving you support. The Americans have got to go. Advisers we don't care about, but there's one American regimental combat team, the 5th Regimental Combat Team [RCT], sitting on the approaches to Seoul.' Today the road to Seoul is built up, but in those days it was open. And the one American unit left in Korea after the summer of 1948 was sitting right astride that route.

Stalin's conditions for assisting the DPRK in invading the ROK were threefold: first, the Americans had to go; second, no sign of intervention could be shown; and the DPRK had to reorganise its army, following the return of DPRK soldiers training in Russia to the Korean Peninsula, to fight the ROK Army, which should ideally be underprepared and ill-equipped to stand up to an attack from the DPRK were it to succeed.[3]

In short, the ROK Army did not defect, and it continued to fight even when its forces were being pushed back towards the Pusan Perimeter. Stalin was requiring all kinds of conditions that were based on the Chinese communist experience. The ROK Army did exactly the opposite. Undergunned, undersupplied, it fought very well. Another of Stalin's conditions was that the Chinese had to promise to give the North Koreans help of some kind, which in fact the Chinese did. They transferred two whole divisions of Korean troops from the Chinese People's Liberation Army (PLA) to the Korean People's Army (KPA). Other Korean veterans of the PLA (there were tens of thousands) came in as individuals, then served as the backbone of at least two other divisions. So, of the seven North Korean divisions, four came from the Chinese PLA. Some historians have argued that Stalin reluctantly approved the North Korean attack under significant pressure from Kim, who won his case by misrepresenting to Stalin the strength of communist guerrillas in the South who would supposedly rise up and provide North Korea with a quick and easy victory. There is also a continuing debate over whether Kim initiated the North Korean attack alone or whether it was a Soviet plot. Indeed, many historians record that, in 1950, the US Government viewed the Korean War as being an initiative of the Soviets.

A year later—with the American troops gone and some signs that all these other preconditions had either been met or would be met if an invasion began—Stalin gave his approval. We have testimony from North Korean officers who later chose to stay in South Korea of exactly how many tanks came in and how many guns. This is not a great mystery. The two officers

---

3   'Telegram from Tunkin to the Soviet Foreign Ministry in Reply to 11 September Telegram', 14 September 1949, History and Public Policy Program Digital Archive, AVP RF, Fond 059a, Opis 5a, Delo 3, Papka 11, listy 46-53, digitalarchive.wilsoncenter.org/document/112132.

who wrote the invasion plan were both Koreans trained by the Soviets. Both of them visited South Korea in their later years and said, 'We don't know what the mystery is. We planned this thing'. The word was out that it was OK to invade.

There is still some debate about the timing of the invasion. The original plan, to the degree that we understand it, called for the invasion to come in August. Now you have to know Korean weather to understand that decision. In late June or early July *changma* begins; this is the rainy season.

Heavy rainfall on the Korean Peninsula is a major military and tactical factor because it is difficult to do armour operations of any kind on the roads, and it is certainly not going to make any kind of air support feasible. The difficulty from the North Korean standpoint was that it looked as if the South Koreans knew there would be an invasion. As a matter of fact, they did. They had infiltrated the North Korean Army and had good intelligence. Many of the Americans of the Korean Military Advisory Group (KMAG) agreed that the ROK Army should go on alert in the first two weeks of June; they went off alert because the ROK Army thought that they needed a little break. Two North Korean officers had defected and revealed the plans. There were four South Korean divisions on the front, and unfortunately the two that were in the path of the attack, Paik Sun Yup's 1st Division and Yu Jae Hung's 7th Division, did go on leave. The 6th Division was at Chunchon, right in the middle of the country, and the 8th Division was on the east coast. Neither of their commanders released their troops. They fought good withdrawals down the coast. The invasion had taken place even though it was raining simply because the North Koreans believed that if they did not go then, the ROK Army would get to a higher state of alert. The ROK would get the four divisions that were in the south, fighting the guerrillas, and bring them north; then maybe the Americans might even decide to intervene.

From a broad historical perspective of the Korean War, this 1950 period provides a narration of the key points throughout the duration of the conflict. The North Koreans thought that if they seized Seoul, the South Korean Government and the South Korean Army would collapse. The South Koreans did not capitulate. That came as a very unpleasant surprise, both to their Soviet advisers and to the North Korean leadership. The thing that begins to turn the war, obviously, is the US intervention, but it was not all that easy. The US Eighth Army was not as ill-prepared as it has often been characterised, but it was unprepared enough. There is no question that UN soldiers—including the ROK Army and the US Army—did not have enough anti-tank weapons until there were medium tanks in theatre, and they got 3.5-inch rocket launchers. The US Air Force (USAF) brought in something like 4,000 3.5-inch rocket launchers and ammunition for them in a period of about eight weeks. By the end of August 1950, the infantry units had a dependable anti-tank weapon. The air force and the US Army actually counted kills of Russian T-34 tanks and came up with almost the same answers. I found this unbelievable. The US Army and US Air Force actually agreed on something. But in fact they found that fewer than half those tanks were destroyed from the air. The others were destroyed by rocket launchers and by artillery and demolitions and other kinds of weapons.

The major military equipment deficit between the UN forces and the communist forces really was not tanks but a disparity in the number of artillery pieces. If you take a look at the engagements, you find that the tanks are a problem; but what really breaks ROK units and breaks up US units is a huge artillery deficit. Divisional artillery was filled out by the fall of 1950, but corps artillery was not in place until the winter of 1951. It took 14 different US National Guard heavy artillery battalions to build a corps artillery component for the allies. The North Koreans had good artillery: it was all Russian, and the North Korean troops were well trained.

Fortunately the weather was not as bad as it might have been. The *changma* rainy seasons in 1951 and 1952 were awful. But in 1950 it was one of the driest *changma* in recorded history. I went through all the records of the Fifth Air Force, and there were only four days, in a period of about three months, in which the air force could not put up at least a hundred sorties. This meant that a road-bound army, which the North Koreans were, was going to be vulnerable to air attack. USAF air attack took out the North Koreans' artillery, as well as counter-battery fire.

The story of the strategic counter-offensive gives too much credit to the Inchon landing to recapture Seoul. Strategically it was an error, because it was the landing that convinced the Chinese that they had to intervene. Critical decisions in China had been made over the nights between 1 and 3 October; then it became a matter of what conditions the Russians and the Chinese would work out between them, not whether or not the Chinese would come into the war. The Russians made a fatal mistake, which Kim Il Sung and others bought. The Russians knew an amphibious landing was probable, but they decided that, in organising the defences, they would emphasise Wonsan. The Russians said, 'We think they're going to Wonsan'. So that is where they laid all the mines. The Chinese war-gamed the problem and told the North Koreans: 'It's not Wonsan. It's Inchon.' Chai Chengwen, who was head of the PLA military mission to the DPRK, insisted that the Chinese gave good advice to the North Koreans, but the Russians countered it. The US X Corps was lucky that Seoul and the approaches to Inchon were not as well defended as they might have been. It was not United Nations Command's (UNC) crossing of the 38th parallel that became critical; it was the Chinese decision that war had become inevitable that led China to intervene.

I want to shift, however, to what is known as the stalemate period, 1951–53, the armistice negotiations period. This is a neglected area; yet, in some cases, the terrain really counts. Both sides wanted to position themselves in such a way that if the armistice broke down, they would hold key terrain that would allow them to continue the war. The Americans wanted first of all to protect Seoul and all the approaches to Seoul. This meant putting good units—the ROK 1st Division, the Commonwealth Division and the US 1st Marine Division—on the northern approaches to Seoul to make sure that the enemy could not go south if they wanted to. This was basically a strategic defence; it was critical to hold onto the base of the Iron Triangle where it sat across the future Demilitarised Zone (DMZ). The Iron Triangle was located between the towns of Chorwon, Kumwha and Pyongyang; it served as an important Chinese troop concentration area, as well as a critical communications and supply area. Up there on Chorwon is one of the few places in Korea where you can see flat ground; it is a fairly open area with roads that go either north-west to Wonsan or north-east to Pyongyang. So if you are thinking about some future campaign, having access to the Iron Triangle becomes an understandable goal.

From the Chinese and North Korean perspective, the concern remained fear of invasion. In 1951 the Chinese decided they were going to have a fortification building program, which was part of their war of attrition. In about 18 months they had their part of the front well-fortified back to a depth of about 20 miles. The next thing they wanted to do was to create counter-amphibious invasion positions up and down both coasts, and these were not completed until the summer of 1953. I think they would not have signed an armistice until they were convinced that the North Korean Army was in good shape and that these fortifications were in place.

From the American standpoint, the key thing was building the South Korean Army. And that took time too. A plan adopted in 1951 would increase that army to almost 15 divisions, then to 20 divisions. Obviously it took time to train and arm this army. The prisoner of war issue was a real one, but it was, I think, defined by the negotiations, not by the general strategic context in which those talks were going on.

Proud of their long history of independence and resistance to invaders, both Koreas asserted that they would seek *Juche*, which can be translated as self-reliance or self-determination. One year after the armistice, with foreign armies still on their soil and scant evidence of recovery, Syngman Rhee and Kim Il Sung had taken political paths they believed were the preconditions for rebuilding their Koreas for the unfinished conflict. Their survival since 1945 had only reinforced their sense of destiny. Their conviction was that they had a divine mission to rule one Korea and build this new Korea upon the wreckage of their ideological rival. True democracy and self-sufficiency in rebuilding their Korea did not really enter their calculations. The Korean people had only left one war behind and entered another kind of irreconcilable conflict.

3

CHINA'S WAR FOR KOREA

Geostrategic decisions, war-fighting experience and high-priced benefits from intervention, 1950–53

Xiaobing Li

From 1950 to 1953, the government of the People's Republic of China (PRC) despatched more than 3 million troops to Korea. In October 1950, when the Chinese launched numerous offensive campaigns trying to drive the United Nations forces out of Korea, it became clear that the conflict was now a war between China and the UN forces. General Douglas MacArthur, commander of the UN forces, reported to Washington that the United Nations faced 'an entirely new war' in Korea.[1] Although still confronting more than a million Kuomintang (KMT) in remnants of the Chinese Civil War on Taiwan and in south-western China (1946–49), Beijing chose to fight the UN forces in a new international war: the 'war to resist America and aid Korea' (*kangmei yuanchao zhanzheng*). With its irregular 'foot soldiers' armed with obsolete weaponry, the Chinese regular army, the People's Liberation Army or PLA (known in the Korean War as the Chinese People's Volunteer Force or CPVF), seemed no match for the UN forces with their vastly superior air, naval and ground firepower.

---

1 W.W. Stueck, *The Road to Confrontation: American Policy Toward China and Korea, 1947–1950*, University of North Carolina Press, Chapel Hill, NC, 1981, p. 3.

This article provides some insight into the PLA's operations and experience in the Korean War, in which China suffered more than 1 million casualties. It offers a Chinese perspective on Beijing's strategic concerns and operational behaviour, and identifies some general patterns among the Chinese commanders facing the most powerful militaries in the world for three bloody years. Even if the details might be forgotten in America, Australia or the rest of the world, the war in Korea is by no means forgotten in China.

Mao's decision

Mao Zedong's decision to send Chinese troops into the Korean War has been one of the most debated controversies since the Cold War ended in 1991. Most Chinese military historians argue that Mao made a rational and necessary decision. It was certainly not a mistake. China's intervention secured the nation's north-eastern borders, strengthened Sino-Soviet relations and saved the North Korean regime. China acted as a great power for the first time since it lost the Opium War to Great Britain in 1840. Some historians, however, challenge this view and condemn Mao for gross miscalculation that cost the lives of hundreds of thousands of Chinese soldiers.[2] Others question whether Mao's war consideration was primarily an ideological or a security concern.[3] More scholars debate the timing of Mao's decision-making, whether it occurred in August, September or October.[4] Their scholarly efforts have laid a solid foundation for a better understanding of the Chinese decision, yet the debate continues.

This new vigour of internationalism revealed a profound change taking place in the 'new China'.

---

2   For example, Yuan Xi, 'The Truth', *Suibi* [Freelance], no. 6, 1999.
3   Yang Kuisong, 'The ideological elements behind China's decision to send troops to Korea', www.yangkuisong.net; Zhang Baijia, 'How China dealt with the Korean War and Vietnam War', *Shijie jingji yu zhengzhi* [World Economy and Politics], no. 3, 2005; Niu Jun, 'Cross the 38th parallel: Political and military considerations and decision for the war to aid Korea and resist the US', *Zhongguo dangshi yanjiu* [CCP History Research], no. 1, 2002.
4   Feng Xianzhi and Li Jie, *Mao Zedong yu kangmei yuanchao* [Mao Zedong and the Resistance against the US and Assistance to Korea], Zhongyang wenxian chubanshe [CCP Central Archival and Manuscript Press], Beijing, 2000, pp. 12–24; Deng Feng, *Lengzhan chuqi dongya guoji guanxi yanjiu* [International Relations in East Asia during the Early Cold War Era], Jiuzhou chubanshe [Jiuzhou Press], Beijing, 2015, pp. 15–17.

Although external Cold War factors might seem the only reasons for this change, in fact the crucial strategic shift came about for significant internal reasons. Modern Chinese history has demonstrated that neither foreign invasion nor the support of an international power can create a strong, centralised national government. Power has depended more on China's own political stability and military strength than on its foreign relations. In this sense, by entering the Korean War, Mao perhaps took the opportunity to continue the communist movement at home and to project the new China's power image abroad.

Mao's strategic priorities included: (1) establishing the legitimacy that the Chinese Communist Party (CCP) needed as the ruling party; (2) national security, winning the last battle of the Chinese Civil War against the KMT on Taiwan; (3) economic recovery; and (4) military modernisation. His decision was perhaps also based on the PLA's superiority in manpower, making Mao and his generals overly confident in their capacity to drive the UN forces out of the Korean Peninsula.

The CCP leaders gave credence to the claim that communist China was founded on and could be maintained by virtue of its military power. After October 1949, Chinese leaders redirected their strategic thinking from winning the Chinese Civil War to building up national security. By early 1950, China had the largest army in the world, totalling 5.4 million men, while the US armed forces had 1.5 million and the Soviet Union's forces numbered 2.8 million, growing to 4.8 million by 1953. The PLA transformed itself from a 'liberation army' into a national force with two new goals: a defence force to fight against foreign invasions, and a security force against internal threats to the new regime.

Mao visited the Soviet Union on 16 December 1949, hoping to achieve what the new China desperately needed through an alliance between the PRC and the USSR. The Soviet leader, among other things, wanted to convince Mao that the Soviet Union had its own difficulties and that there would be no free ride for China. First, preoccupied with European affairs, Stalin needed the Chinese to help with ongoing Asian communist revolutions, including the First Indochina War in Vietnam and the national unification of North Korea. Second, Stalin had no intention of challenging the Yalta agreement, which might cause a direct conflict between the two superpowers. In Moscow in February 1950, Mao, Zhou Enlai (China's premier and foreign minister) and Stalin signed the Sino-Soviet Treaty of Friendship, Alliance and Mutual Assistance. It ensured

Soviet military assistance if China was invaded by an imperialist power—most likely to be the United States or Japan. From the moment that the new China came into being, Beijing's leaders regarded the United States as China's primary enemy and, at the same time, consistently declared that a fundamental aim of the Chinese revolution was to destroy the old world order dominated by the American imperialists.

On 25 June 1950, the North Korean People's Army (NKPA) launched a surprise attack on South Korea, provoking the Korean War. What most surprised Mao and the Chinese leaders was not the civil war in Korea but the US policy shift from a hands-off policy to a hands-on commitment toward the safety of Taiwan. On 27 June, two days after the North Korean invasion of the South, President Harry S. Truman announced that the US Seventh Fleet would be deployed in the Taiwan Strait to prevent a Chinese communist attack on KMT-held Taiwan. Chinese leaders considered the presence of the Seventh Fleet an intervention in the Chinese Civil War and a direct threat to the new republic.

According to Mao's Cold War theory, there would be a clash between the two countries sooner or later. In the 1950s, the United States intruded into and threatened China's security in three areas: Korea, Vietnam and the Taiwan Strait. Mao described American involvement in the three areas as three knives threatening China: America in Korea was like a knife over her head, America in Taiwan was one around her waist, and Vietnam was one aimed at her feet. Thus Korea, not Taiwan, was considered the most immediate threat, leading Mao to adopt an active defence rather than a reactive strategy. Instead of waiting for US forces to invade Manchuria from North Korea, Mao decided to fight the US force in Korea to prevent an invasion of China. It made sense to the Chinese generals: no matter the outcome of their fighting in Korea, they would not be at risk of losing their country. China's final decision to enter the Korean War was not an easy and rapid process; Mao found it difficult to get other Chinese leaders on board. On 8 October, Mao issued orders reorganising the North-east Border Defence Army (NEBDA) into the Chinese People's Volunteer Force (CPVF; Zhongguo Renmin Zhiyuanjun) and appointing Marshal Peng Dehuai as its commander-in-chief and political commissar.

Four offensive campaigns, October 1950 – April 1951

At 5.30 pm on 19 October, the advance guard of the CPVF Fortieth Army removed all identifying Chinese Army insignia from their uniforms, secretly crossed the Yalu River by train over the Andong–Sinuiju Bridge into North Korea, then marched south to meet forward elements of the US I Corps. Before the end of October, two more armies joined the CPVF's first wave, totalling 18 infantry divisions, three artillery divisions and supporting troops—in all about 300,000 men by early November. Late in the month, Chinese forces in Korea totalled 33 divisions and nearly 450,000 men, but this was only the beginning of Chinese involvement. This rapid and unexpected deployment took place without discovery by American forces, since Chinese troops had no trucks and therefore raised no dust. Chinese high command hoped that superior numbers would offset their inferior equipment and technology. It seemed rational to them that a larger force would be a decisive factor for their victory.[5]

The CPVF's first battle in Korea was an unplanned engagement. From 25 October to 5 November, the CPVF's armies had head-on battles with the Republic of Korea's (ROK) 1st, 6th and 8th Divisions, as well as the US 1st Cavalry Division. During this campaign, the CPVF used some of the combat tactics it had perfected during the Chinese Civil War. Among these was the effort to achieve numerical superiority and the element of surprise in order to negate the usually superior enemy firepower. By manoeuvring at night and resting during the day, Peng deployed his first wave of 300,000 Chinese troops south of the Yalu and remained undetected from 19 to 25 October.[6] During the first campaign on 5 November, the CPVF Command expanded its force from 120,000 men to 150,000 in the area north of the Chongchon River, facing 50,000 UN troops. Peng believed that the first campaign was a victory for the CPVF, despite 10,000 Chinese casualties.[7]

---

5 Xu Yan, *Mao Zedong yu kangmei yuanchao zhanzheng* [Mao Zedong and the War to Resist US Aggression and Aid Korea], 2nd edn, Jiefangjun [PLA Press], Beijing, 2006, p. 132.
6 CMC document, 'The circular on the combat characteristics of South Korean troops, 30 October 1950', in *Jianguo yilai Mao Zedong wengao* [Mao's Manuscripts since 1949], ed. CCP Central Institute of Historical Documents, Zhongyang wenxian [CCP Central Archival and Manuscript Press], Beijing, 1993, vol. 1, pp. 630–1.
7 Xu Yan, *Diyici jiaoliang: Kangmei yuanchao zhanzheng de lishi huigu yu fansi* [The First Encounter: A Historical Retrospective of the War to Resist America and Aid Korea], Zhongguo guangbo dianshi [China's Radio and Television Press], Beijing, 1990, p. 47.

After the first encounter with the Americans, many in the CPVF command believed that the over-reliance of the UN and US forces on technology might be to their disadvantage.[8] The Chinese troops quickly gained battlefield experience, assisted immensely by a nucleus of career officers and civil war veterans. For the first time since the Inchon landing, the CPVF stabilised the situation for the North Koreans, providing valuable breathing space by pushing the front line south of the Chongchon. Geography favoured the Chinese. The mountains and forest camouflaged their movements and diluted the effectiveness of UN air attacks. The narrow peninsula made it possible to fortify and defend a relatively short front.

On 25 November, the Chinese People's Volunteer Force launched its second offensive campaign to counter MacArthur's 'home by Christmas' offensive. Before this campaign, Peng had 230,000 men on the western front against 130,000 UN troops, and 150,000 men on the eastern front against 90,000 UN troops, a ratio of nearly two to one.[9] On the whole, the second offensive campaign from 25 November to 24 December was a major victory for the CPVF. US air power forced the Chinese to take to the hills, and much of what the Chinese soldiers required was carried on foot. Most Chinese soldiers had tremendous physical endurance, even though they suffered more than 80,000 casualties.[10] They attacked from the surrounding hills, often establishing roadblocks that not only forced the American troops back but also threatened to cut them off. Amazingly, even in the icy conditions, the Chinese troops found ways of moving artillery to their front-line positions high in the mountains, and in nine days the CPVF pushed the battle line back to the 38th parallel and recaptured Pyongyang, North Korea's capital. The second offensive campaign represented the peak of CPVF performance in the Korean War. Mao's conviction that any battle could be conducted upon the principles of guerrilla warfare dominated Chinese military doctrine during the early offensive campaigns from the autumn of 1950 to the early spring

---

8   China Academy of Military Science [CAMS], *Zhongguo renmin zhiyuanjun kangmei yuanchao zhanshi* [War Experience of the CPVF in the War to Resist America and Aid Korea], Junshi kexue [Military Science Press], Beijing, 1990, p. 28.
9   Hong Xuezhi, *Kangmei yuanchao zhanzheng huiyi* [Recollections of the War to Resist America and Aid Korea], Jiefangjun wenyi [PLA Literature Press], Beijing, 1990, pp. 90–1.
10 Xu, *The First Encounter*, p. 60.

of 1951.[11] These large-scale guerrilla tactics, such as encirclement, proved especially effective in their first two offensive campaigns. Back in China, morale was high and support for the war at its peak during this period.

However, the Ninth Army Group was ill-prepared for combat during the second offensive campaign. The troops came from south-eastern China, believing their next target would be Taiwan in the south, not Korea in the north. Dressed in lightweight canvas shoes and quilted cotton uniforms, the troops were not prepared for the bitterly cold Korean winter. Many became ill and were unable to keep up with the armies, which had marched 120 miles in seven days through mountains and forests. One division lost 700 men to severe frostbite during the first week in Korea.[12] On 27 November, the Ninth Army Group ordered an attack on US 1st Marine and 7th Infantry Divisions around the Chosin Reservoir. The attacking force consisted of eight infantry divisions. Some of the tactics were very successful during the initial attack. First, they achieved a surprise since the Ninth Army Group's entry into North Korea on 11 November, and movement to the eastern front had remained undetected for 10 days. Second, the three Chinese armies had split the US 1st Marine and 7th Infantry Divisions into five parts by the next morning. Third, the 100,000-strong Ninth Army Group was able to surround these fragmented American troops.[13] Even though the Chinese trapped the 1st Marines at Hahwaok-ri (Hagaru-ri) and divided the division into three sections, they could not destroy each section completely. After being divided and surrounded, the 1st Marine Division immediately formed defensive perimeters at three locations. They also constructed a makeshift airstrip for resupply of ammunition and winter equipment, as well as for shipping out their wounded. On 29 November the Marines counter-attacked to break the Chinese encirclement and to unite their scattered units. On 12 December, having broken the Chinese roadblocks to fight through some attacks on its way to the south, the 1st Marine Division met the US 3rd Infantry Division at Hamhung. The Ninth Army Group

---

11 Xiaobing Li, A.R. Millett and Bin Yu (trans. and eds), *Mao's Generals Remember Korea*, University Press of Kansas, Lawrence, KS, 2001, p. 14.
12 Cui Xianghua and Chen Dapeng, *Tao Yong jiangjun zhuan* [Biography of General Tao Yong], Jiefangjun [PLA Press], Beijing, 1989, p. 393.
13 Captain Wang Xuedong, interview, Harbin, April 2000. See also Wang, 'The Chosin Reservoir', in *Voices from the Korean War*, ed. R. Peters and Xiaobing Li, University Press of Kentucky, Lexington, KY, 2004, pp. 117–24.

could not annihilate the 1st Marine Division. During its battle at the Chosin Reservoir, the Ninth Army Group lost 40,000 men in three weeks of fighting, which liquidated three divisions.[14]

On New Year's Eve, the CPVF, while still poorly provisioned (home-supplied food met only a quarter of the minimum needs of the CPVF), launched the third offensive campaign across the 38th parallel against entrenched UN forces, an operation dissimilar to earlier practices. In a matter of nine days, from 31 December 1950 to 8 January 1951, the CPVF crossed the 38th parallel, moved into South Korea, recaptured Seoul and pushed the UN force down to the 37th parallel.[15] The CPVF also faced mounting problems that went beyond the shortages of food and ammunition. CPVF units were exhausted after days of constant movement and fighting, and reinforcements had been delayed. The CPVF and NKPA lost 8,500 men during the third offensive campaign.[16] By this time the US and UN forces had mobilised overwhelming firepower superiority on the ground and in the air, inflicting heavy casualties and serious damage on the CPVF troop movements as well as on their transportation and communication lines. The CPVF needed a more cautious strategy after the third offensive campaign.

Nevertheless, Stalin and Kim Il-Sung pressured the CPVF to launch the next offensive operation immediately in order to drive the UN forces out of Korea with all possible speed. Mao also cabled Peng in January, urging preparation of a fourth campaign to drive the UN forces further south. The CPVF command was under tremendous pressure from the political leaders of all three communist countries for a quick victory. The gap between this political goal and strategic realities became wider at the end of each campaign.[17]

---

14   CMC document, 'Telegram to Song Shilun, and others, 17 December 1950', in *Mao Zedong junshi wenxuan* [Selected Military Papers of Mao Zedong], Jiefangjun zhanshi [PLA Soldiers Press], Beijing, 1981, vol. 2, pp. 682–3.
15   Xiaobing Li, 'China's intervention and the CPVF experience in the Korean War', in *The Korean War at Fifty: International Perspectives*, ed. M.F. Wilkinson, Virginia Military Institute, Lexington, VA, 2004, pp. 144–5.
16   CAMS, *War Experience of the CPVF*, p. 48.
17   Xiaobing Li, 'Chinese Army in the Korean War, 1950–1953', *New England Journal of History* 60, nos 1–3, 2003–04, p. 282.

From 25 January to 21 April, as the CPVF engaged in its fourth campaign in a series of back-and-forth mobile battles,[18] the UN forces appeared to have recovered from their early surprise. On 25 January, US Eighth Army commander Lieutenant General Matthew B. Ridgway launched a counter-attack by leading four US divisions, two British brigades, one Turkish brigade and two Republic of Korea divisions in a two-pronged offensive towards Seoul. The CPVF commanders were unprepared for the UNF's quick transformation from being on the defensive in early January to the large-scale offensive less than two weeks later.[19] The CPVF command deployed its Fiftieth and Thirty-Eighth Armies to build up a defence on the southern bank of the Han River to stop Ridgway's northern advance. The Fiftieth, formerly the KMT Sixtieth Army of Jiang Jieshi (Chiang Kai-shek), which had surrendered to the PLA in the civil war, faced a significant challenge, barely surviving the first week of defence. US Eighth Army forces broke through the Fiftieth Army's defence line on 7 February, forcing the Chinese to retreat north of the Han River.[20] From 7 to 26 February, the Chinese Thirty-Eighth Army stood alone against the US 24th and 1st Cavalry Divisions, suffering heavy casualties. The Chinese Thirty-Eighth Army's 112th Division lost two of its three regiments (the 334th and 336th) in less than 10 days, causing the 38th to give up its defensive positions on 18 February and to withdraw to the north of the Han River.[21]

To alleviate the pressure on the defence of the Han River in the west, the CPVF command ordered six armies to attack the ROK divisions in the east. On 11 February, the Chinese Thirty-Ninth, Fortieth and Forty-Second Armies mounted a massive attack on the ROK 8th Division at Hoensong, while the Sixty-Sixth Army was despatched to envelop the ROK rear and II and V Corps of the NKPA were sent to block the ROK 5th Division's reinforcement.[22] The ROK 8th Division collapsed, creating a salient in the UN forces' front. The US Eighth Army's 2nd Division and

---

18   Xu, *The First Encounter*, p. 80.
19   Hong, *Hong Xuezhi Huiyilu* [Memoirs of Hong Xuezhi], 2nd edn, Jiefangjun [PLA Press], Beijing, 2007, p. 448.
20   Yonghui Jiang, *Sanshiba jun zai chaoxian* [The 38th Army in Korea], Liaoning renmin [Liaoning People's Press], Shenyang, 1992, pp. 301, 363; B.C. Mossman, *Ebb and Flow, November 1950–July 1951: US Army in the Korean War*, US Army Center of Military History, US Government Printing Office, Washington, DC, 1990, pp. 253–4.
21   Jiang, *The 38th Army in Korea*, pp. 301, 327–32, 405–8.
22   Guo Baoheng and Hu Zhiyuan, *Chipin hanjiang nanbei: 42 jun zai chaoxian* [Fighting over the South and North of the Han River: The 42nd Army in Korea], Liaoning renmin [Liaoning People's Press], Shenyang, 1996, pp. 212–21.

the US 187th Airborne Regimental Combat Team supporting the ROK divisions struggled to block the CPVF–NKPA penetration at Wonju. The CPVF attack was successfully halted. On 13 February, at Chipyong-ni, a small town west of Hoensong, three CPVF divisions attacked the US 23rd Regiment and the French battalion, which totalled 6,000 UN troops. US General Ridgway believed that this was a key junction and ordered the defenders to hold it against 32,000 Chinese troops. For two days the Chinese mounted attack after attack against the UN positions, but the defenders refused to surrender. The CPVF was unable to organise another effective attack by 15 February, making the battle of Chipyong-ni a serious setback for the Chinese. Some UN officers considered it the turning point in the Chinese intervention, comparable to the Inchon landing during the North Korean offensive in 1950. The failed attack exposed the CPVF's weakness and convinced US policy-makers that the UN forces could stop the Chinese offensives and stabilise the situation in Korea. The US State Department agreed with the Joint Chiefs of Staff at a meeting in February: 'Generally speaking, military operations in Korea are now stabilized, although there will be a certain amount of give and take … [the current] positions are likely to remain approximately as they are now.'[23]

Unable to break through the US Eighth Army line in central Korea while trying to hold back an Eighth Army drive west of the penetration, on 17 February Peng decided that the CPVF would withdraw to the 38th parallel while organising a few defensive engagements to slow down the UN forces' drive.[24] To make sure Mao understood his difficulties, Peng rushed back to Beijing on 21 February and briefed Mao himself. When Peng pointed out that the Korean War could not be a quick victory,[25] Mao agreed and told Peng, 'Win a quick victory if you can; if you can't, win a slow one'. Peng was relieved to find that Mao had become strategically flexible for the fourth campaign.[26] By March 1951, Mao's strategic goal in the war had changed from driving the UN forces

---

23   US State Department, 'Memorandum for the record of a Department of State–Joint Chiefs of Staff meeting, 13 February 1953', *Korea and China*, Foreign Relations of the United States, 1951, vol. 7, p. 177.
24   Wang Yan, *Peng Dehuai zhuan* [Biography of Peng Dehuai], Dang dai Zhongguo [Contemporary China Press], Beijing, 1993, p. 449.
25   Peng, 'My story of the Korean War', in *Mao's Generals Remember Korea*, ed. Li, Millett and Yu, p. 35.
26   Shuguang Zhang, *Mao's Military Romanticism*, University Press of Kansas, Lawrence, KS, 1992, p. 143.

out of the peninsula for a quick victory to a prolonged war with the goal of eliminating several UN divisions a year. Mao believed that it would 'take several years to inflict casualties of hundreds of thousands of American troops to make them [the United States] beat a retreat in the face of difficulties'.[27] The campaign's goal shifted from a total Chinese victory to a US withdrawal from Korea.

The US forces, however, showed no sign whatsoever of a withdrawal, and instead intensified their northward offensives. On 7 March, the US Eighth Army launched its offensive in the west. The CPVF command ordered a further withdrawal to north of the 38th parallel, and UN forces captured the battered capital of Seoul for the second time. By early April, UN troops had reached the Kansas Line, a few miles north of the 38th parallel. For the UN forces, however, attention now shifted from battlefield to politics: the Truman–MacArthur controversy. On 11 April 1951, Truman relieved MacArthur of command. On 21 April, CPVF troops disengaged after the UN forces stopped their northern advance at positions along the 38th parallel. The Chinese fourth campaign had lasted for 87 days. The CPVF and NKPA suffered total casualties of 53,000 men; of these, the Chinese lost 42,000 and listed 4,379 as missing in action.[28] All China's troops were ground forces, since the CPVF air force had not yet been formally committed to the war.[29]

The decisive battle: The 1951 Spring Offensive campaign

Not until after the CPVF's Fifth Phase Offensive campaign in April–May 1951 did Mao conclude that the goal of driving the UN forces out of Korea was unattainable. In April, considerable disagreement emerged among CPVF officers as to how to execute the fifth campaign. Most of the top commanders disagreed with Peng's idea (imposed upon him by Mao, Kim and Stalin) of striking south.

---

27 Peng, 'My story of the Korean War'.
28 CAMS, *War Experience of the CPVF*, p. 85.
29 Xiaoming Zhang, *Red Wings Over the Yalu: China, the Soviet Union, and the Air War in Korea*, Texas A&M University Press, College Station, TX, 2002, pp. 145–6.

To ensure a victory in their fifth offensive campaign, Mao and the Central Military Commission (CMC) decided to send China's second echelon to Korea, including nine armies with 27 infantry divisions.[30] (The first echelon of the CPVF was nine armies with 30 infantry divisions and three artillery divisions, which had been engaged in Korea since October 1950.[31]) The main strength of the second echelon was the Third Army Group from south-west China, including three armies with nine infantry divisions,[32] and the Nineteenth Army Group from northern China, also comprising three armies with nine infantry divisions.[33] When the second echelon arrived, the CPVF forces in Korea had doubled from 450,000 troops in January to 950,000 by mid-April, including 770,000 combat troops in 42 infantry divisions, eight artillery divisions and four anti-aircraft artillery divisions.[34] The NKPA had about 340,000 troops reorganised into six army corps, bringing communist forces to almost 1.3 million troops. The UN forces comprised about 340,000 men, including 150,000 Americans, 130,000 South Koreans and 40,000 troops from other countries including Great Britain and Australia.[35] Thus, by the eve of their next campaign, the Chinese ground forces alone had a numerical superiority of three to one against the UN ground forces. Peng made it clear to his generals on 14 March that 'the next campaign will be the decisive battle' of the Korean War.[36]

During their planning, the Chinese high command appeared confident of eliminating a large number of UN troops and moving the CPVF into the areas south of the 38th parallel. Mao, Peng and most of the Chinese generals believed that the human factor would determine their victory in the decisive battle. Mao firmly believed that a weak army could win in a war against a strong enemy since he was convinced that man could

---

30 Mao's telegram to 'Filippov' (Stalin), 1 March 1951, in *Mao's Manuscripts Since 1949*, vol. 2, p. 152.
31 Xu Yan, 'Chinese forces and their casualties in the Korean War', in *Chinese Historians 6*, trans. Xiaobing Li, pp. 48–9; R.E. Appleman, *US Army in the Korean War: South to the Nakton, North to the Yalu (June–November 1950)*, Office of the Chief of Military History, Department of the Army, Washington, DC, 1961, pp. 768–9.
32 CMC's telegram to Peng, Song [Shilun], Tao [Yong] and PLA regional commands on 18 February 1951, 'Some changes in CPVF armies rotation plan in Korea', in *Zhou Enlai junshi wenxuan* [Selected Military Papers of Zhou Enlai], Renmin [People's Press], Beijing, 1997, vol. 4, pp. 158–61.
33 CMC telegram to Peng Dehuai on 11 February 1951, 'The counter-attack plan and advance of the 19th Army Group', in *Selected Military Papers of Zhou Enlai*, vol. 4, pp. 154–6.
34 Hong, *Memoir of Hong Xuezhi*, pp. 464–5.
35 Mossman, *Ebb and Flow*, p. 437.
36 Peng, 'Speech at the CPVF Army and Division Commanders Meeting, 14 October 1950', in *Peng Dehuai junshi wenxuan* [Selected Military Papers of Peng Dehuai], Zhongyang wenxian [CCP Central Archival and Manuscript Press], Beijing, 1988, p. 324.

beat a weapon. 'Weapons are an important factor in war, but not the decisive factor,' Mao wrote. He explicitly made the distinction that 'it is people, not things, that are decisive'.[37]

Mao's confidence in a human being's subjective capability to determine defeat or victory in war made sense to the Chinese officers and soldiers. Shaped by the military culture and communist ideology, the Chinese belief in the superiority of humans over technology suggests their unique attitude towards war and ways to fight a battle. The idea that a soldier or a warrior, because of his godliness and virtue, can vanquish stronger opponents is a strong tradition in Chinese culture. The Chinese high command might have found and used a principle of the Sunzi (Sun-tzu): 'Throw [your soldiers] where there is no escape. And they will fight with the courage of the heroes.'[38]

On 22 April 1951, Peng launched the Spring Offensive campaign, which became the largest battle in the PLA's history. The Chinese offensive can be divided into three phases. The first step was the CPVF attack on the US I and IX Corps, to be carried out in the west from 22 to 29 April; the second was the Chinese attack on the US X Corps, to be carried out in the east from 8 to 21 May. The third step was the Chinese withdrawal and defence, to take place from 23 May to 10 June.

At 5 pm on 22 April, the CPVF Ninth Army Group, totalling 250,000 men, launched attacks into the centre of the US IX Corps, and the campaign began. The five armies of the Ninth Army Group attacked a 28-kilometre UN defence line held by the ROK 6th Division, the US 24th and 25th Divisions and the US 1st Marine Division. The Chinese 39th and 40th Armies broke through the UN line held by the ROK 6th Division, penetrating into the central mountainous areas. They separated the Koreans from the Marines and divided the western UN divisions from those on the eastern front. To cut off the US 24th Division's retreat, the Chinese Fortieth Army sent its divisions to attack the British 27th Brigade at the road junction at Kapyong. However, the attacking Chinese troops faced a strong defence by the brigade's 3rd Battalion, Royal Australian Regiment (3RAR). The Chinese divisions could not prevent the US 24th from breaking through their roadblocks nor from withdrawing south.

---

37 Mao, 'On Protracted War', in *Selected Works of Mao Tse-tung*, Foreign Languages Press, Beijing, 1965, vol. 2, pp. 143–4.
38 Ibid.

At 7 pm on 22 April, the CPVF Third and Nineteenth Army Groups, totalling 270,000 men, launched attacks against the US I Corps in the west. Their armies, however, were not ready for such a large-scale offensive and failed to break through the defence lines of the ROK 1st Division and the British 29th Infantry Brigade. At the time Peng issued his order, many troops of the Third Army Group were not yet in their staging positions and had to run for 30 to 60 minutes before they reached their staging positions. This meant that the attacking forces were unable to use artillery barrage against the UN forces' defence. Even after the artillery fire had extended into the UN positions, some of the infantry troops were still unable to reach their staging positions. The main strength of the Nineteenth Army Group did not penetrate deeply enough into the US I Corps' rear and did not reach Uijongbu to complete the encirclement of the US 3rd, 24th and 25th Divisions. This failure made it impossible for Peng to achieve his goal of annihilation, and some of his armies did not perform as well as they did during the Chinese Civil War.

With the UN forces heavily concentrated in the west around Seoul, the east was primarily defended by the ROK troops. Sensing an opportunity in early May, Peng ordered 200,000 troops, including 15 CPVF infantry divisions from the Third and Ninth Army Groups and five NKPA divisions, to attack the ROK 3rd, 5th, 7th and 9th Divisions and US X Corps between 8 and 21 May as the second step of the Spring Offensive campaign. The shock of the Chinese attack caused panic in ROK units, many of which abandoned their defensive positions and fell back. A huge gap opened up on the US X Corps' right flank. Six CPVF divisions struck the US 2nd Division to the left of the salient at Hyeongri, but the US division held its ground and even pushed into the flank of the attacking Chinese forces, as air and artillery pounded the densely concentrated CPVF units. Simultaneously, the US 3rd Division shifted from the Seoul area to block further CPVF movement.

Although the CPVF forces were still managing to continue their attacks, they had run out of strength at nearly every position across the line. After fighting almost uninterruptedly throughout two major offensive operations within one month, all the front-line forces were tremendously battle-fatigued and exhausted. Some of the front-line forces had completely run out of ammunition and food, and many others were approaching the same situation. On 21 May, the CPVF–NKPA joint command issued the order to halt attacks and to conclude the second step of the fifth offensive campaign. On the night of 23 May, the main forces of the Chinese People's

Volunteer Force and the North Korean People's Army began withdrawing to the north while forces assigned to defensive missions began to move into their designated positions.

US Lieutenant General Van Fleet ordered all-out counter-attacks just two days after the CPVF ended its offensive operations, completely catching the Chinese forces by surprise. Peng had expected that the UN forces would launch their counter-attacks no earlier than 10–15 days after the Chinese had stopped their offensive operations. Van Fleet assembled 14 divisions, one brigade and two regiments to launch frontal attacks on the CPVF line of defence. He left three divisions and three brigades in reserve. Most of the US forces launched their full-scale attacks during daylight on 23 May, seven days after the CPVF had initiated its attacks on Hyeongri. This was the UN forces' new strategy: to attack the Sino-North Korean forces on the day their hand-carried supplies would run out.

At that point, 90 per cent of the Chinese forces had nearly exhausted their food supplies and matériel, and were preparing to withdraw to the north. The UN forces' main attacks at the middle and eastern front began at the same time as the CPVF and NKPA were beginning to pull their forces out of combat operations. Moving along the highways, with tank units spearheading the advance, the mechanised UN forces advanced northward more rapidly than the Chinese and North Korean commanders expected. The CPVF formations were badly disrupted by the thrusting UN attacks, especially since they were unable to move during daylight for fear of coming under aerial assault. The Chinese Third Army Group was thrown into chaos and disorder. Its Sixtieth Army failed to mount a defence to cover the Army Group withdrawing to the north. The 180th Division of the Sixtieth Army, deployed in the centre of the Sixtieth's defence, was unable to stop the US attacks and was cut off by the UN forces. By 29 May, the 180th Division had collapsed: only 4,000 troops eventually broke out and returned home. From a roster of 12,000 men, the division lost more than 8,000, including 5,000 captured. It was the largest single loss of the CPVF in the Korean War.

The 1-million-men offensive had failed. The CPVF lost the decisive battle and suffered 85,000 casualties. More important, the front line was pushed farther north. Among the major reasons for the early Chinese setback between 22 and 29 April were certainly that the UN and US forces had established overwhelming firepower superiority on the ground and in the air, and that the UN was inflicting heavy casualties and serious damage on CPVF troops, transportation and logistical supplies. In retrospect, the CPVF command had miscalculated the campaign situation and made three major strategic mistakes. First, Peng and his commanders did not sufficiently prepare their striking forces, rushing them to the offensive. Second, Peng used the same strategy of divide, encircle and annihilate as in the four previous campaigns from November 1950 to April 1951, failing to develop new strategies and tactics for the Spring Offensive. Third, the CPVF command did not improve its methods of transportation or of maintaining supplies. The 1-million-strong CPVF–NKPA offensive campaign caused few losses and minimal damage to the UN forces, but produced unusually high casualties in the Chinese forces, especially the Third and Nineteenth Army Groups. Peng admitted later that the early attack was one of only four major strategic mistakes he had made during his military career.[39] After the collapse of the Spring Offensive campaign, Mao pointed out three major reasons for the CPVF failure: 'too much haste, too large scale, and too far into the [enemy's] territory'.[40]

Mao was right about two of the problems the CPVF faced in late April, as it had launched an immense offensive with neither necessary preparation nor sufficient supplies. But he was wrong about being too far into the enemy's territory, since no CPVF force had ever advanced more than 50 miles (80 kilometres) into UN-held territory in the Spring Offensive campaign. In fact, it was because of their slow movement and lack of deep penetration that the Chinese armies failed to encircle and annihilate the US I Corps. Mao criticised his rigid campaign strategy as another reason for the Chinese setback between 22 and 29 April. In retrospect, Mao's strategy—divide, encircle and annihilate—was inflexible as well as out of date, leading to the disastrous result of the CPVF offensive.

Encirclement and annihilation had proved effective in the first two CPVF campaigns from October to December 1950. The Chinese forces were able to launch surprise attacks, then flank and encircle on both sides one UN unit, cut off its connection and set up roadblocks to stop its withdrawal. During the second offensive campaign in November–December 1949, the Ninth Army Group scored the CPVF's only major encirclement and annihilation success during the three-year war.

---

39   Xie Lifu, *Chaoxian zhanzheng shilu* [Historical Records of the Korean War], World Knowledge Press, Beijing, 1993, pp. 456–8.
40   Du Ping, *Zai zhiyuanjun zongbu: Du Ping huiyilu* [At the CPVF General HQ: Memoirs of Du Ping], Jiefangjun [PLA Press], Beijing, 1988, p. 250.

In early 1951, however, the UN forces had figured out how to deal with the Chinese strategy. They no longer retreated on discovering Chinese troops on both sides or behind. Instead, they quickly reorganised their troops into a stronghold protected by tanks and self-propelling artillery guns. Thomas Fleming points out that 'Ridgway ordered that no unit be abandoned if cut off. It was to be "fought for" and rescued unless a "major commander" after "personal appraisal" Ridgway-style—from the front lines—decided its relief would cost as many or more men'. When UN units were under attack, they called in air raids and artillery, which inflicted such heavy casualties on the attacking Chinese troops that they had to withdraw after a few assaults. The UN operations of attrition under Ridgway's command were very different from its earlier rapid advances for a quick victory, as practised by MacArthur.[41]

The CCP leadership and the high command of the People's Liberation Army realised the limit of China's military power after their troops lost their fifth offensive campaign in the spring of 1951. The communists never again came as close to Seoul, nor mounted another major southward incursion. Their defeat forced Mao to reconsider his political and military aims. Realising the huge gap between China's capabilities and its ambitious aim of driving the UN forces from the peninsula, the Chinese leadership was forced to accept a settlement without total victory. The fifth offensive campaign was the decisive battle as well as the turning point that shaped not only the remainder of the war but also truce negotiations.

Negotiating while fighting: Trench warfare, 1951–53

After that setback, in order to limit casualties and negate the UN forces' firepower, the CPVF command adopted positional warfare, focusing on more cautious defensive tactics. By the summer of 1951, the nature of the war had changed from a large-scale mobile war to a stalemate and trench warfare. Until 1953, Chinese commanders shifted their focus from eliminating enemy units in mobile warfare to securing lines. In a limited battleground such as Korea, it was difficult for either side to overpower its opponent completely, unlike the situations in both the Second World

---

41 W.T. Bowers (ed.), *Combat in Korea: Striking Back, March–April 1951*, University Press of Kentucky, Lexington, KY, 2010, pp. 408–9.

War and the Chinese Civil War. Chinese leaders changed their goal from driving UN forces out of Korea to merely defending China's security and ending the war through negotiations.

By the summer of 1951, the CPVF was no longer expected to recapture Seoul and move into South Korea. While the armies could achieve temporary success in limited sectors, it came at a high cost. The Soviets were ready for peace talks that would secure North Korea's regime and strengthen the Soviet Union's position in Asia. On 23 June the Soviet Ambassador to the United Nations, Yakov Malik, called for discussions on a ceasefire as well as an armistice to end the Korean conflict. In Beijing, the Central Committee discussed the Soviet proposal as well as its next step in Korea. Most committee members considered it proper that the Chinese forces should stop at the 38th parallel but continue to fight while working toward a negotiated settlement. They believed they had already achieved their political goal of driving the enemy out of northern Korea. The pause at the 38th parallel, in fact, was a return to the pre-war status quo that was acceptable to the parties in the war. Presided over by Mao on 2 July, the CMC committed to this 'dual strategy' for the rest of the war.[42] The Chinese had convinced the North Koreans of this new strategy during their visits and communications in the summer of 1951.[43] When Beijing's *People's Daily* endorsed the Soviet proposal, it appeared that the key players in all the warring powers, except South Korea, were ready to negotiate.[44]

On 10 July truce negotiations began at Kaesong, a neutral city between the lines. The UN delegation, however, soon discovered that the Chinese and North Korean delegation was more interested in using the event for propaganda purposes than in negotiating. During the early weeks of the meetings, there was major disagreement over the demarcation line. In August negotiations were suspended. On 25 October, talks resumed at the village of Panmunjom, 8 kilometres from Kaesong. From late 1951 to early 1952, the issue of prisoners of war deadlocked the negotiations. The UN delegation proposed a 'voluntary repatriation' of prisoners, while

---

42 Mao, 'Telegram to Peng Dehuai, 2 July 1951', in *Mao's Manuscripts since 1949*, vol. 2, pp. 379–80.
43 Ministry of Foreign Affairs, 'Lee Xiangchao's visit to Beijing, 17 February 1953', p. 15; '[Zhou Enlai's] Speech (draft) at the third anniversary of the Korean War, 24 June 1953', pp. 24–5, File no. 106-00034-01 (1), Foreign Ministry Archives.
44 Ministry of Foreign Affairs, 'Lee Xiangchao's visit to Beijing, 17 February 1953', p. 25.

3. CHINA'S WAR FOR KOREA

the Chinese and North Korean delegation insisted on the return of their prisoners. The UN delegation believed that the communists held more prisoners (estimated at 65,000) than the 11,559 they admitted to at the negotiating table.[45]

In the meantime, fighting continued. After the end of 1951, when the two sides agreed on the demarcation line, the nature of the war changed. Chinese soldiers did not realise that the war had moved into a period of stalemate and trench warfare.[46] Much bloody fighting lay ahead, but the front lines remained essentially unchanged. Both sides dug in and prepared to stay. In the autumn of 1951, the CPVF had begun an active defence by constructing underground tunnels to strengthen the CPVF defensive capacity and to achieve a favourable negotiating position. The 'underground Great Wall', as it became known, was built along the front line.[47] The Chinese commanders' strategy placed its main emphasis on gaining and retaining the operational initiative in battles. Their trench defence and tunnel system were tested by the sudden onset of the UN forces' Kumhwa offensive in mid-October 1952. The US 7th and ROK 2nd Divisions began intensive shelling of the Chinese Fifteenth Army's positions in the Osong Mountain region on 14 October, and occupied Hills 597.9 and 537.7, two small features collectively known as Triangle Hill. By 16 October, the UN attack had forced the Chinese troops off the ridge and into their tunnels. The 45th Division of the CPVF Fifteenth Army, as the defensive force on the hills, fought a pattern of see-saw actions.[48] During the day, UN troops would force Chinese troops into the tunnels; at night the Chinese would counter-attack and recover their surface positions, only to lose them again the following day. The Battle of Triangle Hill turned into one of the bloodiest of the war. The 45th Division lost 5,200 soldiers on the two hills. The Fifteenth Army suffered a total of 11,400 casualties from late October until early November, when the Battle of Triangle Hill finally came to an end.[49]

---

45   Chai Chengwen and Zhao Yongtian, *Banmendian tanpan* [The Panmunjom Negotiations], Jiefangjun [PLA Press], Beijing, 1992, pp. 200–3.
46   Ibid., p. 46.
47   Xu, *The First Encounter*, pp. 122–5.
48   Captain Zheng Yanman, interview, Harbin, Heilongjiang, August 2002. Also see Zheng, 'The Chinese go underground', in *Voices From the Korean War*, ed. Peters and Li, pp. 177–8.
49   Captain Zheng Yanman, interview, Harbin, Heilongjiang, August 2002.

By December 1952, Chinese forces in Korea had reached a record high of 1.45 million men, including 59 infantry divisions, 10 artillery divisions, five anti-aircraft divisions and seven tank regiments. CPVF numbers remained stable until the armistice agreement was signed in July 1953. Mao committed nearly a quarter of China's military strength to North Korea's defence.[50] Until the end of the war, the CPVF maintained a relatively stable front line, increased CPVF air force, artillery and tank units, and strengthened logistical support. Indeed, the CPVF increasingly became a mirror image of its US counterpart in its prosecution of the war. The Korean War kickstarted China's military modernisation and professionalism in terms of command, organisation, technology and training. In this respect, the United States turned out to be a 'useful adversary' in the Korean War.[51] For instance, Chinese forces gained experience in joint operations, although these did not take place until the last phase of the war. The first joint effort took place on 30 November 1951, when Chinese forces launched an amphibious attack, supported by aircraft, on Dahoo Island, off North Korea's coast. Although the CPVF lost five of nine bombers during the joint attack, the landing succeeded.[52]

Starting in the fall of 1952, the PLA began to rotate Chinese troops into Korea to gain modern fighting experience against US forces while providing much-needed recuperation for CPVF troops there. The Chinese Army had previously fought the Japanese Army and the Chinese Nationalist Army, but its leaders knew little about the US, British, Canadian and other technologically equipped Western forces. Korea became a combat laboratory offering Chinese officers and soldiers essential combat training. By the end of the war, about 73 per cent of Chinese infantry troops had been rotated (25 out of 34 armies, or 79 of 109 infantry divisions). More than 52 per cent of Chinese air force divisions, 55 per cent of tank units, 67 per cent of artillery divisions and 100 per cent of railroad engineering divisions had been sent to Korea.

By the end of the war, the Chinese People's Volunteer Force was emphasising the role of technology and firepower, and the People's Liberation Army respected their technologically superior opponents. To narrow the technology gap, China purchased weapons and equipment

---

50   Xu, 'Chinese forces and their casualties in the Korean War', pp. 52–3.
51   T.J. Christensen, *Useful Adversaries: Grand Strategy, Domestic Mobilisation, and Sino-American Conflict, 1947–1958*, Princeton University Press, Princeton, NJ, 1996, pp. 1–2.
52   Li, 'Chinese Army in the Korean War, 1950–1953', p. 286.

from the Soviet Union to arm 60 infantry divisions during 1951–53.[53] Thereafter, Chinese weaponry became standardised. The Soviets also transferred technology for the production of rifles, machine guns and artillery pieces. In 1952, the Central Military Committee made its first Five-Year Plan for National Defence, emphasising air force, artillery and tank force development.[54] Additionally, Chinese and North Korean armies received foreign aid from Eastern European countries such as Poland, Romania and Czechoslovakia.[55] Romania provided 41 railcars of war materials for the North Korean and Chinese troops in April 1951, including hospital equipment (two railcars) and medicine (10 railcars) for a 100-bed hospital, as well as 22 medical personnel.[56]

The CPVF improved its logistics and transportation by establishing its own logistics department in Korea in the spring of 1951. General Hong Xuezhi (Hong Hsue-ch'i) set up a new configuration system that fitted the CPVF's needs for its new positional warfare doctrine. This new system was aimed at supplying directly to front locations rather than to specific army units.[57] Food and ammunition always lagged behind operations.[58] Hong's new logistics system established area supply depots along the front lines, servicing all troops stationed within that area. The troops moved in and out, but the area supply depot remained and could be used by both Chinese and North Korean troops.[59] The new system improved CPVF logistics capacity at regimental and battalion levels, and increased the front-line troops' combat effectiveness. Chinese solutions to battlefield problems were not elegant, but they were effective.

---

53 Xu Xiangqian, 'The purchase of arms from Moscow', in *Mao's Generals Remember Korea*, ed. Li, Millett and Yu, p. 53.
54 Peng, 'China's military experience in the past four years and the fundamental issues for our future military development', in *Selected Military Papers of Peng Dehuai*, pp. 474–6.
55 Ministry of Foreign Affairs, 'Documents of transporting Poland's first and second shipments of aiding North Korea materials through China, 20 April to 25 October 1951', File no. 109-00161-02 (1), Foreign Ministry Archives.
56 Ministry of Railroad Transportation, 'Reports and documents on assisting Romania transport aiding North Korea materials, 9 April to 4 May 1951', File no. 109-00144-02 (1).
57 Nie, 'Beijing's decision to intervene', in *Mao's Generals Remember Korea*, ed. Li, Millett and Yu, p. 53.
58 Colonel Wang Po, interview, PLA Logistics College, Beijing, July 1994.
59 Ministry of Foreign Affairs to Foreign Affairs Office, Teng Daiyuan to Li Kenong, 'About the rail cars in north-east China halted by the North Korean People's Army, 29 June 1951', File no. 106-00026-02 (1), Foreign Ministry Archives.

The role of air power

In July 1949, the CMC had signed a deal with the Soviet Union to sell 434 military aircraft to the PLA and send 878 aviation experts to China, enabling the establishment of the PLA Air Force. In October the CMC established seven new aviation schools, and on 11 November 1949 the PLA proclaimed the establishment of the Chinese People's Air Force,[60] whose development sped up after the outbreak of the Korean War. Its first division, the Air Force 4th Division, was formed in Nanjing in June 1950, the 3rd was formed in Shenyang in October and the 2nd was formed in Shanghai in November. Each division had three to four regiments, each regiment had four wing commands (*dadui*, battalion) and each wing command had eight to 10 fighters.[61] The 4th Division was the first air force division deployed on the Korean front, and served under CPVF command from January to September 1951.[62] The 2nd, 3rd, 8th and 10th Divisions joined the 4th in November; seven more air force divisions participated in the war through 1953, a total of 60,000 personnel, including pilots, ground personnel and security troops. These air force divisions kept their bases in China proper, while their Soviet-trained pilots flew into Korea to carry out their missions. Soviet air force officers also coordinated Chinese and North Korean air cooperation. By the end of 1953 the PLA had 3,000 fighters and bombers, establishing China's air force as the third largest in the world.[63]

'The Soviet air force (Voemo-Vozushnye Sily; VVS) also participated in the Korean War. General Belov arrived in north-east China in August 1950 with one Soviet air force division; 12 more arrived in China within the next three months, under his command. Their mission was to protect the Yalu bridges, power plants, railroads and airports in an area 50 miles (80 kilometres) south of the Chinese–North Korean border. However, at Stalin's insistence, Russian pilots who flew into Korea had to take off from China. They wore Chinese uniforms and swore never to tell of their Korean War service. They were not allowed to communicate in Russian while airborne and, most importantly, they were not to be taken prisoner,

---

60   Wang Dinglie, *Dangdai Zhongguo kongjun* [The PLA Air Force in Contemporary China] (Beijing: Zhongguo shehui kexue [China Social Science Press], 1989), pp. 17–25.
61   Zhang, *Red Wings Over the Yalu*, pp. 224–46.
62   Ibid., pp. 146–8.
63   Zhang, 'Air combat for the People's Republic', in *Chinese Warfighting*, ed. Ryan, Finkelstein and McDevitt, p. 278.

and were prepared to commit suicide. All Russian aircraft were repainted with Chinese or North Korean marks. On 1 November 1950, seven days after the Chinese engaged the UN forces, Russian fighters began patrolling Korean air space. On that first day, six Yak-9 fighters engaged US fighters and bombers over the Anzhou area, with the Russians claiming to have shot down two B-29 bombers and one Mustang fighter while losing two Russian Yak-9s.[64] General Belov reported to Stalin that his pilots had shot down 23 US aircraft in the first half of November. Stalin was impressed and, as a result, sent 120 newly designed MiG-15 jet fighters to the Korean War.

In January 1951, when three Chinese offensive campaigns had pushed the front southward to the 37th parallel, Peng requested an extension of Soviet air coverage further south to protect the CPVF transportation and communication lines. Stalin immediately agreed and ordered Belov to transfer two more Russian fighter divisions, the 151st and 324th Divisions of the 64th Air Force Army, into North Korea. On 15 March, Stalin telegraphed Mao, informing him that two more fighter divisions would be transferred from China to North Korea.[65] By August, the 64th Air Force Army had deployed 190 MiG-15s and two anti-aircraft artillery divisions to North Korea. Still, Russian aircraft were not authorised to fly over UN-controlled areas, nor be engaged over the front, nor fly south of the 39th parallel. The CPVF Command complained about these restrictions, as Russian fighters were prevented from supporting Chinese ground operations, and no Russian bombers, which were most needed, took part in the war. Chinese forces suffered casualties caused by friendly fire from the Russian fighters, including two Chinese aircraft that were mistakenly shot down by Russian fighters.

But Stalin had his own considerations: the Soviet Union did not want a war with the United States over Korea, nor anywhere in east Asia. The Soviet Union had done what it could for the Koreans. From November 1950 to July 1953, 12 Soviet air force divisions engaged in the war, a total of 72,000 Russian personnel, including pilots, technicians, ground service and anti-air defence troops. Russian involvement peaked in 1952, with 26,000 Russian air force personnel sent into North Korea. According to Soviet official statistics, Soviet fighters shot down 1,097 UN

---

64   Shen, *Mao, Stalin and the Korean War*, p. 330.
65   Ibid., pp. 334–5.

aircraft,⁶⁶ and anti-aircraft artillery forces shot down 212. The Soviet air force lost 335 fighters and 120 pilots, with a total of 299 deaths in the Korean War.⁶⁷

From 19 October 1950 to 27 July 1953, confronted by US air and naval superiority, Chinese volunteer forces suffered heavy casualties; one was Mao's son, a Russian translator at the CPVF headquarters, who died in an air raid. According to Chinese military records, Chinese casualties in the Korean War break down as follows: 152,000 dead, 383,000 wounded, 450,000 hospitalised, 21,300 prisoners of war and 4,000 missing in action—a total of 1,010,700 casualties.⁶⁸ Chinese soldiers who served in the Korean War faced a greater chance of being killed or wounded than those who had served in either the Second World War or the Chinese Civil War. Among the 21,300 Chinese prisoners, 7,110 were repatriated to China in three different groups during September and October after the armistice was signed in July 1953.⁶⁹ Other Chinese prisoners—about 14,200—went to the Republic of China on Taiwan.⁷⁰

Throughout the war, the PRC spent a total of about 10 billion renminbi, equal to US$3.3 billion at the time. The Chinese Government transported into Korea a total of 5.6 million tons of goods and supplies during the intervention. In the years between 1950 and 1953, China's annual military spending represented 41 per cent, 43 per cent, 33 per cent and 34 per cent, respectively, of its total government budget.⁷¹ The Korean War was the first time Chinese armed forces had engaged in large-scale military operations outside China. Except for the thinly disguised title of 'volunteers', the Chinese military went all out in engaging one of the best-equipped militaries in the world.

---

66   Zhang, *Red Wings Over the Yalu*, pp. 202–3.
67   Shen Zhihua, 'The Soviet Air Force in the Korean War', in *Zhonggong dangshi yanjiu* [Studies on CCP History], no. 2, 2000, pp. 27–9.
68   Xiaobing Li, 'Chinese intervention in the Korean War', in *East Asia and the United States: An Encyclopedia of Relations since 1784*, ed. J.I. Matray, Greenwood Press, Westport, CT, 2002, pp. 94–6.
69   Foreign Affairs to Chinese chargé d'affairs in Pyongyang (Gan Yetao), '[Zhou Enlai's] Speech (draft) at the Third Anniversary of the Korean War, 24 June 1953', File no.106-00034-01 (1), pp. 24–5, Foreign Ministry Archives.
70   Xu, *The First Encounter*, pp. 308–10.
71   CAMS, *War Experience of the CPVF*, pp. 233–4.

By 27 July 1953, when the Korean Armistice Agreement was concluded, China had sent nearly 3 million men to Korea (out of 6.1 million PLA troops). Mao judged China's intervention a victory, as it saved North Korea's communist regime, prevented what had been perceived as a US invasion of China, gained more Russian military and economic aid for China, and established the PRC's new world status.[72] As Peng stated, the Korean War began a transformation of the Chinese military into a modern force.[73] Not only did its performance demonstrate that China was a military force capable of fighting the world's powerful forces to a draw, it also proved that Chinese society was secure enough to withstand a terrible conflict.

China's early Cold War experience—as exemplified by China's participation in the Korean War—not only contributed significantly to shaping the specific course of the Cold War in Asia but also, more importantly, helped to create conditions for the Cold War to remain cold. The lessons learned between 1950 and 1953 influenced subsequent developments, including China's decision to make its own atomic bombs. The war in Korea is by no means forgotten by the Chinese. In China, historians and scholars reopened their objective research and academic debate over the Spring Offensive in the late 1990s, departing from the official conclusion that the campaign was another Chinese victory. For political reasons, however, Chinese historians still have a long way to go before they can publish an objective account of the Chinese Spring Offensive campaign in their home country.

---

72   Mao, 'The great victory of the war to resist America and aid Korea and our task', in *Selected Works of Mao Zedong*, vol. 5, pp. 101–6.
73   Peng, 'China's military experience in the past four years and the fundamental issues for our future military development', in *Selected Military Papers of Peng Dehuai*, pp. 468–9.

4

FIGHTING IN THE GIANTS' PLAYGROUND

Australians in the Korean War

Cameron Forbes

In October 1950, people in Melbourne read good news on the front page of the *Age*.[1] The headline was: 'Korean War May End this Month: Capture of Wowan Menaces Red Capital'. The prediction had been made by military sources, almost certainly by staff at Douglas MacArthur's Tokyo headquarters. They were, as usual, tirelessly working to burnish their general's reputation. The previous day, also on page 1, was a short report of one of the stranger episodes in the history of the 3rd Battalion, Royal Australian Regiment (3RAR). The heading was: 'Two Australians Hiked to War'. An American correspondent who was, to use the current term, embedded with the US 7th Cavalry, filed this story:

> Two grimy, stubble-bearded Australian soldiers dug into a foxhole on Saturday and vowed they would be the first foreign soldiers across the 38th parallel. They are Privates Rex T. Wilson, of Adelaide, and Ernest S. Stone, of Melbourne, who arrived in Korea recently with the first detachment of Australian volunteer troops. Wilson said: 'We joined up to fight, but when we arrived we found our unit too far from the front line, so we just took off and headed for the noise of the firing.' Wilson and Stone

---

1   This chapter is based on C. Forbes, *The Korean War: Australia in the Giant's Playground*, Pan Macmillan, Sydney, 2010.

trudged several miles along the dusty road to the north and then got a ride with the leading tank of a northbound convoy. Stone said: 'We wanted to be the first Australians over the parallel. Now it looks as though we might even beat the Americans. Anyway, we are going to try.'

In fact, perhaps seven diggers, members of 3RAR, had hitched a ride on the American tank. They did not make it across the 38th parallel; they were returned to the Australian camp, luckily to face lenient punishment by the commanding officer, Charlie Green, much admired and soon to be much mourned.

When the North Koreans began their blitzkrieg south on 25 June 1950, 3RAR was Australia's rear guard in the occupation force in Japan. The members of the battalion were preparing to say sayonara to the good life, the soft life—to the Japanese house boys and house girls, some of them to their Japanese mistresses, to the cheap beer and the nice earnings on the black market. But 3RAR was understrength, underarmed and undertrained. In the opinion of the Chief of the General Staff, Lieutenant General Sydney Rowell, they were simply not battle-worthy. Yet a month and a day later their fate was sealed. They would be making the short trip to Korea, the land that would become the giants' bloody playground.

Australia's Minister for External Affairs, Percy Spender, moved with unseemly haste to commit Australian ground troops. On 26 July Robert Menzies was safely in his cabin on the *Queen Mary*, on the high seas between Britain and America. Menzies was doubtful about a Korean involvement; he expected it would provoke confrontation with the Soviet Union in Europe and the Middle East. It was the perfect time for Percy Spender to push the commitment. His eyes were on the glittering prize: a security pact with the United States. Despite his misgivings, once the draft of the Australia, New Zealand, United States Security Treaty (ANZUS) was initialled in February 1951—and I am obliged to Professor Robert O'Neill for this anecdote—Menzies, a convert, toasted Spender with his best cognac.

The Korean War, of course, became known as the forgotten war. I shared that general amnesia until my interest was aroused by a conversation with a friend, a documentary filmmaker, about the Battle of Kapyong. In mid-April 1951, 3RAR's commanding officer, Lieutenant Colonel Bruce Ferguson, invited the nearby Turkish Brigade to send representatives to the Australian base in the Kapyong Valley on 25 April.

There, along with the New Zealanders of the 16th Field Regiment, the old enemies, now allies in the world's newest war, would commemorate the 36th anniversary of Anzac Day. Diggers had already gathered wild azaleas from the high hills to weave wreaths; extra beer was laid on. Unfortunately the Chinese Fifth Offensive intervened.

Turks in Korea? Why? Kazim Çeliker, a Turkish veteran to whom I spoke, had not known why when the brigade sailed. He had not even known where Korea was. In November 1950, the Turkish Brigade, hindered by poor communications and faulty intelligence, went into their first action. It was a disaster. Çeliker recalled his commander shouting, 'We are surrounded. Protect yourself. Save yourself. Don't waste your bullets'. Çeliker also recalled:

> We took our *sung* [long knives] and fought the bayonets. Half our group died. We had gone to help the Americans. Nobody came to help us. After the battles there we went back to base. We didn't have any more battles until the New Year because we had so many casualties.

The Turks were in Korea because their government, fearful of Soviet expansionism, wanted membership of North Atlantic Treaty Organization (NATO). When Turkey became a full NATO member on 15 February 1952, a Turkish newspaper wrote: 'There has been a great and honourable share of the blood of our Korean heroes in the signatories' ink.'

Australian soldiers also paid a blood price for a treaty. The first Australian to die in the Korean War was the operations officer of No. 77 Squadron, RAAF, Squadron Leader Graham Strout. On 28 June 1951, MacArthur invited his favoured correspondents—called, with some envy, the 'palace guard'—to accompany him on his personal aircraft, the *Bataan*, when he went to survey the chaos in Korea and to watch Seoul burning. He told Australian Roy Macartney he wanted No. 77 Squadron as escorts: the pilots were first class, and he particularly needed long-range fighters like the squadron's Mustangs. On 2 July Strout led No. 77 Squadron's first mission (anticlimactic, as it turned out) from the Iwakuni base in Japan. On 6 July he had to abort because of engine trouble. The following day he peeled off to rocket a railway station. A few seconds later, his wingman saw a blinding flash near the railway line as Strout crashed.

***

More than three years later, on the night of 25 July 1953, a six-man patrol from 2RAR was pushed up by their mates to the top of the main trench on the Hook, a strategic position on a mountain spur looking across the Samichon Valley to the Chinese lines. Custody of the Hook was shared between 2RAR, 3RAR and the forward troops of the 1st Commonwealth Division. To the left were the US Marines of the 7th Regiment, 1st Marine Division. The patrol was on its way to a forward listening post called Green Finger, on a downward-sloping ridge. The Korean War had been in a bloody, grinding stalemate for two years, but at last discussion of an armistice had begun on 10 July. Day after day in July, 2RAR's war diary had reported troop movements, the weather and the incomings, finishing with the words—and you can sense the relief—'no casualties'. On 22 July, however, the Chinese set up an ambush. As the Australians approached Green Finger, grenades and rifle fire came out of the darkness. Private Frank McDonnell was shot in the back and killed.

So on the night of 25 July the patrol again made the hated scramble to Green Finger, downwards past dead and rotting enemy bodies, tangled barbed wire, unexploded shells and mortar bombs, and discarded grenades. The patrol was in position in the outpost when the Chinese launched a furious assault on the marines, although there was little to gain. 2RAR's war diary records steady Chinese artillery fire during the day, intensifying at 11 pm to 30 rounds a minute, then slowing to a steady beat until a silence at 3 am on 26 July. By that time 20-year-old Corporal Kevin Cooper and 21-year-old Private Ron McCoy lay dead on the Hook. At Green Finger, Private Leon Dawes was hit by a piece of shrapnel that passed through his body. He said only, 'I've been hit in the back'. His mate Jimmy Petrie comforted him for the last three minutes of his short life: Leon Dawes was only 19. He was the last Australian killed in action in the Korean War. The armistice was signed the next day, 27 July. The Australian death toll was 340.

***

The Australians of 3RAR had disembarked from the Aiken Victory on 28 September 1950. It seems they were all looking for a fight. They were all volunteers; they had to be, under military regulations, but there would have been a mixture of motivations. Let us start at the top. Lieutenant Colonel Charles Hercules Green enlisted for the Second World War the day recruiting started. He became a superb soldier and a superb leader of men. Aged 25 in 1945, he was a lieutenant colonel and probably the youngest battalion commander in the war. His widow, Olywn Green, watched him struggle when he returned to Australia in peacetime:

> He couldn't seem to find his home, that place he had yearned for during those long nights in the desert sangars or the jungle pit. Dreams were out of reach. He didn't fit. He was not an innocent lad any more; he was a man who had learned terrible—and wonderful—lessons that nobody else knew. It wasn't comfortable finding himself untrained and unprepared for civilian action; his apprenticeship on rifles and bayonets proved inappropriate for peace.

Green went back to the army and back to war.

Major Ben O'Dowd was a child of the Great Depression, a child of a broken home. He left school at the age of 14, basically uneducated, and was working as an underground miner when the Second World War broke out. 'I decided to annihilate all the King's enemies,' he told me. 'I enlisted straight away.' O'Dowd loved soldiering. He was very good at it, and he was at home in the army structure.

Captain Reg Saunders came from a family of Aboriginal warriors. His father, Chris, fought on the Western Front in the First World War. His uncle, William Rawlings, was first bayonet in a bombing team, and won the Military Medal before being killed in action in 1917. As a child, Reg listened to his grandfather's memories of the killing and dispossession of the Wannon tribe, yet, like his father and uncle before him, he went away to war for white Australia when the country needed him. So did his younger brother Harry. Reg survived 11 months in German-occupied Crete, and in New Guinea he was a superb jungle fighter. It was there that Harry Saunders was killed in action. In 1944, a board recommended a commission for Saunders. The matter was so sensitive in racist Australia that it went to the desk of General Thomas Blamey for approval. After the war, Saunders came back, as surviving Aboriginal soldiers had done since the Boer War, to entrenched discrimination in a land in which he could not vote. In August 1950, with relief, he returned to the equality of the army and went to Korea.

Sergeant Ian 'Robbie' Robertson had been taught marksmanship by his father Jim—who had been a sniper on Gallipoli—as they shot rabbits in paddocks outside Melbourne for food and fur during the Depression.

Robbie, a man of humour and charm, talked matter-of-factly about the art of sniping and about his tally of men killed, somewhere around 85. Robbie had been brought up with memories of war and loss. The men in his family had been soldiers. An uncle had died on Gallipoli. At morning school parades, Robbie declared his love of God and country and pledged to honour the flag and serve the King. During the Second World War Robbie, aged 16, attempted to enlist but was turned down by the recruiting sergeant, a mate of his father's. After he turned 18 he managed to be accepted, but as it was 1945 he joined the ranks of the disappointed: he was too late for the fighting. Korea gave Robbie and many others the war they had missed.

Privates Keith Langdon and Denis O'Brien made an odd couple. Like O'Dowd, Langdon came from a broken home and had had a rough childhood. He had a habit of losing his temper, or 'doing his 'nana'. When the government was calling for K Force volunteers, he had a bad day and a few beers, did his 'nana and decided to go to Korea. O'Brien, on the other hand, came from a warm and close Catholic family, imbued with the spirit of Irish nationalism and rebellion, a socialist family. Young Denis was always searching for a cause. The Second World War recruiting sergeant he faced somehow failed to notice he was a boyish 16, and O'Brien got his war and his battles. In peacetime, he went to the University of Melbourne. He became a protégé of Manning Clark, who introduced him to ideological wars. O'Brien, a Catholic crusader, disappointed Clark by becoming an anti-communist soldier. When the call went out for K Force volunteers, O'Brien sent the children home from his one-teacher school in Victoria's wheat belt and joined up. For him, Korea was a cause. Even after being wounded and repatriated, he chose to go back to the battlefield. He wanted to fight alongside his mates; he wanted to fight communism. Keith Langdon once showed me a photograph of his 12th Platoon mates. He pointed to Denis, saying, 'We sang that song the night before Maryang San'. Keith sang part of it for me. It was a traditional soldiers' song, often a drinking song, sad and defiant, sung by British troops in India, by both sides in the American Civil War, and by Errol Flynn and David Niven in the 1938 film *The Dawn Patrol*. Its chorus went, 'Let's drink to the dead already, and three cheers for the next man to die'. That next man was Denis O'Brien. Ten days before, on leave in Tokyo, he had told Langdon he would be smacked the next time they went into action. A Bren-gunner in the leading section, Denis O'Brien was the first Australian to die in the Battle of Maryang San on 5 October 1951. His 82-year-old sister Barbie still mourned for him as she had given me a copy of a letter that Catholic chaplain Father Joe Phillips had written to her mother Monica, a week after the morning on Maryang San:

> Denis was a most extraordinary character. He had a nature that was simple, sincere and just loveable … It is no wonder that the Good Lord wanted him for himself … He looked upon me as both a friend and a priest. But a few days before the fatal attack he called down at my tent one evening. We had a very long chat. Then he made his peace with God. Next day he was at Mass and Holy Communion. This was most surely a most beautiful preparation and anticipation of the invitation that our Divine Lord was so soon to make of him.

***

As the Australians, with their various motivations, were building up the 3rd Battalion of the Royal Australian Regiment, the Americans already on the ground were having a terrible time of it. It was two months after the North Korean strike, and the mighty American military of the Second World War was skeletal and weak. For the Australians who joined them—a small Australian unit in the giant American machine—there were always going to be problems of operational methods, lines of communication and, in general, military ethos. There was at least the modest umbrella for 3RAR of the 27th British Commonwealth Brigade, commanded by Brigadier Basil Coad. Coad was a large man with a pronounced ruddy nose. O'Dowd assures us that the nicknames 'Plonky' or 'Penfolds' were respectfully appended, and Coad did have a deep concern for the welfare of his British, Australian and Canadian troops. For decades after the end of the Korean War, the British War Office withheld a document from public scrutiny. It was labelled 'top secret', and had printed in red on the front cover 'To be kept under lock and key'. This was the Coad Report, a report on the operations of the 27th Brigade between 29 August 1950 and 31 March 1951.

His report was under lock and key to keep it from American eyes. Coad was critical of American tactics in the field. He wrote, 'As usual, the Americans were not holding properly in the hills, the bulk of their men being along the roads'. Basics were ignored, and Coad directed his anger at the ranking officers: 'Complete lack of control by higher HQ [Headquarters] was a feature of the American command.' The report is sprinkled with the signs of his exasperation, sentences often ending with double or triple exclamation marks and double question marks. Scattered through it are comments on transport and tank support promised but never received, on contradictory orders, on confusion and futile searches for divisional headquarters. He was angered by the lack of communication: 'With very few exceptions the American staff officers never leave their HQs even to visit lower formation HQs, and never in our experience did a staff officer come to look at any ground.' At one point Coad writes: 'To make the position clear, I had seen no superior commander for some ten days. We had no contact with 24th Infantry Division under whom I was serving and [who] knew of course nothing about our right flank.'

The troubled relationship Coad described was not a passing problem. More than 18 months later, 3RAR was part of the 1st Commonwealth Division under the command of British Major General Jim Cassels. Cassels had to deal with the American I Corps commander, General John O'Daniel, known in the usual over-blown fashion as 'Iron Mike'. Sensibly, Cassels was provided by the British hierarchy with a directive instructing him to appeal to the Commander-in-Chief of British Commonwealth Forces in Korea if he were ordered by any American commander to carry out operations that were either inconsistent with the purpose of UN operations or which imperilled the safety of Commonwealth troops to a degree exceptional in war.

Cassels's *1st Commonwealth Division Periodic Report, 2 May–15 October 1952*, demonstrates how valuable and necessary this directive was. He wrote:

> My main trouble during this period was to convince I Corps that, though we were more than ready to do anything that was required we did like to know the reason behind it. On many occasions I was ordered, without any warning, to do things which I considered militarily unsound and for which there was no apparent reason.

Flawed intelligence was endemic throughout the Korean War. The prelude to the Battle of Kapyong was no different.

In early April 1951, 3RAR was in reserve in a pleasant part of the Kapyong Valley the diggers called Sherwood Forest. They deserved a rest; they had fought as vanguard up the peninsula and as rear guard in bitter retreat. Charlie Green, Ben O'Dowd's mentor, was dead. The sad irony is that it was O'Dowd, as second in charge, who had sited Green's tent after the Battle of Chongju in October 1950. As Green rested, a single shell hit a tree and a single fragment pierced the canvas and killed Charlie Green.

4. FIGHTING IN THE GIANTS' PLAYGROUND

On the morning of 23 April, Ben O'Dowd was dozing in the sun. As the battalion's intelligence officer recalled, 'It was a beautiful warm day with clear blue skies. War seemed a long way off'. In fact, it was not far up the valley. The Eighth Army was about to be surprised, despite a plethora of information about Chinese troop movements. Among other signs, a Chinese captive in the 1st Marine Division zone was telling interrogators an attack would be opened before the day was out, which is what happened.

That afternoon 3RAR took up thinly stretched positions. B Company was on a low ridge rising like an island to the west of the valley road. A Company, commanded by O'Dowd, was spaced up a steeply rising spur to the summit of Hill 504, where D Company scraped its position. Saunders's C Company was in blocking position behind them. Four empty kilometres across the valley to the west, on Hill 677, was the 2nd Battalion of Princess Patricia's Canadian Light Infantry. The 6th Republic of Korea (ROK) Division was supposed to be just up ahead.

Keith Langdon and Dennis O'Brien, in a forward position on Hill 504, looked down to see refugees fleeing south along the valley, then, as Langdon put it, 'South Korean soldiers, a mob of them, throwing their guns and rifles and even uniforms to buggery'. Through a long night, 3RAR fought magnificently and invaluably to hold off mass Chinese attacks. The next day O'Dowd, as senior rifle company commander, planned and supervised the retreat of the Australians, which Bob Breen rightly describes as a superb military feat—although, unjustly, O'Dowd received no official recognition for it. D Company evacuated its hilltop with the marvellous aid of the artillery of the New Zealand 16th Field Regiment. Saunders later wrote, 'At last I felt like an Anzac and I imagine there were 600 others like me'.

Thirty-two Australians died at Kapyong. The Korean War set the pattern for Australian involvement in Vietnam, Iraq and Afghanistan. Like Percy Spender in 1950, John Howard in 2001 was eager to get Australian troops on the ground in Afghanistan. For the first time since Spender had lobbied for it, ANZUS was invoked by Australia's government. US Secretary of State Donald Rumsfeld kindly said that the Pentagon would include Australia in the operation 'if we can'.

5

THE TRANSFORMATION OF THE REPUBLIC OF KOREA ARMY
Wartime expansion and doctrine changes, 1951–53

Jongnam Na

This chapter deals with the reorganisation of the Republic of Korea (ROK) Army during the Korean War, in particular during the second and third years of the war. The reorganisation began in earnest in the summer of 1951 in what became a sustained campaign of Americanisation.[1] This campaign transformed, both physically and psychologically, a seriously broken South Korean military. Two programs—General James A. Van Fleet's project to increase the ROK Army's combat effectiveness, and General Mark W. Clark's expansion program to increase the ROK Army's size to 700,000 men and 20 divisions—were most significant in transforming the ROK Army into a reliable Cold War military force. Despite many limitations and difficulties, both Koreans and Americans were finally ready to cooperate towards the same goal.

---

1   In this chapter, the term 'Americanisation' is used to mean the ROK Army's introduction to the US Army's models, including training, tactics, professionalism and military culture. My views on Americanisation borrow from E.S. Rosenberg, *Spreading the American Dream: American Economic and Cultural Expansion, 1890–1945*, Hill & Wang, New York, 1982.

Setting the stage

The ROK Army's inadequacies emerged as a prominent issue between the United States and South Korea from late December 1950. The issue intensified as the ROK Army's repeated collapses in the face of Chinese attacks in early 1951 spread panic throughout the ROK Army. Without significant improvement in combat effectiveness and self-confidence among South Korean forces, the entire UN force could expect grave difficulties in their efforts to turn back Chinese offensives.

Predictably, the ROK Government and US military leaders in Korea differed on how best to improve the ROK Army. Arguing that a shortage of soldiers and insufficient weapons and equipment were his military's gravest problems, President Syngman Rhee requested an increase in the ROK Army's total manpower ceilings, as well as increased logistical support from the United States. Lieutenant General Matthew Ridgway, the US Eighth Army commander at that time, opposed this request because he believed that it would not solve the ROK Army's fundamental problems.[2] Instead, command and combat observation reports of early 1951 had convinced him that the ROK Army's shortcomings resulted mostly from such factors as poor leadership and insufficient training. Ridgway thought that the ROK Army's combat performance would not improve until its officers became better leaders, so he wanted to focus on creating a loyal and professionally competent officer corps. He frequently told Korean military leaders and President Rhee that until satisfactory leadership could be developed, all talk of expanding and equipping the ROK military forces should cease.[3] Rhee disagreed and tried to lobby the US Government directly. However, after the ROK Army's collapse in May 1951, Rhee lost his leverage over the ROK Army, and US military commanders were able to exert control over its reorganisation in the summer of 1951. Ridgway was transferred to Tokyo to take over from General Douglas as commander of UN forces. He was replaced by General James A. Van Fleet, who ended up playing the role of the confident American adviser.

---

2   Ridgway to Collins and JCS, 10 May 1951, RG 218, Geographic Files, 1951–53, Box 31, National Archives, College Park, MD [NA].
3   Ridgway to the Department of Army for Hull, 5 May 1951, RG 218, Geographic Files, 1951–53, Box 31, NA.

Van Fleet had led one of the D-Day spearheads on Utah Beach in June 1944. Promoted to brigadier general in September and to major general in November 1944, he guided his division through heavy fighting at Metz in the Ardennes, at Remagen in the Ruhr and in Austria. In February 1948, he was promoted to lieutenant general and given a tough new assignment as a military planner and educator. As a member of the Greek National Council, Van Fleet directed the building and training of Greek anti-communist forces in Greece's civil war. His experience in creating a strong Greek National Army that successfully suppressed communist guerrillas in Greece between 1948 and 1950 would serve him well in his new mission in South Korea.

Although he agreed with General Ridgway's argument that poor leadership was the gravest problem facing the ROK Army, Van Fleet soon discovered a range of other problems that needed to be addressed urgently. An analysis of the ROK Army's disappointing performance at the front in April and May 1951 by the Korea Military Advisory Group (KMAG) revealed not only a leadership deficit at all levels of the officer corps but also serious training problems, shortages of weapons and equipment, poor logistical support and, most seriously, a lack of confidence.[4] Van Fleet concluded that the ROK Army needed to be comprehensively reorganised from the ground up in order to increase both its combat effectiveness and its self-confidence.

So Van Fleet reversed Ridgway's decision about expanding the ROK Army and increasing US logistical support. Ridgway had thought that the more logistical support the United States handed over to the ROK Army, the more it would be handing over to the enemy.[5] Van Fleet's more optimistic appraisal led him to favour a short-term objective, focusing on ROK Army combat effectiveness as the first step in its reorganisation. Van Fleet also decided that Ridgway's evaluation of the ROK Army's overall performance was too harsh and reflected a failure to understand this 'Asiatic' military and its political leader. For example, Ridgway thought of President Rhee as 'a troublemaker'; he was at best 'standoffish with an oriental and impassive face'. However, Van Fleet believed that the

---

4   CG EUSAK to CINCFE, 'Personal for Hicky from Van Fleet', 20 July 1951, RG 554, United States Military Advisory Group to the Republic of Korea [KMAG], AG Decimal File, 1951, Box 41, NA.
5   Ridgway to the Army, 'Personal for Collins', 1 May 1951, Clay and John Blair Collection [CJBC], Box 62, US Army Military History Institute [USAMHI]; CINCFE to the Army, 'Personal from Ridgway to Hull', 23 July 1951, Van Fleet Papers, Box 86.

South Koreans' help would be essential to any reorganisation program, so he adopted a more cooperative attitude towards Rhee and the ROK Government.[6]

Van Fleet sent his final reorganisation plan to the US Department of the Army (DA) in late July 1951. Although doubtful about Van Fleet's ideas, Ridgway gave his endorsement. The plan emphasised training:

> One will be school and basic training, another will be field training of units up to division size, and the third will be ROK Army frontline operations ... The schools and basic training are fairly well organized now but they will be greatly improved under [the new command] ... All of the ROK divisions need a minimum 60-day intensive cycle of training.[7]

In preparing the master plan for the ROK Army's reorganisation, Van Fleet's experience with the Greek Army and KMAG's accumulated knowledge of the ROK Army were the most essential elements. As the plan made clear, Van Fleet would do for the South Koreans 'the same as we did for the Greek divisions'.[8] Van Fleet had a great deal of support from Washington. US policy-makers realised that if the ROK Army could not confront the communists, the other UN forces—mostly US troops—would suffer heavy casualties. It was probably for this reason that General J. Lawton Collins, US Army Chief of Staff, and Frank Pace Jr, US Secretary of the Army, supported Van Fleet's idea of increasing the ROK Army's combat effectiveness.

Van Fleet's plan enjoyed several advantages in South Korea as well. After the armistice talks began in July 1951, the battlefront became relatively quiet while policy-makers in both Beijing and Washington anticipated an end to hostilities, leaving Van Fleet and the ROK Army free to concentrate on the reorganisation project. Second, South Korean military commanders and senior leaders threw their full support behind the project, while Van Fleet shielded ROK officers from President Rhee's anger.[9]

Van Fleet was aided by the presence of an experienced group of KMAG advisers. In December 1950, even before Van Fleet started his mission in Korea, US military advisers had launched several training programs

---

6   Ridgway to Collins and JCS, 20 May 1951, CJBC, Box 62, USAMHI.
7   Van Fleet to Collins, 13 June 1951.
8   Ibid.
9   Van Fleet to John J. Muccio, US Ambassador to the ROK, 2 May 1951.

for the ROK Army, and prepared a detailed analysis of the ROK Army that helped Van Fleet start his program without serious delay. Realising KMAG's importance to the success of his project, Van Fleet requested an increase in the number of KMAG advisers, whose numbers rose to more than 1,300 in October 1951—four times larger than when the war started.[10]

What made the project truly successful, however, was Van Fleet's sincere effort to maintain good relations with both President Rhee and ROK military leaders. He visited ROK Army units to meet Korean officers and soldiers as often as he could. He also frequently met with President Rhee and the Secretary of National Defence and succeeded in building close relationships with them, just as he had with his counterparts in Greece.[11] As a consequence, less than two years after he arrived, most ROK officers and soldiers liked him immensely and regarded him as the 'father of the modern ROK Army'.[12]

Making a better army

In contrast to earlier stages, when US and Korean goals differed, Van Fleet's project progressed smoothly and swiftly thanks to his clear sense of direction, wholehearted Korean support and KMAG's accumulated know-how. To achieve his top priority—increasing the ROK Army's combat effectiveness—Van Fleet's first concern was to restructure the ROK Army's school and training system, created in 1947 but almost destroyed in the first year of the war. Although KMAG revived part of the system in January 1951, all new officers recruited after the beginning of the war suffered from a lack of both basic and advanced training. According to KMAG reports in early 1951, 12 service schools and two training centres operated almost independently, and most schools conducted their own officers' commissioning courses, officers' basic and advanced courses, and courses for enlisted technicians and specialists.[13] There was virtually no

---

10   R.K. Sawyer, *Military Advisors in Korea: KMAG in Peace and War*, Army Historical Series, US Army Center of Military History, Washington, DC, 1963, pp. 141–51, 161.
11   P.F. Braim, *The Will to Win: The Life of General James A. Van Fleet*, Naval Institute Press, Annapolis, MD, 2001, pp. 272–8.
12   Syngman Ree, address to US Congress, 28 July 1954.
13   K.W. Myers, *KMAG's Wartime Experiences, 11 July 1951 – 27 July 1953*, Camp Zama, Japan, Office of Military History Observer Manuscript, 1958, pp. 132–41; KMAG to Secretary of the Army, 'Korean Army Training Program', 11 April 1951; G-3 to Chief, KMAG, 'Advisors to Korean Army Training Installations', 26 February 1951, RG 554, KMAG AG Decimal Files, 1951, Box 57, NA.

central control or coordination. The Replacement Training Centre on Cheju-do Island to the peninsula's south, the only training centre for ROK enlisted men, was responsible for all replacement training. The lack of qualified instructors, equipment and facilities added to the problems in the service schools and at the Replacement Training Centre.

In August 1951, Van Fleet established the Replacement Training and School Command (RTSC) at Taegue in the south-east region of Yeongnam. Controlling all 12 branch schools and two replacement training centres, this new command would have complete responsibility for training throughout the entire ROK Army. The RTSC sought to standardise the training and education of the ROK Army for the first time, and published training regulations, standard tactics and training manuals.[14]

There remained some functional problems, such as scattered individual schools and poor administrative systems. After intensive inspection, KMAG reported that the ROK Army schools could work more effectively and efficiently in one location. Under Van Fleet's coordination, KMAG and the ROK Army decided to move the RTSC to Kwang-ju, a city in the south-western area of the ROK. Three key combat schools—infantry, artillery and signals—moved to the south-western city of Kwang-ju in the Honam region in early November 1951 and were placed under a new command, the Korean Army Training Centre, located at the Kwang-ju Military Post, while the remaining schools and training centres continued operations at their respective locations under the ROK Army Headquarters control.[15]

The opening of the Korean Army Training Centre on 6 January 1952 helped the entire ROK Army to get over the nightmare of its recent defeats. Serving as a model for future permanent establishments for the army, the Korean Army Training Centre was named Sang Mu Dae, meaning 'hail to the spirit of the warrior knights'. As many Korean officers later confirmed, Sang Mu Dae became the symbol of the new ROK Army's development and provided the basis for future victories over the Chinese in several bloody battles.[16]

---

14 Major Lyle E. Widdowson to Senior Advisor, RTSC, 'Programs of Instruction and Weekly Training Schedules', 18 October 1951, RG 554, KMAG AG Decimal Files, 1951, Box 33, NA.
15 Myers, *KMAG's Wartime Experiences*, pp. 129–30; Sawyer, *Military Advisors in Korea*, pp. 178–9; Addenda, Van Fleet Papers, Box 89.
16 Lee Han-lim, *Heosangrok: Ae-ki-yei geok-rang* [Memoirs: Violent Waves of Time], Plabokwon, Seoul, 1994, p. 224.

The 2nd Replacement Training Centre was established in the western province of South Chungcheon within the city of Non-san in November 1951. Its mission was, according to KMAG, 'to provide Korean Army basic trained infantrymen who were trained as infantry replacements and in all military subjects common to all arms and services'.[17] It had been physically impossible for the 1st Replacement Training Centre, the only replacement centre in the ROK Army until November 1951, to offer training for more than 14,000 recruits, including basic training and some special programs. Because the centre lengthened its training cycles between February and July 1951 from four weeks to eight weeks, then to 12 weeks, its physical capacities, including housing and training facilities, were strained to the limit. With the establishment of the 2nd Replacement Training Centre near the Korean Army Training Centre, the army's replacement training system finally was able to provide well-trained manpower to field and other units without serious delay.

Van Fleet started another pivotal program that aimed to train most ROK units above the regimental level for the first time in their history. Less than a third of the ROK Army units had finished battalion-level training when the war started. Because they had been vigorously engaged in combat since, most divisions had had no opportunity for retraining, and the number of trained personnel in individual ROK units was too low to confront the enemy effectively in combat.

To train ROK Army divisions in combat, Van Fleet started a Field Training Centre program modelled on the one he had developed to train Greek Army units.[18] Its main purpose was to increase the ROK divisions' combat performance through proper unit training. The plan was for each corps in the US Eighth Army to help with this program, with KMAG directing the whole process. The 1st Field Training Centre was organised at Pupung-ni, located in present-day North Korea, in the US I Corps area in August 1951 to train the ROK 9th Division.

Van Fleet instructed all ROK Army divisions to complete the nine-week program, providing divisions with one week of rest and eight weeks of individual and unit training in an area near the UN main line of action. Selected officers and non-commissioned officers were brought in from US divisions to supervise the training. They welcomed the chance to be relieved of combat duty and the opportunity to impart to Korean soldiers

---

17 'Replacement Training Center 1 & 2', KMAG, no date, Van Fleet Papers, Box 90.
18 Braim, *The Will to Win*, pp. 209–10.

the lessons they had learned in combat. In most cases, American officers were surprised to find Korean soldiers willing, cooperative and eager to absorb this training.[19] One Korean division in each of the four corps of the US Eighth Army could undergo training simultaneously. KMAG established three more field training centres after September 1951. When the ROK Army began to expand from June 1952, three field training centres were made part of the Unit Training Centre, which took charge of training newly activated ROK units.

While the ROK Army made rapid progress in its Americanisation under both the new school system and the Field Training Centre program, Van Fleet moved to increase the ROK Army's combat firepower, one of its most serious weaknesses during the first year of the war. During that time, ROK Army divisions had no tanks, heavy mortars or aircraft; it had only one 105-millimetre howitzer battalion.[20] Even after ROK Army units received quantities of artillery and other heavy weapons in April and May 1951, they failed to use these weapons effectively and lost most of them to the enemy.[21] An angry Ridgway had temporarily suspended US military support to the ROK as a result. When Van Fleet and the KMAG began to consider this problem in June 1951, they realised that they had to find a way to increase US military support to the ROK Army and train ROK artillery specialists and units.

They needed first to gauge ROK artillery needs, particularly where units had to operate in rough and mountainous terrain with poor roads that created resupply problems. KMAG developed a plan for ROK Army artillery units that stressed flexibility of organisation and the use of concentrated artillery power. KMAG envisaged creating in each ROK Army division one organic 105-millimetre artillery battalion and six artillery group headquarters, each of which would consist of one 155-millimetre battalion and six 105-millimetre battalions. Each headquarters would be approximately the same size as the US divisional artillery.[22]

19   Myers, *KMAG's Wartime Experiences*, pp. 132–44; A.H. Hausrath, *The KMAG Advisor: Role and Problems of the Military Advisor in Developing an Indigenous Army for Combat Operations in Korea*, US Department of the Army, Washington, DC, 1957, pp. 172–4.
20   Chief, KMAG, to Deputy Chief of Staff, EUSAK, 'Memo', 25 May 1951, Van Fleet Papers, Box 86.
21   Major David E. Wright and Major Fred T. Shelton, Jr., 'Debriefing Report', 10 September 1951; Major Eldon B. Anderson, 'Debriefing report, no. 76', 6 March 1952, RG 550, Military Historian's Office, Organizational Files, Box 61, NA.
22   Sawyer, *Military Advisors in Korea*, pp. 183–4; Myers, *KMAG's Wartime Experiences*, p. 88; J.R. Wheaton, 'Korean artillery', *Military Review* 34, October 1954, p. 55; Widdowson to Commanding General, EUSAK.

Although these ideas seemed simple and straightforward, trial and error would guide the entire development between late 1951 and the middle of 1953. Because KMAG could not handle the increase in US military support to the ROK Army directly, Van Fleet took charge of this agenda from the first, especially focusing on contacts with the Department of the Army, the Joint Chiefs of Staff and the Department of Defense. Although KMAG bore the principal responsibility for training and advising ROK artillery units, US artillery units took charge of training the newly organised ROK units, then providing direct and close supervision of their activities. Additionally, Van Fleet directed US officers to rotate from US Eighth Army units to KMAG and ordered ROK units to be integrated into the US Eighth Army. In this way he hoped to maximise the speed and effectiveness of this program.[23]

Another focus was on increasing the armoured strength of each ROK division. This project encountered strong opposition from some US officers on the ground, who believed that armour was ineffective in the rugged and mountainous Korean terrain. The scarcity of available stocks and a lack of sufficient ammunition also slowed the project. Only 10 armoured companies were authorised for the ROK Army by the end of 1952.[24] Moreover, unlike the artillery units, it took more time for KMAG advisers to train Korean tank personnel because of the tankers' lack of previous experience. Nevertheless, the activation of tank units in ROK divisions had a great psychological impact on all Korean soldiers, which was perhaps more important than the units' actual firepower.[25]

Van Fleet and KMAG also sought to create a professional officer corps in South Korea. As Van Fleet wrote to the US Army Chief of Staff, General J. Lawton Collins, in September 1951, 'The basic problems with the ROK Army at this time are training and development of leadership qualities. This is a long-range project, especially the development of an officer corps, as would be true in any new army'.[26] He gave two programs priority: ROK officers' education at US service schools, and the establishment of two key military schools, the Korea Military Academy and the Command and General Staff College (discussed below).

---

23 Myers, *KMAG's Wartime Experiences*, pp. 98–9.
24 HQ, US Eighth Army, Commanding Officer's reports, September 1952, RG 550, Military Historian's Office, Classified Organization History Files, Box 76, NA.
25 Paik Sun-yup, *Heokorok: Kum kwa Na* [Memoirs: The Army and I], Daeruk Yunguso Chulpanbu, Seoul, 1989, pp. 232–5.
26 Collins, *War in Peacetime*, pp. 315; Van Fleet to Collins, 8 September 1951, Van Fleet Papers, Box 73.

The idea of educating ROK officers at US service schools had come from KMAG as early as 1948. By the start of the war, some 15 Korean officers had studied at US Army schools, mainly at the Infantry School at Fort Benning, Georgia.[27] Once they returned to Korea, they worked as instructors in ROK military schools, teaching what they had learned in the United States. Although this program had been ended abruptly at the outbreak of war in 1950, KMAG had great confidence in the program's value and requested in December 1950 that it resume. They believed that US-educated Korean officers would form the nucleus of a trained, professional ROK officer corps.[28] KMAG failed to make any progress on this project, however, until Van Fleet came to Korea. Although Ridgway had agreed to the basic concept behind KMAG's proposal, he did not give it his active support. Van Fleet, however, did.

KMAG then contacted both the US Army's Infantry and its Field Artillery Schools in the United States. The Infantry School agreed to set up a special 20-week basic course for 150 Korean officers; the Field Artillery School recommended a 20-week course for 100 students. This group of officers—the first to attend US military schools since the war had begun—departed Pusan on 10 September 1951 with 22 interpreters and two KMAG officers. The Department of the Army approved KMAG's request to fund the 250 students in March 1952, and agreed to extend the program over the following years. By April 1952, Korean officers had enrolled in more than 20 US Army service schools. A total of 594 Korean officers attended US schools in 1952, primarily the infantry and field artillery schools, with 829 spaces allocated for 1953 and 1,019 spaces requested for 1954.[29] In the event, no fewer than a thousand Korean officers travelled to the United States annually during the late 1950s and throughout the 1960s to attend advanced military courses.

This training in US service schools contributed in a major way to the overall process of Americanisation. In the opinion of KMAG, the positive effect on the ROK Army far outweighed the expense. One KMAG officer, who was to a large extent responsible for the planning of this program, defined this arrangement as 'a package plan to provide maximum instruction at the least possible expense in the least possible time'.[30]

---

27 Sawyer, *Military Advisors in Korea*, pp. 88–9.
28 Collins, *War in Peacetime*, pp. 315; Van Fleet to Collins, 8 September 1951, Van Fleet Papers, Box 73.
29 Myers, *KMAG's Wartime Experiences*, pp. 174–7.
30 KMAG G-3, General Reference Files, no date, quote from Myers, *KMAG's Wartime Experiences*, p. 180.

5. THE TRANSFORMATION OF THE REPUBLIC OF KOREA ARMY

Brigadier General C.E. Ryan, chief of KMAG, looked for the graduation of Korean students in the United States to produce a 'chain reaction' in ROK training establishments.[31] The effect of this program went well beyond Ryan's expectations. Korean officers competed intensely for this golden opportunity, and those selected were proud of their success and worked hard to learn as much as they could from what they regarded as the best military in the world. To the surprise of their American instructors, the first two Korean classes in the Field Artillery School achieved better scores than US officers in the same course.[32]

Van Fleet also established two symbolically important military schools in Korea: the Korea Military Academy and the Command and General Staff College. President Rhee had first asked General Walker, commander of the Eighth US Army at the beginning of the war, then Ridgway after Walker was killed in December 1950, to revive the Korea Military Academy. Both of these commanders considered Rhee's request impractical, but Van Fleet agreed with Rhee, and in late October 1951 the ROK Army Chief of Staff proposed an academy with a four-year course modelled after the US Military Academy at West Point. KMAG soon created a temporary site for the new school at Chin-hae, near Pusan, and appointed three West Point graduates to oversee this program. Van Fleet sent Brigadier General Ahn Chun-sang, superintendent of the new school, to visit West Point in late 1951 to observe and learn. After he returned from his two-week visit, Ahn wrote to Van Fleet that West Point had left him 'overwhelmed'.[33]

The Korea Military Academy from its inception followed the US model. Its mission was 'to provide the Korean Army with a permanent nucleus of professionally trained junior officers who have the essential qualities of character, leadership and aptitude'.[34] At the school's opening ceremony on 20 January 1951, Major General Lee Jong-chan, ROK Army Chief of Staff, wrote to his US Army counterpart, 'The Korean Military Academy

---

31 Myers, *KMAG's Wartime Experiences*, p. 180; Brigadier General C.E. Ryan, Chief, KMAG, to Chief of Staff, ROK Army, 'Subject: Korean Army attendance at US service schools', 3 November 1951, RG 554, KMAG AG Decimal Files, 1948–53, Box 33, NA.
32 Major General Reuben E. Jenkins, Assistant Chief of Staff, G-3, to Deputy Chief of Staff for Operations and Administration, 'Republic of Korea Army students attending the Artillery and Infantry Schools', 21 November 1951, RG 319, Chief of Staff, Decimal Files, 1951–52, Box 742, NA.
33 Ahn Chun-sang to Van Fleet, 4 July 1952, Van Fleet Papers, Box 72.
34 'Korean Military Academy', United States Military Advisory Group to the Republic of Korea, no date, Van Fleet Papers, Box 90.

is the hope of our people ... We are also assured of our contribution to the new institution by firmly establishing an honourable and respectable tradition like that of your Military Academy in America'.[35]

If the academy was the favourite of the Koreans, the Command and General Staff College was the US priority. Van Fleet and KMAG gave considerable thought to a school system that would improve the quality of leadership among senior officers. The function of the college, which opened in late 1951, was similar to that of the US Army Command and General Staff College at Fort Leavenworth, Kansas. The course of study lasted six months and was patterned after the associate course at Fort Leavenworth. American instructors taught the first cohort of students in English with the aid of interpreters. Instruction for subsequent classes was presented in Korean, 10 students from the first class having been retained as teaching staff. Because a large number of students were having trouble understanding English, a plan was adopted in January 1952 to allocate one hour a day to language instruction. Starting with the second cohort in July, the number of students was increased to 50, the maximum that KMAG believed the ROK Army could spare from combat duty.[36]

The introduction of new, modern warfare tactical and training principles promoted Americanisation in this period. By learning close air support tactics while operating under US units, for example, Korean officers could see how ground forces and air power could coordinate effectively. Also, for the first time they received up-to-date training in nuclear and biological warfare.[37] New administrative systems that Korean officers learned from KMAG effectively supported the ROK Army's growing administration.

A small investment in Americanisation under Van Fleet's command had produced a large benefit for the ROK Army. In this process, both Americans and Koreans finally achieved what they had failed to achieve in the previous period: developing respect for, and confidence in, each other. Based on this mutual regard, Van Fleet's reorganisation programs soon paid off by achieving a rapid increase in the ROK Army's combat effectiveness.

---

35 Lieutenant General Lee Chongchan, Chief of Staff, ROK Army, to General J. Lawton Collins, Chief of Staff, US Army, 5 February 1952, RG 319, Army Intelligence Project Decimal Files, 1951–52, Box 164, NA.
36 Myers, *KMAG's Wartime Experiences*, pp. 205–6.
37 'Chemical, Biological, and Radiological Training', United States Military Advisory Group to the Republic of Korea, no date, Van Fleet Papers, Box 90; HQ, US Eighth Army, Commanding Reports, April 1952, RG 550, Military Historian's Office, Classified Organization History Files, Box 71, NA.

Making a bigger army

If Van Fleet's project was to strengthen the ROK Army's value as a reliable military by increasing its combat effectiveness, General Mark W. Clark's project was to strengthen its role in the global Cold War by increasing its size. Clark's idea was to replace US ground forces in Korea by increasing the ROK Army size to nearly 700,000 men, grouped into 20 divisions. Each division would be combat-effective and led by well-educated officers. Despite many problems, as well as opposition from Washington, Clark was able to proceed with his project, beginning in June 1952.

Since the activation of the Bamboo Plan in early 1946, the US Government had controlled the ROK Army's physical size, keeping it as small as possible. Although President Rhee had argued that increasing the size of the ROK Army would save US manpower in the war, US military commanders in Seoul and Tokyo strongly opposed the idea of increasing the ROK Army's numbers. Ridgway set a limit of 10 divisions, which he thought was the most the ROK economy could support, and he criticised Van Fleet's proposal in late 1951 to double the size of the ROK Army. General Ridgway thought the Japanese Self-Defense Forces, the Nationalist Chinese and US commitments in South-East Asia had higher priority for the United States.[38] Finally, in early 1952, he endorsed Van Fleet's plan to increase the ROK Army's size from approximately 252,000 to 383,000 men, mostly in supplementary units, but Ridgway made clear that in no case would he allow the number of ROK Army divisions to be increased.[39]

Clark dramatically shifted the US position. He suggested increasing the ROK Army to 20 divisions, which would relieve US forces in Korea, with the ROK Army taking charge there. Clark was impressed by the ROK Army's rapid achievements under Van Fleet's Americanisation program: 'I have been favourably impressed with the fighting abilities of ROKA soldiers and with the effectiveness of present ROK Army units. I consider their future potential is high and should be developed to the maximum

---

38 Collins, *War in Peacetime*, p. 314; Hull to Ridgway, 8 April 1952; Ridgway to Department of the Army, 9 April 1952, RG 319, Records of the Office of the Chief of Staff, Top Secret Correspondence, 1948–62, Box 5, NA.
39 Ridgway to Department of the Army, 9 April 1952, RG 319, Records of the Office of the Chief of Staff, Top Secret Correspondence, 1948–62, Box 5, NA.

during this critical period.'⁴⁰ He believed that expanding the ROK Army would result in a corresponding reduction in US casualties and would give US military units increased flexibility for future operations.

Clark's plan to '[bring] American soldiers home' was appealing not only to policy-makers in Washington but also to the American public. But it encountered difficulties, above all because the increase to 20 divisions would be costly, requiring an increase in the budget of the US Government. Europeanists inside the Truman administration opposed transferring funds from what they regarded as the primary European front to the secondary Asian front. Most importantly, Clark had to prove to sceptics the potential value of the ROK Army as a Cold War military force. Although Van Fleet's reorganisation programs had improved South Korea's military dramatically, its value as a reliable military had yet to be tested. US policy-makers could not shake memories of the ROK collapse during the first days of the war.⁴¹

Despite opposition from Washington, Clark started his expansion project in June 1952, and it progressed smoothly and swiftly with strong support from Van Fleet, KMAG and the ROK Government. By stabilising the ROK Army induction system with the cooperation of the ROK Government, KMAG could produce 7,200 men per week from the two ROK Army replacement training centres. This manpower became the most fundamental resource for the new ROK Army units. By transforming the existing field training centres into unit training centres in late 1952, the US Army corps took charge of the newly organised ROK unit training programs. This put the US Army in control of how new units were organised, equipped, trained and prepared to go to the front.

However, expected difficulties soon arose. One was a shortage of personnel and materials in KMAG, in the US Eighth Army in Korea and in the Far Eastern Command in Japan. Another was criticism in Washington that the additional logistical support needed in Korea would hurt the US Army's ability to meet other overseas military commitments. Critics argued that Korea should wait until supplementary US budgetary action provided additional support. Nevertheless, Clark submitted his plan to the Department of the Army on 3 October 1952. It called for a two-year

---

40   Clark to Department of the Army, 23 June 1952, RG 218, Geographic Files, 1951–53, Box 40, NA.
41   Major General Frank E. Lowe to Truman, 15 December 1950, 20 January 1951, 14 February 1951, Frank E. Lowe Papers, USAMHI.

program to increase the size of the ROK Army by 10 divisions so as to reduce the number of UN forces deployed in Korea.[42] Clark argued that this would allow the United States to withdraw five divisions, two corps headquarters and some service troops from Korea; after 1 July 1954, the number of US ground forces in South Korea would have fallen by 70 per cent. Until such time as the ROK Army could assume full defence responsibilities, it would be necessary to retain four US Eighth Army divisions in Korea.

Both the Department of the Army and the Joint Chiefs of Staff finally agreed with Clark that expanding the ROK Army was essential.[43] They were especially attracted by the prospect of reducing US casualties by increasing the number of ROK troops on the battle line. The Joint Chiefs of Staff also agreed that augmenting ROK forces would permit reinforcement of the defensive lines and provide reserves essential to the operational flexibility of the US Eighth Army and the entire US Army.[44] The now-authorised expansion project would bring the ROK Army to 12 divisions and 463,000 men.[45]

With the Joint Chiefs of Staff still needing the president's approval, the presidential campaign settled the matter in favour of expansion. In a speech on 29 October 1952, Republican Party candidate Dwight D. Eisenhower criticised the Truman administration's reluctance to expand the ROK Army. Emphasising the necessity of letting Asians fight against Asians, Eisenhower released a personal letter from Van Fleet that criticised Washington for delaying the decision to increase the size of the ROK Army.[46] Approval now came swiftly. On 31 October, President Truman supported the Joint Chiefs of Staff's recommendation to increase the ROK Army to 14 divisions.[47] Several days later, the Department of the Army asked Clark to prepare a plan to use ROK manpower to reduce demands on

---

42 Major General C.D. Eddleman to Chief of Staff, US Army, 'Proposed Two-year Program for the Augmentation of the ROKA to Reduce United Nations Forces in Korea', 3 November 1952, RG 319, Records of the Office of the Chief of Staff, Top Secret Correspondence, 1948–62, Box 5, NA.
43 JCS to Clark, 30 October 1952, RG 218, Geographic Files, 1951–53, Box 41, NA.
44 J.E. Welch and B.R. Eggeman, 'Joint Chiefs of Staff Decision on JCS 1776/317', 26 September 1952, RG 319, Records of the Office of the Assistant Chief of Staff, G-3, Top Secret Decimal Files, 1952, Box 20, NA.
45 JCS 1776/328, 27 October 1952; JCS 1776/332, 31 October 1952; JCS to Clark, 30 October 1952, RG 218, Geographic Files, 1951–53, Box 41, NA.
46 'Background on Korea Issue Enlivening Presidential Race', *New York Times*, 31 October 1952; 'Lovett Denies Van Fleet's Charge of Delay in Training Korean Troops', no date, Van Fleet Papers, Box S-24.
47 DA to CINCFE, 31 October 1952, from Myers, *KMAG's Wartime Experiences*, p. 62.

US troops while lowering US battle casualties and rotation requirements. Clark was specifically asked what was needed for the Pentagon to cut the number of US troops in Far Eastern Command by 50,000 men, withdraw two US divisions from the Korean front by the end of 1953, and turn the defence of the entire front over to the ROK Army by the end of 1954.[48]

Fearing that the army and the Joint Chiefs of Staff were suddenly moving too fast, Clark began to take a more cautious attitude to the project he had initiated. In submitting his final plan, Clark emphasised that it was feasible only if the stalemate continued in Korea without any substantial increase in enemy forces, and only if adequate and properly phased logistical support was forthcoming from the United States.[49] He also felt that the Department of the Army's 18-month timeline for this project was unrealistic, even dangerous.[50] As a result, the 20-division plan underwent further study in Washington until mid-November 1952.[51]

Once elected, Eisenhower hesitated over the expansion program, and the Department of the Army, Joint Chiefs of Staff and the Defence Department moved in different directions. First, several military studies warned that the US military suffered from serious matériel shortages as a result of budget reductions: to support the ROK Army expansion, scheduled projects in other areas such as NATO and South-East Asia would have to be delayed.[52] Second, US policy-makers worried about the ability of the Korean economy to support the expansion, leaving the US Government to pick up the bill. According to the Joint Chiefs of Staff's staff report, the estimated cost of the expansion was approximately $2 billion in the first year (approximately $19.4 billion today), bringing the total cost of maintaining the ROK Army to $3 billion (approximately $29.1 billion today).[53]

---

48 Eddleman, Assistant Chief of Staff, G-3, to Chief of Staff, 'Proposed Two-year Program for the Augmentation of the ROKA to Reduce United Nations Forces in Korea', 3 November 1952.
49 Clark to the Department of the Army, 28 October 1952, RG 218, Geographic Files, 1951–53, Box 41, NA.
50 CINCFE to DA, 28 October 1952; General Clark to C/S, 1 November 1952, RG 218, Geographic Files, 1951–53, Box 41, NA.
51 Eddleman to Chief of Staff, G-3, 3 November 1952; Eddleman, 'Memorandum for the Chief of Staff, US Army—Subject: Development of Wartime Republic of Korea Army', 4 November 1952, RG 319, Records of the Assistant Chief of Staff, G-3, Top Secret Decimal Files, 1952, Box 20, NA.
52 Omar N. Bradley, 'Memorandum for General Collins', 19 November 1952, RG 319, Records of the Assistant Chief of Staff, G-3, Top Secret Decimal Files, 1952, Box 20, NA.
53 Lovett, 'Memorandum for the Joint Chiefs of Staff'.

While fierce debates continued inside the Pentagon, President Eisenhower, in mid-May 1953, finally granted authority for the ROK Army's support strength to be increased to 655,000 men and 20 divisions. Despite the potential problems, allowing American soldiers to return home by increasing reliance on Korean military forces was the most crucial aspect of this decision. Most policy-makers in Washington hoped the expansion would quiet Rhee's opposition to an impending armistice.[54]

The actual expansion in Korea progressed faster than Clark's schedule. Despite the lack of matériel, the ROK 12th Division was organised, trained and in action at the front by the end of December 1952, while the ROK 15th Division was similarly deployed by the end of January 1953.[55] Once these two divisions were activated, the prospects for other divisions seemed much better.

President Rhee and the ROK government strongly supported this project. Quietly, behind the scenes, Rhee had argued for expansion. He told US Senator H. Alexander Smith, 'We do not want you to sacrifice your own boys. All we ask for is that you give us equipment and that you train our own people. It is much better for Asians to fight Asians'.[56] Making new laws and regulations to start the large induction of manpower beginning in May 1952, the ROK Government supported KMAG's request to implement Clark's plan.

The ROK Army officer corps was the single biggest beneficiary of this project, because the expansion of the army would provide enormous opportunities to Korean officers, including increased chances of promotion, better assignments and higher expectations for their military careers. Promotion from major to lieutenant colonel took less than 10 months in mid-1952. For example, it took just five months for Major Lee Byung-hung to be promoted to lieutenant colonel with a new assignment as G-3 of the ROK Army 2nd Division, a post he had long hoped for.[57]

---

54   Clark to the Department of the Army for JCS, 13 May 1953, RG 218, Geographic Files, 1954–56, Box 44, NA.
55   Myers, *KMAG's Wartime Experiences*, p. 66.
56   Syngman Rhee to Senator H. Alexander Smith, no date, quote from D.C. Skaggs and R.P. Weinert, 'American Military Assistance to the Republic of Korea Army, 1951–1965', draft manuscript, p. II-1, RG 319, Military Historian's Office; unpublished manuscript, 'KMAG in Peace and War', Box 1, NA.
57   Lee Byung-hung, *Yun-dae-jang* [Memoirs: Regimental Commander], Bung-hak-sa, Seoul, 1997, pp. 11–12.

The newly organised units also gave Korean officers useful experience for their future professional careers. Colonel Kim In-chul realised that he was the first man to arrive at his new unit, which would be organised as the 58th Regiment in November 1952 in the north-eastern county of Yang-yang. With help from neighbouring units and KMAG advisers, Kim was able to organise his unit within two weeks. Fortunately, Kim could appoint able and well-trained personnel as his subcommanders, staff officers and even non-commissioned officers from other existing units. After finishing a four-week Unit Training Centre program under the US X Corps, Kim's regiment became one of three in the ROK 20th Division, which was activated in February 1953. Right after the US X Corps' combat inspections in March, this new regiment arrived at the combat line less than six months from its activation.

This and other new units performed impressively in combat. In its first combat mission in April, Kim's regiment scored an impressive victory over the Chinese, for which it won the Corps Commander's decoration.[58] During June and July 1953, the ROK II Corps demonstrated a similar effectiveness against a major Chinese offensive that was meant to influence the final stage of the armistice talks. Although the Chinese first blow in the vicinity of Kum-sung was strong enough to penetrate the defence of two front-line ROK divisions, the 5th and 8th, the other division of this corps, the 3rd, soon filled this gap. While the US Eighth Army provided rapid reinforcement to this area to back up this ROK corps, all three Korean divisions launched counter-attacks less than 24 hours after the enemy's attack had begun. Surprising even US military commanders, this ROK corps inflicted more than 50,000 casualties on the Chinese forces. Many American observers, military and civilian, praised the ROK Army units for standing firm against the communists by themselves. General Maxwell Taylor, who assumed command of the US Eighth Army after Van Fleet retired in December 1952, acknowledged the achievement: 'This is really the first time that the South Korean divisions have been engaged on their own in large-scale operations. They are acquitting themselves magnificently and are holding their main lines which the Communists have nowhere penetrated.'[59]

---

58   Kim In-chul, *Yuk-i-o Jun-jaeng Heokorok: Sam-pal-sun-yei-seo Hui-jun-sun-ka-ji* [Memoirs: From the 38th parallel to the Demarcation Line], Bo-mun-dang, Seoul, 1992, p. 376.
59   Lieutenant General Maxwell Taylor, interview with William Courtenay, 7 July 1953, quoted in Myers, *KMAG's Wartime Experiences*, p. 358.

Conclusion

As early as the summer of 1952, the Republic of Korea Army had become a reliable military, a fact that many observers both inside and outside the ROK Army recognised. In particular battles against the communists, ROK Army units were proving the value of what they had learned and achieved under the US Army's direction. The success of the ROK Army's Americanisation project had two instant consequences for Americans and Koreans. First, as US policy-makers expected, major US ground forces were able to withdraw from South Korea, leaving the Cold War mission to the ROK Army, and enabling the United States to improve its Cold War manpower situation. Koreans also benefited by achieving their old aspirations: with this strong military force, South Koreans could preserve their national pride and security through their own efforts.

During the last two years of the Korean War, the ROK Army underwent a fundamental transformation. Physically, the small and outdated Asian military force became a well-trained and effectively equipped first-class army. No longer Asiatic, it had become Westernised, following predominantly the US Army's model. The Korean War was not only the most decisive turning point but also the best opportunity for the ROK Army's Americanisation. In its first year this war demonstrated the value of military Americanisation to Koreans, who had been suspicious on that point. The war itself served as an ideal classroom for the ROK Army's new learning. Its officers tested in combat what they had learned and affirmed the value of their new learning.

Also significant was the relationship between two field actors, American advisers and Korean advisees. Although policy-makers in both Washington and Seoul decided on the basic framework for this project, details were decided by actors on the ground. As a result, the relationships formed between the US and Korean participants accounted for much of the overall success of the Americanisation efforts. Cultural problems and different expectations led to confrontations at the start, yet US advisers and ROK officers managed eventually to cooperate with each other and to develop friendships, while fighting together against a common enemy to achieve a common goal. Without the so-called perfect partnership between these two sets of soldiers, military Americanisation in the Republic of Korea might have failed.

PART 2

KOREAN SKIES AND KOREAN WATERS

The RAAF transitioned to jet fighters during the Korean War. The Meteor F.8 was outclassed by the MiG-15 in dogfights, but it was an excellent ground attack platform.
Source: AWM JK0242.

The RAN Fleet Air Arm's 21st Carrier Air Group, flying Sea Fury and Firefly aircraft off the deck of HMAS *Sydney* (III), conducted 2,366 sorties over a period of 64 days during the latter months of 1951.
Source: AWM 044801.

HMAS *Sydney* (III)'s deployment to Korean waters was the first time a dominion carrier had been deployed on active service. It was the only time *Sydney* saw active service as an aircraft carrier.
Source: AWM ART28077. Ray Honisett, *HMAS Sydney in Korean waters, 1951–52*.

6

THE AIR WAR IN KOREA

Coalition air power in the context of limited war

Richard Hallion

The Korean air war constituted the last significant non-air-refuelled air war, and this created a major problem at the war's outset for those seeking to employ air power effectively in South Korea's defence. While the air-refuelling issue did not strongly influence United States Air Force (USAF) bomber operations, it had a profound impact upon the USAF's tactical air power application, particularly after the North Korean People's Army (NKPA) had overrun most of South Korea's airfields. As a result, naval aviation power projection from carriers was essential in preventing communist forces from completely overrunning the Korean Peninsula. Air superiority operations, including air-to-air defence intercepts, offensive fighter sweeps and airfield attacks, effectively removed the North Korean People's Army Air Force (NKPAAF) as a significant factor in the war by the beginning of July 1950, permitting, in effect, uninterrupted coalition air power operations from then until the intervention of the Soviet air force (the Voenno-Vozdushnye Sily; VVS) in November. Until then, medium and heavy bombers were able to operate essentially from the onset of the war without significant opposition, all the way up to the Manchurian border.

Operations early in the war were aided as well by North Korea's lack (remedied subsequently) of medium and heavy anti-aircraft artillery. As a result, the combination of available air power forces on land and at sea in the summer of 1950 offset the South's lack of large, in-place, land-power armour and infantry forces, and furnished close air support (CAS) and battlefield air interdiction (BAI). CAS–BAI dramatically reduced the amount of fuel and food available to advancing NKPA forces; destroyed large numbers of vehicles and troops; eased the pressure on coalition land-warfare forces; and substituted for the coalition's own lack of artillery and heavy fire support, particularly during bitter fighting around the Pusan Perimeter and at the Naktong River in August–September 1950. Halting the North Korean advance bought time for reinforcement, reconstitution and the build-up to the invasion of Inchon, the necessary prelude for the subsequent United Nations advance up the Korean Peninsula.

When Mao sent the People's Liberation Army (PLA)—renamed the 'Chinese People's Volunteers Force' (CPVF)—into North Korea in November 1950, this same combination of air-power forces again proved crucially important. Air force fighter operations kept MiG depredations to a minimum, pending arrival in theatre of the North American F-86 Sabre. Strategic bombers, medium bombers and naval attack aircraft struck at bridge, road and rail targets (although many bridges were dropped, there was alas something of a 'closing the barn door after the horse has bolted' quality to much of these actions). In this crisis, the airmen of the United States Navy (USN) and United States Marine Corps (USMC) again distinguished themselves in ensuring the safe extraction of UN forces and refugees from the port of Hungnam, and covering the withdrawal of Marine and coalition units breaking out from the Chosin Reservoir. Afterwards, land- and sea-based air power functioned much as it had six months earlier (although with far better coordination and organisation), again with steady attrition of advancing CPVF forces, to the frustration of the PLA's Korean leadership and troop-level cadres. After the war stabilised along a relatively static Main Line of Resistance (MLR) in 1951, land- and sea-based air power forces furnished persistent observation, surveillance, reconnaissance, interdiction, battlefield air attack, CAS and artillery and naval gunfire control until the Korean armistice in July 1953.

6. THE AIR WAR IN KOREA

Military aviation, 1945–53

The two great revolutions that transformed aviation at mid-century were the development of the jet engine and the derivation of high-speed aerodynamic design theory (typified by the swept-back wing), which enabled flight at speeds approaching and exceeding the velocity of sound. Both promised, and then made possible, the era of 600-plus miles per hour (960-plus kilometres per hour) flight speeds. However, integrating the jet aircraft into the force structure of leading air-power nations proved difficult and time-consuming. Early turbojet aircraft had very high fuel consumption rates, in contrast to slower, long-loitering propeller-driven designs. Mixing older propeller-driven and newer jet aircraft in common strike packages required creative planning to ensure that the slower aircraft were not left unprotected over a target area, while the faster aircraft did not run out of fuel too soon. (This problem, incidentally, affected both the United Nations Coalition and the VVS and PLAAF in their own air operations, sometimes with disastrous results.) Command and control of the new jet aircraft posed its own problems, for ground controllers were used to the behaviour of petrol-fuelled, piston-powered aircraft, not kerosene-guzzling jets. As one fighter test pilot recalled, controllers 'did not understand how altitude affected range and endurance. We pilots measured fuel in pounds and minutes, and the controllers measured it in gallons and hours. We would climb to 35,000 feet, and they would vector us to intercept a bogey at sea level and then wonder why we never had enough fuel'.[1]

Operating from land bases, the USAF had less difficulty adapting to the jet age, but even so, the peculiarities of early generation jet engines took a high operational toll on pilots. This stemmed particularly from the engines' low-thrust and slow throttle-response (reflecting slow spool-up time, or rotative acceleration), leaving aircraft with a generally sluggish slow-speed performance. Exacerbating this were the low-speed aerodynamic deficiencies of early swept-wings, which lacked the lift-enhancing technologies available to later aircraft. Both the Soviet MiG-15 and North American F-86 possessed vicious deficiencies in their handling qualities that could bite the unwary with a vengeance.

---

1   D.D. Engen, *Wings and Warriors: My Life as a Naval Aviator*, Smithsonian Institution Press, Washington, DC, 1997, p. 102.

Integrating jet aircraft into an operational construct was a particular challenge for naval aviation. Early jet aircraft lacked the rapid throttle-response characteristics of propeller-driven aircraft, and had nowhere near the rapid throttle transient characteristics of later fighter aircraft such as the F-15 and F/A-18. Their lower-aspect-ratio wings (a concession for speed) endowed them with higher sink rates (rate of descent) than their propeller-driven, higher-aspect-ratio predecessors. Only after Korea did the USN introduce swept-wing fighter aircraft into operational service. The Royal Navy's Fleet Air Arm and France's Aéronavale introduced them even later. Thus, the US Navy fought Korea with straight-wing jet aircraft, typified by its Grumman F9F Panther. While these were more than adequate to deal with the NKPAAF's propeller-driven Yak fighters in the summer of 1950, the Panther was seriously outclassed by the Soviet-flown swept-wing MiG-15 when it appeared in Korean skies in November 1950. So too was the straight-wing, twin-engine McDonnell F2H Banshee. Fortunately, the quality of naval pilots was such that, one-on-one, USN airmen generally evaded opposing MiG fighters, and in some cases shot them down.

The safety statistics for both the USAF and US Navy in the 1940s and 1950s reveal the very high loss rates associated with early jet aircraft operations. During the Korean War, the USAF lost 787 aircraft to enemy action and 960 others in non-combat losses: 1,747 aircraft, or approximately one lost per 456 sorties. In the same time period, the US Navy and US Marines lost 567 aircraft in combat and 684 in non-combat losses: 1,251 aircraft, or approximately one lost per 240 sorties. Naval aviation was thus almost twice as dangerous as land-based aviation, largely an indication of the inadequacies of both the straight-deck carrier in the early jet era and of the turbojet aircraft that operated from it. As an example of naval loss rates in Korea, the carrier USS *Essex* went to war in August 1951: less than a month later it returned to Japan, having lost 18 aircraft (more than 20 per cent of its air group), eight aircrew and seven maintainers, including one horrendous deck-landing accident that killed eight, injured 16 and destroyed four aircraft.[2]

Then there were basic problems with combat execution owing to the erosion of skills after the Second World War. In January 1949, all of the USAF Strategic Air Command's bombers flew against Dayton, Ohio,

---

2   Essex action report, 8 August–21 September 1951, pp. 2–4, Naval History and Heritage Command archives, Washington Navy Yard, Washington, DC.

practising bombing from 30,000 feet: analysis indicated that, if they had actually dropped bombs, the average bomb would have hit 10,090 feet (more than 3 kilometres) from the aim point. About the same time, a naval Corsair squadron in Seattle flew cross-country to visit another in Denver. None of its pilots managed to find Denver, instead landing in twos and threes across various states. For a service that had routinely sent its fighter pilots out from carriers against enemy fleets and shore targets, it was, as one naval officer characterised it, 'beyond belief'.[3]

Oddly enough, and as touched on in an earlier chapter, the greatest threat to UN air superiority in Korea—the MiG-15—owed a considerable debt to Great Britain. In 1946, Britain sold 55 Rolls-Royce Derwent and Nene jet engines to the Soviet Union, a controversial decision that ANU historian Joan Beaumont judged as 'manifestly against Great Britain's and the West's strategic interests'.[4] (Allegedly, Stalin wondered aloud: 'Who's stupid enough to sell his secrets?'[5]) Both the Derwent and Nene were reverse-engineered and placed into production for use in new Soviet jet fighters and bombers.[6] At that time, the Royal Air Force (RAF) did not possess any operational swept-wing aircraft of its own. Instead, its finest fighter was the subsonic straight-wing, twin-engine Gloster Meteor F.8, 94 of which the Royal Australian Air Force (RAAF) received in 1951 as replacements for the RAAF's even more obsolescent propeller-driven Mustangs.[7]

Then there was the state of air power on the Korean Peninsula. Military ties with the United States were ostensibly strengthened in 1948, but excluded air power. At a time when the Democratic People's Republic of Korea (DPRK) gained a surprisingly robust air arm of more than 160 propeller-driven fighters and attack bombers, the Republic of Korea (ROK) was allowed just a token air service less than a tenth the size of North Korea's. It consisted of 13 light, fabric-covered Piper L-4

---

3   A.S. Crossfield with C. Blair, *Always Another Dawn*, World Publishing Co., Cleveland, 1960, p. 117; he was one of the pilots involved.
4   J. Beaumont, 'Trade, strategy, and foreign policy in conflict: The Rolls-Royce affair 1946–1947', *International History Review* 2, no. 4, 1980, pp. 603, 616.
5   Y. Gordon, *Early Soviet Jet Bombers*, Midland Publishing, Hinckley, Leicestershire, 2004, p. 4.
6   A.S. Yakovlev, *Fifty Years of Soviet Aircraft Construction, NASA TTF-627*, Israel Program for Scientific Translations & National Aeronautics and Space Administration, Jerusalem, 1970, pp. 103–4. Klimov design bureau engineers so closely copied the Nene that, after inspecting one, its designer, Sir Stanley Hooker, remarked, 'They even copied the mistakes!'
7   A. Stephens, *Going Solo: The Royal Australian Air Force, 1946–1971*, AGPS, Canberra, 1995, pp. 229–32.

and Stinson L-5 liaison aircraft and three North American T-6 trainers, offering no combat capability whatsoever. So muddled was US policy over the future of South Korea and its air capabilities that President Syngman Rhee sought the advice of retired Major General Claire L. Chennault on forming a force like the Flying Tigers—American volunteers who flew in China in 1941–42 under Chennault's command. He responded by crafting a plan for a 99-plane force built around a core of F-51 Mustangs, but it did not come to pass. The last US military forces left Korea at the end of June 1949. Six months later, Secretary of State Dean Acheson artlessly explained the United States' perception of its security responsibilities in the western Pacific, seemingly consigning South Korea to a zone beyond US interests. Six months after that, North Korean tanks rumbled across the arbitrary line separating the two Koreas, launching an outright invasion of the South.

Air power at war

For airmen, Korea was a war of many images: the MiG v. Sabre duels in what became known as 'MiG Alley'; the day-to-day routine of interdiction, air pressure and CAS strikes; the night strategic bombing war and the night-fighter crews of the US Marine Corps, US Navy and Far East Air Forces (FEAF) that supported it; and the operations at sea of the USN's Task Force 77 (TF77) and the light carrier forces. Often neglected but crucially important were maritime patrol operations that watched for communist submarine forces and North Korean mine-layers. Here, too, it was a coalition effort, with three RAF Sunderland squadrons partnered with the 'patrons' (patrol squadrons) of the USN. Helicopter crews earned special respect for their 'can do' attitude and willingness to take rudimentary and woefully underpowered and underprotected craft into enemy territory.

Crucial to the conduct of combat operations in Korea was control of the air. Overall, the UN coalition began the war with air parity, moved rapidly to assert air superiority and never lost that superiority over the duration of the conflict. But the story is more complex than that. In the fall of 1950, the introduction of the MiG-15 and their Soviet pilots dramatically transformed the air war. Only its short range (in its initial models) and the Stalin-prescribed policy that the Soviet air force, the VVS, limit its operations to MiG Alley prevented the MiG from having an

6. THE AIR WAR IN KOREA

even greater influence. It immediately rendered obsolete all other fighter aircraft in theatre. Had the quality of its pilots been up to that of the UN coalition—and some MiG pilots were quite experienced—the impact on UN operations would have been extraordinary. If the communist air leadership had succeeded in persuading the Soviet Union to allow the VVS to take a greater role over North Korea, the battle for air control could have moved south to the Main Line of Resistance (MLR) and east and west to the coastal waters of Korea, denying FEAF and naval aviation forces much of the freedom they enjoyed to conduct routine operations so close to hostile territory.

Undoubtedly the coalition benefited from the availability of the F-86 Sabre in its swept-wing platform. The Sabre was far from a perfect fighter aircraft, but it had sufficient advances to enable it to dominate the MiG-15 in the high-speed arena, thanks largely to a better flight control system and better basic aerodynamics. The MiG-15's tendency to enter unrecoverable spins seriously constrained its combat utility: in 32 observed combat spins, 29 of the MiGs involved continued spinning into the ground.[8] A flight test evaluation on a NKPAAF defector's MiG, delivered to Kimpo after the war, confirmed the Sabre's basic superiority over it, but noted as well other aspects in which the MiG's performance, particularly its acceleration, was better. Overall, the USAF credited the F-86 with shooting down 810 MiGs for the loss of 78 Sabres, a victory-to-loss ratio of more than 10:1. In the years since, the merit of this number (and the 14:1 ratio for experienced Sabre pilots against tyros with new VVS or PLAAF units) has been hotly debated. Undoubtedly, as in any air war, both sides engaged in overclaiming, usually a result of misinterpreting what one sees happening at the time. In any case, many aircraft (on both sides) carried as operational losses because of disappearances or other unexplained losses were in any case lost on air combat operations. Certainly the Sabres performed at far better than air parity, and to this author, a victory-to-loss ratio of about 8:1 seems a completely reasonable figure.

Even so, it must be noted that the F-86, for all its merits, was hard pressed, particularly as its early models lacked the power (and hence thrust-to-weight ratio) one would have desired in a transonic jet fighter. RAF Squadron Leader William 'Paddy' Harbison, an experienced fighter pilot, MiG-killer and noted fighter tactician, was sent to Korea in February

---

8   W.T. Y'Blood, *MiG Alley*, Air Force History and Museums Program, Washington, DC, 2000, p. 38.

1952 and flew combat missions with the 4th Fighter Wing. His classified comparative study concluded: 'The relative superiority of the present F-86E pilot–plane–weapon "team" is not likely to continue forever. In point of fact, it is the considered opinion of most pilots that, given the present MiG-15 advantages of combat location, the rising proficiency of the MiG-15 "team" will eventually void our present superiority.'[9] In fact, the USAF introduced the F-86F, and it retained its dominance over the MiG-15 to the end of the war.

But the air war over MiG Alley was far from a sure thing. Brigadier General Michael De Armond recalled in 2000: 'At times it was pretty grim ... I don't want you to think that we stood back there and knocked the MiGs down out of the sky without losing a lot of very, very good people.'[10] Harbison was quite correct that the moment of the Sabre's superiority over the MiG-15 was passing. It is interesting to contemplate what might have happened, had the air war continued into 1954, if the MiG-15 force in Korea was augmented, then replaced, by the later MiG-17. Deceptively similar to the early MiG-15 in appearance, the MiG-17 totally outclassed the F-86F, and would have been at worst equivalent to the slightly later F-86H.

Achieving and holding air superiority was primarily the responsibility of the USAF, as the USN and coalition air forces lacked an aircraft equal to the MiG-15 and the F-86 until after the war. Nonetheless, those forces played a role in the battle for control of Korea's skies. TF77's F9F and F2H Panther pilots provided top cover for B-29 bombing strikes going to the far north of Korea near the Soviet frontier, and routinely provided cover for their fellow naval aviators on strikes on the periphery of, or into, MiG Alley. As well, they capped the fleet; that is, they provided combat air patrol cover for naval assets. Early in the afternoon of 18 November 1952, at least seven VVS MiGs left an airfield near Vladivostok and flew on a direct course towards TF77, attacking four F9F-5s, the latest and most powerful model of the veteran Panther. The superior training of the navy

---

9   Sqdn Ldr W. Harbison, *The F.86 v. the MiG-15*, RAF Central Fighter Establishment, West Raynham, Norfolk, 1952, AIR 8/1709, National Archives, Kew, Great Britain [TNA]. I thank retired RAF Air Vice Marshal Paddy Harbison for his contributions to my understanding of the air war over North Korea.
10 Statement of DeArmond in *Silver Wings, Golden Valor: The USAF Remembers Korea*, ed. R.P. Hallion, USAF, Washington, DC, 2006, p. 34. DeArmond was shot down and taken prisoner in the war.

airmen, and the better gunsight and gun system of the F9F-5, saved them from loss; three (perhaps four) MiGs were shot down at the price of one Panther seriously damaged. VVS airmen never again approached TF77.

The RAAF pitted its Meteor F.8 fighters (which had replaced No. 77 Squadron's Mustangs in early 1951) against the MiG, losing four but shooting down five MiGs in return. The Marines furnished Yalu patrols for B-29 night strikes, shooting down several MiG-15s with their Douglas F3D-2 Skyknights. The US Navy and Marines teamed to furnish air defence for Kimpo, Seoul and other South Korean advanced locations, which came under extensive heckling attacks by Korean People's Army Air Force Polikarpov Po-2, Yak-18 and legacy ex-Imperial Japanese Army Air Force Tachikawa Ki-9 light aircraft; one Corsair pilot received credit for five victories over the annoying little attackers.

The air-to-ground war

The single most controversial aspect of Korean air operations was the conduct of close air support (CAS) in the first year of the war. By late July it seemed possible that UN forces would be thrown off the peninsula by an army that had not even existed five years previously. At the heart of the problem was that, while joint terminology defined 'close tactical air support' as 'air action against hostile surface targets which are so close to friendly forces as to require detailed integration of each air mission with the fire and movement of these forces', there was no agreed joint operating doctrine covering such operations. Instead, the marines and the navy had developed one system and the army and the air force another, each to achieve different ends.

Mirroring their origins as a lightly equipped landing force, the US Marines employed their aircraft as a substitute for battlefield artillery. The USMC–USN system delivered CAS from the line of contact back to the artillery line, similar to Great War trench strafing.[11] The army had a layered support system, rooted in army and air force experience gained in air–land operations during the breakout across France in 1944.[12] Army

---

11 A. Millett, 'Korea, 1950–1953', in *Case Studies in the Development of Close Air Support*, ed. B.F. Cooling, USAF, Washington, DC, 1990, pp. 345–410; and P.B. Mersky, *US Marine Corps Aviation: 1912 to the Present*, Nautical and Aviation Publishing Company of America, Annapolis, MD, 1983.
12 D.N. Spires, *Air Power for Patton's Army: The XIXth Tactical Air Command in the Second World War*, USAF, Washington, DC, 2002.

doctrine granted both land and air commanders equal authority in setting priorities for tactical air support, and carved out an artillery-only zone in front of the line of contact, extending back approximately 1,000 metres to a so-called artillery line. This ensured that army artillery could freely engage enemy forces unhindered by air force air support aircraft.[13] Thus, the USAF would not routinely deliver air support inside the artillery line. Beyond the artillery line, the army–USAF system allowed coordinated air support from the artillery line to an army-designated bomb line. While both the army and the air force then defined this as CAS, it was, to use more recent parlance, battlefield air interdiction (BAI). Working together, both systems furnished complementary coverage that denied any area of sanctuary for the foe, from the line of contact to the bomb line, and air operations beyond the bomb line extended that zone of vulnerability across the enemy's rear areas.

The CAS challenge became acute in August and early September 1950, as NKPA forces closed in on the contracting Pusan Perimeter. USMC Corsair pilots flew their first CAS missions from the carrier USS *Sicily* on 3 August, the beginning of a particularly acute period in the fight to save South Korea. Here the doctrinal, equipment, training and exercise shortfalls of the postwar period took their greatest toll, for combat operations quickly revealed numerous deficiencies, particularly a lack of effective communication. Maps lacked the proper grid references to ensure accurate positional reference. Serious deficiencies, incompatibilities and differences existed among the services' communication systems. Inadequate ship-to-shore circuits hindered communication between TF77 and Fifth Air Force. Korea's hilly terrain and old equipment limited the ability of army–USAF tactical air control party radio jeeps to communicate with strike aircraft. In the air, things were somewhat better, as USAF and Marine forward area controllers had modern multi-channel radios, but poor radio discipline and extraneous chatter saturated the net.

---

13   USA, *Air–Ground Operations: Field Manual*, War Department, Washington, DC, 1946, pp. 31–5; W.T. Y'Blood, *Down in the Weeds: Close Air Support in Korea*, USAF, Washington, DC, 2002; W.T. and B.C. Nalty, *Within Limits: The USAF and the Korean War*, USAF, Washington, DC, 1996. M. Lewis, *Lt Gen. Ned Almond, USA: A Ground Commander's Conflicting View with Airmen over CAS Doctrine and Employment*, School of Advanced Air Power Studies, Air University, Maxwell AFB, June 1996.

In August, nearly 30 per cent of all navy CAS sorties were cancelled because pilots could not contact controllers.[14] Carrier commander Admiral John Thach recalled years later, 'The pilots would come back and say, "We couldn't help. We wanted to. We were there and we couldn't get in communication with people."'[15] Fortunately, this changed over time, but until it did, many pilots took off on solo 'road recce' missions in search of targets, which, at this point in the war, were relatively plentiful. 'A typical two-aircraft combat recce flight,' one recalled subsequently, 'would yield three or four trucks, a bus, and perhaps a locomotive.'[16]

However imperfect, the two competing CAS systems first caused attrition to, then blunted, then halted the North Korean advance, often inflicting hundreds of casualties, particularly if used against massed-formation infantry attacks. By mid-August, the NKPA advance came to a halt along the Naktong River, stopped by the resolute defenders of the Pusan Perimeter and by the combination of deep air attack, robbing NKPA forces of food, fuel and ammunition, and battlefield air attacks supporting ground defenders.

By now the steady supply attrition caused by the Far East Air Force's (FEAF) bridge-bombing campaign had inflicted serious shortages in the NKPA forces. For the period between 25 June and 1 November 1950, 21 per cent of NKPA prisoners attributed their low morale to lack of food (a product of both air strikes on northern supply lines and a local famine in the South), while another 18 per cent attributed it to fear of aircraft attack. Battlefield air interdiction, by dropping bridges, destroying vehicles and forcing movement at night, greatly hindered supply of front-line NKPA forces, whose individual food ration fell from 800 grams per soldier per day at the onset of the war to just 400 grams (primarily rice) by the time the NKPA advance stopped at the Naktong. Rail strikes so disrupted transport that it took a month for reinforcements to journey from Pyongyang to the Pusan front, moving at an average slightly less than 10 miles (16 kilometres) per day, as trains hid in tunnels during the day.[17]

---

14   US Pacific Fleet Operations Comander in Chief US Pacific Interim Evluation Report No. 1: 25 June–15 November 1950, www.history.navy.mil/research/library/online-reading-room/title-list-alphabetically/k/Korean-War-Interim-Evaluation-No1.html.
15   Admiral John S. Thach, USN (retd), interview with Cmdr Etta-Belle Kitchen, US Naval Institute Oral History Program, p. 533; copy of transcript in US Naval Academy Library, Annapolis, MD; see also USN, Interim evaluation report no. 1, vol. 3.
16   Engen, *Wings and Warriors*, p. 116.
17   E. Mark, *Aerial Interdiction: Air Power and the Land Battle in Three American Wars*, USAF, Washington, DC, 1994, pp. 280–2.

Truck losses caused particular concern because they engendered cascading effects, including shortages of food, ammunition and fuel, that triggered problems in morale, fitness and combat effectiveness. The 'high casualty rate among truck drivers led to numerous desertions', one analyst noted; the NKPA resorted to forcing prisoners to drive their trucks. Ordnance and ammunition shortages grew as the average tonnage delivered to NKPA divisions dropped from 166 tons per day in late June 1950 to just 17 tons per day in mid-September.[18] Although it tried, the NKPA could not resume its offensive.

On 15 September 1950 General Douglas MacArthur oversaw the Inchon landing, the largest amphibious operation since the Second World War. In the two weeks of Inchon-related operations, the UN air coalition, spearheaded by naval air power but supported as well by FEAF interdiction attacks, coalition air attacks and aerial supply by FEAF's Combat Cargo Command, furnished protection, direct attack, indirect support and logistical assistance. Further south at Pusan, a similar air assemblage accomplished the same for the Eighth Army. Withdrawing NKPA forces both at Inchon–Seoul and at Pusan were mercilessly bombed, strafed, rocketed and napalmed by near-constant air attacks that took a fearsome toll of NKPA forces. Air attacks along the Naktong killed thousands, including 1,200 in a single strike on NKPA soldiers attempting to cross the river.[19] Afterwards, the NKPA was in headlong retreat.

Having broken out, the US Eighth Army advanced north from Pusan and linked up with X Corps near Osan. Both moved north, crossing the pre-war border, overrunning both the North Korean capital at Pyongyang (thereby forcing Kim Il Sung to decamp for Sinuiju on the Yalu River across from Andong) and the strategic port of Wonsan. As the bomb line moved north towards the Yalu, so too did the air campaign.

Halt phase redux

Unknown to MacArthur and his commanders, as revealed earlier, three Chinese armies under General Peng Dehuai had already crossed into North Korea, and three more were on the way, encouraged by the expectation that, unlike the North Koreans earlier, they would receive active air

---

18   USAF HD, *USAF Operations in the Korean Conflict, 25 June–1 November 1950*, p. 46.
19   Futrell, *USAF in Korea*, p. 162.

support from the Soviet air force, the VVS. (Stalin, as Xiaoming Zhang has noted, 'never intended to offer the support the Chinese expected'.[20]) In late October, isolated captures of Chinese soldiers occurred on the US Eighth Army's front. Alarmed, MacArthur ordered airmen to sever the Yalu River bridges linking North Korea to Manchuria. FEAF Bomber Command's B-29s and TF77's Douglas AD-4 Skyraider aircraft took on the task. The first B-29 raid, launched on 8 November against Sinuiju's bridges and the city itself, failed to drop any spans; but the bombers burned out 60 per cent of the city, killing 2,000, and shocking a group of visiting VVS generals watching from across the river at Andong. During the B-29 strike, MiGs attacked its F-80C escort. In the dogfight that followed, the air force claimed its first victory over the speedy Soviet jet. The next day, navy pilots shot down another, marking the first aerial victories over the MiG.

Air force and navy bridge attacks ultimately dropped five bridges in total, but to little immediate effect, as approximately 180,000 Chinese People's Volunteers (CPVF) had already crossed into North Korea. On 25 November, Peng Dehuai launched a devastating assault against the US Eighth Army in the west; the next day his troops attacked the US X Corps in the east. By 28 November, MacArthur's invasion forces were in retreat, triggering an emergency need for tactical air support.[21] Interdiction and continued bridge attacks assumed greater importance in an effort (largely successful, in contrast to popular myth, as will be discussed) to rob CPVF forces of sustenance, matériel and firepower. In the west, the US Eighth Army collapsed so rapidly that Peng could not press his advantage, but eastern Korea was potentially far more disastrous. The burden of covering that withdrawal fell to just two USN carrier air wings, one carrier-deployed USMC Corsair squadron, and USMC air ashore (i.e. an air unit based on shore), supported by USAF and coalition airlift for supply and casualty evacuation.

On 1 December, the Marines began their breakout. It is likely that the Marine withdrawal would have ended in disaster except for the efforts of naval and USMC airmen, who flew a total of 2,200 CAS–BAI sorties from

---

20 Xiaoming Zhang, *Red Wings Over the Yalu: China, the Soviet Union, and the Air War in Korea*, Texas A&M University Press, College Station, TX, 2002, p. 73.
21 D. McCullough, *Truman*, Simon & Schuster, New York, 1992, pp. 817–22; see also S.L.A. Marshall, *The River and the Gauntlet: Defeat of the Eighth Army by the Chinese Communist Forces, November 1950, in the Battle of the Chongchon River, Korea*, William Morrow & Co., New York, 1953, which relates the collapse in harrowing detail; and Zhang, *Red Wings Over the Yalu*, pp. 91–2.

1 to 11 December, furnishing 24-hour air support.[22] Coalition airlifters evacuated more than 1,800 seriously wounded Marines from Hagaru-ri and Koto-ri, and an intense USAF–USMC air supply and airdrop effort kept the Marines supplied—including bridge sections so that a crucial bridge could be repaired, permitting the Marines to withdraw their vehicles, many laden with wounded and weary troops. The Marine column linked up with Marine reinforcements from the coast on 10 December, and arrived safely at Hamhung the next day.[23] The withdrawal had been costly, with 718 dead and many more wounded or incapacitated by frostbite and other injury, but it could have been far worse. Battlefield air support devastated CPVF forces. The USAF introduced the swept-wing F-86A into combat on 15 December, and two days later, it claimed its first MiG-15. With the introduction of the F-86A, the USAF redressed the technological disparity. While the UN coalition would never be able to claim that it had air supremacy over the entire Korean Peninsula, it clearly possessed it over the main line of resistance between NKPA, CPVF and UN forces.[24]

As the CPVF made their way south, constant UN air attack took a steady toll, and as its effects grew more pronounced, so too did Peng's pleas to Mao for help. (In response, Mao urged him onwards with vague promises of possible Soviet air support that never came.) The CPVF forced the UN coalition back, but could not achieve a breakthrough, taking fearsome casualties, one of whom was Mao's own son, killed in an air strike. By the end of January 1951, the front had stabilised in a rough line running from south of Osan in the west, to a point south of Samchok in the east. A frustrated Peng returned to China, complaining to Mao that air attacks had limited his forces to receiving only 30 per cent of what they needed to prosecute an offensive. Peng's deputy commander, General Hong Xuezhi, reported combined air attack and artillery robbed the CPVF of 43 per cent of its trucks.[25] Prisoner interrogations indicated that CPVF soldiers were surprised at the strength of UN air power, had lost faith in their leaders and had lost hope of a CPVF victory. One last offensive

---

22 K.W. Condit and E.H. Giusti, 'Marine air at the Chosin Reservoir', *Marine Corps Gazette* 36, no. 7, 1952, pp. 18–25; Giusti and Condit, 'Marine air covers the breakout', *Marine Corps Gazette* 36, no. 8, 1952, pp. 20–7.
23 W.M. Leary, *Anything, Anywhere, Anytime: Combat Cargo in the Korean War*, USAF, Washington, DC, 2000, pp. 17–23.
24 The best analysis is K.P. Werrell, *Sabres over MiG Alley: The F-86 and the Battle for Air Superiority in Korea*, Naval Institute Press, Annapolis, MD, 2005.
25 Mark, *Aerial Interdiction*, note, pp. 27, 303.

gambit in late April also proved a failure. Finally, on 24 June, the Soviet Union suggested armistice talks, in recognition that Mao and Kim could not unify the North with the South by military means.[26]

Afterwards, a CPVF study team concluded that, with control of the air, 'we could have driven the enemy into the sea and the protracted defensive battles ranging from 25 January to 22 April … should have been avoided'.[27] UN senior commanders concurred. The US Eighth Army's General Walton Walker stated, 'Had it not been for the outstanding work of the Air Forces, we would most certainly have been pushed out of Korea'.[28] Although generally an air sceptic, General Matthew Ridgway (who replaced Walker as the Eighth's commander) agreed, writing years later, 'Not only did air power save us from disaster, but without it the mission of the United Nations forces could not have been accomplished'.[29]

Interdiction, air pressure and the path to armistice

With the CPVF and its supporting NKPA elements stopped, the United Nations turned to regaining lost ground, establishing a MLR, with fortifications and trench works echoing the Great War, running diagonally north-east from Munsan in the west to Kosong in the east. As armistice talks commenced and progressed, Sabres and MiGs duelled over the Yalu, and UN airmen undertook a series of interdiction campaigns to rob front-line NKPA–CPVF forces of the food, ammunition and other supplies they required to fight. At the main line of resistance, around-the-clock battlefield air support by UN airmen proceeded without fear of communist air intervention.

The greatest dangers facing UN coalition air attackers were large anti-aircraft cannon; light flak, predominantly 37-millimetre cannon, and 12.7-millimetre and 7.62-millimetre machine guns; as well as barrage

---

26 Zhang, *Red Wings Over the Yalu*, pp. 113–17.
27 Report of the Chinese Special Aviation Group, in USAF, Far East Air Forces intelligence round-up, no. 69, 22–28 December 1951, AFHRA Archives.
28 Futrell, *USAF in Korea*, p. 146. It is clear, from the context of this and some of his other comments, that his judgement encompassed the contributions of naval aviation and coalition forces.
29 M.B. Ridgway, *The Korean War: How we Met the Challenge, How All-out Asian War was Averted, Why Macarthur Was Dismissed, Why Today's War Objectives Must be Limited*, Doubleday & Co., Garden City, NY, 1967, p. 244.

fire from rifles, machine pistols and carbines. North Korean forces also often strung cables between hills to deter low-level night attackers. In the first six months of 1951, flak shot down 190 UN coalition aircraft, an average of more than one per day. April, coinciding with Peng's last push, was particularly costly; that month, among other losses, cost the UN coalition 30 Corsairs (two-thirds of which were Marine) and 30 F-51s, an indication of the vulnerability of slower, propeller-driven strike aircraft to light anti-aircraft fire.[30]

As fighting continued into the summer of 1951, interdiction operations against supplies assumed top priority, and after 20 September 1951 interdiction assumed such a priority that Far East Air Force removed TF77 from any CAS responsibilities except in tactical emergencies.[31] Korea's interdiction campaign involved three separate efforts: Operations Strangle I (mid-1951), Strangle II (late 1951) and Saturate (1952). Interdiction largely involved daytime bridge attacks and rail cuts, and hazardous night attacks against trucks and trains moving supplies south.[32] Bridge attacks undoubtedly discomfited the CPVF—Peng repeatedly complained of the delays and denial of supply they caused—but they were a far greater source of frustration to the UN airmen who attempted to destroy the bridges. As they dropped, the number of work-arounds proliferated, and supplies continued to get through. Results from rail strikes were mixed; by October 1951, attackers were destroying North Korea's western rail network so rapidly that repair crews could not keep up, forcing North Korean authorities to concentrate on keeping the line from Sinuiju to Pyongyang in service. A month later, all direct lines from Manchuria into central North Korea had been closed, while in the east TF77 had closed rail traffic into Wonsan, forcing communist forces into time-consuming (and harrowing) journeys. But the proliferation of their anti-aircraft artillery and light flak, coupled with the new MiG-15s equipped with range-extending drop tanks, endangered coalition operations north of Pyongyang, reversing this situation.[33]

---

30 W.H. Rankin, *The Man Who Rode the Thunder*, Pyramid Books, New York, 1961, pp. 40–66.
31 R.P. Hallion, *The Naval Air War in Korea*, Nautical and Aviation Publishing Company of America, Baltimore, MD, 1986, p. 92.
32 B. Tillman and J.G. Handelman, 'The Hwachon Dam and Carlson's Canyon: Air Group 19's Princeton Deployment of 1950–51', *The Hook* 12, no. 1, 1984, pp. 32–7. These attacks have gone down in history as the Battle of Carlson's Canyon. They inspired arguably the greatest combat aviation novel ever written, James Michener's *Bridges at Toko-ri*, Random House, New York, 1953.
33 Mark, *Aerial Interdiction*, pp. 312–17.

Interdiction posed a serious challenge. The fighting from May 1951 was largely positional jockeying along the MLR. Hence the amount of matériel getting through, however slight, was more than sufficient to keep the communist forces well supplied for combat. The targets themselves were not susceptible to nodal damage effects: rail cuts were easily filled in, highway cuts even more so, and bridges often were so low to the ground, or on such flat land, that temporary repairs, detours and pontoon bridges could easily replace them. A rail cut could be typically repaired in a few hours (rarely longer than a day), and bridge cuts often could be bypassed or patched with heavy timber framing. As Eighth Army Commander Lieutenant General James A. Van Fleet (who had succeeded Ridgway) noted after the war, 'We won the battle to knock out the bridge, but we lost the objective, which was to knock out the traffic'.[34]

Night interdiction over Korea's mountainous terrain posed particular challenges. The air force, navy and Marine Corps vigorously prosecuted a night air war, but the hazards of hunting for trains and trucks, then manoeuvring to attack them, posed serious challenges and safety risks. The murky circumstances of night attack led to over-claiming, as bomb and napalm eruptions were mistaken for exploding vehicles and trains. A USAF operational analysis found night intruders were only destroying 1.8 trucks for every 100 bombs they dropped, and strafing accuracy was at best 1–2 per cent of all rounds fired.[35] There is no reason to believe that USN and USMC results were any better than those of Far East Air Force.

In the spring of 1952, FEAF's Deputy for Operations, Brigadier General Jacob E. Smart, had prepared a plan for selective air pressure strikes against key North Korean targets, starting with power generation. General Mark Clark (who had become UN forces commander in May) strongly endorsed the plan, ordering Smart and Navy Admiral J.J. 'Jocko' Clark to work together. Their first air pressure strike targeted the Suiho hydroelectric facility on the Yalu with almost 200 US Air Force, Navy and Marine aircraft on 23 June 1952. When the smoke cleared, Suiho was knocked out of the war. Simultaneously, other USN, USAF and Marine attackers hit smaller power generation facilities at Chosin, Fusen and

---

34   J.A. Van Fleet, *Rail Transport and the Winning of Wars*, Association of American Railroads, Washington, DC, 1956, p. 35.
35   Mark, *Aerial Interdiction*, pp. 317–18.

Kyosen, destroying 90 per cent of North Korea's electrical power grid.[36] Afterwards, Smart and Clark continued their joint operations, targeting military facilities in and around Pyongyang, then North Korea's extractive and processing industry, including the Sindok lead and zinc mill, a magnesium carbonate plant at Kilchin, a supply centre at Changpyong-ni, the Aoji oil refinery, industrial and power-plant targets at Munsan and Chongjin, and a rail centre at Kowon.[37] The air pressure strikes seriously disconcerted the communist leadership and exacerbated growing divisions between the three parties—Soviet, Chinese and North Korean—over what the future course of the war and the proper role of communist air power should be.

In May 1953, the USAF and USMC attacked North Korea's Toksan and Chasan irrigation dams, releasing water that destroyed eight bridges and miles of rail line and roads, flooded ripening rice paddies and rendered at least one airfield unusable. This apparently demoralised North Korea's Kim, already upset at the unwillingness of the Soviet Union and China to defend North Korea's airspace more aggressively, and encouraged his growing desire to bring the conflict to a close.[38] Fighting continued for a further six weeks, victory being defined for both sides as securing commanding terrain along the MLR.

In the fighting from the fall of 1952 through the armistice, the tempo of the ground war gradually increased, as both sides jockeyed for favourable position. The interdiction campaign had until then proved a disappointment, as the relatively low level of communist logistical expenditure meant that the losses inflicted upon the NKPA and the CPVF were not enough to have much influence. But now that changed, for the ammunition and supply demands of the NKPA and CPVF gradually rose as well.

In May 1953, Jocko Clark made a familiarisation flight along the front, just behind the line of contact and out of reach of enemy anti-aircraft fire. As he overflew allied supply areas, located out of reach of communist

---

36 Quote from Naval History and Heritage Command, 'Korean Combat Action Reports for USS *Boxer* (CV/CVA 21)', 9 June–8 July 1952, p. 5; for raid, see Futrell, *USAF in Korea*, pp. 449–52, and Zhang, *Red Wings Over the Yalu*, p. 188.
37 Futrell, *USAF in Korea*, p. 495; see also Cagle and Manson, *Sea War in Korea*; and Naval History and Heritage Command, 'Korean Combat Action Reports for USS *Essex* (CV/CVA 9)', 5 September–1 November 1952, pp. 1–2.
38 Zhang, *Red Wings Over the Yalu*, p. 197.

artillery, he realised that if the communists had had the ability to project air power over the front, such open storage would have been impossible. But the NKPA and CPVF had to have large caches of supplies at the front, simply to sustain the pace of day-to-day artillery barrages and savage infantry assaults. Any supply caches destroyed at the front would be hard for them to make up. Thus, Clark concluded, the communists must have supplies lying in the region beyond UN artillery range but below the bomb line.[39]

It was a brilliant insight and deduction. Subsequent reconnaissance sorties confirmed that the communists had numerous supply facilities, using tunnels or burrowed into hillsides. He immediately arranged for joint USN–USAF strike missions, which were dubbed 'Cherokee strikes' in honour of his Native American ancestry. The Cherokee strike program began in early October 1952. From then until the end of the war, the navy flew an average of three Cherokee missions per day, and night attacks as well. Eighth Army commander General James Van Fleet held the view that if the Cherokee strikes had been coupled with a major UN ground offensive, the NKPA and CPVF forces at the front would likely have fallen back.[40]

Of course, neither side intended to launch massive offensives at this point in the war. Both the Soviet–Chinese partnership and the UN coalition had effectively achieved their major aims: North Korea would not succumb to the South, and South Korea would not succumb to the North. Instead, as other chapters have noted, the fighting was really over positional advantage along the MLR, a battle for local (if strategic) real estate. As an armistice drew nearer, fighting reached a crescendo, and Jocko Clark, as a precaution, journeyed to Tokyo to meet theatre commander General Mark Clark and request that tactical nuclear bombs be placed on TF77's carriers. General Clark concurred, and they were; fortunately, conventional means of waging war continued to carry the day.[41]

On 19 July, word reached FEAF that an armistice was imminent, and on 22 July, FEAF shot down its last MiG. At 10 am on 27 July, a truce was signed, effective later that night. To prevent any last-minute surprises, FEAF flew a maximum effort, putting as many Sabres into the air as it

---

39   As narrated in J.J. Clark, *Carrier Admiral*, David McKay Co., New York, 1967.
40   Cagle and Manson, *Sea War in Korea*, p. 469.
41   Discussed in Clark, *Carrier Admiral*.

could over North Korea, one of which caught an Ilyushin Il-12 transport near the Yalu (loaded, as it emerged, with VVS senior officers) and shot it down. Strikes continued along the MLR all day, and UN airmen ceased combat operations as deep night fell over the Korean Peninsula. An uneasy and imperfect peace has remained between North and South Korea to this day.

Conclusion

Although precise numbers are surprisingly difficult to reconcile across various international data sets, overall, analysis indicates that coalition airmen flew almost 1.2 million sorties—an average, across the war, of more than a thousand sorties per day.[42] Figure 1 (in the Appendix) offers a perspective on the overall coalition air effort. The armed forces of the United States flew approximately 94 per cent of all these, with other UN airmen flying the remaining 6 per cent. It should be pointed out that while the USAF flew 73 per cent of sorties, US Naval and Marine aviation played a crucially important role, one still not fully appreciated. US Navy and Marine airmen flew 41 per cent of US combat sorties in the Korean War, including 40 per cent of interdiction sorties, 53 per cent of close air support (CAS) sorties, 36 per cent of counter-air (air superiority) sorties and 30 per cent of reconnaissance sorties. Approximately 80 per cent of all combat sorties furnished direct or indirect combat support to Korea's ground warriors: as live fire, ISR (intelligence, surveillance and reconnaissance) or matériel. Although the USAF performance in Korea has been largely seen through the simplistic prism of Sabre versus MiG, and B-29 operations against the North, in fact counter-air sorties accounted for only 14 per cent of all air force combat sorties, and strategic bombing (despite all the publicity surrounding it) not quite a tenth of 1 per cent.

---

42 Based upon data found in USN, Office of the Chief of Naval Operations, Combat Activity of Naval Aviation (April–July 1953), Table 15, 71, Korean War Naval Aviation Records Collection, Headquarters, Naval History and Heritage Command, Washington Navy Yard, Washington, DC; USAF, *USAF Tactical Operations: World War II and Korea* (USAF Historical Division Liaison Office, Washington, DC, May 1962), Table 101, 106, 108, 162, Archives of the Air Force Historical Research Agency, Maxwell AFB, AL; R.F. Futrell, *The United States Air Force in Korea, 1950–1953* (Duell, Sloan & Pearce, New York, 1983), p. 690; J.R.P. Lansdown, *With the Carriers in Korea: The Fleet Air Arm Story 1950–1953* (Severnside Publishers, Upton-upon-Severn, UK, 1992); and HMAS *Sydney* patrol reports, May 1951–December 1953, AWM 78, Folders 329/5 and 329/6.

The relative contribution of all the coalition air forces is shown in Figure 2 (in the Appendix). While deceptively small, the participation of non-USAF coalition air forces had, at various points in the war, a decisive effect all of its own, and often at tremendous cost. The RAAF and South African Air Force, flying with rare dedication and skill, stand out as two air services that materially affected the outcome of the war. The RAAF's No. 77 Squadron established an extraordinary record for the commitment and achievement of its pilots. That record came at a fearful price. The squadron lost 13 Mustangs from the time it entered combat to the time it transitioned into Meteors, then lost a further 46 Meteors from combat and operational losses before the end of the war. Forty of its pilots died, 30 of them in combat, and others were captured and subjected to a brutality that is shocking even by the standards of a later and more jaded world. The steadfastness, courage and performance of the RAAF strengthened further the bonds forged by mutual combat in the Pacific less than a decade previously, and served as a foundation for stronger ties between the United States and Australia in the years ahead.[43]

Finally, there is the legacy of air power in the Korean War itself. Traditionally, armies fear an enemy air force far more than they respect their own. During and after the war, many critics took anti- or pro-air power positions claiming to prove either that it was decisive or that it had failed. In truth, the circumstances of the Korean War shaped the use of air power in important ways. Given the constraints and the sanctuaries, it simply could not be employed in the free-ranging form it had been in the Second World War. That said, while critics since the war have made much of the Manchurian sanctuary, the United Nations had sanctuaries as well, notably Japan and Okinawa. Fortunately, the restrictions placed upon airmen in Korea were far less than those of South-East Asia a decade later.

On balance, the judgement of air power in Korea, and certainly of naval air power in Korea, is that, overall, it worked. It could not be decisive on its own, nor was it expected to be. But thanks to the control of the air that coalition airmen secured, all other tasks in the war were made easier (as Ridgway, Walker, Van Fleet and others amply noted). Beyond question, the tremendous psychological and physical power of air attack over the battlefield prevented, on numerous occasions, the CPVF and NKPA from overwhelming the South and its defenders, as is evidenced

---

43   The combat record of No. 77 Squadron is well told in Stephens's *Going Solo*, pp. 225–41.

by the communications by and among Stalin, Mao, Kim and the commanders and troops of their forces. To that degree, air power certainly fulfilled what was expected of it, and if not overwhelmingly decisive in all applications, it was decisive enough in the most critical phases of the war, consistent with its performance in both earlier and later conflicts. Of air power can be said what the prophet said of old: 'You show your might when the perfection of your power is disbelieved, and in those who know you, you rebuke insolence.'[44]

---

44 Book of Wisdom, 12:13, pp. 16–19.

7

OFFENSIVE AIR OPERATIONS OVER KOREA
The first challenge for Australian naval aviation

Jack McAffrie

The Royal Australian Navy's Fleet Air Arm was formally established on 28 August 1948 with the commissioning of the 20th Carrier Air Group at Royal Naval Air Station Eglinton in Northern Ireland.[1] A little over three years later, the Fleet Air Arm was at war, with HMAS *Sydney* (III) and her Carrier Air Group deployed off the coast of the Korean Peninsula.

By any measure, the establishment of the Fleet Air Arm, and its rapid progress to being a highly efficient and effective operational entity, is a remarkable story. There were political, bureaucratic, financial, manpower and timing challenges, any one of which might have brought the process to a halt, especially in the early stages. That *Sydney* and her air group deployed to Korea and performed so well was the result of determination on the part of the RAN leadership, enlightened political decision-making, and a mix of experience and youthful enthusiasm among all concerned.

---

1   A version of this paper was first published in *Sea Power Ashore and in the Air*, ed. D. Stevens and J. Reeve, Halstead Press, Sydney, 2007.

Reflecting on the performance of the Fleet Air Arm in Korea—and indeed of the destroyers and frigates, which also distinguished themselves—the RAN would have had every reason to look to the future with confidence. Yet a mere seven and a half years after *Sydney* returned from Korea, and only 11 years after the establishment of the Fleet Air Arm, its demise was announced by the government in November 1959, scheduled for 1963. Clearly, operational excellence was not sufficient on its own to ensure organisational survival.

Formation and workup

Early planning anticipated that the first carrier would be commissioned in June 1948, and the second would follow in 1949 or 1950.[2] The RAN also expected that the Royal Navy (RN) would provide the majority of the aviation and air group personnel at first. The RAN also began its own training programs. No. 1 Naval Air Pilots Course began in HMAS *Cerberus* on 7 December 1947, and nine of the 14 starters graduated at RAAF Base, Point Cook, on 29 July 1949. They then undertook operational conversions in the UK on both Fireflys and Sea Furys, completing in April 1950.[3]

The second pilots' course began in August 1948; the RN also loaned a number of observers and telegrapher air gunners to the RAN. The first group of ex-naval (RN, RAN Volunteer Reserve and Royal New Zealand Navy) and ex-RAAF aircrew joined HMAS *Cerberus* on 6 February 1948 for a six-month orientation course. They then travelled to the United Kingdom for further flying experience and to join either the 20th or 21st Carrier Air Group.[4]

The Fleet Air Arm was established on 28 August 1948, and four months later HMAS *Sydney* was commissioned in Devonport, England, with Captain Roy Dowling as commanding officer. Air Group workup in the UK entailed the full run of proficiency and operational flying, including deck landing practice in RN Fireflys and Sea Furies. Lieutenant

---

2 A. Wright, *Australian Carrier Decisions: The Acquisition of HMA Ships Albatross, Sydney and Melbourne*, Papers in Australian Maritime Affairs, No. 4, pp. 151, 157, www.navy.gov.au/sites/default/files/documents/PIAMA04.pdf.
3 Australian Naval Aviation Museum friends and volunteers, *Flying Stations: A Story of Australian Naval Aviation*, Allen & Unwin, Sydney, 1998, p. 53.
4 Ibid., p. 54.

7. OFFENSIVE AIR OPERATIONS OVER KOREA

Danny Buchanan caused some excitement on 17 March 1949 while landing on HMS *Illustrious*. His Firefly missed the wires, jumped the barrier, destroyed four other Fireflys in the forward deck park and was itself also destroyed.[5] Nevertheless, no one on deck was hurt, and as he himself walked away without a scratch, the landing must be recorded as a good one.

Eventually, the 20th Carrier Air Group and HMAS *Sydney* sailed for Australia on 12 April 1949 and arrived in Jervis Bay on 25 May. Flying for the air group began from the newly commissioned Nowra Naval Air Station in June, and there were two embarked periods between then and April 1950.[6] *Sydney* then returned to the UK to bring home the 21st Carrier Air Group, arriving in Australia in December 1950. This transport task meant that the ship and the air group were unavailable to reinforce the Commonwealth effort in the Korean War, which had broken out mid-year.[7] There had been some consideration of replacing HMS *Theseus* with *Sydney*, and there was an expectation that the issue might be raised again.[8]

Indeed, by March 1951 the Chief of the Naval Staff, Vice Admiral Sir John Collins, had received a request from the First Sea Lord for *Sydney* to replace HMS *Glory* in Korea in late 1951. Consequently, in May 1951 the navy decided to form an air group from Nos 805 and 808 Sea Fury Squadrons and No. 817 Firefly Squadron, and workup plans began immediately. Most air group members were RN personnel, but most of *Sydney*'s ship's company were Australian. The workup was costly in aircraft, with weather contributing to several deck crashes. Ultimately *Sydney* sailed for Korea, with HMAS *Tobruk* in company, on 31 August 1951.[9]

En route to Korea, preparations continued for the forthcoming operations. This included rehearsal of bombardment spotting procedures, lectures on escape and evasion, planning conferences and small arms practice. Additionally, a number of officers had gone ahead of the ship to observe RN flying operations in Korea.[10]

---

5   Ibid., p. 59.
6   Ibid., pp. 73–4.
7   Ibid., p. 75.
8   Ibid., p. 76.
9   Ibid., p. 84.
10 C. Jones, *Wings and the Navy 1947–1953*, Kangaroo Press, Kenthurst, NSW, 1997, p. 75.

In fact, Australia experienced a major problem in responding credibly to the initial calls for military assistance at the outbreak of war, as other chapters illustrate. There were severe shortages of defence personnel, money was scarce, and the army had fewer than a thousand infantrymen in the regular force—and most of them were in the British Commonwealth Occupation Force (BCOF) in Japan, from which Australia wanted to withdraw anyway.[11] Additionally, No. 77 Squadron, RAAF, was in Japan and HMAS *Shoalhaven* was in Japanese waters.

Neither the services nor the Australian prime minister wanted to become involved in Korea. Provision of forces to Malaya had been a consideration in May, and Britain was urging Australia to commit ground and air forces to the Middle East, which was seen as a higher priority in the event of any Soviet attack.[12] Yet General MacArthur had indicated that he wanted both No. 77 Squadron and the 3rd Battalion of the Royal Australian Regiment (3RAR), the army unit based in Japan. As Robert O'Neill noted in Chapter 1, the Minister for External Affairs, Percy Spender, was keen for Australia to become involved, as he had in mind a future security pact with the United States. Eventually No. 77 Squadron was committed on 30 June and 3RAR on 26 July.

On the naval front, the United States Navy (USN) was not well placed to respond at the beginning of the war. It only had a few ships in Japanese waters, but most of the Seventh Fleet, itself by no means a powerful force then, was in or around the Philippines. On the other hand, the RN was much better placed. A major portion of the Far East Fleet, 22 ships, including a light fleet carrier, was in Japanese waters, escaping the heat of Hong Kong and Singapore.[13] This force was placed under MacArthur's control.

For the RAN, HMAS *Shoalhaven* was to be relieved by HMAS *Bataan*, but both ships remained in theatre initially. They were joined by Canadian and New Zealand units, and all of them operated within the RN force. This British Commonwealth Naval Force formed the West Coast Support

---

11   Ibid., pp. 31–2.
12   Ibid., pp. 38, 41.
13   R. O'Neill, *Australia in the Korean War 1950–1953*, vol. 2: *Combat Operations*, AWM & AGPS, Canberra, 1985, p. 416.

Group (Task Group 96.8), while the USN made up the East Coast Support Group (Task Group 96.5), and the Seventh Fleet's carrier force (Task Force 77) operated wherever it was needed.[14]

Shoalhaven was assigned to escort duties between Sasebo and Pusan at first and was relieved by HMAS *Warramunga* on 31 August 1950. The RAN had consistent problems in replacing ships in Korea, because of shortages of suitable ships and of people.[15] Other tasking for the surface forces included support for amphibious operations and shore bombardment, often in the face of a significant mine threat, and sometimes with the fear (ultimately unrealised) of a Soviet submarine threat.

From the outset of the war, carriers were in heavy demand, not least because the United States Air Force (USAF) aircraft were in short supply and because North Atlantic Treaty Organization (NATO) and domestic US demands limited the availability of reinforcements. Other factors making carriers attractive were the lack of suitable operating airfields in Korea and the limited time over target for tactical aircraft operating from Japan.[16]

Normally TF77 operated in the open Sea of Japan off the east coast of Korea. The British light fleet carrier force (TE [Task Element] 95.11) normally operated in the more restricted waters off the west coast. Their contribution in aircraft numbers was not great, but it did permit the maintenance of a continuous air offensive off both coasts. After December 1950, a USN light fleet carrier also joined the west coast operation, thereby allowing each of the RN and USN carriers to rotate on station about every 10 days.

In the first year of the war, UN air and sea power prevented almost all enemy movement at sea and fought off the first MiG-15 challenge. With general control of the air, UN forces limited North Korean movements to the night hours.[17] Generally, the carriers were not attacked, but there was constant anti-submarine screening by escorts.

---

14 Ibid., pp. 417, 461.
15 Ibid., p. 425.
16 Ibid., p. 464.
17 Ibid., p. 465.

HMAS *Sydney* in Korea

The aircraft

HMAS *Sydney*, like the RN carriers, operated a mix of Fairey Firefly and Hawker Sea Fury aircraft. The Firefly was a single-engine, two-seat anti-submarine reconnaissance and strike aircraft, also in widespread RN service. It had a maximum speed of more than 350 miles per hour (560 kilometres per hour) and an endurance of more than six hours. Weapons included four 20-millimetre cannon and two bombs of up to 1,000 pounds (450 kilograms) each.[18] The RAN had both Mark 5 and Mark 6 aircraft, and because only the Mark 5 had the cannon armament, the RAN took 12 of those aircraft to Korea with No. 817 Squadron, where they also carried two 500-pound bombs for strike missions.[19] For ASW (anti-submarine warfare) missions, depth charges were substituted for the bombs.

The Sea Fury was a single-engine and single-seat fighter bomber, the last piston-engine fighter to serve with the RN Fleet Air Arm and the only one to serve with the RAN. Its top speed was more than 450 miles per hour (720 kilometres per hour), and it had a range of up to 1,000 nautical miles (1,850 kilometres) with two drop tanks. Armament consisted of four wing-mounted 20-millimetre cannon, and it could carry a mix of either eight 60-pound (27-kilogram) rockets or two 1,000-pound bombs. In Korea, the Furys usually flew with eight rockets and two drop tanks, and had about 125 rounds per gun.[20] The Sea Fury served with No. 805 and No. 808 Squadrons in Korea.

During operations in Korea, HMAS *Sydney* also embarked, for the first time, a Sikorsky S51 Dragonfly helicopter. With a crew of two, the Dragonfly had a maximum speed of 95 miles per hour (150 kilometres per hour) and a range of 300 nautical miles (550 kilometres). This helicopter was used for search and rescue, for plane-guard duties and inevitably for mail runs. At first the helicopter came from HMS *Glory*, but for most of the deployment it was provided by the USN. Colloquially it came to be

---

18   O. Thetford, *British Naval Aircraft Since 1912*, 6th rev. edn, Naval Institute Press, Annapolis, MD, 1991, pp. 185–6.
19   S. Wilson, *Sea Fury, Firefly and Sea Venom in Australian Service*, Aerospace Publications, Weston Creek, ACT, 1993, p. 81.
20   Jones, *Wings and the Navy*, p. 86.

known as 'Uncle Peter' because of its identification letters. The Dragonfly performed sterling service for *Sydney*'s aircrew during their Korean War deployment.

The ship

Under the command of Captain D.H. Harries and with Commander V.A.T. Smith as executive officer, *Sydney*'s ship's company worked hard and kept the ship in as good a state as was possible under the prevailing conditions. *Sydney* did not operate as a flagship, although the Flag Officer Commanding the Australian Fleet, Rear Admiral J.W.M. Eaton, did spend three days in the ship in January 1952. Rear Admiral A.K. Scott-Moncrieff, RN (Commander West Coast Blockade Force), also spent time in the ship on occasion. Morale for the most part was very good, although behaviour ashore was not always what was expected. Leave-breaking was a problem, and relations with the ships' companies of other UN force ships were also strained at times.[21]

HMAS *Sydney* had a single hydraulic catapult, and although free take-offs had often been used before the Korean War, the catapult was invariably used in wartime operations, not least because of the higher take-off weights at which aircraft were operating. The catapult proved to be reliable, with the only failure occurring on 1 January 1952. Even then, 51 sorties were flown that day after the catapult was repaired.[22] The average time between launches was 42 seconds, although lower times were recorded. This was a level of flight deck performance that the RN carriers found difficult to emulate.[23]

With a straight deck, *Sydney* was more prone to deck landing accidents than the later angled-deck carriers. Nevertheless, her record during the Korean deployment was very good. During the patrol that ended on 13 November 1952, there was only one deck landing accident in more than 400 landings. The fact that no night flying was conducted undoubtedly contributed to the good figures. Pilots averaged one and a half sorties each day in the war zone; but taking into account that not every pilot was always available to fly, most pilots flew two sorties on the days they were available.

---

21   O'Neill, *Combat Operations*, p. 486.
22   Ibid., p. 480.
23   Ibid., p. 477.

With three squadrons totalling 38 aircraft embarked, *Sydney*'s flight deck and hangars were always crowded. Flight deck operations, never to be taken lightly, were invariably made more complex by the need to have 20 of the aircraft always parked on deck. These aircraft were manned and started for every flying event, so that any unserviceable aircraft could be replaced immediately.[24] After every recovery, unserviceable aircraft were parked forward or taken below for maintenance, while the serviceable ones were taken aft for fuelling and arming. At the end of every flying day, all deck-parked aircraft had to be heavily lashed in case of inclement weather. The handlers, armourers and maintainers worked hard under often difficult conditions. Aircraft maintenance was a never-ending task. On average, 38 per cent of aircraft returned unserviceable—although the figure varied from 29 up to 66 per cent.[25] All flak damage was repaired overnight.

Air operations in Korea

Sydney operated mainly in the Yellow Sea and alternated on station with the USS *Rendova* and USS *Badoeng Strait*. At that time Operation Strangle was underway. This involved the UN Command (UNC) air forces in interdicting the removal northwards of large North Korean supply dumps and the movement south of combat supplies by the North Koreans. The latter interdiction task proved more difficult because of the North Korean capacity to repair damaged supply routes.[26] The carrier operating cycle was nominally nine days on patrol and nine days for return to Sasebo and replenishment there. Frequently, however, one of the on-station days was taken up with replenishment at sea, which provided a welcome break for aircrew. The missions flown by the air group were mainly strike, armed reconnaissance, close air support, naval gunfire support spotting, combat air patrol and ASW. Some time was also spent in convoy escort.[27]

---

24   Ibid., p. 471.
25   Ibid., p. 485.
26   Ibid., p. 350.
27   Major M.B. Simkin, 'HMAS *Sydney* in Korean Waters', Report by the Carrier Borne Ground Liaison Officer, held by Sea Power Centre—Australia, undated, pp. 1–3.

Strike operations

Strike operations were a major component of *Sydney*'s contribution to the war. Target location proved to be difficult, especially at first, because of excellent camouflage by the North Koreans. As the operation continued, the most reliable targeting information was normally photographic or visual reconnaissance provided by *Sydney*'s own aircraft.[28] Targets varied a great deal and included North Korean artillery positions, coastal shipping (including junks), troop concentrations, road and railway bridges, railway tunnels, buildings and supply vehicles, including ox carts.

A lot of effort went into determining the best method for the Fireflys to bring down bridges—for which direct hits were necessary. Dive-bombing was tried at first, diving from 8,000 feet and releasing at 3,000 feet. Ultimately they settled on 10-degree dive-bombing at low altitude along the length of the bridges, in flights of four aircraft.[29] This was the typical ASW depth-charging profile.[30] With experience, a flight of four Fireflys proved able to bring down three bridges in one sortie. But, however satisfying dropping bridges was to the aircrew, the North Koreans managed to repair them quickly in most cases. This led to the following assessment by the Carrier Borne Army Liaison Officer (CBALO): 'It is of interest to note that the hard night-working Communists have already repaired the large hole we knocked in the rail bridge only three days ago. The Australian Country Roads Boards could well do with a few of these gentlemen!'[31]

North Korean gunners certainly enjoyed some success against RAN aircraft. Aircraft were hit by flak 99 times and nine aircraft were shot down—seven of them Sea Furies.[32] The gunners did not use tracer and did react to changing aircraft operating patterns, but for the most part aircraft were shot at only after they had passed over enemy positions. The flak could be astonishingly good, and at times equally bad. On the other hand, the aircrew were extremely keen to press home attacks, and some

---

28 Jones, *Wings and the Navy*, p. 89.
29 Ibid., p. 86.
30 F. Lane, 'Naval aviation in the Korean War', *Naval Officers Club Newsletter*, No. 60, 1 March 2005, p. 18.
31 72 CBAL Section, HMAS *SYDNEY*, War diary—Korean operations, 21 October 1951.
32 O'Neill, *Combat Operations*, p. 483. The actual number of aircraft lost varies among sources. Taking account of enemy action and all other causes, 13 aircraft appear to have been lost: nine Sea Furys and four Fireflys.

consideration was given to setting minimum altitudes (below which it was not permitted to fly) and a maximum number of attack runs. This became more of an issue as anti-aircraft fire increased.[33]

Other operations

During the voyage to Korea, much time was spent in practising naval gunfire support spotting techniques. The time was well spent, as the subsequent results while in Korea were impressive. The aircrews especially enjoyed working with the big gun ships, such as USS *New Jersey*, because of the much greater accuracy of their guns.[34]

Twenty per cent of sorties—about 10 each day—were flown as combat air patrol over *Sydney*, because of the proximity of North Korean airfields. The extent of the self-defence effort led to a view that the carriers would be more effective if operating in pairs or in larger groups.[35] No *Sydney* combat air patrol ever intercepted an enemy aircraft.[36]

Normally, just one Firefly was assigned to ASW, because of the low level of threat. The same aircraft was also often used for surface contact identification and for search and rescue assistance.[37]

Sydney's patrols

Sydney's first patrol began on 5 October 1951, as part of the operation to push the front back from the Han River and the approaches to Seoul.[38] She flew 47 sorties on each of the first two days, a rate that was considered quite high for a ship new to the theatre. During this first patrol, *Sydney* was ordered to join a special force under Rear Admiral Scott-Moncrieff on the east coast. She subsequently flew strikes against positions south-east of Wonsan, but without clear details of the purpose of the overall mission. Later, the operation proved to have been a demonstration for the benefit of Admiral Sir Guy Russell, RN, visiting from Hong Kong.[39]

---

33 Ibid., p. 484.
34 Australian Naval Aviation Museum, *Flying Stations*, p. 89.
35 O'Neill, *Combat Operations*, p. 472.
36 Lane, 'Naval aviation in the Korean War', p. 16.
37 O'Neill, *Combat Operations*, p. 472.
38 Jones, *Wings and the Navy*, p. 77.
39 O'Neill, *Combat Operations*, p. 470.

Captain Harries set a demanding daily sortie rate, but one that was achievable and sustainable: 54 sorties, spread over five events or waves. The shortness of the winter days and the distance to targets made any more than five events difficult to achieve. This followed some quite exceptional flying performances, such as that on 11 October, when 89 sorties were flown. At one time, late in the day, 31 aircraft were airborne at the same time.[40] This sortie rate was a record for the light fleet carriers, but was subsequently bettered by HMS *Glory*.

The second patrol, which began on 18 October, was quite eventful. It involved attacks against railway bridges and tunnels as part of a major interdiction campaign, and strikes against enemy troops and coastal shipping. It was during this patrol that the first close air support sorties were flown, for the British Commonwealth Division on 21 October. This sometimes included providing cover for South Korean troops and irregular forces, and was most popular when ordered in support of Australian troops.

Although the pilots really enjoyed this work,[41] it was not without hazard; on 25 and 26 October, for example, three aircraft were shot down. Lieutenant Col Wheatley's Fury ditched off Chinnampo; Lieutenant Commander J.C. Appleby's Fury was badly damaged by flak but he managed to get it to Kimpo. Then Sub Lieutenant Noel Knappstein's Fury crash landed on mud flats in the Han River estuary.[42] The pilot was rescued by HMS *Amethyst*, but before being picked up he had removed some salvageable equipment from the aircraft. Then, showing commendable enterprise, he sold the remains of the aircraft to some local Koreans. It was a very satisfied Sub Lieutenant Knappstein who returned on board *Sydney* with a thick wad of Korean notes. The supply officer duly changed them into coin of the realm and presented him with … one shilling and ninepence.[43]

On 18 November *Sydney* left Sasebo in company with HMS *Belfast*, HMAS *Tobruk* and several USN ships for Operation Athenaeum. This was to be a major bombardment of Hungnam on the east coast. In two days *Sydney* launched 113 sorties, of which 75 were against Hungnam coastal batteries and 38 were defensive combat air patrols for the ships.

---

40   Jones, *Wings and the Navy*, p. 78. Reference to the 72 CBAL Debriefing Reports shows that in fact 93 aircraft sorties were flown on that day.
41   72 CBAL Section, HMAS *SYDNEY*, War Diary—Korean Operations, 31 October 1951.
42   O'Neill, *Combat Operations*, p. 474.
43   Jones, *Wings and the Navy*, p. 84.

The operation was not notably successful, and *Sydney* returned to the west coast for operations in poor weather. Returning to Kure at the end of this patrol on 30 November, *Sydney*'s air group had flown 966 offensive and 360 defensive sorties; 43 aircraft had been hit, and four had been lost.[44]

In mid-December, HMAS *Sydney* became involved in convoy escort, after the UNC decided to exchange the operational tasking of the US Fifth Air Force with that of the west coast carrier force. Convoy escort was a task the aircrew found intensely frustrating, mainly because it almost invariably proved to be boring. During this particular patrol, before the change to convoy protection, much more flak damage was taken, with 25 aircraft damaged and five destroyed between 6 and 18 December. This was more than half the total number of aircraft lost to enemy action in the entire deployment.

After Christmas in Kure, *Sydney* began her sixth patrol on 28 December, this time conducting more airstrikes in the area of Cho Do and Sok To. Targets included North Korean artillery and junk concentrations. Sorties were also flown in support of South Korean troops and irregular forces.[45] On 4 January 1952, Rear Admiral Scott-Moncrieff personally briefed attacks on gun positions along the Yesong River, close to Panmunjom. Lieutenant Peter Goldrick was wounded during this operation but managed to bring his aircraft back and land safely on *Sydney*. Navy Office was informed of the incident, and in its reply to the ship displayed the kind of humour that we have all come to associate so readily with head office. Navy Office directed that Lieutenant Goldrick's flying pay was to cease from the moment he had been wounded, as he was then temporarily unfit to fly and might never fly again.

The seventh and final patrol began on 16 January. Bad weather and poor coordination between the blockading force and convoys affected the flying rate. Nevertheless, North Korean gunners still managed to damage 10 aircraft. During this patrol, strike targets were switched from rail infrastructure to water towers, on the basis that water towers would take longer to repair.[46] No flying was possible on the final day of operations, 25 January. Cold and the overnight snow had rendered all deck-parked aircraft unserviceable. The five forward-most Furys were almost totally covered in frozen salt water.

---

44   72 CBAL Section, HMAS *SYDNEY*, War Diary—Korean Operations, 30 November 1951.
45   O'Neill, *Combat Operations*, p. 480.
46   Ibid., p. 482.

All in all, during the deployment *Sydney*'s Air Group flew 743 Firefly sorties and 1,623 Sea Fury sorties. Nine aircraft were destroyed and a further 90 aircraft were damaged by flak.[47]

The Carrier Borne Army Liaison Section

One of the most important behind-the-scenes organisations in *Sydney* was the combined Carrier Borne Army Liaison (CBAL) Section, which was manned by officers and men from 71 and 72 Sections. It comprised two majors, one of whom, M.B. Simkin, had flown to Korea ahead of the ship, two warrant officers class 2 and two corporals. En route to Korea, as well as conducting bombardment spotting practice, the CBAL Section also provided briefings on escape and evasion and Owen gun practice for Firefly crews.[48]

Once on operations, each of the majors briefed and debriefed alternate flying events. They also undertook target assessment, and on each evening proposed a target list for the following day's operations to the commander (air), the air group commander and the operations officer. The section also kept up-to-date situation and flak maps and maintained target dossiers and files of briefing photographs. A store of more than 200,000 maps and charts was also maintained by the section.[49] Other specific tasks for which the CBAL Section was responsible included the provision of army advice to the captain, through the commander (air); the provision of all intelligence information to aircrew; and the collection and assessment of all flak information.

Busy as they undoubtedly were, the army personnel were not entirely oblivious to their surroundings. They developed a comprehensive handover process for replacement personnel, which included a set of 'How to survive the Navy' instructions: (1) Never sign for anything. The Naval Supply Branch never forgets; (2) enjoy your food, eat ashore; (3) treat all parts of the ship as though they have been freshly painted— they probably have been; (4) if you should require a drink after the bar shuts, follow the trail of Air Group officers to cabin G67.

---

47   Jones, *Wings and the Navy*, p. 90.
48   72 CBAL Section, HMAS *SYDNEY*, War Diary—Korean operations, 5 September 1951 and 3–4 October 1951.
49   Ibid., 5 October 1951.

Other challenges

Quite apart from the dangers associated with carrier aviation and low-level flying in the war zone, there were several other matters that made life difficult from time to time. Of these, weather was probably the most significant and most frequent.

Sydney's first real taste of what was in store came on 14 October, when all Commonwealth ships in Sasebo were ordered to sail in order to ride out the approaching Typhoon Ruth. Some in HMAS *Sydney* wanted to remain in harbour, noting that Sasebo was surrounded by mountains 2,000 feet high. Nevertheless, she did sail and met the full force of the storm with 18 aircraft lashed down on the flight deck. Chocks and fastening lugs were torn away from aircraft, and the heavy movement of the ship collapsed some undercarriage legs. Minor electrical fires broke out in the ship as seawater shorted out ventilator fan motors.[50] Four aircraft broke free and were washed overboard, and many others were damaged.[51] The ship itself survived pretty well.

As the winter progressed, intense cold, low cloud and snow also caused problems. Snow tended to settle only on the forward and aft sections of the flight deck, as the relative warmth from the hangars melted it elsewhere. Aircraft often had to be thawed below decks, and engine oil in deck-parked aircraft often had to be diluted at night so that engines could be started in the morning. Propellers and wing leading edges were coated with an anti-icing paste that made the deck slippery. Cold also damaged propeller seals and coolant hoses.[52]

These conditions of course made working on aircraft on the flight deck extremely difficult. Often, fine work requiring the removal of gloves could not be done for more than five minutes at a time. For the aircrew, immersion suits were always needed, and map reading was a constant challenge over snow-covered country. There were also days when the weather was simply too bad to allow flying—low cloud, wind and snow being the usual culprits.

---

50   O'Neill, *Combat Operations*, p. 472.
51   Ibid., p. 473. Fred Lane disputes this figure, claiming that only one Firefly was lost overboard, together with a motor boat and a forklift. See Lane, 'Naval aviation in the Korean War', p. 18.
52   O'Neill, *Combat Operations*, p. 473.

Although it did not necessarily affect individual aircrew, command and control was a periodic headache for the command. Much of the problem was cultural, with the RAN and RN ships generally unhappy with the degree of prescription and detail contained in USN operation orders. There was also an underlying friction between Rear Admiral Scott-Moncrieff and his USN superiors, Vice Admiral Dyer or Vice Admiral Joy, and which preceded *Sydney*'s arrival in Korea. More often than not the cause of the friction was an unfortunate level of mutual misunderstanding. Scott-Moncrieff was sceptical of the value of some US-proposed operations when weighed against the risk to his ships. He was also mindful that the smaller navies, like those of Australia and Canada, could ill afford to lose ships in such operations.[53] The USN hierarchy, in contrast, felt that the RN had a half-hearted approach to the war and was prepared to allow the USN to take the risks so that British forces could be conserved.

During *Sydney*'s time, the most significant such issues arose with the UNC's decision to institute a temporary exchange of duties between the US Fifth Air Force and the west coast carrier force. Admiral Joy had argued for the switch on the ground that it would be sensible for the naval aircraft to take over the convoy escort role between Japan and Korea if the Fifth Air Force took over the strike and ground support roles of the carrier force.[54] Scott-Moncrieff disputed the move because of the familiarity his aircrews now had with the terrain of north-west Korea and because of the monotony associated with the convoy protection task. Through all of this, Harries was in full agreement with Scott-Moncrieff.[55]

The rescue of downed aircrew was another major challenge associated with operations in Korea. Robert O'Neill noted that the air war virtually ceased until downed aircrew were located and, where possible, rescued.[56] *Sydney* made her own unique contribution. The first innovation was to provide pilots with fluorescent panels, two feet (60 centimetres) square, coloured red and yellow. They could be laid out on the ground to indicate the condition of aircrew, the location of enemy troops and the intentions of the aircrew.[57] The second element was a message bag that could be dropped to downed aircrew. Both innovations were taken up by other air forces in Korea.

---

53   Ibid., p. 453.
54   Ibid., pp. 478–9.
55   Ibid., p. 479.
56   Ibid., p. 486.
57   72 CBAL Section, HMAS *Sydney*, War Diary—Korean Operations, 29 October 1951.

Effectiveness and achievements

During her Korean War deployment, *Sydney* spent 122 days in Korean and Japanese waters. Of these, 42.8 days were spent on flying operations, 11.7 days were lost to poor weather, 29.5 days were spent on passage or in replenishment and 38 days were spent in harbour.[58]

Financially, it was a costly deployment, but carrier air power was a necessary counter to North Korea's land force predominance and a lack of suitable air bases in Korea. Fortunately, *Sydney* lost only three aircrew killed. The three, all Sea Fury pilots, were Lieutenant Kenneth Clarkson and Sub Lieutenants Dick Sinclair and Ron Coleman. Looked at in terms of the damage caused to North Korean infrastructure, logistics support and the number of troops killed, the result is mixed. The official figures (although sources do vary a little) are: 3,000 enemy troop casualties, 66 bridges destroyed—many of them more than once, seven tunnels damaged, 495 junks and sampans sunk or damaged, and 15 artillery pieces damaged or destroyed.

As Chapter 6 attests, battle damage assessment was quite difficult, and *Sydney*'s aircrew and the CBALO's staff took a notably conservative view of their achievements. For example, unless bodies could be counted, rockets had to be seen to hit known numbers of troops before kills were accepted.[59] That the approach was conservative was confirmed by 'Leopard', the US leader of an irregular ground force group. His assessments on the ground indicated that RAN aircrew were underestimating their impact. That they were doing so had important ramifications in that it contributed to the US dissatisfaction with the performance of the Commonwealth forces. On the other hand, RAN aircrew were said to have been bemused by the American penchant for figures of often doubtful reliability.

Issues such as these might well have contributed to a degree of frustration that had emerged among the aircrew by the end of the deployment. A much more significant cause, however, might have been the inability to shut down the North Korean supply lines completely. This inability simply reflected the realities of the limits of air interdiction, seen also in Vietnam in the 1960s.[60] Some of the aircrew involved bemoaned what seemed to

---

58 O'Neill, *Combat Operations*, p. 485.
59 Australian Naval Aviation Museum, *Flying Stations*, p. 86.
60 Jones, *Wings and the Navy*, p. 89.

be the exchange of North Korean oxcarts and peasants for UN aircraft and aircrew. The significance of this criticism is evident in the decision by US and RN authorities to switch from tactical targets to strategic ones, such as petrochemical installations and powerhouses. Only then, after *Sydney* had departed, did the North Koreans begin to show flexibility in the armistice talks.[61]

Yet, although there might have been some disappointment at their inability to close down North Korean supply lines, the RAN aviators should have been satisfied with their efforts. They created significant problems for North Korean logistic support, and ensured that most, if not all, such movements took place only at night. They also provided ground troops with consistently accurate close support. Perhaps unknown to them at the time, *Sydney* and her air group at the political level enabled Australia to avoid having to commit additional ground forces to the conflict.[62] For their efforts they were awarded three Distinguished Service Crosses and one Bar, one Distinguished Service Medal and two US Legion of Merit awards. As the CBALO, Major Simkin, noted in his official diary, 'Australian Naval Aviation can be justly proud of its first major war effort'.[63]

The aftermath

The Korean War heralded a new Australian naval construction program, announced in February 1952. It was to include six River Class frigates, one replenishment ship, three boom defence ships and four coastal minesweepers. It was also to include modernisation of the cruiser HMAS *Hobart*, the three Tribal Class destroyers, and conversion of the Q Class destroyers to fast anti-submarine warfare frigates.[64]

The Fleet Air Arm was not forgotten in the program. HMS *Vengeance* was offered on loan to the RAN while HMAS *Melbourne* was being modernised. Additionally, Sea Venom and Gannet aircraft were ordered in 1951 and 1952, respectively. Schofield's airfield also became HMAS *Nirimba* on 1 April 1953, with two reserve air squadrons, a repair base and the captain (air).[65]

---

61 Australian Naval Aviation Museum, *Flying Stations*, p. 84.
62 O'Neill, *Combat Operations*, p. 486.
63 Simkin, 'HMAS *Sydney* in Korean Waters'.
64 Jones, *Wings and the Navy*, p. 95.
65 Ibid., pp. 101–2.

The personnel element of this program was planned to see the navy grow from 10,252 Permanent Naval Forces (PNF) and 4,943 citizen force members in 1950 to 17,000 PNF and 10,000 national servicemen. The closest it got to that target was a strength of 14,144 PNF and 7,398 citizen force members in 1953.

Circumstances, however, conspired to curtail the program. Hostilities ceased in Korea in 1953, and the focus of Australian defence efforts changed from the Middle East—a Commonwealth commitment—to South-East Asia. As well, high inflation in 1954 saw the imposition of cuts in the defence program. These resulted in cancellations and delays to building and modernisation activities.

Nevertheless, HMAS *Melbourne* entered RAN service in 1955, together with her Sea Venom and Gannet aircraft. But *Sydney* was not modernised and ceased to be a front-line aircraft carrier. Additionally, a mere four years after *Melbourne* entered service, seven years after *Sydney* returned from her successful wartime deployment (and a mere 11 years after the Fleet Air Arm was established), the government decided that carrier aviation would have no further place in Australia's defence and that the carrier and its aircraft would be paid off in 1963. A reprieve was subsequently granted, but for the carrier and fixed-wing aviation it lasted only until 1982–83.

There is a question as to whether Australia could have done more to ensure the survival and growth of naval aviation. The question is relevant, as the nation recently acquired two large amphibious ships (HMAS *Canberra* and HMAS *Adelaide*) with flight decks as big as any ever before in the Australian inventory. Some questions remain about whether Australia will make the most of the aviation potential of these ships.

PART 3
FROM GENERALS TO LIEUTENANTS
Command in the war

Senior Australian army officers in Korea, c. April 1953.

From left to right: Lieutenant Colonel Arthur MacDonald, CO 3RAR; Lieutenant General Henry Wells, Commander-in-Chief British Commonwealth Forces, Korea; Brigadier John Wilton, commander 28th British Commonwealth Infantry Brigade; Lieutenant General Sir Sydney Rowell, Chief of the General Staff; and Lieutenant Colonel George Larkin, CO 2RAR. The experiences of Australia's senior commanders in Korea shaped the Australian Army for a generation after the war.

Source: AWM HOBJ4338.

IN FROM THE COLD

The dogged defence by Australians, Canadians and New Zealanders at Kapyong was instrumental in blunting the Chinese drive on Seoul, and helped to save the city from falling into communist hands again.
Source: AWM 147844.

8

AUSTRALIAN HIGHER COMMAND IN THE KOREAN WAR
The experience of Brigadier John Wilton

David Horner

Australian higher command in the Korean War is not just a matter of esoteric interest. Rather, from the time of the First World War, higher command arrangements have been a crucial element during most of Australia's military commitments. They have been both a means by which the Australian Government has exercised its sovereignty and an expression of the degree to which Australia has been able to have that sovereignty recognised. The command arrangements in the Korean War have had ramifications that continue to the present. This chapter discusses those higher command arrangements, then focuses on Brigadier John Wilton's command of the 28th British Commonwealth Brigade.

The classic starting point in any discussion of this subject is the First World War. Major General William Bridges, General Officer Commanding (GOC) of the 1st Australian Division as well as commander of the Australian Imperial Force (AIF), was responsible to the Australian Government for the administration of the Australian army forces overseas. But his force came under British command for operations, and the Australian Government had so little control over its deployment that it first learned that the Australians had landed on Gallipoli after the event. When Bridges was mortally wounded in May 1915, the GOC of the Anzac Corps, Lieutenant General Sir William Birdwood, a British officer, took command of the AIF, retaining the appointment until the end of the war. By that time the five Australian divisions on the Western Front had been grouped into the Australian Corps, under Lieutenant General Sir John Monash, but he still remained under a British Army commander for operations.

Learning from this experience, early in the Second World War the Australian Government appointed Lieutenant General Sir Thomas Blamey as Commander of the Second AIF, with a charter that made him responsible to the Australian Government for the administration of his force. He was also given authority to challenge orders from the British Commander under whom his force was placed, and to appeal to the Australian Government if he thought his force was being risked unnecessarily.[1] It was a declaration that Australia was an independent nation whose forces remained under its command even when operating under a British commander.

The situation became more complicated after Japan entered the war and the American General Douglas MacArthur was appointed Commander-in-Chief of the South-West Pacific Area, which included all Australian forces in and around Australia. By this time Blamey was back in Australia as Commander-in-Chief of the Australian Army, but his advice to the government could be overridden if the government accepted contrary advice from MacArthur, as at times happened. Nonetheless, Australian Army officers commanded at army and corps level in the field.

Higher command in the Royal Australian Air Force (RAAF) in the Second World War was less satisfactory. Nineteen RAAF squadrons served in Europe and the Middle East under British command, but few Australian officers commanded at higher than squadron level. In the South-West Pacific the RAAF, like the army, came under MacArthur's command. Similarly Royal Australian Navy (RAN) ships operated under British command in the first part of the war and later operated under American command.

---

1 Blamey's charter said that, with regard to the employment of the AIF in an emergency, he might 'take a decision on such a question, informing the Commonwealth Government that he is doing so' (quoted in D. Horner, *Blamey: The Commander-in-Chief*, Allen & Unwin, Sydney, 1998, pp. 136–7).

Australia learned several lessons from the experience of the two world wars. First, and ideally, the Australian Government needed to have some say in the process of developing imperial or allied grand strategy. In practice this proved extremely difficult. Second, Australian higher commanders needed to be able to influence the plans of the allied theatre commanders. This too proved difficult, unless Australia provided a large proportion of the forces in the relevant theatre. Australia could, however, influence the theatre commander's plans by the simple, if controversial, practice of denying forces to him—as Blamey did when he denied MacArthur's request to use the 6th Division for the invasion of Java.[2] The third lesson was the need to aggregate Australian forces into large groups under an Australian commander, thereby giving that commander more influence and also more experience of higher-level command.

These higher command problems were not surprising, given that Australia was a small country operating in a larger allied coalition. Big-power jealousies were difficult to overcome. In the South-West Pacific, the United States was loath to place its army formations under Blamey, as Commander, Allied Land Forces, even though his appointment was difficult to challenge, given that Australia provided 12 and the United States only two of the 14 infantry divisions in that theatre.

Similarly, Britain was reluctant to cede to Australian military leadership, even when the Australians were in superior numbers. Nonetheless, after the war Australia insisted on providing the Commander-in-Chief of the British Commonwealth Occupation Force (BCOF) in Japan. BCOF included a British–Indian division of two brigades, an Australian brigade, a New Zealand brigade and considerable numbers of Australian administrative troops. The Commander-in-Chief of BCOF came under American operational control (the Americans being in charge in Japan), but for policy and administrative matters he reported to the Australian chiefs of staff, who were supplemented by representatives from the other Commonwealth countries involved. The decision to appoint an Australian officer as Commander-in-Chief of BCOF was to have significant ramifications for higher command in the Korean War.

Unlike the situation in the South-West Pacific in 1942–43, when Australia provided the majority of General MacArthur's ground troops, Australia's military commitment to Korea was relatively modest. We might note in

---

2   Ibid., pp. 502, 516–17.

passing that in 1950 the Australians in Korea were still serving under MacArthur's command, as he was Commander-in-Chief of the United Nations Command.

Except for the 28th Brigade, to be discussed shortly, Australia's military commitment to Korea was generally at unit level. As noted earlier, soon after the outbreak of the war, the Australian destroyer HMAS *Bataan* and the frigate HMAS *Shoalhaven*, then serving in Japanese waters, joined a British naval task group operating off the coast of Korea. Australia attempted to maintain two ships on station for the remainder of the war; a total of nine RAN vessels served there, some returning for a second tour. As noted by Jack McCaffrie in Chapter 7, the aircraft carrier HMAS *Sydney* also served in Korean waters from October 1951 to February 1952. In each case the RAN ships operated as part of British task groups. Sometimes, when an Australian destroyer was commanded by a senior captain, he commanded a task group of Allied ships, thereby gaining valuable higher command experience, albeit at the tactical level.[3]

As mentioned by Richard Hallion in Chapter 6, Mustangs from the RAAF's No. 77 Squadron began operations over South Korea in 1950; the squadron served in Korea until the end of the war, generally operating as part of a US Air Force wing. No Australian air force officer was able to command at higher than squadron level.

The 3rd Battalion, Royal Australian Regiment (3RAR), arrived in Korea in September 1950 and joined the 27th British Brigade, which thereby became the 27th British Commonwealth Brigade. As part of the brigade, 3RAR took part in the advance into North Korea in late 1950, the subsequent withdrawal, the gallant defensive battle at Kapyong in April 1951, then, as part of the 28th Brigade, in the brilliant attack on Maryang San in October 1951. The battalion remained part of the 27th Brigade until April 1951, when the 28th British Commonwealth Brigade was formed. In June 1952, the 1st Battalion, Royal Australian Regiment (1RAR), joined 3RAR in the 28th Brigade, which, with two British battalions, had four infantry battalions. An Australian brigadier, Thomas Daly, took command of the brigade. In turn, Daly was succeeded by Brigadier John Wilton, whose experiences will be described later.

---

3   R. O'Neill, *Australia in the Korean War 1950–53*, vol. 2: *Combat Operations*, AWM & AGPS, Canberra, 1985, p. 528.

Therefore, until Daly took over, successive commanders of 3RAR were the highest ranked Australian Army operational commanders in Korea. One should not discount the additional responsibility borne by an Australian battalion commander operating in an allied army in a period of intense fighting. Major General David Butler, who served as a platoon commander in 3RAR in 1950 and later commanded an infantry battalion in South Vietnam, has commented that Lieutenant Colonel Charles Green, who commanded 3RAR in 1950, had a period of command 'without parallel in the history of the Australian Army':

> No-one has been invited to put together a unit in such a short time and take it into action so quickly. The actions he fought were in a sense quite solitary and not only because he was commanding a lone Australian battalion. No Australian CO in either world war experienced encounter battles of the kind Green faced.[4]

After Green was killed, Lieutenant Colonel Bruce Ferguson commanded the battalion in the bitterly cold withdrawal and in the Battle of Kapyong in April 1951. According to Ferguson's intelligence officer, Alf Argent, a contributing factor in Ferguson's relief as commanding officer in June 1951 was his reluctance to replace officers and men with reinforcements from Japan at a time when, in his view, such replacements would have gravely affected his battalion's fighting efficiency.[5] Further, when there was a dispute over giving leave to soldiers, Ferguson could not explain to the headquarters in Japan how short of men he was on the ground. As Butler put it: 'Unfortunately it was a national matter, which his British brigade commander could not take up on his behalf.'[6] So while Green, Ferguson and his successor, Frank Hassett, were tactical unit commanders, they had the additional burden of national responsibilities.

On the other side of the equation, the British commander of the 27th Brigade ordered 3RAR to withdraw after its successful defence of Kapyong because he was 'aware that he was responsible to the Australian Government for the safety of its battalion, and that searching questions would be asked if the only Australian ground force in Korea was wiped out'.[7] It seems that the Australian battalion commanders were never given

---

4   D. Butler, A. Argent and J.J. Shelton, *The Fight Leaders: A Study of Australian Battlefield Leadership*, Australian Military History Publications, Loftus, NSW, 2002, p. 70.
5   Ibid., p. 111.
6   Ibid., p. 149.
7   J. Grey, *The Commonwealth Armies and the Korean War: An Alliance Study*, Manchester University Press, Manchester, 1988, p. 85.

any directives that would allow them to appeal against orders in which their troops might be placed at risk, perhaps because the Australian chiefs of staff believed that, as will be explained shortly, the Commander-in-Chief British Commonwealth Forces Korea, an Australian general, would keep watch on such problems.[8]

So to an extent the Australian battalion commanders were not completely without moral support, and they had another avenue of support as well. At the outbreak of the Korean War, 3RAR, No. 77 Squadron, RAAF, and Australian administrative units were serving as part of BCOF in Japan. By this stage the British, Indian and New Zealand elements of BCOF had left Japan, and Australia was preparing to withdraw its forces as well. The Commander-in-Chief of BCOF, the Australian Lieutenant General Sir Horace Robertson, who had been there since 1946, was still in command. When 3RAR and No. 77 Squadron were deployed to Korea, BCOF provided a convenient administrative base in nearby Japan. Further, when the 27th British Brigade went to Korea, and 3RAR became part of it, the Australian, British, Canadian and New Zealand governments agreed that Robertson would take up the appointment of Commander-in-Chief British Commonwealth Forces Korea. Robertson had the command infrastructure that could be readily adapted to provide administrative support for the Commonwealth forces deployed to Korea.

The 27th Brigade was under the operational control of an American division, with ultimate operational control stretching back to MacArthur in Tokyo. But according to his directive, Robertson was required to maintain the forces in Korea and Japan and to interest himself 'in the operational tasks allotted to the United Kingdom, Australian, New Zealand and Canadian Forces'.[9] He was to maintain close contact with the Commonwealth commanders in Korea and to represent their cases to MacArthur. Robertson was also to report to the Australian Chiefs of Staff Committee, which for the purpose was augmented by representatives from the other Commonwealth countries.

The British Commonwealth base at Kure in Japan was commanded by an Australian, Brigadier Ian Campbell, who was also commander of the Australian Component of the British Commonwealth Forces Korea. Robertson took a keen interest in the operations of all the Commonwealth

---

8 Ibid., p. 107.
9 Ibid., p. 110.

forces in Korea. It was he who appointed Walsh to command 3RAR when Green was killed in November, and he accepted the decision of the British brigade commander to dismiss Walsh from his command and to appoint Ferguson just over a week later.[10] According to Major General Ron Hopkins, Robertson was present in Korea when part of the British 29th Infantry Brigade was overrun by superior Chinese forces in April 1951; Robertson insisted, without success, that he visit the forward British battalions. He returned to Japan 'and peremptorily ordered his staff to round up all available reinforcements in Japan'. By noon the next day reinforcements were arriving to strengthen the 29th Brigade.[11]

In October 1951, another Australian officer, Lieutenant General William Bridgeford, succeeded Robertson as Commander-in-Chief British Commonwealth Forces Korea. In February 1953, Lieutenant General Henry Wells succeeded Bridgeford. After this appointment, Wells became Chief of the General Staff, then, at the end of that appointment, in 1958 he became Australia's first separate Chairman of the Chiefs of Staff Committee. While the successive Commanders-in-Chief held a significant appointment, their ability to influence high-level decision-making was undermined by the fact that Britain appointed a senior officer, Air Vice Marshal Cecil Bouchier, as liaison officer at MacArthur's headquarters in Tokyo.

Although the position of Commander-in-Chief British Commonwealth Forces Korea sounded grand, the most important operational position was that of the Commander of the 1st Commonwealth Division. This division was formed in July 1951, bringing together the 28th Commonwealth Brigade (which included 3RAR), the British 29th Brigade and the Canadian 25th Brigade, along with support troops, including some from India and New Zealand. The commander of the division was a British officer, Major General James Cassels.

There is plentiful evidence of Cassels's disputes with his American corps commander, Lieutenant General John ('Iron Mike') O'Daniel, over his belief that at times he was asked to undertake operations that would unnecessarily cause casualties. As Cassels wrote in October 1951, his main trouble was convincing O'Daniel that, 'although we were more

---

10   O'Neill, *Combat Operations*, pp. 60, 64.
11   R. Hopkins, 'Lieutenant-General Sir Horace Robertson: Commander-in-Chief British Commonwealth Occupation Force', in *The Commanders: Australian Military Leadership in the Twentieth Century*, ed. D.M. Horner, George Allen & Unwin, Sydney, 1984, p. 295.

than ready to do anything that was required, we did like to know the reason behind it. On many occasions I was ordered without warning to do things which I considered militarily unsound and for which there was no apparent reason'.[12] Cassels was a first-rate officer. He had commanded a brigade in Normandy during the Second World War and a division in Palestine on counter-insurgency operations in the late 1940s. Later, with the rank of field marshal, he was British Chief of the General Staff. Unlike the American division commanders, he was prepared to argue with his corps commander in Korea and, as the historian Jeffrey Grey has written, he 'managed to talk O'Daniel out of most of his wilder flights of fancy'.[13]

This rather long introduction provides a necessary background to the discussion of Brigadier John Wilton's role as commander of the 28th Brigade.

It has sometimes been thought that Wilton was a consummate staff officer and that his posting in Korea was designed to give him command experience before he went on to higher rank in the Australian Army. By contrast, it might be noted that his predecessor in command of the 28th Brigade, Tom Daly, had commanded the 2/10th Infantry Battalion in the landing at Balikpapan in Borneo in 1945. In fact the opposite was the case. In the first 10 years of his military service, Wilton spent more time in command appointments than any of his Australian Army contemporaries.

Partly this came about because, after graduating from Duntroon in 1930, he joined the British Army, no position being available in the Australian Army. After his initial artillery training in Britain, in June 1931 he joined an artillery regiment that five months later embarked for India. In February 1935 he transferred to a mountain battery and served, with a small amount of action, in Burma. By early 1939 he was serving in a coastal battery at Karachi, and when he returned to the Australian Army in mid-1939 he went to the Australian Army's largest permanent unit, the 1st Heavy Brigade in Sydney, and was soon commanding a coastal battery.

When Wilton joined the Second AIF in May 1940, he was given command of a field battery, which he led in Palestine and Egypt until February 1941. He then became brigade major of the 7th Division artillery, serving in that

---

12   Quoted in Grey, *The Commonwealth Armies and the Korean War*, p. 138.
13   Ibid., p. 141.

role in the Syrian campaign. Wilton had an almost unbroken period in command, admittedly much of it at a junior level: just short of 10 years. Wilton was General Staff Officer Grade One (GSO1) of the 3rd Division during the Salamaua campaign in New Guinea in 1943, and when the headquarters of the 5th Division took over the campaign, its GSO1 was none other than Thomas Daly. When Daly was commanding the 2/10th Battalion at Balikpapan, Wilton was on the operations staff of General Blamey's advanced headquarters at Morotai. When, after the war, Wilton was Director of Military Operations and Plans at Army Headquarters, Daly was Director of Military Art at Duntroon.

Despite this rather impressive background, when he arrived in Korea in March 1953 to take over from Daly, Wilton was conscious that his British colleagues had even more impressive credentials. Major General Mike West, who had succeeded Cassels as commander of the 1st Commonwealth Division, had commanded a brigade at Kohima in 1944—the bloodiest battle of the war in Burma. Brigadier Douglas ('Joe') Kendrew, commander of the 29th Brigade, had won three Distinguished Service Orders (DSO) as a battalion and brigade commander in the Second World War. Brigadier Jean Allard, who arrived a little later to take over the 25th Canadian Brigade, had also won three DSOs commanding a battalion and a brigade in the Second World War. Wilton had won only one DSO. Allard would later become Chief of the Defence Staff of the Canadian Forces.

The division had strong artillery support, and the commander of the divisional artillery, Brigadier Guy Gregson, DSO, MC, had Canadian, British and New Zealand field regiments, a British light regiment and a British medium battery. The 16th New Zealand Regiment was in direct support of the 28th Brigade, but in defensive battles the brigade would be able to call upon not only the divisional but also the corps artillery. Wilton was pleasantly surprised to find that the commanding officer of the 20th Field Regiment Royal Artillery was Lieutenant Colonel Geoff Brennan, one of his fellow Duntroon graduates who had transferred to the British Army with him back in 1931.

With two British and two Australian battalions—1st Battalion, Royal Fusiliers (1RF), 1st Battalion, Durham Light Infantry (1DLI), 3RAR and the newly arrived 2RAR—Wilton's brigade was the strongest in the division, and also included units from most countries of the Commonwealth. As mentioned above, its direct support regiment was from New Zealand, and the 60th Indian Field Ambulance also supported it. The battalion commanders were capable and experienced infantry officers. Lieutenant Colonels Peter Jeffreys, DSO, OBE (1DLI), and Dick Stevens, OBE (1RF), had commanded brigades of their own in the Second World War. By contrast, the Australian battalion commanders had less command experience, although they were no less able; they had much experience as staff officers on active service. Lieutenant Colonel Arthur MacDonald (3RAR) had served with Wilton at Army Headquarters (AHQ). Wilton observed that MacDonald, who would become Chief of the Defence Force staff in the 1970s, had 'settled down quite well and is fit and full of confidence as ever'. George Larkin, who commanded 2RAR, was 'having quite a job getting his battalion settled down and used to the new conditions'.[14]

Wilton formally took command on 25 March 1953, and on 7 April the Commonwealth Division began to move forward to take over from the US 2nd Division in the Jamestown Line. The 28th Brigade occupied the right-hand sector, including Hill 355, the Canadian 25th Brigade was in the centre, and the 29th Brigade was on the left, defending the Hook. Wilton deployed 1DLI on Hill 355 and 1RF on Hill 159, and the two Australian battalions in reserve. The US 2nd Division had taken to heart the injunction to avoid clashes with the enemy. Before long, both of Wilton's forward battalions were in contact, and in a patrol clash on 23 April, 1RF lost one killed, two wounded and one missing.[15]

With no offensives to plan and a generally static defence line, at first glance there seemed little for the higher commanders to do. According to Brigadier Allard:

> [A] brigade commander could not, on his own initiative, mount an offensive that would involve more than a platoon. To attack with a company we had to obtain permission from the army corps commander—the divisional commander did not have that power of decision—and the corps commander had to have the blessing of the army commander to involve more than one company.[16]

---

14   Wilton to Helen, 25 March 1953, Wilton family papers.
15   War diary, 28th Brigade, April 1953, TNA: WO 281/711.
16   J.V. Allard, with S. Bernier, *The Memoirs of General Jean V. Allard*, University of British Columbia Press, Vancouver, 1988, p. 173.

As a result, the brigade commander could not test the defensive capability of his opponents or the offensive capability of his own troops. Further, if the enemy dominated his defences, he could not mount an attack to drive him off his forward positions.

The brigade commander's prime duty was to remain ready to deal with a Chinese offensive while maintaining the morale and efficiency of his units. On the night of 14 April, a 1DLI patrol clashed with a Chinese patrol; Wilton took the opportunity to rehearse his battle procedure, communications and counter-attack plans. As he wrote to his wife, he thought that 'all went off very well': 'I'm quite confident now about this job and except on rare occasions when there is a minor "flap" on about a patrol clash etc I shall have a fairly easy time unless the Chinaman decides to carry out a big offensive.'[17]

Wilton knew that it was important to keep a close watch on activities in the line and to be seen by the troops. The best time to visit was in the early morning. Most of the troops were awake at night, manning the forward positions and sending patrols into no man's land. So if he was to see the troops, he needed to arrive about an hour before they stood down after the night's work. Further, if he drove up to the front line in his jeep during the day, the enemy would shell him. Hence, two or three times per week he woke at 4 am, drove to one of the forward battalions, then sent his jeep back to his headquarters. After completing his morning inspection, he would then walk back through the communication trenches, which, he assured his wife, was 'quite safe but fatiguing'.[18]

Wilton's other concern was to establish his reputation. He was conscious that he was the only brigadier in the division who had not commanded a unit in combat. As he confided to his wife, his problem was 'to obtain and maintain the respect of the British COs, both of whom are very experienced infantry officers who in the last war both commanded brigades of their own': 'So you can see that my relations and attitude towards them must be different to that which I can adopt towards MacDonald and Larkin. However, I'm not unduly concerned—it's merely a matter of time and handling them carefully.'[19] To the divisional commander he was also an unknown quantity, but by 18 April he thought that his relations with

---

17 Wilton to Helen, 18 April 1953, Wilton family papers. For the patrol clash, see war diary, 28th Brigade, April 1953, TNA: WO 281/711.
18 Wilton to Helen, 12 April 1953, Wilton family papers.
19 Ibid.

West were good. 'We are getting to know each other better. I naturally feel that he is watching me very closely to make sure that I'm up to the job and that is normal of course. He is very friendly and helpful and ready to give advice.' In the first week of May, Wilton ordered his two Australian battalions to relieve the British battalions in the forward positions. On 14 May a Chinese propaganda broadcast welcomed the Australians to the front line, adding, 'We hope you will preserve the good names of the previous two battalions'.[20]

It was not long before both battalions were in action with fierce patrol clashes in no man's land and ambushes by both sides. The Chinese shelled the forward positions, and one Australian patrol received casualties in one of their own minefields after straying into it while in contact with the enemy. The 29th Brigade, defending the Hook on the left flank of the division, came under sustained attack beginning on 8 May. Shelling increased on 20 May, and a full-scale assault began on 28 May. The 29th Brigade received an estimated 10,000 incoming rounds of artillery, but the divisional artillery replied with 32,000 rounds plus a further 5,000 from the corps artillery and 500 from the Royal Tank Regiment. The 29th Brigade repulsed the Chinese brigade-sized attack, inflicting heavy casualties—estimated by Major General West at 250 killed and 800 wounded.[21] Wilton confided to his wife that Brigadier Kendrew was a 'good solid chap although I would not say he is a clever chap by any means'; all the same, Kendrew understood how to fight a battle and was awarded another DSO for this action.[22] Referring to the Chinese artillery attack, Kendrew commented: 'In the whole of the last war I never knew anything like that bombardment.'[23] The 28th Brigade's casualties in May were 20 killed, 116 wounded and seven missing in action, mostly incurred by the Australian battalions.

Wilton's brigade major, Bill Morrow, had served with Brigadier Daly for three months and was in an excellent position to compare the two brigade commanders. He thought that both were 'very fine' commanders. Daly was 'more gregarious' and would talk easily with the soldiers. Wilton was 'very intelligent and very quiet'. Morrow was impressed by Wilton's 'very

---

20 War diary, 28th Brigade, May 1953, TNA: WO 281/711.
21 Despatch by Major General M.M.A.R. West, p. 10, private papers of General Sir Michael West, GCB, DSO, Imperial War Museum, Documents, 11300.
22 Wilton to Helen, 9 June 1953, Wilton family papers.
23 A.J. Barker, *Fortune Favours the Brave: The Battle of the Hook, Korea, 1953*, Leo Cooper, London, 1974, p. 143.

cool, calm and collected manner' in moments of tension. The Battle of the Hook was a good example. The Chinese artillery had been building up during the latter days of May until the final assault beginning on 28 May. As the night progressed, Morrow awakened Wilton to tell him about the attack. As Morrow recalled, 'he was wonderfully cool'. He replied, 'Well, there is not much we can do at this stage. Keep your eye on it and give me a call when things develop'.[24]

In late May, 1DLI relieved 3RAR, and on 16 June 3RAR relieved 2RAR. The patrol clashes, ambushes and artillery bombardments continued; during the month the brigade suffered 20 killed, 133 wounded and six missing—distributed equally among 1DLI, 2RAR and 3RAR.[25] Wilton was now well into his stride as a brigade commander, and in a letter to his wife on 21 June he reflected on his responsibilities:

> I must say that if this phoney sort of war goes on much longer I am going to get very bored because there is no scope for much initiative for a brigade commander. The battalion commander has the interesting and busy job and my main job is to see that the battalion commanders do theirs properly and to coordinate their activities.[26]

In the second week of July, Major General West reshuffled his brigades. The 28th Brigade moved across to take over the left flank position, including the Hook. The Canadian 25th Brigade relieved the 28th Brigade, and in turn the 29th Brigade occupied the centre position.

Wilton was now responsible for the division's most threatened area. The Chinese had made frequent attacks against the Hook, aware that if they could take this feature they could dominate the Imjin River, 4 kilometres to the south. Wilton deployed 2RAR into the left forward area, on the Hook. 3RAR was on its right, overlooking the Samichon River, 1DLI was on the opposite side of the Samichon, and 1RF was held in reserve to deal with major enemy penetrations of the brigade's defences. The Turkish Brigade had previously held the position to the left of 2RAR, but the 7th Regiment of the US Marines 1st Division had now replaced it.

---

24 Brigadier W.J. Morrow to author, 21 November 2002.
25 War diary, 28th Brigade, June 1953, TNA: WO 281/711.
26 Wilton to Helen, 21 June 1953, Wilton family papers.

This was a difficult time for the troops. On 8 June, UN and Chinese negotiators signed an agreement on the exchange of prisoners, and only the final details of the demarcation line remained to be concluded. By mid-July, South Korea had agreed to accept the terms of the armistice and a final truce seemed near. Meanwhile, on the night of 19/20 July the Marines were driven off two positions near 2RAR, exposing its positions further. Patrol clashes indicated that the Chinese were building up for yet another assault. To the troops in their trenches, it seemed futile to risk their lives.

At 6.15 in the evening of 23 July, Wilton called his battalion commanders together to inform them that the signing of the armistice agreement was imminent and that they were to send out only those patrols essential to the security of their positions. The following evening, the Chinese bombardment of the Marines and the left flank of 2RAR grew in intensity. Large bodies of Chinese were seen on the forward slopes of the 2RAR positions, while enemy forces surrounded a 2RAR bunker on the left flank. The Marine liaison officer at brigade headquarters reported that Chinese were probing the Marine positions. Sitting quietly in his command post, at 9.10 pm Wilton ordered one company of 1DLI to occupy a reserve position on the 2RAR left flank, to the rear of the US Marine Division, and the reserve company of 3RAR to be 'embussed and ready to move in event of emergency'.[27] Nineteen-year-old Sergeant Brian Cooper, commanding a section from the 2RAR machine gun platoon on the extreme left flank within the Marine perimeter, called down the Commonwealth Division artillery around his own and the Marines' position to break up the enemy attacks.[28] One of Cooper's mates well remembers the feeling of being let down as the Marines filed past their position, pulling out: 'Then there was the realisation that when they were gone, there was just us!'[29]

Throughout the next day, the Chinese maintained a slow but persistent shelling of the Australian positions, stepping up the intensity in the evening. That night the Marines on the nearby hills came under a fierce assault, necessitating a counter-attack. At 12.45 am Wilton ordered the

---

27 War diary, 28 Commonwealth Brigade, July 1953, TNA: WO 281/712.
28 B. Cooper, 'Recollections of Korea, July 1953', in *Korea Remembered: The RAN, ARA and RAAF in the Korean War of 1950–1953*, ed. M. Pears and F. Kirkland, Doctrine Wing, Combined Arms Training and Development Centre, Georges Heights, NSW, 1998.
29 'Ron' Walker, 'Last days on the "Hook"—1953', in *Korea Remembered*, ed. Pears and Kirkland, p. 163.

reserve company of 3RAR to move across to occupy the position behind 2RAR, and at 2.18 am he placed one company of 1DLI on five minutes' notice to move to a blocking position. By dawn the Chinese attack had been repulsed, and Wilton went forward to visit 2RAR, 3RAR and 1DLI. During two nights, 2RAR had lost five killed and 24 wounded, while in the same period the Marines had 43 killed and 316 wounded. Over three nights the Commonwealth Division's artillery fired almost 23,000 rounds, and the Marine artillery fired a similar number. By contrast, the 28th Brigade recorded only 2,700 incoming rounds.[30]

There were no further contacts on the night of 26 July, as news came that the armistice would be signed at 10 am the next day, to come into effect at 10 pm. In the morning of 27 July, Wilton boarded a light aircraft to fly to Panmunjom. There, on behalf of Australia, he witnessed the signing of the armistice documents.

At dawn on 28 July, West and Wilton went forward to inspect 2RAR's forward positions. Standing on the bunkers, he studied the Chinese positions. He wrote later:

> The floor of the valley between the Hook and the Chinese position was almost covered with dead Chinese who had been caught by our deadly defensive-fire artillery concentrations. On the immediate approaches to 2RAR the bodies literally carpeted the ground sometimes two deep. It was a terrible sight which I will never forget.[31]

We are never likely to know the numbers of Chinese killed in the 2RAR area. Whatever the actual numbers, it was a salutary illustration of the power of concentrated artillery and the wastefulness of massed attacks. As a professional gunner, Wilton later reflected on the fact that in normal circumstances nothing can stand in the way of a 'solidly packed' human wave attack on a front of about 500 to 1,000 metres, except if the defender has access to a large amount of artillery support.

---

30   War diary, HQ RAA, 1st Commonwealth Division, July 1953, TNA: WO 281/728; P. Meid and J.M. Yingling, *US Marine Operations in Korea 1950–1953*, vol. V: *Operations in West Korea*, Historical Division, Headquarters US Marine Corps, Washington, DC, 1972, p. 388. The 1st Commonwealth Division, *Periodic Report, 1 April 1953–1 August 1953* (TNA: WO 308/65), claimed that 4,000 rounds fell on the divisional position on 25 July, mainly on the Hook and point 121.
31   Quoted in O'Neill, *Combat Operations*, p. 282.

The Australians' last battles at the Hook received little notice in the histories of the war (except for the Australian official history).[32] During two weeks on the Hook, 2RAR lost 17 killed and 32 wounded. By comparison, in the celebrated Battle of Long Tan in the Vietnam War in August 1966, the Australians lost 18 killed and 24 wounded, inflicting, by Australian records, 245 enemy deaths.[33] In May 1968 in Vietnam, the Australian task force, with two battalions deployed, fought what the official history describes as 'their largest, most hazardous and most sustained battles of the war'. Australian casualties were 20 killed and 95 wounded. Enemy casualties from the Australian operations numbered more than 200.[34]

Wilton had fought his last battle; but he remained in Korea commanding his brigade until February 1954. He found the time in Korea to be a worthwhile experience. He later reflected:

> If I hadn't had that experience in command of operations in the field at that level I wouldn't have been as well equipped as I should be later on when I became a general and, subsequently, head of the Army. You can't have a bloke heading the Army who hasn't commanded anything more than a small unit in the field.

Of course, he was not tested in fast-moving operations. As he later explained, the decision-making was 'not very difficult because you had plenty of time to work out your dispositions and counter-attack plans and fire plans, and it was just a question of which one to put into effect according to where the attack came from'.[35]

He learned much about cooperation with allied armies. He had already had considerable service with the US Army, but the experience in Korea confirmed his critical views about the American approach to war—a view that would colour his thinking when dealing with the Americans in Vietnam 10 years later. Further, he met 'a lot of American and British

---

32 The British official history deals with the battle in one sentence; see A. Farrar-Hockley, *The British Part in the Korean War*, vol. 2: *An Honourable Discharge* (HMSO, London, 1995), p. 383. Farrar-Hockley (p. 383) also claims that Lieutenant Colonel Jeffreys of 1DRL had planned a counter-attack on 26 July to recover a company area, and that Wilton left it to him to decide whether to do so. This seems unusual as 1DRL was in a reserve position.
33 I. McNeill, *To Long Tan: The Australian Army in the Vietnam War 1950–1966*, Allen & Unwin/AWM, Sydney, 1993, pp. 356, 368.
34 I. McNeil and A. Ekins, *On the Offensive: The Australian Army in the Vietnam War, January 1967–June 1968*, Allen & Unwin/AWM, Sydney, 2003, pp. 349, 396.
35 Transcript of interviews conducted by J. Wilton and J. Eisenberg, pp. 79–80, McNeill papers, held by the author.

officers' whom he was to meet again in the Southeast Asian Treaty Organization (SEATO), Malaysia and Vietnam.³⁶ One of these was General Maxwell Taylor, commander of the US Eighth Army, who would become Chief of Staff US Army, special adviser to President Kennedy, Chairman of the US Joint Chiefs of Staff, and later US Ambassador in Vietnam.³⁷ Operationally, Wilton particularly noted the value of helicopters; the Commonwealth Division had none, but the US Army made its own available when needed. Years later he would fight for the Australian Army to have its own helicopters.

The problem of maintaining one and later two battalions in Korea was another crucial lesson. Because there was no ready replacement at the time, 3RAR remained in Korea throughout the war, being sustained by a process of individual replacement as soldiers completed their 12 months service. As Wilton wrote later, each unit was 'in a constant process of change, and no sooner had the subunits and units built themselves up as a team when half the team went away'.³⁸ By comparison, 1RAR was completely relieved by 2RAR. In the lead-up to the Vietnam War he would argue for a larger army, and would lay down the policy for the relief of complete units.

Wilton's experience commanding the 28th Brigade therefore taught him much more than the relatively straightforward (but nonetheless vitally important) mechanics of commanding a brigade in action. It gave him an important background for his later commands. As Chief of the General Staff from 1963 to 1966, he set the parameters for the Australian Army's commitment to the Vietnam War. Then, when he became Chairman of the Chiefs of Staff Committee in 1966, he assumed overall responsibility for the commitment to Vietnam, which almost simultaneously grew from a mainly army affair to a tri-service commitment. In all this, the management of relations with allies was a key feature.

Finally, we should note that Wilton's predecessor as commander of the 28th Brigade, Thomas Daly, succeeded Wilton as Chief of the General Staff from 1966 to 1971, and was therefore responsible for maintaining the Australian Army in Vietnam. Frank Hassett, who commanded 3RAR in the Battle of Maryang San in 1951, rose to become the first Chief of the

---

36 Ibid., p. 79.
37 Wilton Diary, Wilton Papers, ADFA Library.
38 'Commonwealth Division in Korea', address by Wilton, undated, Wilton Papers, folder 23, ADFA Library.

Defence Force staff. He was succeeded in that role by Arthur MacDonald, who had commanded 3RAR in 1953. Ron Hughes, who commanded 3RAR in 1951–52, commanded the 1st Australian Task Force in Vietnam and was commander of the 1st Division in the 1970s. The Australian Army's higher command experience in the Korean War therefore influenced the Australian Army, and indeed the Australian Defence Force, for a generation beyond the end of the war.

9

THE RELIVING OF MINOR TACTICS
Reflections of a platoon commander's war in Korea

Colin Kahn

Former United States Chief of Army General Bruce Clarke wrote: 'The paramount concern of the Army is the ground combat soldier. It will be a sorry day for us all in this supersonic, nuclear age should the ground combat soldier ever be deprived of his rightful place in the hearts and minds of the military forces and the people.' This chapter focuses on those responsible for the tactical fighting of Australian-conducted operations in Korea: infantry rifle sections and platoons, for this was primarily an infantry soldier's war.

Although I will concentrate on the activities of rifle platoons, the infantrymen who served in Korea can never forget the contributions and support given by other arms and services, especially artillery, which frequently proved to be battle-winning contributions that led to success or survival. While it did happen, it was rare that Australian rifle platoons fought without support.

When preparing this chapter I was reminded of Montaigne's words, 'I have gathered a posy of other men's flowers, and only the string that binds them is mine'. I participated only in the static, patrol phase of the war in 1952; for the mobile and attack phases, I have relied on the flowers provided to me by the experienced, outstanding warrant officers and senior non-commissioned officers (NCOs) with whom I have served, and with whom I have instructed on the topic of Infantry Minor Tactics, both at the School of Infantry in Singleton, NSW, and in Canberra at Duntroon. Incidentally, most of these NCOs served in Korea with our 3rd Battalion, Royal Australian Regiment (3RAR). They never let me forget that if you did not serve in the 3rd Battalion, you did not really serve in Korea; and even then, if you were not in the first mobile phase with the 3rd Battalion, when they had the fun of going up and down the peninsula, you still did not really serve in Korea.

In Korea, indeed as ever, good platoon commanders put their individual stamp on the workings and the life of their platoon. This stamp, this mark, made on all successful platoons, included the stamp of high morale, of aggression, of example and the adaptation of tried and known minor tactics to his own platoon. As a result of this individualism, one must tend to generalise when talking of platoon activities. However, because of our training in proven minor tactics, learnt during the Second World War at platoon and company level, application was generally common; and what one subunit of the RAR did well (or, on rare occasions, not so well) would or could have been done by any other Australian subunit. This leads us into considering the building blocks in the structure and application of how we operated.

The men — composition

First among these blocks were the men who comprised our subunits. Company commanders generally had Second World War experience, as did some platoon commanders. The majority of platoon commanders were, however, recent Duntroon graduates, well trained in minor tactics and leadership, and anxious to prove themselves in battle. Hence this ingredient of minor tactics was present in Korea: uniform, tried battle experience, or highly trained, enthusiastic young officers.

The soldiers were a mixture. Some were Korea Force volunteers—men, in the main Second World War veterans, who specifically enlisted for the duration of the Korean War, something rather unique. They came not only from Australia but also from overseas, especially the United Kingdom, and many were not ex-soldiers but were ex-airmen or ex-sailors; I had two in my platoon. These men were mature and in the main battle-

9. THE RELIVING OF MINOR TACTICS

hardened to varying degrees. Next were the young regular soldiers, many 18 or 19 years old, of the recently formed Australian Regular Army. This blending of experience and youth proved to be a great success in battle.

Weapons and equipment are clearly two major determinants of minor tactics. With the end of the Second World War less than five years before, it was no surprise that we went to Korea with what was left over from the Second World War. There was nothing that was new. The basic Australian infantry weapon was the bolt-action, single-firing .303 rifle and bayonet; each section had one Bren light machine gun and M36 grenades. Meanwhile infantry section commanders and most platoon commanders had Owen submachine guns, which were used extensively in the Second World War. At times, within the platoon there was a 3.5-inch rocket launcher and a 2-inch mortar, in addition to the platoon commander having an 88 set radio for communications with his company commander; communications between sections was by voice or hand signals. It is also important to remember that all movement was by foot, by truck, by jeep or on tanks; there were no lift helicopters.

As the war progressed, and trading with the Americans increased, platoon weapons slightly changed. Major changes occurred during the static phase of the war, when platoons armed themselves with more light machine guns and submachine guns for patrolling purposes. But primarily platoon weapons remained the same as in the Second World War.

The effect that clothing had on minor operations became very clear in the freezing conditions of Korea. Initially our troops went in Second World War clothing (some of it from the Middle East) and web equipment: slouch hats, leather studded boots, web gaiters and old field dress. Gradually, platoons were more appropriately attired with British and US underclothing, smocks, fleecy caps, winter boots, gloves with firing fingers, sleeping bags and so on. Lack of suitable clothing restricted the time troops could spend out in the cold; and without suitable gloves, fingers stuck to gun metal.

The old saying 'as you train, so will you fight' stayed true. The training of soldiers and NCOs was generally sound, with many in the 3rd Battalion having trained and/or served in Japan with the British Commonwealth Occupation Force (BCOF). Reinforcements trained at home for up to six months—from 1952 onwards, they were trained by Korean veterans.

All troops on arrival in Japan went to the British battle school in the mountains at Hara-Mura in Nagano prefecture where they were trained by veteran instructors.

While many section commanders brought Second World War experience with them, and NCO courses were run in New South Wales and Victoria, much still remained to be done under the guidance of experienced company sergeant majors and platoon sergeants, almost all of them with Second World War experience. Not all leadership training was uniform or extensive, however. A well-known retired warrant officer class 1 wrote to this author recently: 'I joined the Army at 21, in January 1950; I was in Korea by September and was immediately made a lance corporal, and within two weeks I was a corporal section commander. Most of my training and leadership skills as a section commander was on-the-job learning from old K Force veterans in my section.'

Mobile phase

An understrength 3RAR in Japan needed reinforcements and further training to get it to Pusan in September 1950, and in October the first major engagements with the North Koreans occurred at the Apple Orchard and the Broken Bridge. The mobile phase of the war for Australian troops was well underway.

These advance operations, going up the peninsula, were identified with infantry platoons mounted in trucks, on tanks or on foot, clearing advance centre lines and flanks; and when enemy positions were encountered, they mounted quick assaults, frequently with grenade and bayonet, to force the enemy to withdraw. These were classical advances to contact, identified by quick off-the-march assaults, frequently across open paddy fields at section level, and supported by artillery and US air power. Some of the terrain encountered during this advance in central North Korea included steep ridges covered in pine forests, causing platoons to revisit fighting experienced in the Second World War, up ridge lines in New Guinea. At times, advance frontages were restricted to two or three men, or less.

The advance operations went on for six months, then the units became involved in withdrawals from North Korea in the face of massive Chinese intervention. Rear guards and temporary defensive positions were established in defiles, at crossroads and bridges, to cover withdrawals of

United Nations (UN) troops mixed in with refugees. In the many major and minor encounters during this phase, the operations of the infantry subunits were characterised by quick, aggressive action that enabled orderly withdrawal with minimum losses.

Defensive battle—Kapyong

As the major defensive Battle of Kapyong is covered elsewhere in this book (especially chapters 3 and 4), this chapter will refer briefly to the actions of platoons to indicate how the leadership and aggression shown at junior levels in the previous mobile phase was repeated by platoons in defence. Generally, 3RAR companies and platoons were in widely dispersed, unprepared defensive positions on hilltops around Kapyong valley, and were attacked by wave after wave of Chinese assaults. Forward companies were cut off, with further confusion caused by refugees and others fleeing through the area.

Being a hastily occupied defence, deep weapon pits or trenches were replaced by hastily prepared shell scrapes or protective mounds of stones. Sections relied primarily on .303 single-shot rifles, with automatic fire from one light machine gun and one submachine gun per section. More automatic weapons were needed to defeat mass assaults. The Chinese assaults—almost always preceded by whistles and bugles for communication—normally consisted of Chinese soldiers closing to grenade range, followed by charges with rifles and burp guns.[1] This major defensive battle was won by resolute and aggressive defence by sections and platoons holding their positions; or, when these were lost or overrun, conducting local counter-attacks, frequently without support, but using grenade and bayonet to regain lost weapon pits.

Overall, this major battle was supported by US air, especially Corsairs dropping napalm, and by US Sherman tanks that provided fire support, brought up ammunition and evacuated casualties. On one night, however, there was no artillery or other support available to 3RAR, and the companies and platoons repelled several major night assaults, using only their own infantry weapons: rifles and light machine guns. Dead and

---

1   A burp gun is a Russian-made submachine gun; see 'The burp gun was ugly—but damn did it spray lead', *War is Boring*, 15 October 2014, medium.com/war-is-boring/the-burp-gun-was-ugly-but-damn-did-it-spray-lead-cc4730dadfe8.

wounded from forward weapon pits were taken to rear positions and replaced by fit men from the rear. Some section strengths were reduced to fewer than four men. Eventually, companies were forced to withdraw, under pressure, by leap-frogging sections and platoons back while they covered each other. This battle was fought and won at section, platoon and company level by resolute and aggressive defence.

Chinese tactics

As explained by Xiaobing Li in Chapter 3, the initial tactics of the Chinese forces in 1950 involved using mass numbers—even launching daylight attacks—until losses caused by overwhelming air and artillery support caused them to revert to movement and attack primarily at night. Attack tactics were to close on UN forces as closely as possible, avoiding detection, then to charge, using grenades and burp guns, with movements frequently controlled by whistles and bugles. Preliminary stick grenade assault was standard. Some UN and Australian reports speak of enemy assault waves not having any weapons at all, but relying on picking up the weapons of Chinese soldiers killed in earlier waves.

In a conversation with a Chinese colonel who had been a staff officer with a division in Korea in 1950–51, he confirmed that there was an initial shortage of radios and that Chinese forces did use bugles to communicate and control assaults. He also pointed out that they had reverted to night attacks, but would not agree that unarmed soldiers were sent into battle. He said weapons were picked up only if they were better than the one the soldier was carrying.

Later discussions with staff colleagues at the Canadian Army Staff College, members from Princess Patricia's Canadian Light Infantry who had fought at Kapyong, echoed the platoon experiences of 3RAR.

Attack battle

Australia had only one major attack battle in Korea, which was at Maryang San: Operation Commando, which must rank as one of the most successful battalion battles fought by Australian troops. It is covered by Bob Breen in Chapter 10 of this book, so again I will provide a brief overview.

The outstanding success of Operation Commando, putting aside the brilliance of the battalion commander's actions, was again due to the professionalism and the aggressive leadership shown by experienced company commanders—and by so many professionally trained young platoon commanders and battle-experienced warrant officers and NCOs, leading soldiers of high morale and good training. Australia subsequently took most of these same warrant officers and NCOs to Vietnam, together with a new generation of similarly professionally trained young officers and soldiers (both regulars and national servicemen) of high morale and aggression. In that war, with such men, it is no wonder we did as well as we did.

Operation Commando was the epitome of infantry minor tactics, a battle of basic fire and movement, of aggressive assault, of defence against counter-attack, of aggressive leadership and determined response by troops to get what they were after. This was a classic infantry battle, fought and won at platoon level, with platoons passing through platoons to sustain pressure on the enemy and keep the momentum of the assault going, while other platoons gave covering fire. Frequently, Bren gunners would take over faltering assaults to maintain the momentum of attacks, followed by Australian troops attacking enemy positions with grenades, then charging with bayonets. This was a six-day attack battle, up ridges against an entrenched enemy, where assault frontages were at times reduced to a few men on ridge lines. Again, assaults were successful with the assistance of great artillery support. Time was always of the essence. Instant obedience to orders by all in the attack, the willingness to press on under fire, and for soldiers to assume command when section commanders were wounded, all led to success.

The static war

As other chapters have attested, in the last one and a half years of the war Korea moved from high-level tactics of divisions, brigades and battalions to a platoon-level, tactical war—or, more correctly, a patrol commanders' war. It was a war of artillery and mortar duels, of trenches and dugouts, of patrols and raids to capture prisoners, the occupation of high ground; a war of mines and barbed wire; a war in which Australian battalions would commit at least a quarter of their strength, night after night, to protect positions by dominating no man's land with patrols of all kinds—fighting, ambush, reconnaissance, standing, protective, listening posts—and by applying tactics learnt from the two world wars.

It became a war in which enemy artillery and mortar fire could be as intense as our own, and in which our tanks supported patrols, not by moving with us, but by firing from static positions and sniping against enemy bunkers. Enemy patrolling and reaction was frequently as aggressive and as successful as ours, and a well-armed enemy negated our air superiority by mounting major operations only at night. It remained, for us, a war led by experienced Second World War company commanders and a great proportion of four-year-trained young professional platoon commanders. The impact of this patrol war can be gauged by considering that of the 30 members of my Duntroon class who went to Korea, more than 60 per cent were killed, captured or seriously wounded during that patrol phase of the war.

The static period of the Korean War was interspersed with several operations above platoon level, including when the 1st Battalion, Royal Australian Regiment (1RAR), launched a conventional daylight company attack against the well-defended enemy Hill 227, and a night company attack on a hill behind enemy front lines near Hill 355. Both were at company level and involved classic company attacks, designed to capture prisoners; both ended without success. Heavily supported, they reached their objectives, and occupied enemy-held trenches and assaulted the enemy with bayonets and grenades. As David Horner points out in Chapter 8, during the last three days of the war, the 2nd Battalion, Royal Australian Regiment (2RAR), and US Marines fought a major defensive battle on the Hook against massed Chinese attacks.

The period of static defence during the Korean War was defined by a number of key characteristics that influenced the tactics of Australian forces. Frequently, infantry would be required to support air attacks against enemy positions by firing across the valley into enemy bunkers to prevent them firing against UN air assets. This was one of the few instances, so far as I know, when the army supported the air force. Australian forces also used tanks and riflemen to act as snipers, while search lights were critical in illuminating no man's land and assisting defensive patrols. Night sentries were normally present in every section and included at least two soldiers. Defensive locations were based on platoons and were connected to company headquarters by communication trenches. While forward, platoons were generally on isolated hilltops, and beyond this were small standing patrols or listening posts. These forward listening and observation posts were responsible for raising the alarm if the enemy was approaching and to count Australian patrols going out and coming back. The posts were connected to their platoon and company by land telephone line.

In the closing stages of the Korean War, some defensive positions had become complex and sophisticated. Such defensive positions had extensive overhead protection; troops could withdraw and call down friendly fire on top of their own position if the enemy were there. Mines were laid in front of defensive locations but were of mixed benefit because they rarely stopped enemy probes and tended to limit their own movements—patrols had to go out through known mine gaps, and come back the same way, which the enemy got to know. Confusion was caused by differing layouts used by the various UN units. Minefields were delineated by fences, which could be destroyed by fire or hidden by vegetation. Markers were lost. Disoriented patrols returning from a contact would wander into their own minefields, resulting in casualties. Reinforcements were not always aware of the locations of minefield gaps, but the enemy knew them all. At times minefields included drums of fuel detonated by trip wire or by explosive bullets. As in the First World War, barbed wire proved to be a formidable defensive obstacle and was often placed at the front of trenches to slow down enemy forces.

Artillery played a critical role for both sides during the Korean War. Australian forces were often supported by extensive defensive fire from behind their lines. North Korean and the Chinese forces frequently knew where the Australian defensive fire would fall, having previously located the locations through patrol contacts. Artillery support was also an essential aid to Australian patrol commanders navigating their way through no man's land and identifying enemy positions.

Patrols during the static war period

The patrol war gave junior leaders the opportunity to use their own tactics of movement, with formations and use of weapons that were best suited to individual tasks and the abilities of the leaders and their platoons. Formations varied, depending on the platoon commander: single file, file, arrowhead, blob or box formation. Patrol leaders decided how many automatic weapons to take with them and how many they had to leave in their position for the defence of their defended localities. They decided where to place those weapons, what action the patrol would take on contact with the enemy, the use of grenades, and the use and layout of ambush formations. Patrol leaders also decided how to establish firm bases, from which they would frequently detach small reconnaissance or snatch groups to take prisoners from enemy lines.

Box formation was one popular patrol grouping, with men moving out spaced in a rough rectangular shape, with the commander in the centre. This allowed good control and communication within the patrol, aggressive immediate assault action on contact with the enemy and a ready-made, all-round ambush formation.

1st Battalion, Royal Australian Regiment patrols: Hill 355

A good example of how and why Australian troops patrolled, the intensity they experienced and the enemy tactics they encountered, is an operation undertaken by 1RAR on Hill 355 in October and November 1952.

Hill 355, which had been taken as part of Operation Commando, was considered to be divisional 'vital ground'. Not surprisingly, Chinese forces decided to recapture it from the defending UN unit. The enemy had detected that little patrolling was being done by the UN unit. Over a number of nights, the enemy crossed no man's land in the valley and was unhindered as it dug caves and tunnels big enough to shelter large numbers of troops from artillery fire around the base of Hill 355. Attacking troops infiltrated, without interception, across the valley into these caves before attacking the hill. When the attack started, UN artillery defensive fire, which might have caught enemy troops crossing the valley, was largely ineffective, as the enemy was already protected and on its objectives. Before the attack was defeated, the enemy captured the forward UN company position on the hill, and our battalion was sent to relieve the UN unit the next morning. This meant clearing and restoring the completely demolished forward company positions and starting an intensive patrol program to dominate no man's land.

The program immediately implemented by 1RAR was to saturate no man's land with fighting patrols. Many platoons conducted two fighting patrols each night for around two weeks. The platoon commander would take half the platoon from last light to midnight, then the platoon sergeant would take the other half from midnight to dawn. The caves used by Chinese forces for their attack were destroyed, and minefields and barbed wire were restored. Although some contacts with enemy patrols occurred, no other Chinese raid or attack was mounted on Hill 355 for the duration of our time there. I think it is fair to say that this can be largely attributed to the fact that we dominated no man's land.

Chinese defensive patrol tactics

Chinese patrol tactics were similar to Australian defensive patrol tactics. Chinese patrols were well armed and reacted with aggression. There are numerous examples of the enemy rapidly reacting to our patrols, by artillery fire and despatching their own patrols, sometimes at platoon strength, to attack our firm bases, which we had set up before sending off recce or snatch groups. The enemy closely followed up and attacked our withdrawal from these firm bases.

Frequently Chinese forces would set up ambushes near entrances to (or even inside) our minefields in order to catch patrols that had relaxed and let their guard down after a night's operations. One tactic Chinese forces used to their advantage was heavily bombarding our positions around last light to prevent Australian patrols moving out—for it was frequently a race to get into no man's land first to establish ambush positions. Under cover of artillery, the enemy could get patrols into the valley after the artillery fire had lifted, then ambush our patrols coming out, at times catching us silhouetted against the skyline as we came down the ridges.

Conclusion

It is fair to conclude that minor tactics, the movement and operation at platoon level in Korea, were remarkable only because of their similarity to proven tactics of previous wars. This was largely because the weapons and technology in use had changed little. While the terrain was adapted to, the cold was perhaps the only new major influencing factor.

A major difference, for Australian troops at least, was the existence of an almost entirely well-trained force led by experienced or well-trained professionals at junior levels of leadership. Tried and tested tactics of the desert and jungles of the Second World War were mirrored in actions in 1950 and 1951, while conditions and operations of the First World War were evident from 1952 to 1953.

I would like to conclude with a quote about infantry in the Second World War. The words are from the Australian company commander Joe Gullett's book, *Not as a Duty Only*. On my return from Korea, he gave me a copy of his book with some areas marked. I quote his words, as I believe they epitomise the actions and the spirit of our rifle platoons in Korea:

> An infantry battalion in being implies a state of mind—I am not sure it is not a state of grace. It involves a giving and a taking, a sharing of almost everything—comforts, possessions, trust and confidence. It implies doing a hundred different things together—marching to the band, marching all night long, being hungry, thirsty, dirty, being near to but never quite mutinous. It involves the spirit to carry things through to the butt and bayonet and the determination that what we go for, we get and what we get, we hold.[2]

This was the spirit shown by Australian infantry platoons in Korea.

---

2 H. Gullett, *Not as a Duty Only*, Melbourne University Press, Melbourne, 1976, pp. 1–2.

PART 4

THE WAR ON THE GROUND

New Zealand artillerymen provided accurate and devastating firepower in attack and defence to various nationalities of the United Nations Command.

Source: National Library of New Zealand—Te Puna Mātauranga o Aotearoa Ref: K-1216-F.

Lieutenant Colonel Frank Hassett (centre) took over 3RAR during a period of change and, with support of his junior officers, welded the battalion into a fine fighting unit.
Source: AWM 044485.

In the early hours of 3 October 1951, the start of Operation Commando, A and B Companies, 3RAR, crossed this valley floor and captured Hill 199.
Source: AWM 044744.

PART 4

British units in Korea were brought up to strength with national servicemen and men from other battalions. Private Bill Speakman of the Argyll and Sutherland Highlanders served with the King's Own Scottish Borderers and was awarded the Victoria Cross.
Source: AWM HOBJ2808.

Wounded soldiers were often sent to Japan for further treatment and convalescence. Pictured is Second Lieutenant William Purves of the King's Own Scottish Borderers, resting at the Commonwealth Forces Convalescent Depot in Kure, Japan.
Source: AWM LEEJ0057.

Captain Perditta 'Dita' McCarthy, of the Royal Australian Army Nursing Service, served at the British Commonwealth General Hospital at Kure during the Korean War and took part in aeromedical evacuation flights to Korea.
Source: AWM HOBJ0204.

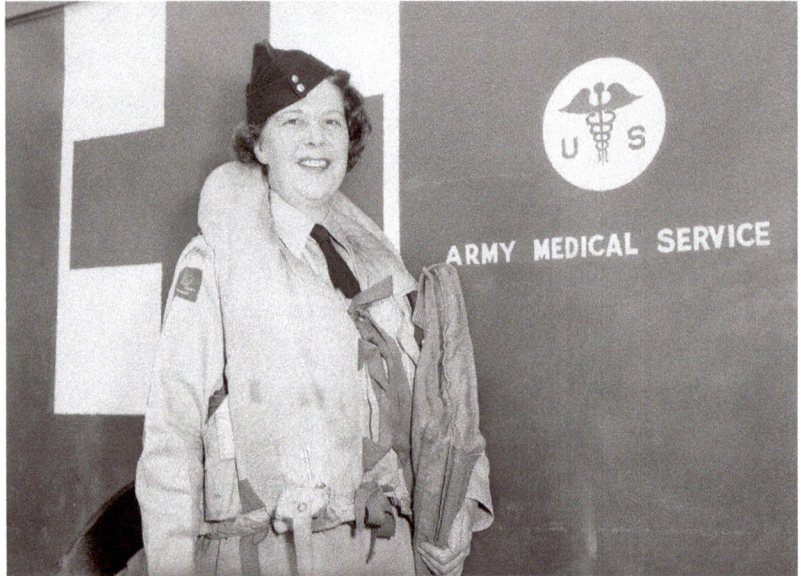

Sister Betty Washington, of the Royal Australian Air Force Nursing Service, had over a period of 10 months amassed 259 hours on casualty evacuation flights between Kimpo and Japan.
Source: AWM FEAF0656.

The morning after the armistice came into effect, Australian soldiers stand above their front-line trenches at the Hook. For the first time in more than three years the front line was silent.
Source: AWM P04641.105.

Defence in depth was vital in case of a Chinese breakthrough. Here men from 2RAR unload timber baulks to construct bunkers, most likely on the Hook.
Source: State Library of Victoria H2001.200/2747.

10

THE BATTLE OF MARYANG SAN
Australia's finest feat of arms in the Korean War?

Bob Breen

The Korean War was the first test of the fighting qualities of the newly named Royal Australian Regiment. After the arrival of 3rd Battalion, Royal Australian Regiment (3RAR), a series of encounter battles during the United Nations forces' advance to the Yalu River in North Korea in late 1950 and two deliberate battles at Kapyong and Maryang San in 1951 stand out as fine feats of arms that took place during the manoeuvre phase of the Korean War.[1] Participation in the Battle of Kapyong has the most prominent place in Australia's Korean War military history because American, Australian, British, Canadian and New Zealand troops delayed a major Chinese thrust towards South Korea's capital, Seoul, from 24 to 26 April 1951 and won a US Presidential Citation. The defensive determination of outnumbered Australians and their fighting withdrawal prompted enduring national and international recognition.

---

1   R. O'Neill, *Australia in the Korean War 1950–1953*, vol. 2: *Combat Operations*, AWM & AGPS, Canberra, 1985, chapters 6 and 8.

The capture of a peak known as Maryang San as part of an effort by UN forces to secure high ground and straighten the line before an armistice in early October 1951 has received far less attention. Fighting for territory is less interesting and noteworthy than saving Seoul from advancing Chinese troops. Although seized and defended against a Chinese counter-attack by 3RAR, Maryang San was later lost and never recovered by UN forces. It stands unoccupied in the Demilitarised Zone between North and South Korea to this day. However, this battle merits consideration as Australia's finest feat of arms in the Korean War. For those who know the battle, such as Professor Robert O'Neill, the official historian for Australia's participation in the Korean War, there is little doubt:

> In this action 3RAR had won one of the most impressive victories achieved by any Australian battalion. In five days of heavy fighting 3RAR dislodged a numerically superior enemy from a position of great strength. The Australians were successful in achieving surprise on 3 and 5 October, the company and platoon commanders responded skilfully to [Commanding Officer] Hassett's directions, and the individual soldiers showed high courage, tenacity and morale despite some very difficult situations ... The victory of Maryang San is probably the greatest single feat of the Australian Army during the Korean War.[2]

Lieutenant General John Coates, the Australian Chief of the General Staff in 1991, echoed O'Neill's assessment:

> The scale of manoeuvre of the rifle companies of 3RAR during the action-packed five days of the battle—by night, in fog, across rugged terrain and for much of the time under artillery and mortar fire—can only challenge contemporary Australian infantrymen to strive for similar levels of excellence. The display of endurance, courage and aggression during the battle are timeless benchmarks for offensive operations.[3]

General Peter Cosgrove, former Chief of the Australian Defence Force, opined in the foreword to John Essex-Clark's biography of General Sir Francis Hassett, 'No other major battle in the Army's modern history more aptly underpins the qualities the Army strives for today'.[4]

---

2   Ibid., p. 200.
3   Lieutenant General H.J. Coates, Chief of the General Staff, foreword to B. Breen, *The Battle of Maryang San*, Headquarters Training Command, Balmoral, NSW, 1991.
4   J. Essex-Clark, foreword, *Hassett, Australian Leader: A Biography of General Sir Francis Hassett*, Australian Military History Publications, Loftus, NSW, 2005.

10. THE BATTLE OF MARYANG SAN

Against the odds

The comments of O'Neill, Coates and Cosgrove suggest that 3RAR must have been an experienced, superbly trained, cohesive and well-equipped battalion to have achieved in five days what American and British battalions had failed to achieve in other costly attacks.[5] Not so. Lieutenant Colonel Frank Hassett, a 33-year-old Duntroon graduate, had taken command in July 1951 without meeting his predecessor.[6] He had 10 weeks to adjust to working within a newly formed 28th British Commonwealth Brigade under its inaugural commander, Brigadier George Taylor.

The strength of 3RAR lay in the experience of individuals, not in unit cohesion. By the end of September, many of those who had fought during the winter campaign were returning to Australia at the end of their 12-month tour of duty. Hassett described the battalion as 'a "transit camp" in action … [I]n August/September there were perhaps over 200 replacements and this continued up to and including the battle'.[7] Fortunately, many of the replacements were experienced Second World War veterans, but others were new. Hassett described the unblooded reinforcements as 'K Force volunteers, patriotic and adventurous young men fired up by the experiences and stories of the Second World War'. There were differences and rivalries between the older veterans and the newly arrived enthusiastic infantrymen. He opined later that 3RAR 'was basically an organised collection of well-trained individuals which had been strung out in a defensive position for the past three months and was quite unpractised as a unit in the battle procedures and techniques required for a battalion in attack'.[8]

The preparedness of the companies for offensive operations was low. Ahead was a multiphased attack against well-fortified positions occupied by experienced troops who had repelled US battalion attacks with heavy casualties. They would also repel British attacks during what was called Operation Commando.[9] Major Jack Gerke, commanding C Company, had a small number of non-commissioned officers and soldiers with some previous experience in action. He was the only officer in the company who

---

5   O'Neill, *Combat Operations*, p. 184 (American attacks) and pp. 186–7 (British attack).
6   Essex-Clark, *Hassett, Australian Leader*, p. 170.
7   Ibid., p. 23.
8   Breen, *The Battle of Maryang San*, pp. 7–8.
9   Essex-Clark, *Hassett, Australian Leader*, p. 6.

had been under fire.¹⁰ Two of his platoon commanders were Lieutenants Maurie Pears and Arthur 'Bushy' Pembroke, who had both graduated from Duntroon in December 1950 and arrived in Korea in July 1951. Major Jack 'Basil' Hardiman, commanding D Company, remembered that his heart stopped for a second when Hassett told him that he was to be first in the assault on Maryang San. His company was down to 72 men from its entitlement strength of 140. The other companies of 3RAR were also well below full strength. He later noted: 'I thought how unprepared we were for such an operation—too many new faces, lacking some items of equipment and not fit enough for a long, tough attack. We [had] spent the last three months in defence. In attack you use entirely different muscles to defence.'¹¹

Bold attack plans

Brigadier Taylor's attack plan worried his two British battalion commanders, one of whom reportedly feared it might cost a thousand casualties.¹² Taylor had little choice but to accept the objectives given to him by his divisional commander, Major General Jim Cassels.¹³ Cassels's promise of the division's artillery, together with US batteries from Corps and Eighth Army, as well as close support from Centurion tanks, should have comforted Taylor's British subordinates. Hassett trusted Cassels and Taylor, and kept his own counsel.¹⁴

For phase 1, Taylor directed Lieutenant Colonel John Barlow, commanding 1st Battalion, King's Shropshire Light Infantry (KSLI), to drive Chinese defenders from three hills south of the phase 2 objective, a large hill (Hill 355) known locally as Kowang San and nicknamed 'Little Gibraltar'.¹⁵ Lieutenant Colonel John MacDonald, commanding 1st Battalion, King's Own Scottish Borderers (KOSBs), had the mission of seizing Little Gibraltar in phase 2. For phase 3, Taylor ordered the Australians to capture Maryang San, a towering hill that rose sharply to a pinnacle located across a valley north of Little Gibraltar. Taylor gave

---

10   Breen, *The Battle of Maryang San*, p. 10.
11   Ibid., pp. 11–12.
12   Essex-Clark, *Hassett, Australian Leader*, p. 9.
13   A. Farrar-Hockley, *The British Part in the Korean War*, vol. 2: *An Honourable Discharge*, HMSO, London, 1995, p. 218.
14   Breen, *The Battle of Maryang San*, pp. 13–14.
15   Farrar-Hockley, *An Honourable Discharge*, pp. 219–20.

1st Battalion, Royal Northumberland Fusiliers—a unit seconded from the British 29th Infantry Brigade and scheduled to leave Korea after Operation Commando—the task of capturing a hill adjacent to Maryang San, nicknamed 'the Hinge', after seizing a heavily fortified Chinese position on Hill 217, located on the ridge line south of the Hinge.[16]

Hassett matched Taylor's audacious plan with one of his own. Despite his youth, Hassett was a veteran of the South-West Pacific campaign in the Second World War, and he had seen Australian battalion commanders use ground and timing effectively against Japanese defensive positions.[17] He persuaded Taylor to withdraw his direction for the Australians to attack Maryang San frontally across the valley. Hassett wanted to surprise and split the fire of the Chinese, in both the timing and direction of attack by assaulting out of the morning gloom along a line of knolls from a flank (nicknamed by the British as Victor, Whiskey, Uniform and Tango). At the same time, he would distract them with a noisy diversionary attack from Major Jim Shelton's A Company, positioned in the valley with Centurion tanks from the 8th Royal Irish Hussars.[18] Hassett's plan obliged his assault companies to navigate silently by night, over rough terrain (hills with thick timber and long grass) and creep up to Chinese fortifications, taking advantage of first light to assault over a short distance and be among the defenders with grenade, bullet, butt and bayonet before everyone was awake: close combat through a labyrinth of trenches, foxholes and bunkers.[19]

Adaptability

The Australians and the KSLI successfully captured the forward Chinese positions on 2 October, and the remainder of the brigade deployed for phase 2, but Taylor's plan faltered the next day when the KOSBs failed to take the heights of Little Gibraltar (or Kowang San). Early on 4 October, Taylor directed Hassett to support a renewed attack by the KOSBs by driving the defenders from two hills close to the main Chinese fortifications. Chinese flanking fire from these two hills had worried the

---

16 O'Neill, *Combat Operations*, pp. 183–5.
17 Ibid., p. 184; see also Essex-Clark, *Hassett, Australian Leader*, p. 15.
18 Breen, *The Battle of Maryang San*, pp. 18–22, and O'Neill, *Combat Operations*, pp. 185–94.
19 For a detailed description of Hassett's thinking at the time, see Essex-Clark, *Hassett, Australian Leader*, pp. 18–27.

KOSBs the day before.[20] Twenty-one-year-old Lieutenant Maurie Pears's platoon led Jack Gerke's C Company's assault at first light after a pre-dawn approach march. The element of surprise resulted in the first hill falling quickly, and the second fell after heavy fighting. Maintaining momentum as the Chinese withdrew in front of them, the Australians raced to high ground on top of the north-eastern end of Little Gibraltar.[21]

As it happens, whether 3RAR could claim to have taken Little Gibraltar that morning is highly contested, as Chapter 11 by Nigel Steel explains. Steel suggests that Australian authors were influenced by nationalistic bias. For his part, Bob Breen, who wrote his monograph on the Battle of Maryang San on the basis of interviews with Australian veterans of the battle and Robert O'Neill's Australian official history, clarified Australian claims in 2011.[22] He observed that Little Gibraltar had two peaks that were assaulted simultaneously and occupied by British and Australian forces at different times. No one would know who arrived at one of the peaks first without also knowing the exact time artillery fire was lifted from the peak to allow infantry to occupy. Michael Hickey, a British military historian, wrote accurately, 'Both units were to claim, correctly, that they had taken "Little Gibraltar", for neither would have got there without the unseen support of the other'.[23]

Nonetheless Taylor's two-pronged Australian–British attack during the second attempt to capture Little Gibraltar split the enemy fire. Fearing being overrun by simultaneous Australian and British assaults, the Chinese defenders withdrew north to the Maryang San defensive positions. The KOSBs fought up three ridge lines and moved through, bagpipes playing, to occupy vacated Chinese defensive positions around the heights.[24] The Australian attack had been 'of considerable assistance to 1 KOSB in the final stages' of the capture of Little Gibraltar.[25] Taylor

---

20 O'Neill, *Combat Operations*, p. 187; also D. Butler, A. Argent and J. Shelton, *The Fight Leaders: A Study of Australian Battlefield Leadership: Green, Ferguson and Hassett*, Australian Military History Publications, Loftus, NSW, 2002, p. 132.
21 O'Neill, *Combat Operations*, pp. 187–8.
22 B. Breen, 'The Battle of Maryang San: Australia's finest feat of arms in the Korean War?', www.awm.gov.au/visit/events/conference/korea.
23 M. Hickey, *The Korean War: The West Confronts Communism 1950–53*, John Murray, London, 1999, pp. 256–9.
24 J.F.H. MacDonald, *The Borderers in Korea*, Martin's Printing, Berwick-upon-Tweed, UK, 1954, pp. 32–3.
25 Directorate of Infantry, AHQ, 'Operation Commando, Korea, 2–8 Oct. 1951', *Australian Army Journal*, no. 34, March 1952, pp. 5–13; quote from p. 7.

was delighted with the Australians' performance.[26] His attack plan was one day behind schedule, but he had succeeded in taking the first of the brigade's three objectives—one of the most important in General Cassels's overall plan.

For phase 3 of the brigade's attack, Hassett regrouped his companies and adapted his plan to accommodate his reserve company's casualties. The Australians prepared for their assault on Maryang San on 5 October, and the Fusiliers prepared to attack towards the Hinge via Hill 217. Although Hassett did not know it then, the Australian assault force of 320 men (approximate numbers in A, B, C and D Companies)[27] faced a fresh, well-equipped and well-supplied regiment of three battalions (571st Regiment), numbering about 2,000 men. Of this force, a battalion of at least 600 or 700 men awaited the Australian and British infantrymen on Maryang San and the Hinge.[28] It would have been unthinkable for an Australian national commander to have signed off on this attack plan during recent operations in Iraq or in Afghanistan in the 2000s. The preference at the time was for the ratio of attackers to defenders to be 3:1, not 2:1. Taylor depended on indirect firepower (approximately 120 guns, howitzers and mortars), as well as tank and medium machine-gun fire to make up the difference, while using age-old tactics such as deception, surprise and different axes of assault.[29]

Resilience

On the morning of 5 October 1951, four companies made up of three platoons of less than 25 men each set out to meet their fate through the night and fog—a navigational nightmare but a tactical godsend. The fog lifted by mid-morning as D Company, the forward assault company, found themselves less than 50 metres from the edge of the Chinese positions.[30] B Company, the other assault company, had become lost during the approach march and took no part in the attack, but provided useful flank security for D Company. A Chinese medium machine gun fired into Major Hardiman's D Company headquarters as the fog lifted, wounding

---

26 Breen, *The Battle of Maryang San*, p. 105.
27 Various sources put Australian rifle companies at between 70 and 90 strong on 2 October. The figure of 320 is reached by multiplying the average (80) by four companies.
28 O'Neill, *Combat Operations*, p. 184.
29 Ibid., p. 184.
30 Ibid., p. 190.

him and one of his platoon commanders, Geoff Leary. Another platoon commander, Lieutenant Jim Young, took command of the company. Its three platoons were now being led by sergeants, one of whom, Sergeant Bill Rowlinson, went on to earn a Bar to the Distinguished Conduct Medal that he had won at Kapyong in April.[31] The company regrouped under new commanders and attacked the Chinese positions, inflicting heavy casualties as they went—savage, close-quarter fighting with point-blank shooting and the use of grenades and bayonets, accompanied by the yells of men killing surprised Chinese defenders, and roaring orders and warnings to each other.

Endurance

Young and his men took the first knoll leading to Maryang San, sustaining further casualties but inflicting many more. Hassett and his New Zealand direct support battery commander, Major Arthur Roxburgh, prepared an artillery and mortar-fire plan to support a further attack on a second knoll, but Hassett feared that Young and his men would be spent if they succeeded, and would therefore be unable to assault the final objective, the peak known as Maryang San. Another company would need to punch through after Young took his next objective. Hassett turned to Jack Gerke, his reserve company commander who had been so aggressive on the approaches to Little Gibraltar the day before, and ordered him to get in behind Young's men and move through them to assault Maryang San after they had taken their objective.[32] Gerke's men headed out for a forced march as Young's men waited for the end of the artillery bombardment of the Chinese positions ahead of them.

During D Company's earlier assault, Major Jim Shelton's A Company attacked the Chinese positions from the south-west to draw fire away from the main assault by D Company. His was the dangerous task of assaulting forward with tank and machine-gun support to get close enough to draw Chinese fire without risking significant casualties. Shelton's forward platoons, led by Kapyong veterans Sergeant George Harris and Lieutenant 'Freddy' Gardiner, emulated the aggression of their compatriots in C and D Companies and penetrated the Chinese defences, causing heavy enemy casualties in savage, close-quarter combat.[33]

---

31   Breen, *The Battle of Maryang San*, pp. 50–5.
32   O'Neill, *Combat Operations*, pp. 193–4, and Breen, *The Battle of Maryang San*, pp. 66–7.
33   Breen, *The Battle of Maryang San*, pp. 60–3.

When artillery and mortar fire lifted, Young and the remnants of D Company commenced their assault against the stunned Chinese, whose machine guns were pointed south and did not have time to turn and fire on the Australians: surprise, speed and aggression won the day. Nearly 70 Chinese defenders lay dead. More than a hundred wounded and 30 dazed prisoners fell into Australian hands. Three Australians were killed and 14 wounded. Just over 35 exhausted men remained unscathed.[34]

The victorious Jim Young and his men clapped and cheered as Gerke and his warriors pushed through their lines towards Maryang San. Ahead of the final Australian assault, artillery and mortars pounded the peak, shattering the enemy's confidence; they abandoned the heights now that the eastern approaches were in Australian hands. The Australian assault was an anti-climax of climbing on hands and knees to the summit for a grand view of the surrounding countryside. The honour of taking a second summit in 24 hours fell to Maurie Pears.[35] Hassett consolidated his blackened, bedraggled and exhausted troops around his prize, and for the first time in four days of fighting and moving with heavy loads, the Australians had a night of rest interrupted only by sentry duty.

The next morning Lieutenant Arthur 'Bushy' Pembroke's platoon attacked a Chinese company occupying an adjacent feature on the Maryang San ridgeline (Sierra) to give the Australian position some depth before expected counter-attacks. Pembroke's dawn attack without preliminary artillery or mortar bombardment caught the Chinese by surprise; he and his 21 men, outnumbered and outgunned, drove off more than a hundred startled Chinese defenders, inflicting casualties in a brisk action.[36]

The Hinge

Once again, Taylor's attack plan faltered. This time the Fusiliers failed to capture the Hinge on 5 October or during a second attempt the following day.[37] He turned to Hassett again. This time Hassett assigned Captain Henry 'Wings' Nicholls's B Company to form up behind the position of Pembroke's platoon on Sierra and to assault the Hinge after an

---

34 Ibid., pp. 55–60.
35 Ibid., pp. 68–70.
36 Ibid., pp. 78–80.
37 O'Neill, *Combat Operations*, pp. 195–7; Breen, *The Battle of Maryang San*, pp. 82–6.

artillery bombardment once the morning mist had lifted. The assault was successful, but the ensuing retaliation from Chinese artillery and mortars forced Nicholls and his men into the Chinese trenches. Indeed, the whole Maryang San position had become perilous as the Chinese pounded it in preparation for a major counter-attack.[38]

Defence of Maryang San, 7–8 October

By this time, the Australians had been moving and fighting for almost five days without respite, and had sustained more than a hundred casualties—almost a third of their starting number. Taylor had overextended them to occupy the Hinge. Hassett later recalled:

> Platoons were now down to 15 to 20 strong, too low for orthodox tactical use. It was not just the casualties. Most were physically exhausted. Lack of sleep and battle stress apart, just moving under heavy load, let alone fighting, in hilly, difficult terrain was most demanding. The Battalion was just about spent.[39]

The Chinese had given the Australians some respite on the night of 5/6 October before shelling them on 6 and 7 October. Hassett and his men now dug in on Maryang San and the Hinge, evacuating wounded and running the gauntlet to supply everyone with ammunition, rations and water before the coming battle. For this dangerous work, stoical Korean porters made round trips under steady Chinese artillery and mortar fire. As night fell on 7 October, Chinese assault formations crept stealthily to the edge of Australian positions on the Hinge. The time had come to test whether the Australians were as good at defending as they were at attacking.

At 8 pm Chinese artillery and mortars began a 45-minute preparatory bombardment, followed by the first assault.[40] Like a battle cry, the Australians shouted to each other, 'Watch your front!' The Chinese attacked twice more during the night. Low on ammunition, the Australians took to the enemy as they arrived in pitiless hand-to-hand fighting, kicking, strangling and bayoneting many to death. While under fire, brave Korean porters carried ammunition in and wounded Australians out on

---

38 O'Neill, *Combat Operations*, p. 197.
39 Breen, *The Battle of Maryang San*, p. 88.
40 Ibid., pp. 92–3.

stretchers.[41] American, British and New Zealand artillery and mortars scythed through the ranks of attacking Chinese, leaving more than 120 bodies and hundreds of body parts strewn in front of the Australian positions the next morning.

Taylor decided to relieve the Australians with the KOSBs after their night of battle; they had done enough after six days of forced marches and combat. After dawn on 8 October, Hassett permitted Chinese medical orderlies and stretcher parties to come forward and collect scores of wounded under a flag of truce. The Australians began to withdraw from their hard-won territory later that day. Taylor recalled later that Frank Hassett and his men had exemplified the attacking spirit required take Maryang San and the terrain leading to its peak. 'It was a very emotional moment for me when I went to see the battalion after it occupied new positions to thank all ranks from the bottom of my heart for the great part they had played in ensuring victory in a very tough battle.'[42] During the six days of fighting, 3RAR suffered 20 killed in action and 89 wounded in action, with 15 of the wounded remaining on duty.[43] In combination with artillery, mortar and tank fire, it was estimated that two Chinese battalions had been decimated and a brigade forced to withdraw from well-prepared defensive positions.

The final word goes to General Sir Francis Hassett:

> Unquestionably, the soldiers won the Maryang San battle, not just because they were brave, but because they were smart also. They recognised that if they were to get 317 [Maryang San] at all, let alone without massive casualties, then they had to move quickly. This they did. There were no heroes' welcome home for these warriors. They left from Australia [in 1950 and 1951] as individuals or in small groups and returned the same way, unheralded and unsung. Somehow, it did not seem to matter. There was much quiet satisfaction just knowing that one had fought at Maryang San.[44]

---

41 Ibid., pp. 96–100.
42 Ibid., pp. 100–1.
43 Breen, *The Battle of Maryang San*, pp. 111–12.
44 Ibid., p. 125.

11

CONQUERING KOWANG SAN, ASSAULTING UNITED

Myth and misunderstanding in the shade of Maryang San, October 1951

Nigel Steel

Without doubt the story of the capture of Maryang San or Hill 317 by the 3rd Battalion, Royal Australian Regiment (3RAR), is a superlative tale of leadership, command and control, determination and aggression. But I am uneasy at the way some histories portrayed the wider British contribution to Operation Commando. The war diaries and other published records of the two main British battalions involved—the 1st King's Own Scottish Borderers (the KOSBs) and the 1st Royal Northumberland Fusiliers (RNF, or the Fusiliers)—contain sharp conflicts of evidence with many of the accounts in Australia, which is what I want to address in this chapter. I do so in a spirit of intellectual investigation and not in any way to score points or denigrate anyone's performance.

Regrettably there is no space to give anything but the gist of Operation Commando, which aimed to place the Commonwealth Division on a series of heights west of the Imjin River, close to the current Demilitarised Zone (DMZ). As Map 4 shows, the 28th British Commonwealth Brigade's primary objective—Hill 355, known as Kowang San—was allocated to the KOSBs. To the south were a series of hills (referred to by the British as Points) named after their heights in metres as Hills 208, 209, 210 and ultimately 227. These were to be taken by the 1st King's Shropshire Light

Infantry (KSLI). To the north, Hill 317, better known as Maryang San, was the target of 3RAR, supported by a subsidiary attack against Hill 217 by the Fusiliers. Holding Hills 355, 317 and 217 was a full Chinese regiment, with one battalion on Hill 355, another in the area of Hill 317 and a final in reserve. A battalion from a separate regiment held the ridge to the south of Kowang San.

The commander of the 28th Brigade, British Army Brigadier George Taylor, devised a bold and ambitious plan. The terrain over which the brigade was to attack was difficult and complicated and, according to a later account by the KOSB's commanding officer, chiefly 'consisted of steep-sided hills of rock and sandstone, for the most part covered by dense pine forests'.[1] British units, including the 28th Brigade headquarters, used a series of distinctive names for the operation's main features. In particular, as the ridge leading north onto Hill 317 was to be assaulted by men from Northumberland, the features were called in turn Newcastle, United, Football and Club. But those closer to Hill 317 were later renamed, with Football eventually becoming known as the Hinge and Club as the Knoll.

The KOSBs formed part of the 28th Brigade and the assault on Hill 355 was their first major battle. They were to assault the hill's southern and eastern flanks. On the right, B Company would move directly against Finger Ridge, which led up towards the two 220-metre features later assaulted by 3RAR's C Company. On the left, the KOSBs' C Company was first to take the operational features of Long, then Kidney. The remainder of the battalion would finally swing north-west onto the summit of Hill 355 itself.

The battalion moved off shortly before 7 am on 3 October. B Company made steady progress, 'despite heavy artillery and mortar fire', the KOSBs commanding officer noted,[2] and the battalion's war diary recorded that by 8.55 am it had reached its 'objective with no contact'.[3] To the south, C Company, 3RAR had more trouble against Long. By 8.27 am, it had covered half the distance to Long, but 'became engaged in fierce hand-to-hand fighting. The enemy was holding the feature in considerable strength and offered fanatical resistance from well-prepared and

---

1 J.F.M. Macdonald, *The Borderers in Korea*, Martin's Printing Works, Berwick upon Tweed, UK, 1954, p. 31.
2 Ibid., p. 32.
3 1st King's Own Scottish Borderers [KOSB], war diary, 3 October 1951, 0855 [hours], National Archives [TNA], WO281/484.

ingeniously concealed positions'.[4] It was not until 11.15 am that the KOSB's C Company reached the crest of Long. But 2nd Lieutenant William Purves explained some years later that as they did so, he believed, they made a basic error:

> That was my first real attacking position and the secret, of course, is that you don't stop at the top. You've got to go over the hill, even though that exposes you to enemy fire, you've got to go over the hill and see what's on the other side, and whether the enemy is dug in on the other side. And while we did it to some degree, I make the excuse that we were all exhausted. But this enabled quite a significant body of Chinese to creep up on us when we were trying to recover from our climb.[5]

Already hit by heavy Chinese mortar fire, the KOSB's C Company were assailed by a series of close-quarter Chinese counter-attacks, mostly by grenade. Under this pressure, C Company was ordered back to regroup at around 12.20 pm before making another effort to take Long.

Realising that C Company was unlikely to be able to succeed on its own, the KOSB battalion commander, Lieutenant Colonel John Macdonald, ordered A Company to link up with C Company for the assault. Arriving in the area as C Company fell back, A Company's commander, Major George Duncan, realised something extra was needed to bolster his own men's morale. One of his junior officers, 2nd Lieutenant Jock Foulis, remembered:

> The first thing he did was to send for the Pipe Major. He then led us to the position, and he and the Pipe Major—he wielding his walking stick, which was his trademark—he and the Pipe Major led the company with the Pipe Major playing the regimental charge, which I think historically is probably the last time that anybody went into action in a Scottish regiment led by a piper playing the regimental charge. It was a slightly unusual happening! … He had two platoons down on the right, a platoon down on the left, and George was silhouetted on the ridge line, with the piper, leading the company into the attack. And he was unscathed, the Pipe Major was unscathed and the company never stopped. There has to be a relationship between those things.[6]

---

4   Macdonald, *The Borderers in Korea*, pp. 31–2.
5   Sir William Purves, Imperial War Museum, Sound Archive (IWM SR) interview 20471, reel 2, 05:21.
6   Jock Foulis, IWM SR interview 19661, reel 3, 18:59.

At 2.15 pm, the KOSB's A and C Companies renewed the attack on Long. Within an hour it had been taken. According to the 28th Brigade war diary, 'The enemy by this time had been completely outfought'.[7] Leaving C Company to hold Long, at 4.35 pm A Company moved off to assault Kidney; by 5.15 pm it was firmly established on this feature. By the time the position was consolidated, the CO pointed out, 'it was already getting dark'.[8] It was agreed that the KOSBs would remain in position along Finger Ridge, Long and Kidney, and renew the attack on Hill 355 the following morning.

The intention had been to capture Hill 355 on the first day of Operation Commando; on the second day, the Canadians were set to launch a parallel assault to the south at 6 am. To maintain the full weight of the Commonwealth Division's artillery in support of the KOSBs when they renewed their assault, the Canadian attack was now delayed until 11 am. Further support was also to be given to the KOSBs by the KSLI, who would complete the capture of Hills 210 and 227, by the Fusiliers' 3-inch mortars and by an air strike. The 28th Brigade also ordered 3RAR to send a company to attack two hills, both 220 metres high, which stood to the east of Hill 355 and from which the Chinese had levelled small-arms fire on the KOSBs throughout 3 October. The commander of 3RAR, Lieutenant Colonel Frank Hassett, decided to send C Company from his reserve.

But what task was C Company, 3RAR intended to undertake? 28th Brigade headquarters did not envisage the Australians joining the assault on Hill 355; they were there to support the KOSBs as the KOSBs completed this objective. The 28th Brigade initially noted the Australian company as being told to move onto the first of two 220-metre hills standing to the east of the summit,[9] recording clearly that 3RAR's company 'will not go over 18 grid line Westing', which meant it should not cross the line on the contemporary 1951 battle map that ran clearly north–south through the second 220-metre hill some way east of Hill 355.[10] The 28th Brigade's

---

7   28th Brigade, war diary, November 1951, TNA, WO281/140 [hereafter 28th Brigade, war diary], Appendix B, Lieutenant C.W. Crossland, 'The Battles of Kowang San and Maryang San', typescript narrative, p. 3.
8   Macdonald, *The Borderers in Korea*, p. 31.
9   28th Brigade, war diary, located as map reference 183198 on G7901 R1 s25 Sheet 6528 II NE, p. 143, s3-ap-southeast-2.amazonaws.com/awm-media/collection/RCDIG1027454/bundled/RCDIG 1027454.pdf.
10 28th Brigade, war diary, 4 October 1951, 0705 [hours].

war diary narrative talks about C Company, 3RAR 'assisting by attacking the Wangying Myon feature [the map name for the area around the first 220-metre hill[11]] and the small, strongly held hill to the south [the second 220-metre hill] that commanded the approach into the rear of Hill 355'.[12] Confusingly, Robert O'Neill's official history talks about Hassett being ordered to 'make a company attack on a 220-metre hill 700 metres northwest [*sic*] of the summit of Hill 355'.[13] But this cannot be so, as neither of the 220-metre hills lies 'north-west' of Kowang San. In a significant departure from the orders issued to it by the 28th Brigade, 3RAR's summary of operations notes the battalion's objective as being 'to make a company attack on feature 178192',[14] and possibly it is this feature to which O'Neill is also referring. But this map reference, well to the west of the 18 grid line, is not one of the two 220-metre hills. It is the north-eastern shoulder of Hill 355 itself, which is where C Company ended up. Both the battalion summary of operations and the official history appear simply to be confirming what actually happened, not what 3RAR was told to do. But even if this is so, this position lies directly north-east of Hill 355, not north-west of it.

C Company, 3RAR moved off at 5.45 am; at around 9.15 am they were cresting the first 220-metre hill,[15] where the 28th Brigade noted they 'completely routed' the Chinese.[16] At 9.45 am, the KOSBs began their assault—just as the Australians finished clearing the first 220-metre hill. Shortly after 10 am, the Australians moved on towards the second 220-metre hill. 3RAR's war diary noted, 'Heavy opposition met. C Company at 1015 hrs [10.15 am] were attacking enemy along ridge. Action lasted till 1215 hrs [12.15 pm]'.[17] The 28th Brigade recorded at 11.40 am that C Company, 3RAR was involved in 'hand to hand fighting' along the saddle connecting the two 220-metre hills.[18] The Australian

---

11   28th Brigade, war diary, located as map reference 183198, p. 143.
12   Map reference on 1951 battle map as 181191. See 28th Brigade, war diary, Appendix B, p. 4.
13   R. O'Neill, *Australia in the Korean War 1950–53*, vol. 2: *Combat Operations*, AWM & AGPS, Canberra, 1985, p. 187.
14   3RAR, war diary, October 1951, AWM85 4/34 [hereafter 3RAR, war diary], Appendix 10, typescript, 'Operation by 3RAR—2 Oct–8 Oct 51, "Commando I and II"', p. 2, para. 19. See also second report in Appendix 12, typescript, 'Summary of 3RAR ops 1 Oct—9 Oct', p. 2, para. 10.
15   3RAR, war diary, gives 5.45 am on map traces. O'Neill, *Combat Operations*, gives the time as 5.30 am.
16   28th Brigade, war diary, October 1951, Appendix M, typescript report, 'Operations against the enemy by 28 British Commonwealth Infantry Brigade on the 3rd to the 7th October 51', p. 1.
17   3RAR, war diary, annotation on map traces, dated 4 October 1951.
18   28th Brigade, war diary, 4 October 1951, 11.40 am.

official history also has the second 220-metre hill firmly 'in Australian hands' by 12.15 pm.[19] All sources consistently show C Company, 3RAR close to hitting 'its final objective' immediately adjacent to the 18 grid line shortly after midday.[20]

By this time, D Company of the KOSBs had taken Hill 355 and was dispersing its platoons across the summit. The documentary evidence for this is quite clear. The 28th Brigade war diary records: at 10.25 am, the KOSBs' forward troops were ascending the steep slope from Kidney to Hill 355; 15 minutes later, at 10.40 am, they were nearing the summit; at 11.04 am, '1 KOSB forward troops captured Pt 355 [Hill 355] at 1100 hrs [11 am]—one Platoon on 173189 [the summit of Hill 355], one Platoon at 176189 [forward slopes to the east of the summit leading towards the second 220-metre hill]'.[21]

The battalion's war diary confirms the capture of Kowang San (Hill 355) at 11 am and 30 minutes later corroborates it with the clear statement, 'D Company firm on Point 355 [Hill 355] with Battle Patrol remaining on 170187 [westward shoulder of Hill 355]'.[22] An hour later, roughly the same time that C Company, 3RAR was consolidating its hold on the second 220-metre hill, the 28th Brigade recorded the location of the KOSBs' companies: A Company still on Kidney, C Company on Long, D Company and the battalion's 'Battle Patrol' on Hill 355, and B Company moving up from Finger Ridge towards the north-eastern shoulder of Hill 355 at map reference 176191—almost the same map reference as the final objective for C Company given by 3RAR's summary of operations.[23]

It seems clear from all the available contemporary documentation that the KOSBs were on the summit of Hill 355 by 11 am and had firmly consolidated their hold by 12.30 pm. Yet this contradicts one of the prevalent Australian views that it was C Company, 3RAR that took Hill 355. How has this come about?

If you look closely at the few timings given in contemporary Australian documents, they do not clash with the British diaries, and the map traces at the end of 3RAR's war diary refer only to the two 220-metre hills, not to

---

19 O'Neill, *Combat Operations*, p. 187.
20 Ibid. The map reference 181191 is labelled 'final objective'.
21 28th Brigade, war diary, 4 October, 11.04 am.
22 KOSB, war diary, 4 October 1951, 11.30 am.
23 28th Brigade, war diary, 4 October 1951, 12.28 pm.

11. CONQUERING KOWANG SAN, ASSAULTING UNITED

Hill 355. Nor does 3RAR's summary of operations make any mention of 'taking' the hill, talking only of capturing the edge of Hill 355.[24] Referring to 'the area 178192'—which is the north-eastern shoulder of Hill 355—it goes on to state: 'This feature commanded the approach into the rear of Point 355 [Hill 355] and was strongly held. C Company carried out this attack at 0530 hours [5.30 am] in a very efficient manner and pressed it with great determination.'

The 28th Brigade's war diary makes it clear how important this attack was in supporting the KOSB's own assault. It concludes:

> This action was of considerable assistance to the Borderers who were attacking 355 with D Company and their Battle Patrol … Under the pressure of constant artillery fire and the subsidiary attack of C Company, 3RAR, they [the Chinese troops on 355] finally put up only token resistance to the assaulting Scots [KOSB's] who gallantly scaled the precipitous approaches.[25]

3RAR's move is clearly happening simultaneously with the main attack by the KOSBs, but is not the central element in clearing the summit.

At this juncture I must acknowledge a crucial point made to me in person by Maurie Pears, one of the junior officers of C Company, 3RAR, who was at the forefront of the action, and who, when prompted to reflect on the events covered by this chapter, highlighted the importance of the shape of Hill 355 in explaining many subsequent differences of opinion. I trekked up to the Demilitarised Zone in 2007 to look at Hills 317 and 355 from afar. The mist from the Imjin River was so thick that, to my intense disappointment, I could not see either feature. But Maurie Pears was there and saw for himself during the battle. I am sure he is right to say that the shallow crest line of Hill 355, rising and falling some 50 metres around the summit or highest point, is the reason why so much misunderstanding seems to have arisen. The nature of the crest prevents anyone from seeing clearly what is happening on the other side.[26]

The claim that it was 3RAR that took Hill 355 seems to be based largely on personal perception and testimony. In 1985, Robert O'Neill's official history noted that, after arriving on the crest of Hill 355, C Company's commander, Major Jack Gerke, radioed Hassett around 2 pm 'that the

---

24 3RAR, war diary, Appendix 12, p. 2, para 10. See also Appendix 10, p. 2, para. 19.
25 28th Brigade, war diary, November 1951, Appendix B, p. 4.
26 Maurie Pears, MC, conversation with author, 7 October 2011.

KOSBs were still below the summit, making their way steadily upwards'.[27] Yet, as we have just seen, by 2 pm the KOSBs had been on the summit of Hill 355 for three hours, and its B Company had set off 90 minutes earlier for the same north-eastern shoulder where Gerke apparently was. In addition, although O'Neill observes that 'it was a moment of triumph for Gerke to stand on the crest of that great, round hill which dominated the battlefield of Operation Commando', he also describes Gerke's final assault on Hill 355 as being against 'the eastern end of the summit of Hill 355', not the very peak of the hill itself.[28]

However, it is clear that Gerke believed he had taken the hill. In Bob Breen's monograph, *The Battle of Maryang San*, Gerke is cited as saying, 'I reckoned we had taken 355 but I did not stress this with the CO when I spoke to him at 1600 hr [4 pm]. He, of course, was well aware of the fact'.[29] Gerke's account, and the other accounts in Breen's book, are all legitimate oral history. There is no reason to doubt the memory or recollection they record. But we should question whether they can be reconciled with the documentary evidence. Is what they thought happened what actually did happen?

Once contextualised in a narrative, this kind of recollection is soon established as truth. Setting out C Company, 3RAR's memories in his own text, Breen states:

> After clearing the Chinese off the summit and north-eastern approaches to Little Gibraltar [Hill 355] … at about 1400 hr Gerke reported to Hassett that he held Little Gibraltar. At this time Gerke's men could hear the Borderers making their way up the south-eastern and western slopes accompanied by the jaunty sounds of their bagpipers playing traditional Scottish marching tunes.[30]

---

27 O'Neill, *Combat Operations*, p. 188.
28 Ibid., p. 187.
29 B. Breen, *The Battle of Maryang San*, Headquarters Training Command, Balmoral, NSW, 1991, p. 34. By 1998, Gerke's opinion had not changed. See M. Pears and F. Kirkland, *Korea Remembered: The RAN, ARA and RAAF in the Korean War of 1950–1953*, Doctrine Wing, Combined Arms Training Centre, Georges Heights, NSW, 1998, p. 68.
30 Breen, *The Battle of Maryang San*, p. 41.

Annotating map 3 in his monograph, Breen is even more explicit: 'Gerke's men were in possession of Little Gibraltar when the Borderers completed their assault.'[31] Yet none of this agrees with the contemporary documentation.

These facts, once established in print, start to be perpetuated with increasing certainty but without any apparent reference to contemporary sources of evidence. In his *Atlas of Australia's Wars*, Lieutenant General John Coates makes no mention at all of the KOSBs being involved in taking Hill 355: 'In a series of quick attacks along the ridge, they [C Company, 3RAR] not only captured their preliminary objective (a second 220 m feature) but also went on to capture Kowang San itself.'[32] The British official history's attempt to mediate in the matter[33] is rejected by Brigadier Jim Shelton in his trenchant chapter about Hassett in *The Fight Leaders*. He writes, 'The KOSB claim [to have taken 355] is not accepted by 3RAR or by the 16th New Zealand Field Regiment. The forward elements of the KOSB did not reach Gerke's position on the summit until at least one hour after the Australians'.[34] Even in a recent Australian account of the Korean War, written by Cameron Forbes and published in 2010, the image is repeated of the Australians on top of Hill 355 watching and hearing 'the pipers playing the Borderers up the south-eastern and western slopes'.[35]

Immediately following his account of Gerke reaching the summit of Hill 355, Breen goes on to add a further point of great significance: 'Subsequently, [the KOSB CO] Macdonald never sought the opportunity to meet Gerke or to acknowledge his part in the capture of Little Gibraltar.'[36] This same point is later reiterated by Shelton, who adds that Macdonald 'never acknowledged the contribution C Company [3RAR] had made in assisting the KOSB in the attack on Point 355 [Hill 355]'.[37] There is clear resentment that Macdonald never said thank you. But from the KOSBs perspective, why was this necessary? All the units involved— the KOSBs, the KSLI, the Fusiliers and 3RAR—were working to the

---

31 Ibid., map 3, following p. 42.
32 J. Coates, *An Atlas of Australia's Wars*, Oxford University Press, Melbourne, 2001, pp. 316–17, text 3.
33 See A. Farrar-Hockley, *The British Part in the Korean War*, vol. 2: *An Honourable Discharge*, HMSO, London, 1995, p. 223.
34 D. Butler, A. Argent and J.J. Shelton, *The Fight Leaders: A Study of Australian Battlefield Leadership*, Australian Military History Publications, Loftus, NSW, 2002, p. 132.
35 C. Forbes, *The Korean War*, Pan Macmillan, Sydney, 2010, p. 406.
36 Breen, *The Battle of Maryang San*, p. 41.
37 Butler, Argent and Shelton, *The Fight Leaders*, p. 132.

same plan issued by the 28th Brigade and, if the timings of the war diaries are to be believed (as they were at the time), the KOSBs' work finished well before the forward elements of C Company, 3RAR arrived on the north-eastern shoulder of Hill 355.

How has it then come to be claimed that 3RAR took the hill itself and gifted it to the KOSBs? I now think the shape of the hill, as Maurie Pears suggested to me, is ultimately the key to this riddle.[38] Men positioned on either side of the summit cannot see each other and can easily be unaware of events on the other side of the crest. In addition, I think there was a degree of misunderstanding at the time. At 4.10 pm, the 28th Brigade war diary noted, '1KOSB reported 3 Platoons arrived on Point 355 [Hill 355] simultaneously led by Lt C.K.W. Wilson, 2/Lt J.W. Lindquist and 2/Lt Henderson'.[39] Now, if the earlier details had not been received or noted, this report might have appeared as the first record of the KOSBs arriving on the summit, leading to a belief that they did not reach it until 4 pm. This would fit with Gerke's view of the situation and his perception that he had arrived first, much earlier in the afternoon. But, within the full context of the diary, it is clearly a retrospective report. I also believe, using the evidence of the war diaries, that the men Gerke saw moving up towards him on the north-eastern shoulder were those of the KOSBs' B Company climbing up from Finger Ridge, not the main body of the battalion, which had arrived on the summit some hours beforehand. There are too many reports in both the brigade and battalion diaries, as well as in the supporting written and personal accounts, to claim that 4 pm was the time that the KOSBs first arrived on Hill 355.

And what of the second part of this story, the fighting for the ridge Newcastle–United–Football–Club? The capture of Hill 217 on 5 October, and the subsequent exploitation up to what were later better known as the Hinge and the Knoll, was tasked to the Fusiliers. The Fifth Fusiliers, as the Northumberlands are traditionally known,[40] were brought in to supplement the strength of the 28th Brigade at the start of October. They had been in Korea since November 1950 and had already seen considerable action. Their original commanding officer, Lieutenant Colonel Kingsley Foster, had been killed on the Imjin on Anzac Day 1951

---

38 Maurie Pears, MC, conversation with author, 7 October 2011.
39 28th Brigade, war diary, 4 October 1951, 4.10 pm.
40 The traditional name of the 1st Royal Northumberland Fusiliers is the 5th (Northumberland) (Fusiliers) Regiment of Foot. The unit is referred to in the war diaries of the time as the 'Fighting Fifth'.

and was replaced in the field by the second in command, Miles Speer. By the end of September 1951, the Fusiliers knew that their tour was up and they would soon be leaving Korea. One member of the battalion, Ashley Cunningham-Boothe, later pointed out, 'We'd had more battles than any other British battalion in the Korean War and enough was enough. We were all ready to go home, to be posted out of the theatre. In fact some of the reservists had actually got a date for sailing; that's how close we were'.[41] To support 3RAR's assault on Maryang San, the Fusiliers were to take Hill 217 by first moving along a lateral ridge further south known as Crete. Y Company would then move onto Saw, while Z Company attacked to the north-west against Hill 217, or Newcastle. Once taken, the remaining companies would continue pushing up the ridge through United to Football and join 3RAR at Club.

At 6 am on 5 October, the forward elements of the Fusiliers moved west to Crete. According to the Fusiliers' war diary, they were hampered by the same 'thick ground mist' that was enveloping 3RAR's B and D Companies at the base of the ridge leading up to Hill 317. 'Shortly before mid-day', the diary noted, the mist cleared. Y Company established itself on Saw, having encountered 'little trouble other than sniping'.[42] Z Company reached the base of the steep, narrow slope leading up to Hill 217. It was difficult ground, as the war diary explained:

> From Saw leading north the ridge was very steep on both sides, for the most part heavily wooded with thick undergrowth, but with occasional bare patches of rocky outcrop. Thirty yards before reaching Point [Hill] 217 (or Newcastle), however, the trees on the top and east flank thinned out and, as a result of our artillery preparation, were at the time practically non-existent except as stumps to give a hand-hold in the most awkward places. The top itself was a rocky knife-edge some twenty yards long, while the western face, having avoided the ministrations of our artillery by virtue of its steepness, was again thickly wooded.[43]

---

41 Ashley Cunningham-Boothe, IWM SR 19913, reel 4, 20:00.
42 1st Royal Northumberland Fusiliers, war diary, September–October 1951, TNA, WO281/452 [hereafter RNF, war diary], part I, Appendix K, typescript report, 'Action fought for Point 217, 5–8 Oct '51', p. 1. (A copy of this report was published in A. Perrins (ed.), *'A Pretty Rough Do Altogether': The Fifth Fusiliers in Korea, 1950–1951*, Trustees of the Fusiliers Museum of Northumberland, Alnwick Castle, Alnick, Northumberland, 2004, pp. 200–6.)
43 RNF, war diary, p. 1.

Holding defensive positions among the trees, rocks and long grass was a Chinese company deployed in a series of deep bunkers, well armed with automatic weapons, including a section of heavy-calibre machine guns,[44] which were clearly marked on a sketch attached to the Fusiliers' battle report:

> The location of the machine guns shown in the sketch was confirmed by the slits and empty cartridge cases; other machine guns reported may have been moved from place to place or may have been the Chinese version of the Sten gun. There was no doubt that the enemy, particularly during the last counter-attack, was liberally armed with automatic weapons. The trench work also marked on the sketch was filled with boxes of grenades to a scale which was quite fantastic judged by our own standards.[45]

When Z Company advanced towards Hill 217, 11 Platoon on the right emerged out of the mist and surprised a number of Chinese in the open who were 'apparently coffee-housing on the border of the trees immediately below the summit'.[46] On the left, 12 Platoon deployed on the edge of thick trees and undergrowth and met a fearsome response. The platoon commander, Lieutenant Paddy Baxter, recalled:

> Two platoons had gone up to my right. I was going into a saddle to their left, to clear that saddle … And as we came up into that saddle, there were a fair number of Chinamen down below us, on the ridge below us, and of course as you sky-lined, so you hit the target. It was one of these things. I got a bullet in my chest, my sergeant got a bullet in his stomach and my good friend Corporal Bland took the platoon on.[47]

Although both platoons established tentative holds on their objectives, any attempt to join hands was knocked back. The Fusiliers' war diary explained, 'A period now ensued which lasted some ninety minutes and which may seem to the reader to be a period of stalemate though to those on the ground it was packed with sufficient interest and excitement to fill a story in itself'.[48] The Chinese seemed armed with endless stocks of grenades, which rained down on the British in clutches of four or five. Well supported by artillery and air strikes, the Fusiliers fought back.

---

44 28th Brigade, war diary, October 1951, Appendix M, 'HMG Coy on 217', p. 2.
45 RNF, war diary, Appendix K, p. 4 with later detail on p. 7.
46 Ibid., p. 2.
47 Paddy Baxter, 12 Platoon commander, IWM SR 13145, reel 2, 06:36.
48 RNF, war diary, Appendix K, p. 2.

But their own supplies were limited. Grenades were soon running short, as were stocks of Bren gun ammunition. In the early afternoon, after Z Company's casualties had reached 50 per cent, the company commander pulled his men back towards Crete. The Fusiliers' first attempt on Hill 217 had failed.

With Maryang San in Australian hands by the end of 5 October, this left Hill 217 as the only objective of Operation Commando that had not yet been achieved. Believing it was imperative that Hill 217 should still be taken as soon as possible, at 7.30 pm the 28th Brigade ordered the Fusiliers to send a company overnight from Crete to Hill 317 and in the morning to push this company through the Australians to take Football (the Hinge). At the same time, the rest of the battalion would renew its attack on Hill 217. To redouble their determination, Brigadier Taylor sent the Fusiliers a personal letter:

> I look to you to complete the brilliant actions of the capture of Hills 210–317 and 355. You will recapture 217 and move up the ridgeline to join hands above; united with your Australian comrades on Hill 317, who will do their best to help you. I know the fighting Fifth can do it.

Then in a final note he added, 'Watch the ammunition'. No receipt of the letter was noted in the Fusiliers' war diary.[49] Instead the Fusiliers' commanding officer, Lieutenant Colonel Speer, pointed out to the 28th Brigade that two of his companies had already been involved in heavy fighting that day and the other two would be needed for the new assault on 6 October. As a result, the order to send a company to Maryang San (Hill 317) 'was rescinded'.[50]

Already committed to making a renewed attack on Hill 217 the next morning, Speer decided to make a direct assault from the south, head on against the main Chinese position. This was a strange decision and reminiscent of the way the Americans had tried to capture Hill 317 earlier in the year by assaulting directly out of the valley against the southern face. The 28th Brigade's battle narrative included a description of how strong the defences were:

---

49 28th Brigade, war diary, Appendix F.
50 Farrar-Hockley, *An Honourable Discharge*, p. 228.

> The two medium machine guns on the extreme northern end of the ridge fired at very short range at anything approaching from the south whilst from the west (defiladed from the east and south) ran a trench system containing yet another two medium machine guns which were able to shoot obliquely from the north-west on to the ridge approaching 217. A plentiful number of enemy serving as a counter-attack force with ample supply of grenades were hiding in the dead ground just to the west of 217.[51]

It was precisely to avoid a frontal assault on these kinds of positions that Hassett had decided to 'run the ridges' and take Maryang San from the flank.

The Fusiliers moved off at 9.15 am on 6 October.[52] Y Company established itself back on Saw. But the narrowness of the ridge leading onto Hill 217 meant that W Company could attack with only a single platoon forward. When W Company advanced at 10.40 am, the Military Cross citation for its commander noted that the assault was heralded by a cheer that 'could be heard clearly more than half a mile away'.[53] The 28th Brigade's war diary succinctly encapsulated what happened next:

> W Company assaulted [Hill] 217 and captured it except one knob which contained a bunker with three medium machine guns. W Company was counter-attacked and one Northumberland Fusiliers' Platoon was pushed off. Position restored with aid of one Platoon from Y Company. 2nd counter attack on W Company beaten off. 3rd counter attack broken up by artillery. X Company then took over from W Company due to W Company's casualties. X Company made two attempts to take the enemy bunker.[54]

In its battle report, the 28th Brigade concluded, 'Although the Fusiliers got within 15 yards of the [machine gun] nest, they never managed to clear it up and another immediate counter-attack by a reinforced Chinese company forced X Company to withdraw'.[55] By early afternoon, the Fusiliers were finished. In two days, they had suffered 20 killed and 93 wounded, four more even than 3RAR. Yet, unlike 3RAR, they had been unable to overcome the Chinese defences. Although the results

---

51   28th Brigade, war diary, Appendix B, p. 6.
52   Ibid., 6 October, 9.15 am.
53   Major Reginald David Brook, company commander, W Company, 1RNF, Military Cross citation, cited in 'A Pretty Rough Do Altogether', ed. Perrins, p. 365.
54   28th Brigade, war diary, 6 October, note at end of day.
55   Ibid., Appendix B, p. 6.

were disappointing, as the British official history points out, 'their own persistence had not been futile. An important element of the enemy holding Maryang-san [sic] had been occupied continuously over two days',[56] and prevented from moving to the area of Football (the Hinge) and Club (the Knoll).

By the end of 6 October, it was clear that the only way to remove the Chinese from the ridge between Hill 217 (Newcastle) and Football (the Hinge) was to work down from the north. The following day, after A Company of the KOSBs had moved to Maryang San to bolster 3RAR's strength, Hassett despatched B Company, 3RAR against Football (the Hinge). After a day's heavy fighting, the Chinese launched their heaviest counter-attack but were repeatedly driven off by B Company from its new positions. By 8 October, there were signs that the Chinese were beginning to pull back from the ridge. At 12 noon, the KOSBs patrolled down to United and found the Chinese positions empty, with its diary recording simply the patrol made 'no contact'.[57] The Fusiliers then patrolled up to Hill 217 (Newcastle). In meagre consolation for their earlier frustrations, its diary noted, 'At five o'clock in the evening the Intelligence Officer and two sections of the Assault Pioneers walked onto Newcastle unopposed'.[58]

In studying the operations of the Fusiliers on 5 and 6 October, perhaps the most pertinent question is why did 3RAR succeed when the Fusiliers did not? Probably the most important factor was that the Fusiliers' time in theatre was up. On 1 October, the day before the Fusiliers moved over to join the 28th Brigade, Lieutenant Michael Kerney, the battalion's assistant signal officer, wrote in a letter:

> At last we have two days rest after having been in the line 22 days. A record for us. Only another fortnight until we finish here for good … The strain at the moment is terrific and we can only wait for the time when we are relieved and can breathe again in peace.[59]

Many Fusiliers felt that they had already done their bit for Korea. There is also the vital question of command. Lieutenant Colonel Speer was a brave and able commanding officer. But, looking at the way the battalion

---

56 Farrar-Hockley, *An Honourable Discharge*, p. 229.
57 KOSB, war diary, 8 October, 12 noon, 'make no contact'.
58 RNF, war diary, Appendix K, p. 3.
59 Quoted in *'A Pretty Rough Do Altogether'*, ed. Perrins, p. 198.

undertook its attacks on Newcastle, maybe he did not have the flair or creativity of Frank Hassett. But how many men do? Hassett's command of the assault on Maryang San was truly inspired. Faced with the reality of how strong the defences of Hill 217 were, one cannot help but wonder what Hassett would have done.

The same might also be said about the individual soldiers. Despite their initial reluctance, none of the Fusiliers shirked their duty. They fought well, like their commanding officer. But, on the whole, the Australian soldiers seem to have fought better, again like their commanding officer. There was an edge, a hardness, a sense of daring in the gritty actions along Hill 317 or against the Knoll and the Hinge that just seemed to tip the balance each time in the Australians' favour in a way it did not for the Fusiliers in the battle for Newcastle, despite their persistence. There was also probably an element of luck, and it failed to shine on the Fusiliers.

A perception of the disappointing performance of British units during Operation Commando is intrinsic to the overall Australian understanding of Maryang San. In part this derives from 3RAR's wider situation within the Commonwealth structure in Korea. A justifiable sense of injustice, for example, emanates from Australian anger over the quota of decorations and awards for the operation, summed up by Robert O'Neill's observation that 'the KOSBs had gained more decorations in losing Maryang San to the Chinese on 4 November than they, the Australians, had received for winning it on 8 October'.[60] This was exacerbated when the capture of Maryang San was not originally recognised as a separate battle honour but absorbed into the wider 28th Brigade honour of Kowang San—perhaps adding another reason why it was necessary to be able to claim that this objective was really taken by 3RAR—and made worse when the honour 'Maryang San' was used to recognise the loss of the hill in November.[61]

Another key factor was the personality of the KOSB's Lieutenant Colonel Macdonald. He was not to Australian tastes, being described as 'a Calvinistic Scot, averse to tobacco and strong drink and a professional soldier to the core'.[62] But Macdonald was highly regarded as a commanding officer by his own officers. A strict disciplinarian he might have been, but one officer believed Macdonald to be the 'best commanding officer I ever

---

60 O'Neill, *Combat Operations*, p. 200.
61 See Breen, *The Battle of Maryang San*, pp. 129–30.
62 M. Hickey, *The Korean War: The West Confronts Communism, 1950–1953*, John Murray, London, 1999, p. 257.

had', adding, 'I never had a finer CO in my life'.⁶³ Macdonald's perceived failure to acknowledge what C Company, 3RAR had done for him on 4 October, like so many other things, was then compounded after the loss of Maryang San in November. By then Macdonald was commanding the 28th Brigade. Apparently indifferent to Australian sensibilities, he published a tactless message to his old battalion rightly praising them for their efforts in the battle that lost the hill, but inevitably rubbing salt into the still smarting wounds of 3RAR that had been reopened by the loss.⁶⁴

Macdonald's ascendancy to the command of the 28th Brigade was also controversial. From an Australian perspective, he seemed to have been central in getting Brigadier George Taylor sacked, although the conspiracy against Taylor was driven not only by the British but by the New Zealanders as well. This was seen as a hard judgement on a man who had delivered all of his objectives and placed the 1st Commonwealth Division successfully on the new Jamestown Line. Hassett later wrote to Taylor, 'I think one of your senior officers was very ambitious. Perhaps that was part of the trouble'.⁶⁵ Taylor was popular with the Australians. He has been described as 'the product of an old North Country Catholic family, gregarious, extrovert, a lover of good food, wines and jovial company'.⁶⁶ When he left the 28th Brigade with little warning, 3RAR seemed to have felt they had lost a friend. Sending Taylor a copy of Breen's monograph in 1992, Hassett explained that it contained a degree of 'criticism of some British units, the KOSB in particular': 'Much of this flows from the KOSB having Macdonald as its CO. He disliked the Australians, a sentiment they returned in full measure. I consider him a poor CO and a worse Brigade Commander.'⁶⁷

Combined, these factors have coloured the way Australians remember Operation Commando. As a result, the assault and capture of Kowang San and Maryang San have become yet another chapter in Britain and Australia's shared military heritage, which stretches back over more than a hundred years, through both world wars, to the war in South Africa. History is used to build the foundations of nationhood. Even in Britain,

---

63   Jock Foulis, IWM SR interview 19661, reel 1, 21:30 and 23:52.
64   Brigadier J.F.M. Macdonald, Special Order of the Day, 7 November 1951, reproduced in Macdonald, *The Borderers in Korea*, p. 39.
65   Brigadier G. Taylor DSO, letter from Hassett, 14 May 1987, Imperial War Museum, Documents Section [IWM DOCS], 96/12/1.
66   Hickey, *The Korean War*, p. 257.
67   Brigadier G. Taylor DSO, 96/12/1, letter from Hassett, 27 February 1992, IWM DOCS.

where people pretend this is not the case, the way the two great wars of the twentieth century were fought is integral to the way most people see themselves and Great Britain's place in the world. But this makes the responsibility of the historian all the greater. In writing and researching history, particularly when it lays the foundations of national myth, we need to look ever more carefully at the contemporary documentation. We have to seek a definitive statement of what happened based on all the records and try to avoid a selective interpretation based on national bias.

With the Korean War, this is particularly difficult to achieve. I am reminded that the war did not take place all that long ago; it is living memory. Contributors to this volume lived through it; some were there. But eyewitnesses only see one part of the bigger picture. What people see, what people remember, is not necessarily wrong until conclusions are drawn from these recollections and from them alone. As historians, we know that oral history has to be used carefully. It has to be substantiated by firmer documentation and contemporary, primary evidence. Personal testimony can be used to support and embellish, but it is often too fragile on its own to form the foundations of history.

12

THE BATTLE FOR HILL 317 (MARYANG SAN)
One man's account

William Purves

Nigel Steel, in Chapter 11, provides a detailed review of the tactical and operational detail of a multibattalion brigade plan in a divisional setting, which was part of a much larger war effort. This chapter takes a different but complementary view: the view of a British soldier. From the perspective of a British soldier of the Korean War, it is important to understand the composition of the British forces in Korea. Conscription in Britain was in force during the 1940s and 1950s. On my eighteenth birthday, an envelope came through the door, 'on His Majesty's service', telling me that in a few months I would be called up for my two years' National Service. In May 1950, it happened. For some reason I was badged into the Black Watch and sent to Fort George near Inverness for basic training. While there, I was fortunate enough to pass an officer selection board and went to Eaton Hall, where the infantry officers were trained. The training course ran about two months, and during that time I managed to talk my way out of the Black Watch into my territorial regiment, the King's Own Scottish Borderers (KOSBs). I suppose I did so because I thought it would be quite nice to do some travelling at the King's expense, as the KOSBs were in Hong Kong. So I duly arrived as a very raw, young-looking second lieutenant in Hong Kong, and soon afterwards my regiment was mobilised to go to Korea.

Earlier in 1950, after a UN resolution, the British Government was under pressure to send forces to Korea. British Prime Minister Clement Attlee said he was not prepared to reduce the garrison in Hong Kong, so two battalions were earmarked to go to Korea. Apart from the mobilisation, they were not allowed to go by sea and, as you know, the North Korean advance down the Korean Peninsula was so fast that the war might have been over before they got there. So, on 18 August, Brigadier Coad got a message to say that the Argyll and Sutherland Highlanders and the Middlesex Regiment were to go immediately to Korea.

They were both understrength, and a company of the Queen's and East Surreys were sent to bolster the Middlesex Regiment. At least 60 per cent of the troops were national servicemen. Having been told on 18 August that these regiments were to move, we actually embarked on 25 August and reached Pusan on 29 August, by which stage the perimeter had shrunk considerably. We had no vehicles and were dependent on US help for transport. The battalions were sent up to the edge of the perimeter and, as you know, late in September, we were joined by the 3rd Battalion, Royal Australian Regiment (3RAR).

The Argylls and Middlesex were ordered to break out of the perimeter with some US forces on 16 September, and they had to cross the Naktong River. Within 10 days, the Argylls had suffered a terrible accident. A US aircraft napalmed one of the companies, and the company and support troops suffered 90 casualties, 20 of whom were killed. It was there that one of their company commanders, Major Kenny Muir, won his posthumous Victoria Cross.

Soon afterwards there was the Inchon Landing, which took the pressure off the perimeter very quickly. Over two or three days, the two battalions were lifted by air to Kimpo and 27th Brigade joined the race north. The roads became jammed and infantry got onto tanks, and up they went through Pyongyang almost to the Yalu River. Most of the actual fighting, I think at that stage, took place with 3RAR, which stopped short of the Yalu River, and in late October, China entered the war.

There was fighting at Pakchon in the second half of November. Then started what I suppose is the biggest bug-out in history, and the UN troops raced back and were severely attacked in the Uijongbu corridor in early January. They crossed the 38th parallel on 11 December, coming south, and re-established a line well below Seoul. Of course, the biggest enemy in January and February was really the cold. Forty degrees below zero at night, and one had to be careful. If you removed your mitten and picked up a jerry can or something metallic, the skin froze immediately and would get torn off. We were facing north, as you can imagine, and the blizzards from Mongolia and beyond really came down very severely. So it was a very difficult period. The platoon commander every morning had to inspect each man's feet to make sure that we did not get frostbite. By the time you had done that for a couple of weeks, you did not need to look at the Jock's face; you knew who he was from his feet.

Then, as far as the British forces were concerned, the 29th Infantry Brigade was formed under Brigadier Tom Brodie. It arrived in Korea, and not long afterwards was involved in the battle of the Imjin River between 22 and 25 April 1951, in which the 1st Battalion of the Gloucestershire Regiment was essentially wiped out. Any prisoners taken after three days of fierce fighting—by which time they had run out of ammunition—were marched north where they either died or endured more than two years in appalling prison camps. The other two battalions were the Royal Northumberland Fusiliers and the Royal Ulster Rifles. They were mainly reservists, with a few national servicemen, and I think it is fair to say their hearts were not really in it. Many of them were called back to the colours about two weeks before their reserve years were due to end. They had young families at home, and I think it was extremely difficult for them to go to war. Most of them had been involved in the Second World War; they were not volunteers, unlike the Australians; and they found it very difficult to get morale up to the peak that was required. The Gloucestershires were led by Colonel Carne, who was captured and eventually given a VC for his battlefield efforts.

Chapters 3 and 4 of this volume explore the Battle of Kapyong at the end of April 1951. I was not involved so all I will say is that it was well recognised in British circles that it is thanks to 3RAR and the 2nd Battalion of Princess Patricia's Canadian Light Infantry (2PPCLI) that those attacks were repelled.

By the end of April, the 27th Brigade had been renumbered to become the 28th, with Brigadier Taylor in charge. The KOSBs and the King's Shropshire Light Infantry (KSLI) relieved the Argylls and Middlesex, who returned to the United Kingdom; and 3RAR and 2PPCLI moved from the 27th Brigade to the 28th Brigade. In July 1951, the Commonwealth Division was formed under Major General Jim Cassels. He was highly respected by everyone, and soon the division really began to operate as an effective member of the UN forces. Before that, individual battalions had been pretty well left to manage as best they could.

We were, of course, supported by the New Zealand gunners, and they did a marvellous job for us. They were nearly all Second World War veterans. We then moved north of the Imjin River to straighten out the line, and did not really meet a great deal of opposition in the process until we mounted a major attack in October 1951. Then the brigade started to prepare for Operation Commando, taking first Hill 355 (Kowang San), and on 3 October, I and my platoon, 7 Platoon of C Company, started off at dawn to climb the foothills of Hill 355. It was steep, and there was quite a lot of fire from various sources coming towards us. We were held up and suffered quite a number of casualties. The rest of the company passed through and, by 3.30 pm that afternoon, had taken and established themselves on ground higher up.

I guess that my platoon was marooned a little bit there. My platoon and D Company went up the western side of Hill 355 while the Australians came up the eastern side. My regimental war diary says that D Company was further along to the west of us at 11.30 that morning. There was no peak to the hill, as you have read. I went up on the following days to look at the situation from the top of Hill 355, and frankly there did not seem to be a high point. One side was the same height as the other. So I do not think my regiment, anyway, got into any kind of argument as to who took the hill first. We were delighted to see the Australians at the other end of the summit.

Then on 5 October the Australians moved, in this brilliant move that you have read about, flanking round from the right, from the east. I was quite interested, because that morning there was heavy fog lying right along the valley. We were on top of 355 and could see the top of 317 (Maryang San) and some of the other hills; we might call them foothills. They were all pretty steep. And it was there that A Company of 3RAR were moved off, and I don't know whether there is any truth in it, but it is said they got a bit lost in the fog. They certainly took some time to be able to participate in the subsequent battle. Well, the speed at which 3RAR moved was quite remarkable.

12. THE BATTLE FOR HILL 317 (MARYANG SAN)

I think that the Chinese were expecting an approach from a different angle, but by the end of the day on 6 October, all the high features of Hill 317 were held by the Australians, who then suffered two days of severe counter-attack. On 9 October, by which time they must have been quite exhausted, my regiment moved in to take over from them and they were able to have a rest.

What was supposed to happen from there, of course, was that the Northumberland Fusiliers were supposed to take Hill 217, also known as Newcastle. They nearly got to the top on 5 October but failed to take it until the following day. But 3RAR held all the main positions around the top of Hill 317, and the KOSBs took over from them on 9 October.

The KSLI were in reserve. Hill 217 was heavily defended, which proved to be quite an obstacle to the Northumberland Fusiliers attempting to take it. The KOSBs stayed on Hill 317 until early November. My platoon was on one of the summit knolls, reinforced by a platoon of D Company. The rest of Charlie Company and B Company were up on the high ground, with A Company in reserve. For the next few weeks we were engaged in wiring, patrolling and generally preparing for potential counter-attacks. The patrolling was by and large ineffective because the Chinese were so good at camouflaging and holding back and only working at night.

On 28 October, I had a significant observation post near the crest. And we had heard some tracked vehicles moving forward the previous night, but on that afternoon at about 4 pm, a shell obliterated the observation post and both men in it were killed. I guess we had become a bit slack in moving in and out, and the enemy could see us, because we had a marvellous view of the valley. From 28 October until 4 November, there was heavy patrolling, generally through the Hinge, with fighting patrols going out to the north.

I think it was on 2 November that I was asked to take a patrol down the valley to our north, which was very open, with a village at the far end, which only had a few houses still more or less intact. I began to get the impression I was being watched as we went down there with an 88 wireless. Generally speaking they were useless, but we had to keep radio silence anyway. I got down to the village with six men and started to have a look round. There was evidence of meals and cooking, all quite recent. There was one particular house with a straw roof, and lying below it was a ladder. It was a two-storey house in remarkable condition so I decided to have a look into it. I put the ladder up, slid open the wooden door—and you might not believe me, but there in front of me was a rather beautiful young lady. Of course, we had heard about comfort girls quite near the front line for senior Chinese officers. It told us one thing: that there was a major concentration of Chinese building up. It flashed through my mind that if I did not get the hell out of it, I certainly would not get back to my position. I did not tell the Jocks (KOSBs) what I had found.

We gingerly went back as fast as we could, and by that time I was absolutely certain that we were being watched. I suppose we were not wiped out because it would have spoiled the enemy's surprise attack, which was launched on the evening of 4 November. During 2 and 3 November there was a lot of digging. And in the area below the Hinge, the land was quite soft, so there were trails dug in, and it was from that source that the major attack took place at nightfall on 4 November. The main Chinese attack came from the north, the north-west and the north-east.

We were really well wired up round our positions, and those of you who have been on it will know that the top of Hill 317 is bare and rocky. I think one reason the platoon of D Company up there was pushed off was because they had very little wire out in front of them. The sheer volume of attack here started with blowing of bugles, yelling and, before that, heavy artillery bombardment. Then it lifted, and waves of Chinese infantry came right over the position. In B Company, there was the headquarters and two platoons and one platoon on a small feature. This platoon was never heard of again. I believe that three of them were taken as prisoners of war, but I do not have proof of that. But the regular lieutenant and the rest of his platoon were clearly wiped out. Quite a number of our troops from B Company and C Company came under attack. I was sitting up on a knoll, and I could see people running down to the south, which was a bit disconcerting, to say the least of it.

As the hours went on we were able to hold this position. It was quite steep, and we had a good supply of M36 grenades; they were effective and a lot of Chinese were killed round here. D Company was not like that. A platoon from D Company was attacked here, and Lieutenant Barney Henderson was in command of it. He was wounded early on, so I took command of the two platoons. And about 11 o'clock or midnight, I began to realise we were being strafed. We were receiving friendly aircraft fire from our own gunners, who were trying to obliterate the entire area. I managed at some stage to get a message through to D Company, which had fallen back a bit,

12. THE BATTLE FOR HILL 317 (MARYANG SAN)

that we were still there. And although we suffered some casualties, they were all wounded, not killed, but there was no further communication—as I say, the 88 wireless was pretty useless. Then at about 2 am I managed to establish contact with somebody in D Company and reported that we were firm and holding quite well.

At about 3 am I got a direct order to evacuate the position, which we started to do. Not very easy; it was dark, quite steep. We found a path down somehow, and we managed to bring out the wounded on stretchers. We had some strong Korean porters who were in similar uniform to ourselves. I was surprised to see that 3RAR's porters were in white, because of course you could see white from miles away. These porters managed to carry the stretchers. There were three carrying five people, and at some stage, instead of turning right, I discovered there was nobody behind me and they had started to go up here. I ran after them and managed to stop them. All I could hear at that stage was noisy jabbering in Mandarin or Korean.

We got down. There was quite a lot of firing still going on but somehow or other it missed us. The platoon from D Company was reunited with the rest of the company, and my own platoon came down to battalion headquarters. Having handed over to someone else, I was evacuated to hospital with wounds, so I have no idea what happened immediately after that. Attempts were made to recapture Hill 317, but it remained under Chinese control.

I was evacuated to Japan, had some patching up and, in the middle of January 1952, got back to Korea, where the war had become entirely static and the patrolling carried on. I would add that one of the difficulties was the water in the valley had frozen and you know what happens: the ice stays on top, and there's nothing underneath. As you walk down on patrol, if you stood on a bit of ice, it went 'bang'. It was like a shot being fired, and everybody was alerted, and the Chinese put up flares, so you had to freeze. If you showed any movement, then you were under fire. So it was a bit tricky. I have to tell you that on a couple of occasions, once after seeing the girl and once having been caught out in the middle of no man's land with flares all over, I felt very lonely indeed.

At any rate, as the months went on, the static phase of the ground war started, and the KOSBs and KSLIs were relieved in May 1952. The brave troops that followed us were the Duke of Wellingtons and the Black

Watch, then the Devons and the Camerons. The war, of course, had changed in April, with May 1952 being entirely static, which is described very effectively by Robert O'Neill in Chapter 1 of this volume.

The citation for the Distinguished Service Order that I received, recommended by my brigade commander and General Cassels, during the Korean War reads:

> Number seven Platoon of C Company 1 King's Own Scottish Borderers, commanded by Second Lieutenant Purves, was holding the western portion of the knoll feature when the enemy attack on 1 Battalion of the Borderers developed at 16.15 hours on 4 November. The remainder of C Company was some 300 yards to the west of the knoll, whilst a platoon of D Company under operational command of C Company was adjacent on the east side of the knoll. Ignoring the fact that the rest of C Company had been forced off their positions by 18.00 hours, thereby completely exposing his left flank, Second Lieutenant Purves unhesitatingly fought on with his platoon. At about this time the commander of the D Company platoon having become a casualty, Second Lieutenant Purves also assumed command of that platoon. The platoons were repeatedly attacked by large numbers of enemy, each of their onslaughts being prepared by intense mortar and artillery fire. Although in great pain from a serious wound in his right shoulder, Second Lieutenant Purves was undaunted. Under heavy fire of all natures, he dashed from section to section in both platoons encouraging them, directing their fire, and himself hurling grenades at the enemy in the wire. Although it was apparent that point [Hill] 317, which completely dominated his position from 400 yards to his right, was in enemy hands by 21.00 hours, Second Lieutenant Purves, with his position now completely isolated, fought on. It was not until 01.45 hours that Second Lieutenant Purves got a message through to battalion headquarters reporting the situation and asking for information. He was then ordered to try and extricate the platoons towards the rear platoon of D Company, south of point [Hill] 317. Though under heavy mortar fire and under the very nose of the enemy on point [Hill] 317, Second Lieutenant Purves carried out this manoeuvre with great skill and coolness, bringing down the precipitous feature 12 wounded men and all the platoon's arms and equipment.

12. THE BATTLE FOR HILL 317 (MARYANG SAN)

At 04.15 on the 5th of November, Second Lieutenant Purves reported to the battalion command post that his platoon was outside, fully equipped, and ready to fight. It was not until he received a direct order from his commanding officer to report to the regimental aid post that he gave any consideration to his severe and obviously painful wound. The outstanding leadership, personal bravery and resource of this young officer of 19 years of age, together with his exceptional sense of responsibility, was an inspiration to all, whilst the stubborn defence of his feature contributed materially in preventing the battalion from being overrun.

At times, under constant bombardment from communist artillery and small arms fire, we did run short of ammunition on the front line, and of course, there was often no question of resupply during a battle. We often had to stockpile ammunition grenades before a battle over the weeks. I was issued with a cheap Sten gun, and I hope that the Owen guns used by the Australians were better because our Sten guns were next to useless. Whenever you found yourself with the Chinese in front of you, the thing jammed. They were hopeless.

During the battle for Maryang San the artillery fire seemed to be coming from both sides. These features were quite narrow, and I dare say that is why we survived. Even the Kiwi gunners could not land many shells on the top; a lot of them went over and exploded underneath the other side, and a lot of them landed on the back slope. We were sprayed with shrapnel, and I was hit in two or three places, but little bits of shrapnel do not actually blow your head off, so we were quite fortunate because of the terrain—unlike the Hinge, which was relatively flat and where the initial charge dislodged so many of our men. The communist forces artillery was very effective, the Chinese mortars in particular.

In terms of how effective our defensive positions were, we unfortunately did not have overhead cover and everything was through trenches, which were often not very deep because of the rocky terrain. But you learned to keep your head down when there was incoming fire. And if there were wounded, they simply had to stay where they were. There was one young man who was in my headquarters and was in charge of the 2-inch mortar. I rather think that as the ammunition went down, he picked up a mortar bomb that would have already been fired and had not exploded. Anyway, it exploded in the barrel, and he received a bit of shrapnel, which went through his eye and came out the back of his head. And that was a nasty mess, to say the least of it. He was a little fellow from Perthshire, a joiner and roofer. I thought there was no way he was going to make it; I pumped some morphine into him for the first and only time in my life. We all had a couple of shots of morphine, as platoon commanders. When the time came to pull out, he was very light, and I was able to put him on top of somebody else who was on a stretcher. We got him out, but I never expected to see him again. Well, many years later, I met him and his wife. An artificial eye, a great hollowed-out bit of his skull, but there he was alive, and he still had a functioning brain, despite the seriousness of his injury.

In general, the morale of British troops during the Korean War, including those under my command, was remarkably good. Unlike Australian forces in the Korean War, it is important to remember the vast majority of British soldiers were national servicemen. I had lost my platoon sergeant so our sections were led by corporals or lance corporals—again, most of them were national servicemen. As a result of us being relatively the same age, we got to know each other pretty well over the months. There was definitely a sense growing between me and the other ranks, particularly because we had one or two lucky escapes, I guess, when we were patrolling. So somehow or other, I felt that they were with me and we were a team.

13

THE SAMICHON
A final barb in the Hook, 24–27 July 1953

Michael Kelly

At 10 pm on 27 July 1953, the Korean War—which had raged for three years, one month and two days—came to an uneasy end. The front line, which had still been active almost until the armistice came into effect, was now silent. The previous three days, however, had seen a battle fought in the Samichon Valley by men of the 1st Commonwealth Division and the US 1st Marine Division against Chinese forces hell bent on securing strategically important high ground and pushing the UN forces back beyond the Imjin River.

The scale of men and matériel committed to this battle was greater than the Australians had experienced at Kapyong, and the shelling by Chinese artillery was greater than experienced by the men at Maryang San. Arrayed against the Chinese was a force that, despite being numerically inferior, had superior artillery strength and coordination. It was also able, depending on the weather, to provide air support, and it had tanks dug in at key locations to provide direct fire support.

The UN and Chinese intelligence arms were highly attuned and knew of troop movements into the front lines. For the soldiers of the United Nations Command, signals intelligence and human intelligence—in the form of information extracted from prisoners and deserters—was vital in being able to detect and prepare for this last offensive of the war.

Gaining the UN positions of the Jamestown Line that dominated the Samichon Valley was the key reason that the Chinese launched this last offensive. Their objectives were to gain a strategic advantage over the UN troops, and possibly open the corridor for an offensive drive on Seoul. Located 48 kilometres north of Seoul, the Samichon Valley is today part of Korea's Demilitarised Zone (DMZ), but in 1953 it was the front line in a very active war. The terrain, like much of Korea, is mountainous, with steep-sided features giving commanding views into the valleys for those who held the high ground. The valley floors, which had been prime rice-producing agricultural land, were fiercely contested battlegrounds in the nightly patrol war as the belligerent parties vied for the upper hand.

For centuries the Samichon Valley has been a traditional invasion route for armies moving north and south. It was no different in the early hours of 25 June 1950 when soldiers of the North Korean People's Army (NKPA) crossed the 38th parallel and began their drive on Seoul, starting the war.[1] Over the next 12 months, the Samichon Valley changed hands several times as the war ebbed and flowed. After the Chinese Fifth Phase Offensive ended soon after the Battle of Kapyong in late April 1951, the soldiers of the United Nations Command (UNC) went onto to the offensive in early May. Subsequently, limited offensive actions took place until early October; these saw Chinese and NKPA forces pushed back to a line skewed across the 38th parallel. In October 1951, the United Nations conducted a successful offensive, known as Operation Commando (as recounted in Chapter 10 by Bob Breen, Chapter 11 by Nigel Steel and Chapter 12 by William Purves) in which five infantry divisions, including the 1st Commonwealth Division of I Corps, advanced to, captured, then largely held the Jamestown Line. Part of this new line encompassed the Samichon Valley.

---

1   R. O'Neill, *Australia in the Korean War 1950–53*, vol. 2: *Combat Operations*, AWM & AGPS, Canberra, 1985, p. 274.

13. THE SAMICHON

The most dominant feature in the Samichon Valley was Height 146, which became known to the soldiers of the UNC as 'the Hook'. Whoever occupied the Hook was afforded commanding 360-degree views that encompassed the Samichon Valley and back to and beyond the Imjin River. As a result, the Hook was one of the most brutally contested locations in the Korean War. This position quickly gained an evil reputation, and by the end of the war it was said that it was not possible to dig on the Hook without turning up body parts. The stench of death was ever-present.

Six months after Operation Commando, in April 1952 the US 1st Marine Division was transferred from X Corps on the eastern side of Korea to I Corps in the west. The division's new area of responsibility originally stretched from the coast to the Sami'chon (or Sami River) and encompassed the Hook. A series of combat outposts were established forward of the US front line, known as the Main Line of Resistance (MLR), to provide a forward defence buffer.

From early 1952 until the end of the war, the Chinese maintained constant pressure on the UN front line. On the western side of the Korean battlefield, the Samichon Valley was the scene of many hard-fought actions in no man's land, along with numerous attempts by the Chinese to capture the Hook from its defenders. A number of the outposts were either captured or destroyed as the Chinese inexorably closed in on the UNC front line.

The first battle of the Hook began on 26 October 1952 when Chinese forces attacked the US Marines of the 7th Regiment. The Marines were pushed back off the Hook, but soon regained it when they launched a counter-attack. After two days of fighting, the Chinese forces withdrew. Once the Marines regained the Hook, the divisional boundary between the 1st Marine Division and the 1st Commonwealth Division was moved 2 kilometres to the west. As a result, the Commonwealth Division took over responsibility for the ground from the Samichon River to the saddle between Hill 121 and Hill 111 in early November. This slightly compressed the Marines' defensive frontage, which still extended some 55 kilometres from Hill 111 to the west coast of Korea. It was a major undertaking for the Marines who, due to casualties and troop rotations, were already well under the division's nominal strength.

With his division's increased frontage, Major General Michael West, General Officer Commanding (GOC) 1st Commonwealth Division, placed all three of his brigades into the line for the first time. The British 29th Infantry Brigade, already occupying the Commonwealth Division's left sector, took control of the new territory. It was the 1st Battalion, Black Watch, that took over the Hook from the Marines. They faced an uphill struggle to repair positions that had been entirely devastated, but they managed the task just before the next Chinese attack.[2]

The Chinese wasted no time in trying to dislodge the new occupants. The second battle of the Hook began the evening of 18 November 1952, when several companies of Chinese infantry attacked the Hook, and concluded more than 11 hours later when the Chinese were finally driven off the feature. The Black Watch's forward positions had been overrun, but men holed up in bunkers fought ferociously to deny the Chinese retaining a foothold. Artillery was also called down on the Black Watch's forward positions, which helped dislodge the Chinese and retain the position as part of the UNC front line. The Black Watch suffered 107 casualties—killed, wounded and missing. The Chinese suffered at least 100 dead and around 600 wounded.[3]

During a second stint on the Hook in April and May 1953, the Black Watch defeated a Chinese attack of company strength on the night of 7/8 May.[4] The attack lasted less than half an hour, including the 10 minutes of Chinese preparatory artillery fire, during which around a thousand Chinese shells fell on the Hook positions. The following day a Chinese propaganda broadcast 'promised sterner things in the future' for the occupants of the Hook.[5] Fortunately for the men of the Black Watch, their Korean War was over soon after. The battalion was replaced in the 29th Brigade, but instead of a well-earned break, the Scotsmen were sent to the British Kenya Colony to help quell the Mau Mau uprising.[6]

---

2   T. Carew, *Korea: The Commonwealth at War*, Cassell, London, 1967, pp. 266–8.
3   Headquarters, Commonwealth Division, G Branch, November 1952, p. 12, AWM373 Class WO281/76.
4   Carew, *Korea*, pp. 272–4.
5   Headquarters, Commonwealth Division, G Branch, January–June 1953, 8 May 1953, p. 593, AWM373 Class WO281/700.
6   Black Watch, 'Post War, 1945–2006', theblackwatch.co.uk/history/.

13. THE SAMICHON

The 1st Battalion, Duke of Wellington's Regiment (known colloquially as 'the Dukes'), was the next battalion to occupy the Hook. This battalion, forewarned of an impending Chinese attack, again through signals and human intelligence, maintained an alert posture. The only information they lacked was the date of the attack. The Chinese launched their heaviest attack on the Hook on the evening of 28 May. The Chinese infantrymen swiftly gained the front-line positions. Stubborn resistance from small parties of Dukes fighting from bunkers and tunnels—with the Commonwealth Division's artillery support and a counter-attack by the Dukes' reserve company—restored the position and forced the Chinese to withdraw.

Throughout the night the Chinese fired some 10,000 shells onto the Hook and surrounding features. Trenches that had been 10 feet deep in places were now no more than ankle height or had been levelled completely. All of the bunkers had been damaged or destroyed, and the defensive wire had largely ceased to exist. The Dukes suffered 149 casualties, of which 28 were killed. Chinese casualties were estimated to be 250 dead and 800 wounded.[7] Having failed to capture the Hook by *coup de main*, the Chinese focused their attention on the adjacent bastion known as Boulder City. Throughout June the patrol war in front of the Marines' and Commonwealth lines intensified.

To replace the exhausted Dukes, Major General Michael West instituted a divisional move in place. Known as Operation Emperor, the move saw all three brigades of the Commonwealth Division move areas of responsibility. Starting on 9 July, the 28th Brigade moved from the right flank to the left, the 29th Brigade moved from the left flank to the centre, and the Canadian 25th Brigade moved from the centre to the right flank. The operation was successfully carried out and concluded on 12 July.

The US 1st Marine Division had begun returning to the MLR on the morning of 6 July, replacing the US 25th Infantry Division and the attached Turkish Brigade. The 7th Marine Regiment was first to return to the line, their sector encompassing from Boulder City to Hill 111. The Chinese were aware of the handover and tried to take advantage of the situation. Heavy mortar and artillery fire fell on the Marines' front line and the two combat outposts forward of this line, known as Berlin and East Berlin. In the evening, a reinforced Chinese battalion attacked the two outposts and briefly captured East Berlin, but were ejected after fierce fighting.

---

7   A.J. Barker, *Fortune Favours the Brave: The Hook, Korea, 1953*, Leo Cooper, London, 1974, p. 142.

The 28th Commonwealth Infantry Brigade, commanded by Brigadier John Wilton, was faced with an area of operations divided by the Samichon River, which would lend its name to the forthcoming battle. Wilton gave his two strongest battalions, the 2nd Battalion, Royal Australian Regiment (2RAR), and the 3rd Battalion, Royal Australian Regiment (3RAR), the responsibility for the Hook and surrounding positions. The 1st Battalion, Durham Light Infantry was placed to the right of the river. The 1st Battalion, Royal Fusiliers,[8] after having already served, albeit briefly, on the Hook to bolster the Dukes, became the reserve battalion.

The first priority for the Australians was the rebuilding of the Hook and surrounding positions. The defensive wire and minefield fences had to be almost entirely rebuilt and, by necessity, all the work had to be conducted at night. It is a testimony to the officers and men of both 2RAR and 3RAR's assault pioneer platoons that, despite the Chinese artillery, the front-line defences were repaired and in good order before the impending Chinese attack. Particularly noteworthy was Lieutenant Patrick Forbes, 2RAR's assault pioneer platoon commander. He and his platoon not only rebuilt a destroyed minefield fence but also traversed that field—which was unmapped—at night and managed to survive the experience, having suffered no casualties as a result.

During the same period, Australian patrols clashed frequently with the Chinese and suffered several casualties. The area of greatest contact was on a feature forward of the Hook known as Green Finger. Unknown to the Australians, the Chinese had established a cave on the reverse slope. Chinese patrols would race from this location to a small hill nearby, while the Australian patrols would also attempt to gain the same feature. The contacts were fierce and often at close range.[9]

From the beginning of July there was a distinct increase in Chinese radio network activity, as new gun batteries were brought into line in preparation for one last offensive. Along with the signals intercepts, and increased net traffic, numerous Chinese soldiers deserted to the Australians and Americans. The intelligence that they provided quite clearly pointed to an imminent offensive. The Chinese had enough artillery and ammunition available for the coming offensive and were not above using an artillery

---

8   Not to be confused with the Royal Northumberland Fusiliers, which left Korea after Maryang San.
9   H.R. Downey, 'The Second Battalion, the Royal Australian Regiment, Korea, 1953–1954', www.koreanwaronline.com/history/oz/2rar/2rarA.htm.

piece as an over-sized sniper rifle. Private Douglas Cruden of A Company, 3RAR, was killed in such a manner after he was spotted above the skyline in the forward positions. A Chinese 76-millimetre round landed at his feet, killing him instantly.[10]

The weather on any battlefield can cause all manner of problems to those conducting operations. July in Korea is normally the wettest month of the year. The country receives up to 60 per cent of its annual rainfall during July, flooding is common, and July 1953 was no exception.[11] Heavy monsoonal rains from early to mid-July caused the Imjin River to rise 20 metres, destroying Spoonbill Bridge and closing Teal and Harlequin Bridges and Widgeon Ferry for three days.[12] Road traffic was largely brought to a halt, forcing supplies and ammunition to be transported by six-wheel-drive US Marine amphibious vehicles (DuKWs).[13] Wounded men were sometimes evacuated on the return journey.

On the night of 14 July, heavy rain drenched the Samichon Valley, causing several bunkers to collapse in the Australian positions. On at least one occasion, a bunker's occupants had to be rescued after becoming trapped.[14] Trenches were turned into something resembling the Western Front in the winter months of the First World War, but in this case conditions were hot and very humid, the other extreme of the front-line misery scale. For the men working on the construction and repair of bunkers, the conditions were hellish.

On 19 July, negotiations for an armistice were concluded at Panmunjom. The date for the signing was set for 27 July. In the evening of 19 July, the Chinese attacked and captured the Berlin and East Berlin outposts from the US Marines. To limit any form of assistance to the Marines, the Chinese shelled the 2RAR Medium Machine Gun (MMG) section on Hill 111 and the battalion positions on the Hook, killing one man and wounding three.[15]

---

10   3rd Battalion, Royal Australian Regiment, war diary, July 1953, AWM85 4/55 [hereafter 3RAR, war diary], p. 6.
11   'Historical weather for 1953 in Seoul, South Korea', Weather Spark Beta, weatherspark.com/history/33287/1953/Seoul-Seoul-Jikhalsi-South-Korea.
12   L. Ballenger, *The Final Crucible: US Marines in Korea*, vol. 2: *1953*, Potomac Books, Washington, DC, 2002, p. 230.
13   Headquarters, 28 British Commonwealth Infantry Brigade, war diary, May–July 1953, AWM85 1/1, p. 83.
14   2nd Battalion, Royal Australian Regiment, war diary, July 1953, AWM85 3/5 [hereafter 2RAR, war diary], p. 10.
15   Ibid., p. 16.

Throughout the day of 24 July, Chinese artillery had been limited to harassing fire on 2RAR's and the Marines' positions. But at 8 pm, with heavy rain falling, the Chinese artillery fire increased to a barrage focused on positions at the Hook, Hills 121 and 111, and a position known as Boulder City. Soon after, the Australian standing patrol on Green Finger called in an artillery strike on a group of 50 Chinese infantrymen who were moving towards the Hook and Hill 121. The New Zealand gunners responded, using variable timing fuses on their shells to create airbursts, and the Chinese attack was driven back with heavy casualties.

Although several more attempts were made by the Chinese over the next few hours to attack the Hook and Hill 121, the New Zealanders' artillery fire was so effective that the attackers did not even get close to the defensive wire. However, they did manage to get spotters into a position between Hills 121 and 111 from where they called accurate fire down onto 2RAR's mortar baseplate position and rear areas.[16] The Chinese shelling caused a number of Australian casualties: 2RAR lost two men killed and several others wounded. One of those killed was Corporal Albert Wells of D Company. Corporal Jack Philpot, on his second tour in Korea, was next to Wells when a shell hit their position. He described the moments immediately after:

> 'Hey, turn off that bloody tap, what's going on, I can't see!!' I came out of a state of unconsciousness to find that the man next to me had half his head blown off. An enemy shell had scored a direct hit on our trench. The sound of the tap was his life blood pouring out onto the floor of the trench.[17]

Even before the Chinese barrage lifted from Hill 111, their infantry, who were believed to have been lying up at the toe of the 'Betty Grable' feature or in the 1.5-metre-high rushes in the paddy fields, charged through their own artillery in an attempt to overrun the Australians and Marines on the hill. They used satchel charges against bunkers and quickly captured the Marines' front-line positions.[18]

---

16   H.R. Downey, 'The Second Battalion, the Royal Australian Regiment: Korea, 1953–1954', *Korean War Online*, www.koreanwaronline.com/history/oz/2rar/2rarA.htm.
17   J. Philpot, 'Return to Korea', unpublished manuscript, AWM MSS1447.
18   2RAR, war diary, July 1953, p. 211.

Sergeant Brian Cooper, in charge of the MMG section, organised his men into all-round defence, and kept his two Vickers guns on their intended trajectory covering Hills 121 and 146. He placed a Bren gun facing the Marines' positions, which had now been overrun. Eleven surviving Marines had joined Cooper and his men in their positions and assisted in holding off the Chinese. Several Marines took cover in one of the gun bunkers, and Corporal Ron Walker was heard to say, 'Get out of there, you bastards!' Walker placed the Marines in a firing position between a machine-gun post and the command post, with orders to help defend the position.

Private Dan Mudford and Corporal Doug 'Kipper' Franklin were wounded during the Chinese assault. Mudford had dirt and sand blasted into his face and eyes and was temporarily deafened by an explosion. He was taken to the Marines' aid post by Walker.[19] Franklin was shot in his left upper arm as he defended the Australian positions when the Chinese attempted to overrun them. He was thrown back into the trench, blood spurting from a severed artery. After being stabilised, he took himself to the Marine aid post at the rear of Hill 111. Here he joined Mudford, and his wound was assessed and treated by a Marine corpsman. There were also a dozen wounded Marines in the aid post, all requiring evacuation.[20]

The mode of evacuation arrived in the most unlikely form. Corporal Les Pye, a New Zealander on secondment to the 1st Battalion, Royal Tank Regiment, arrived as crew commander of a Centurion MKI tank, which had been converted from a gun tank to an ammunition carrier/recovery vehicle, known as 'the Tug'. The vehicle's turret had been removed and two steel doors welded in place. A crew commander's structure had been added, to which a Browning .30-calibre machine gun had been mounted as a defensive weapon. Pye recalled the heavy incoming fire and the curses of his driver as hot brass flew into his compartment from the .30 calibre as Pye test-fired the weapon.[21] The Australian and Marine wounded were evacuated through 2RAR's Regimental Aid Post to the Indian Field Ambulance and on to the Norwegian Mobile Army Surgical Hospital.

---

19   R. Walker, 'Last days on the "Hook"—1953', in *Korea Remembered: The RAN, ARA and RAAF in the Korean War of 1950–1953*, ed. M. Pears and F. Kirkland, Doctrine Wing, Combined Arms Training and Development Centre, Georges Heights, NSW, 1998, pp. 159–63.
20   D.G. Franklin, letter to Olwyn Green, Papers of Charles and Olwyn Green, AWM PR0466, 6/32.
21   L. Pye, email to author, 3 July 2014; D.G. Franklin, letter to Olwyn Green, Papers of Charles and Olwyn Green, AWM PR0466, 6/32.

As the fighting intensified, Chinese porters were observed bringing up supplies of small arms, grenades and other matériel, making it obvious to those on Hill 111 that the Chinese intended to take and hold the position. In the nearby Contact Bunker, located between C Company's positions on Hill 121 and the MMG Section on Hill 111, Lance Corporal Ken Crockford noticed Chinese troops in front of his position. He and his section engaged them, forcing the Chinese to retire after a short firefight. With the situation on Hill 111 becoming dire, Cooper called a 'box me in' barrage onto his position.[22] The New Zealand gunners—again with their excellent gunnery and the deadly variable timing fuses on their shells—stopped the Chinese attack in its tracks. For the remainder of the night, Cooper and his men fought off repeated Chinese attempts to overrun his position, but just before sunrise the attacks ceased.[23]

The night had been desperate for the Marines on Boulder City. The initial Chinese barrage devastated the defensive wire and minefields and destroyed much of the Marines' trenches, bunkers and fighting positions. As at Hill 111, the Chinese attacked through their own barrage in what seemed to be overwhelming numbers.[24]

The Marines' artillery, ably supported by batteries from the US Army's 25th Infantry Division, the Turkish Brigade and the 1st Commonwealth Division (especially the 16th Field Regiment, Royal New Zealand Artillery) pounded Chinese forming-up points and their attack routes, but the situation was still dire for the Marines. During the night they were forced off the forward slope in a bitter hand-to-hand struggle in which platoons, fire teams and lone Marines fought to hold on to their positions. Others, cut off, simply played dead until they could make their way back to friendly positions. During the first night of the battle, more than 3,000 Chinese troops had assaulted the Main Line of Resistance between the Hook and Boulder City.

As dawn on 25 July broke, the Australians and Americans on the front line took stock. The positions on the Hook had not been directly attacked, although there had been casualties to the patrol on Green Finger and in the C and D Company positions of 2RAR. Chinese forces had taken the forward trenches to the west of Hill 111—what was left of them. Some

---

22 Brian Charles Cooper, interview with author, 3 November 2014.
23 Ibid.
24 P. Meid and J.M. Yingling, *US Marine Operations in Korea, 1950–1953*, vol. 5: *Operations in West Korea*, Historical Division, Headquarters, US Marine Corps, Washington, DC, 1972, p. 385.

Chinese troops had holed up in bunkers, including one near the MMG section. This was discovered when Ron Walker and Private Cranston conducted a reconnaissance into the Marines' communication trench to the west of the Australian positions. On approaching a bunker, Walker and Cranston were greeted by a Chinese grenade. The shrapnel from the resulting explosion wounded Cranston in the buttocks, but he remained on duty. The Chinese soldier refused to surrender, and Cooper ordered grenades thrown into the bunker, killing the Chinese soldier.

The Marines went to work clearing Chinese infantry out of their positions to the left of Hill 111 and on Boulder City. It took most of the day to reclaim their positions, which had further deteriorated through the Marines' use of a 3.5-inch rocket launcher borrowed from Cooper's position, as well as flame throwers and fire support from their M-46 Patton tanks used to clear the area.

While the fighting to reclaim the Marines' positions went on, Chinese stretcher parties approached the Marines' and Australian positions to collect their wounded and dead. These stretcher parties were left alone as they were non-combatants. However, those Chinese carrying weapons and moving about were engaged.[25] Ron Walker recalled sitting outside his dugout, watching Marine bodies being stretchered to the rear and feeling quite upset by it.[26] The now-depleted MMG section was relieved that afternoon by another section from 2RAR's MMG Platoon.[27]

Throughout the day, the Chinese kept up sporadic artillery fire on Australian and American positions. Once again, as evening fell the artillery fire intensified to a barrage, and Chinese forces once more advanced to attack. The US and Commonwealth artillery again opened fire on Chinese form-up points and attacking waves of infantry as they stormed forward to attack Hill 111 and Boulder City.[28] The Chinese forces again quickly gained the Marines' front lines and surrounded the Australian position on Hill 111. Lance Corporal Ken Crockford's position was also surrounded, and Chinese infantry were engaged in hand-to-hand fighting in the trenches and bunkers, which lasted well over an hour. Crockford,

---

25 Cooper, interview.
26 Walker, 'Last days on the "Hook"—1953', pp. 162–3.
27 Cooper, interview.
28 2RAR, war diary, p. 31.

like Cooper the night before, was forced to call artillery onto his position to avoid being overrun. The New Zealand gunners again responded, and the Chinese attack through the gap to Hill 121 was stopped.[29]

Fighting still raged on around Hill 111, where five men of the replacement MMG section were wounded during the night.[30] Chinese troops attacked in greater numbers than on the previous night, and again the artillery of the 1st Commonwealth Division, the US Marines and the US Army proved decisive. As on the day before, the Marines spent much of 26 July reclaiming their forward positions.[31] The Chinese attacked Boulder City and Hill 111 again that evening. These attacks were not driven home with the intensity of the previous two nights, and the Chinese forces were easily repulsed.

Just after midnight Chinese forces again attacked the Marines on Boulder City. Judging from the after-action reports in the 1st Battalion 7th Regiment's war diary, this attack was of company size and did not appear to the defenders to have been driven home with any great enthusiasm. The Marines, however, held nothing back. With artillery and tank support, they inflicted heavy casualties on the Chinese, who were forced to withdraw.[32]

The last infantry actions of the war occurred later in the morning when platoon-sized Chinese forces attacked Boulder City and Hill 111, in what were thought to be covering actions to allow their stretcher-bearers to retrieve wounded comrades.[33] During these actions the Chinese suffered further casualties. The fighting continued as the armistice was being signed a little over 8 kilometres away at Panmunjom by US and North Korean delegates, who could no doubt hear the fighting still going on.

Although Hill 111 had come under attack again, the Australians suffered no further combat casualties. The only casualty listed in 2RAR's war diary that morning was a member of the MMG section on Hill 111 who had been shot and wounded by a Marine when he was caught 'souveniring' items from Marines' packs. The man survived his wounds and, after some time recovering in Japan, was flown home to Australia.[34]

---

29   O'Neill, *Combat Operations*, p. 281.
30   2RAR, war diary, p. 34.
31   Meid and Yingling, *Operations in West Korea*, pp. 388–91.
32   Ballenger, *The Final Crucible*, p 257.
33   Cooper, interview.
34   2RAR, war diary.

During the day, the Australians and Americans took fire from Chinese artillery but received no further casualties. The New Zealanders fired a number of rounds of counter-battery fire throughout the day, and the Americans fired as many mortar, artillery, tank and small-arms rounds as they could at the Chinese positions.[35] At 10 pm the front lines fell silent as the armistice took effect.

The sounds of war had been a continuous presence for those on the front line. For many, the silence that descended on the battlefield seemed ominous. Still expecting an attack to materialise, they ensured that weapon pits remained occupied, and a watch was kept on the Chinese. As dawn broke on 28 July, the men on the Hook wondered whether the war really was over and whether the Chinese would respect the ceasefire. The ceasefire held, and over the next three days both sides dismantled their front-line defences and withdrew the required distance (2 kilometres each), thereby creating the DMZ, which is still extant at the time of writing.

During the Battle of the Samichon, leading up to ceasefire, 2RAR suffered five men killed and 24 wounded, two of whom died from their wounds. The US Marines suffered 43 men killed and 316 wounded. The Chinese casualty figures will likely never be known, but witnesses who saw the situation forward of the Australian positions on 28 July, such as Brigadier (later General Sir) John Wilton and Captain (later Major General) David Butler, estimated that 2,000–3,000 had been killed and up to 10,000 wounded.[36] Wilton's oft-quoted letter paints a vivid picture: 'the floor of the valley between the Hook and the Chinese positions was almost covered with dead Chinese … on the immediate approaches to 2RAR the bodies literally carpeted the ground sometimes two deep … It was a terrible sight which I will never forget.'[37] Since arriving on the Hook, 3RAR had suffered two men killed, including a member of the Korean Service Corps, and two wounded. 2RAR had suffered nine men killed or died of wounds and had 31 men wounded. The Marines had, over a similar period, suffered considerably greater casualties, with 181 killed and 1,430 wounded.

---

35   Meid and Yingling, *Operations in West Korea*, pp. 396–7; '11th Marine Regiment—Command Diary—July 1953', www.koreanwar2.org/kwp2/usmc/089/m089_cd24_1953_07_2479.pdf, p. 25.
36   Wilton quoted in O'Neill, *Combat Operations*, p. 282; Major General David Matheson Butler (retd) quoted in D. Horner, *Strategic Command: General Sir John Wilton and Australia's Asian Wars*, Oxford University Press, Melbourne, 2005, p. 157.
37   Wilton quoted in O'Neill, *Combat Operations*, p. 282.

Had the Hook or Boulder City fallen into Chinese hands, the consequences for the UNC forces on the Jamestown Line might well have been dire. Major General West believed that a withdrawal of 4,000 yards (3.7 kilometres) would have been necessary. Senior UN commanders also believed that had the Chinese achieved their objectives, they could have forced a renegotiation of the armistice agreement or, failing that, launched a new offensive towards Seoul.

Although the Chinese sent an elite division, supported by an increased strength in artillery and mortars, they were unable to effect a breakthrough of the Marines' or the Australian positions. Despite having the numbers in infantry, the Chinese lacked several key elements that the Australians and Marines possessed.

Over the two main nights of the battle, the Chinese infantry faced well-coordinated artillery, mortar and rocket fire; tanks, providing direct fire support; and, after the first night, when the weather cleared, air support, which delivered bombs, rockets and napalm onto the Chinese attackers. But it was the men in the trenches who had fought tenaciously, often in hand-to-hand actions that prevented the Chinese from gaining an enduring hold on the Hook, which they could have further exploited.

The Battle of the Samichon River ranks as one of the heaviest actions to which Australian soldiers were exposed during the Korean War. The scale of Chinese artillery arrayed against the men of 2RAR and 3RAR was greater than that experienced at Maryang San, but the combined-arms might of the US and Commonwealth forces was brought to bear in greater strength than at Kapyong. The coordination and support between allied nations proved decisive in bringing the Korean War to an end on the battlefield and keeping the corridor to Seoul safely closed.

14

CONTINUING THE LEGACY AND BEGINNING A NEW ERA
Australian nursing in the Korean War

Rebecca Fleming

Reflecting on the influence of the Australian nursing sisters who served in the First World War, Major Dulcie Thompson, a veteran of the Second World War and the Korean War, explained the sense of legacy felt by those who followed the First World War sisters:

> They came back and it was still very evident at the beginning of the Second World War that those women ... were something special and I think that helped them raise the status of civilian nursing ... But it was quite evident to us when we came into the army in the late 1930s and '40s that we had a great legacy from those women.[1]

As deputy matron in charge of Australian nurses at the British Commonwealth General Hospital (BCGH) in Kure, Japan, Thompson ensured that this legacy was inherited by nurses in the Korean War. As their predecessors had done, they carried out their work with a sense of professionalism, resourcefulness and dedication to the care of their patients. In many ways their experiences of war shared continuities with

---

1   Dulcie Thompson, interview with Jan Bassett, 16 July 1987, AWM S01811.

experiences of earlier conflicts. However, the Korean War also heralded an era of transition for Australian military nursing, and it is this balance of continuity and transition that is the focus here.

This chapter outlines the significance of the Korean War in the history of Australian military nursing, while highlighting the contribution made by Australian military nurses to that war. This contribution, although limited in numbers, was significant. The nominal roll of Australian veterans of the Korean War lists 34 Royal Australian Army Nursing Corps (RAANC) sisters and 21 Royal Australian Air Force Nursing Service (RAAFNS) sisters as serving in the Korean War between 1952 and 1956.[2] But military nursing's contribution to the war went beyond that. The major support base and hospital for the British Commonwealth troops was at the BCGH in Kure, Japan, and that is where the majority of Australian army nurses were based.[3] The army nursing staff there included trained nursing sisters, who were officers, and other-rank nursing assistants. The other ranks were formerly members of the Australian Army Medical Women's Services (AAMWS) staff who were incorporated into the military nursing hierarchy after the closure of the AAMWS when the army nursing service was made a corps in 1951.[4]

Not all of the army nurses stationed in Japan also served in Korea. The monthly reports for the BCGH in Japan included a nominal roll of staff, but there are gaps in the collection, as not all reports have survived. As a result, the exact number of army nurses who supported the Korean War from the BCGH in Japan is not known. However, an examination of BCGH reports reveals that more than 180 RAANC officers and other ranks served in Japan between 1951 and 1956.[5] As the reports for 1950 are not available, the true figure is perhaps higher than 180. Of these, 34 served in Korea, usually for two-month rotations.[6] Combined with the 21 RAAFNS sisters, the records indicate that at least 201 Australian military nurses supported the Korean War in either Japan or Korea.

---

2   Nominal Roll of Australian veterans of the Korean War, nominal-rolls.dva.gov.au/.
3   H.C.H. Robertson to Secretary Chiefs of Staff Committee, 31 October 1951, British Korea Medal, MP927/1, A81/1/187, National Archives of Australia [NAA].
4   J. Bassett, *Guns and Brooches: Australian Army Nursing from the Boer War to the Gulf War*, Oxford University Press, Melbourne, 1997, p. 180.
5   British Commonwealth Base General Hospital, Army Component, 1950–56, AWM52, 11/2/45.
6   Betty Lawrence (née Crocker), interview with Rob Linn, 22 May 2002, J.D. Somerville Oral History Collection, OH 644/7, State Library of South Australia.

The work carried out by nurses varied, depending on their location and service. At the BCGH in Kure, Australian nurses worked alongside British and Canadian nurses in an integrated hospital.[7] The BCGH staff worked in medical and surgical wards as well as in theatre.[8] Shifts mirrored those in the civilian sector, with the exception that staff stayed on duty to assist when convoys of patients arrived.[9] Other ranks carried out nursing assistant duties, while sisters either were rostered on to manage the wards or assisted surgeons as theatre sisters. RAANC sister Betty Lawrence (née Crocker), who worked as a theatre sister, recalled that she was occasionally called on to complete sutures if the surgeons were called to a more urgent task. This kind of work was not normally assigned to nurses in the civilian sector.[10]

Injuries ranged from bullet and shrapnel wounds to abdominal wounds and frostbite, but the injuries that stood out for all the nurses were the severe burns, often the result of fires lit by soldiers in dugouts to keep warm in the freezing Korean winter.[11] Dulcie Thompson recalled that these burns were so 'frightful' that she ensured nurses were not rostered to be with burns patients for long periods.[12] Betty Hunt-Smith's recollection of treating one particular patient confirms the emotional difficulty for the nurses:

> I had to deal with a patient and I walked towards him and I stopped, and I almost turned and walked out again, because he had been burnt by flamethrower, so that his entire face and his ears and hands were totally burnt. So I had to just pull myself together and go to him, talk to him.[13]

Duties at the British Commonwealth General Hospital occasionally extended beyond the hospital, with sisters being rostered onto convoy duty, which was rotated between the three Commonwealth nations. Convoy duty involved caring for patients in a train carriage as they were transported from Iwakuni airbase to the hospital in Kure. The journey was

---

7   Margaret (Peg) Webster (née Nicholson), interview with Jan Bassett, 3 November 1986, AWM S01820.
8   Colonel E.J. Bowe, visit to Japan, Korea and Hong Kong, 26 April to 31 May 1954, RAANC clothing in Korea, NAA, MP927, A61/1/55.
9   Margaret (Peg) Webster, interview.
10 Betty Lawrence, interview.
11 Barbara Probyn Smith, 'Sis', unpublished manuscript, PA Box 58 01/144, State Library of Victoria.
12 Dulcie Thompson, interview.
13 Betty Hunt Smith, interview with Bill Bunbury, 26 November 1998, AWM S01910.

about 50 miles (80 kilometres), over which nurses did their best to ensure a smooth transition, and the comfort of patients, between the airbase and hospital. There were no doctors rostered to the convoy, so nurses were responsible for making key medical decisions during the trip and advising of medical and triage information at the handover.[14]

From September 1952, RAANC sisters were stationed in Korea for two-month rotations, working alongside Canadian and British nurses in the British Commonwealth Communications Zone Medical Unit (BCCZMU) in an old school house in the suburbs of Seoul, some 30 miles (48 kilometres) from the Korean front line.[15] Conditions were difficult, and at first there was neither running water nor sheets for the beds.[16] By 1955 running water had been installed on the top and ground floors, but water still had to be transported by buckets to the centre floor.[17] The work at the BCCZMU was, as Lawrence described it, 'advanced first-aid'.[18] As there were no facilities for surgery, the BCCZMU worked as a transit hospital in which patients were stabilised for the flight to Japan.[19]

Unlike the hospital duties carried out by RAANC nurses, the main role of RAAF sisters in the war was working on air evacuation flights. RAAFNS sisters worked on DC-3 Dakota aircraft. These planes were equipped to carry 24 litter patients or 27 walking patients, usually a combination of both. The Dakotas flew between the base at Iwakuni in Japan and Kimpo airbase near Seoul in Korea, where the casualties were picked up. The flight between Iwakuni and Kimpo took three to four hours. An RAAFNS sister and a male medical orderly accompanied all flights.[20] As there were no doctors on board, the RAAF sister was responsible for the welfare of patients on the flight and had final say on whether or not the patients were to fly.[21]

---

14   E.J. McNair, *A British Army Nurse in the Korean War: Shadows of the Far Forgotten*, Tempus, Stroud, Gloucs, 2007, p. 141.
15   Bassett, *Guns and Brooches*, p. 183.
16   koreavets.tassie.net.au/espie.htm (site no longer exists).
17   Colonel E.J. Bowe, visit to Japan, Korea and Hong Kong.
18   Betty Lawrence, letter to Darryl McIntyre, in R. O'Neill, *Australia in the Korean War 1950–1953*, vol. 2: *Combat Operations*, AWM & AGPS, Canberra, 1985, p. 571.
19   Betty Lawrence, interview.
20   N.M. Kater, 'Air evacuation of casualties in the Korean War', *Medical Journal of Australia*, vol. 2, issue 3, 1953, p. 95.
21   Catherine Thompson (née Daniel), interview, 7 August 2007 (tape in possession of author).

The RAAFNS sisters also accompanied patients between Japan and Australia, escorting Australian patients home. RAAFNS sisters would also occasionally accompany British patients as far as Singapore, where they would hand them over to British nursing sisters and enjoy some leave on the British base there.[22] The flights to Australia were run fortnightly through Qantas. Escort duty to Australia was long, exhausting work for 27–30 hours of flying time; it was unlike anything that the nurses had performed in the civilian sector.[23]

In addition to flight duty, RAAFNS sisters staffed a holding ward at Iwakuni airbase. Here, they washed and fed incoming patients, attended to their dressings and administered any medication needed.[24] Their contact with the patients was transitional, the main priority being to facilitate the evacuation process.

In all, between February 1951, when the RAAF took over the evacuation of British Commonwealth casualties from Korea, and June 1956, when the last two RAAF sisters left Japan, RAAF sisters assisted in the evacuation of 14,924 casualties between Korea and Japan, 884 casualties between Japan and Australia, and 1,806 casualties between Japan and the United Kingdom.[25]

In many ways the experiences of the Korean War nurses mirrored experiences in earlier conflicts. Those who nursed at the BCCZMU in Korea faced the challenges of working with limited facilities and equipment. Perditta McCarthy recalled carrying out night rounds with the aid of a hurricane lamp[26]—sisters of the Australian Army Nursing Service (AANS) had faced similar challenges on Lemnos in the First World War.[27] Climate has often posed challenges for military nurses—the AANS sisters who served in the First World War faced extremes in climate, from the freezing winter in France to extreme heat in Egypt.[28] Korea posed similar

---

22   Ibid.
23   No. 91 Composite Wing monthly medical report for August 1952, British Commonwealth Forces Korea, NAA, A705, 132/2/866.
24   Catherine Thompson, interview.
25   Report of medical section of RAAF transport flight for June 1956, British Commonwealth Forces Korea, NAA, A705, 132/2/866, Part 1.
26   R. Siers, 'Perditta McCarthy: A remarkable lady, with an indomitable spirit and a wonderful sense of humour', 15 March 2012, www.awm.gov.au/articles/blog/perditta-mccarthy-a-remarkable-lady-with-an-indomitable-spirit-and-a-wonderful-sense-of-humour.
27   K. Harris, *More Than Bombs and Bandages: Australian Army Nurses at Work in World War I*, Big Sky Publishing, Sydney, 2011, p. 62.
28   Ibid., p. 69.

challenges. Betty Lawrence recalled that the temperatures were so cold in Korea that sisters would carry penicillin in the pockets of their parkas to prevent the medication from freezing.[29]

In addition to nursing duties, some RAANC officers in Japan were also rostered on three-month rotations in the role of mess sister, during which they managed catering and events for the officers' mess. After managing functions ranging from social dinners to weddings, Nell Espie recalled that she felt like 'quite the caterer'.[30] This role had also been carried out by AANS sisters during the First World War.[31] In some ways, however, the Korean War signalled an era of transition for military nursing. The key transition in this period was mirrored in the broader Australian military: the increasing professionalisation of military nursing and a move towards career military nursing, rather than recruitment for the duration of a conflict.

A sign of these changes is evident in the motivations of the nurses who joined for the entire Korean War. The decisions of some nurses mirrored those of earlier generations of nurses and of other K Force volunteers. Richard Trembath identified five main motivations of K Force volunteers: a desire for adventure; career advancement; to combat communism; and the final two factors were linked—economic motivation and a feeling of what Trembath called 'restlessness' or social dislocation.[32] In line with other K Force volunteers, RAAF Sister Pamela Leahy cited the opportunity for adventure as one of the reasons for her enlistment,[33] as had AANS sisters of the Second World War.[34] RAAF sister Cathie Thompson (née Daniel) saw Korea as an opportunity to serve in war after having missed the chance to join during the Second World War, a motivation shared by some K Force volunteers.[35]

In some ways the motivations of Korean War nurses aligned with those of earlier generations, but it was the opportunity for career advancement that distinguishes some Korean War nurses from their predecessors.

---

29 Betty Lawrence, interview.
30 Nell Espie, interview, 5 December 2007 (tape in possession of author).
31 Harris, *More Than Bombs and Bandages*, p. 62.
32 R. Trembath, *A Different Sort of War: Australians in Korea 1950–1953*, Australian Scholarly Publishing, Melbourne, 2005, p. 97.
33 Department of Veterans' Affairs, *Korea Biographies Official Veteran Representatives: 50th Anniversary 2001 Commemorative Mission*, Department of Veterans' Affairs, Canberra, 2001, p. 28.
34 Bassett, *Guns and Brooches*, p. 114.
35 Catherine Thompson, interview, and Trembath, *A Different Sort of War*, p. 97.

Betty Lawrence was reading through a newspaper on nightshift at Northfield Hospital in Adelaide when she noticed an advertisement recruiting nurses for K Force:

> And at that time it was the end of the polio epidemic and I was just beginning to sort of think, what will I do now? And I don't know whether it was because of my father—I knew he'd been in the First World War but I hadn't heard much about it—or what, but I thought, 'Well, I've got the qualifications, I'll apply.' I felt that I was the sort of person they were looking for; I thought I'd be useful.[36]

In one sense these motivations clearly align with those of the male K Force volunteers, in that Lawrence saw joining the RAANC to serve in Korea as an opportunity for career advancement. However, in another sense the kind of career advancement being sought was quite distinct. As a trained nursing sister, Lawrence was seeking to advance her nursing career, not a career in the military. She also viewed her contribution to the war as that of a skilled career professional.

This emphasis on career advancement and travel were also themes drawn upon in the recruitment campaigns of the era. During the 1950s, the campaigns for the women's services adopted a new focus—not concentrating on service for a particular conflict, but rather promoting long-term career prospects. Career development was now promoted by the defence forces as a reason to join. This signalled a new era in military nursing, in which a permanent nursing service could now be seen as a long-term career for single women. Women were, however, still required to be discharged on marriage.[37] Where recruitment campaigns of the Second World War called on women to 'join us in a victory job', campaigns in the Korean War era drew attention to opportunities for career advancement.[38] One poster, aimed at recruiting other ranks nursing assistants, explicitly drew upon the legacy of army nursing but still used career opportunity as its key emphasis.[39] The advertisement noted that no experience was needed and highlighted attractive pay and conditions,

---

36 Betty Lawrence, interview.
37 Pay and Allowances—Women's Services, memorandum, 29 August 1950, NAA, MP927/1, A247/1/38.
38 M. Oppenheimer, *Australian Women and War*, Department of Veterans' Affairs, Canberra, 2008, p.186.
39 Recruiting women's services including the Royal Australian Army Nursing Corps [RAANC]—Women's Royal Australian Army Corps [WRAAC]—Women's Royal Australian Naval Service [WRANS]—Women's Royal Australian Air Force [WRAAF], NAA, B1552, 605.

promoting the opportunity for a 'satisfying and rewarding career'.[40] Another recruitment poster, aimed at officers, balanced traditional motivations for joining, including 'the prospect of adventure, travel, and advancement', with professional development opportunities, including 'post-graduate courses at the College of Nursing Australia [e.g. Tutor Sister] and participation in refresher courses in all branches of nursing'.[41] Neither poster was specifically targeted at recruitment for Korea, but both give an indication of the strong shift towards longer term career development and professionalisation.

Military nursing training during the Korean War also underwent a significant change, and it was through induction courses that a more militarised culture began to be introduced to Australian military nursing. Newly enlisted officers and other ranks were instructed in military discipline. Other ranks were also given training in basic nursing care.[42] Betty Lawrence recalled that her training at the School of Army Health at Healesville, Victoria, included training in 'military discipline, military administration, military law, expected behaviour at military functions and of course parade ground drill and marching'. In addition, she explained, 'nursing officers were trained in procedures normally outside the range of civilian nurses such as suturing, intravenous transfusions, anaesthetic techniques, assessment and classification according to military rules of injuries, and transportation of wounded'.[43] For some nurses who had joined the army before the Korean War, this new emphasis on military discipline was not a transition always openly embraced. Nancy Hummerston, for example, disliked the new rules requiring nurses to salute when they were not in indoor dress uniform: 'I didn't like all that. I used to avoid … if there was a senior officer anywhere, hav[ing] to salute.'[44]

The training for RAAFNS also changed during the Korean War era. In the Second World War, only an elite group of women were trained in medical air evacuation duties, as part of the Royal Australian Air Force Medical Air Evacuation Transport Unit.[45] Following the remobilisation of the RAAFNS, the new training procedures incorporated air evacuation

---

40 Oppenheimer, *Australian Women and War*, p. 186.
41 Ibid.
42 'Initial Training—RAANC Ors CMF Block Syllabus of Training—12 months', Women's services—introduction of Women's Royal Australian Army Corps as staff officers, NAA, K1214/1, 241/1/018.
43 Betty Lawrence to Darryl McIntyre, letter, 4 April 1982, AWM137.
44 Nancy Hummerston, interview, 6 December 2007 (tape in possession of author).
45 Oppenheimer, *Australian Women and War*, p. 102.

training for all recruits. In addition to a three-week basic course, recruits undertook an aeromedical evacuation course, which included a demonstration of air-to-sea rescue, a dinghy drill and training flights.[46] Unlike in the Second World War, all RAAF sisters deployed in Korea served on medical air evacuation duties, so the new emphasis on aeromedical evacuation in the training course reflected an expansion in the role of RAAF sisters as flight nurses.

Training for the deployed nurses also became more formalised, particularly for the other ranks, now formally part of the corps. A number of professional development initiatives were implemented at the BCGH in Kure, ranging from lectures and educational visits, to broader work opportunities such as working as an assistant in theatre. In her 1954 report of her visit to Japan and Korea, Matron-in-Chief Colonel Bowie noted the value of such an opportunity: 'At present one officer and one other-rank RAANC are included in the theatre team in order to gain more experience and training in this highly specialised work.'[47]

Although the other ranks no doubt benefited from the increased professional development that came from being part of the corps, the change in status that came with moving from AAMWS to other ranks, which occurred while many were supporting the Korean War in Japan in 1951, caused some distress. Stationed in Japan as part of the AAMWS, the nurses had more or less been treated as officers, and when their status changed to other ranks they were no longer afforded this status. Dulcie Thompson, who was matron at the time, explained the challenge of this cultural change:

> They were not allowed to come into the Officers' Club. My attitude was that I thought that you could have made an exception for the region, as long as the club changed their rules to let all or any of them come in. But the rule was that they could come in if they were invited and I thought that was not fair. Because there were some people who would be invited all the time and some who [would not] … It was a difficult situation to resolve and nobody was very happy about it … But as those people went home and the new ones came up they didn't really give much thought to it at all.[48]

---

46   E.J. Bowe and C. McRae, 'Nursing in the Australian military services', *American Journal of Nursing*, vol. 58, no. 3, 1958, p. 379.
47   Colonel E.J. Bowe, visit to Japan, Korea and Hong Kong.
48   Dulcie Thompson, interview.

A key element that linked the Korean War nurses with earlier generations was their relationship with the wounded men. The nurses' accounts of their patients demonstrate the centrality of these men to their experience of war. While soldiers might recall the enemy, the landscape and the weapons, for nurses the central narrative of their stories is the patients and their wounds. Korean War nurses tended to refer to their patients as 'boys', as military nurses had done in earlier conflicts, often constructing the nurses' role in a maternal light.[49] Marjorie Ford captured this spirit when she commented fondly that they were 'lovely boys … Lovely young men. If you would've been their mother you would have been proud of them'.[50] Ford not only referred to her patients as 'boys' but also explicitly adopted a maternal subjectivity when speaking of them. The nurses were sometimes older than their patients, but not usually old enough to be their mothers.

What stands out as unique among Korean War nurses is their fondness for their British patients. In earlier wars, Australian nurses tended to express a particular fondness for Australian patients.[51] While Korean War nurses were equally fond of their Australian 'boys', the British patients held a special place in many of their hearts. The reason for this special relationship was that many of the British patients were national service conscripts and were often very young. RAANC other-rank Shirley McEwen explained her feelings on the issue:

> You know when you get 18-year-olds in with some horrific wounds. I used to get on a bit of a soapbox about it. I couldn't change it. I couldn't fix it. But I could sound off about it. And we all did. We felt it quite strongly, most of us.[52]

The combination of youth and conscription greatly affected the nurses and foreshadowed political sentiments that would be expressed in Australia during the Vietnam War.

---

49 K. Holmes, 'Day mothers and night sisters: World War I nurses and sexuality', in *Gender and War: Australians at War in the Twentieth Century*, ed. J. Damousi and M. Lake, Cambridge University Press, Cambridge, 1995, p. 46.
50 Marjorie Ford, interview, 23 April 2008 (tape in possession of author).
51 In letters home, First World War Sister Narrelle Hobbes, for example, expressed a distinct preference for nursing Australian soldiers; see M. Oppenheimer, *Oceans of Love*, ABC, Sydney, 2006, p. 19.
52 Shirley Bennetts, interview with Bill Bunbury, 1998, AWM S01904.

14. CONTINUING THE LEGACY AND BEGINNING A NEW ERA

Australians served in the Korean War as part of the United Nations force. For RAANC nurses, this meant serving in an integrated hospital alongside British and Canadian nurses. In earlier conflicts, Australian nurses had worked with other nursing services, particularly the British, usually seconded from their own Australian units or having joined through the British military nursing system. Kirsty Harris has estimated that only 800 of the approximately 2,700 AANS personnel who served during the First World War did so in purely Australian units.[53] The distinction in the Korean War was that Australian nurses served in an integrated force from the beginning.

For the most part, the records and reflections of the nurses suggest that this system worked well. The wards were set up so that each ward was staffed by a particular nursing service, while specialists and other medical staff were allocated from a different country.[54] This ensured that the wards were not segregated by nationality and that nurses could work alongside colleagues who had been trained under the same system. Official reports and anecdotal evidence from the nurses emphasised that teamwork played a large role in the success of the unit.

As was the case in earlier wars, the Australian nurses felt that the British sisters adhered more closely to military rules. This occasionally frustrated the Australians, who considered themselves more practically focused. Nora Hayles recounted one story in which she was frustrated by the need to show deference to a British sister:

> Now for instance I can remember one ward. The sister had taken her day off and there was an English sister there, and [we] had a patient who had put in for a leave pass. He was on a strict diet, mind you, and he'd asked for a day's leave pass. And I said, 'You better get the major to either cancel his diet or cancel his pass.' 'Oh,' she said. 'Oh no, I couldn't ask him that.' … I don't say they're all like that, but this one … couldn't ask them to change anything.[55]

---

53   K. Harris, 'Red rag to a British bull? Australian trained nurses working with British nurses during World War One', in *Exploring the British World: Identity, Cultural Production, Institutions*, ed. K. Darian Smith, P. Grimshaw, K. Lindsey and S. Macintyre, RMIT Publishing, Melbourne, 2004, p. 126.
54   N.C. Davis, 'Surgical aspects of the Korean War, March 1951 to February 1952', *Medical Journal of Australia*, vol. 2, issue 11, 1952, p. 372.
55   Nora Trethewie (née Hayles), interview with Jan Bassett, 23 May 1987, AWM S01809.

IN FROM THE COLD

Although the Korean War represented a shift towards a more militarised culture in army nursing, this story illustrates that Australian nurses were not completely absorbed into a military culture; they still valued their practicality.

Another key aspect of the Korean War that embodied a change in military nursing was that many of the nurses were or would become veterans of more than one war. The Australian nurses who served in Korea were a combination of newly recruited members and veterans of the Second World War, as was the case with the broader K Force contingent. The RAAFNS in particular benefited from the experiences of women with experience of a previous war, such as Helen Cleary, Lucy Marshall and Phyllis Scholz, who had undertaken pioneering aeromedical evacuation work in New Guinea during the Second World War. These veterans now served in Korea, mentoring new members.[56] Cathie Thompson, who enlisted in the RAAFNS for the Korean War, fondly recalled working with Helen Cleary, a more experienced nurse, and admired the work she had done in Singapore. She recalled that Cleary had lots of tales, some sad and others funny.[57] As the Korean War came so soon after the Second World War, it gave the opportunity for new nurses to learn directly from those with conflict experience.

Many of the RAAF sisters who served in Korea went on to have significant military careers. For example, Helen Cleary had joined the RAAFNS in 1943 and was one of the earliest members to be involved in medical air evacuation duties, serving in New Guinea, Borneo and Singapore in the evacuation of prisoners of war, as well as teaching the first Australian postwar medical air evacuation course. From 1952 until mid-1953 she was the senior sister at Iwakuni. After the war she continued a career in the RAAFNS, reaching the position of matron-in-chief in 1967 and retiring from that position and the RAAFNS in 1969.[58] RAAFNS sisters Betty Bristow Docker and Betty Edwards, who both also rose to the position of matron-in-chief, had also served in Japan and Korea.[59]

---

56   'Brief on nursing career in RAAFNS', in O'Neill, *Combat Operations*, p. 582, and RAAFNS historical events photographs and news items (scrapbook), 1940–64, part 3, AWM137, 3/3.
57   Catherine Thompson, interview.
58   G. Halstead, *Story of the RAAF Nursing Service, 1940–1990*, Nungurner Press, Metung, Vic, 1994, pp. 381–4.
59   Ibid., pp. 385–402.

14. CONTINUING THE LEGACY AND BEGINNING A NEW ERA

A number of RAANC officers who served in Korea also went on to have distinguished military careers. Two examples are Nell Espie and Perditta McCarthy. Espie joined the corps in July 1951 and served in Japan and Korea from July 1952 until April 1954. Following the Korean War, she built a successful military nursing career, serving in Malaya and Vietnam and culminating her service with an appointment to lieutenant colonel and matron-in-chief of the RAANC in January 1971.[60] The creation of the RAANC in 1951, together with the new emphasis on career within the RAANC, was a major shift in the conception of the role of Australian military nurses. Espie was one of the first career military nurses. Her fellow Korean War RAANC officer, Perditta McCarthy, who had also served in Papua New Guinea and with the British Commonwealth Occupation Force in postwar Japan, was the first Australian army nurse to be promoted to the rank of brigadier.[61]

Of course, not all the nurses who served in Korea continued a military nursing career. Some married and raised families, others pursued civilian nursing careers. For some, such as Nora Hayles, a career in the army in a period of peace did not offer the same challenges as wartime nursing. After returning from Japan, Hayles worked at a camp hospital at Puckapunyal, caring for national servicemen. The nursing work was quite different from that which she had undertaken in Japan. She recalled that it was mostly medical, with little surgical work. The lack of surgical work apparently influenced her decision to leave the army, saying that she left because 'there wasn't the work to do'.[62] So although military nursing was increasingly being promoted as a long-term career during this period, it did not necessarily offer the challenges associated with nursing in a war zone.

On her return from Korea, RAANC sister Dorothy Wheatley stayed in the corps to develop her interest in nursing education, which she had developed by working with United States Army nurses in Korea. While still in the army, Wheatley completed a Diploma in Education at the Royal College of Nursing, Australia, then went on to work at the School of Army Health at Healesville, Victoria. After 10 years with the RAANC, she decided it was time to move on. She met a former colleague who offered her a position as a nurse educator at Sir Charles Gairdner Hospital

---

60 Espie, Nellie Jane, NAA, B2458, F64.
61 Oppenheimer, *Australian Women and War*, p. 189.
62 Nora Trethewie, interview.

in Perth. For the next 25 years this position provided her the opportunity to pursue her passion for nursing education. During her time at the hospital she was involved in the transfer of nursing training from hospitals to a university-based system, and she retired when the last hospital-based school closed.[63] Wheatley's nursing career from the Korean War onwards was focused on the change to the university-based system, which she had admired while working with American nurses during the war. Although she did not remain in the RAANC, Wheatley's experiences in the Korean War were clearly influential in her later nursing career.

For women such as Shirley Bennetts (née McEwen), the connections made with the patients they nursed influenced their personal and political views. Reflecting on how she was changed by the war, Bennetts said:

> I think growing up during the war, I thought to go and fight for your country was a very brave heroic wonderful thing, but by the time I got up there and saw what it was, I didn't think it was quite so good … Seeing these young men. Seeing the injuries, the burns, the amputations, from treading on landmines. And I just thought, what a waste of young men.[64]

The Korean War undoubtedly changed the lives of all who were touched by it, and the Australian Korean War nurses were no exception.

---

63 Dorothy Wheatley, interview, 7 January 2008 (tape in possession of author).
64 Shirley Bennetts, interview.

PART 5
LEGACIES

A Chinese officer, Hshwang Shon Kwang, presents a red 'peace' flag to Douglas Bushby, an Australian war correspondent, in no man's land, the day after the ceasefire in Korea took effect. Jamestown Line, the Hook, 28 July 1953.

Source: AWM P04641.119. Image courtesy of Douglas Bushby.

A Republic of Korea military policeman stands guard at Panmunjom in 2001. South Korean and North Korean guards still continue to face off, only metres apart, at Panmunjom.

Source: AWM P03529.001.

The Korean War remains unfinished. As yet, no peace treaty exists between the West and North Korea. This propaganda poster, produced after the armistice in July 1953, remains relevant today. c. 1953.
Source: AWM ARTV08071.

The long-lasting individual and social influences of the Korean War on Australia are remembered and recognised at the Australian National Korean War Memorial in Canberra, Australia.
Source: Image courtesy of Liam Brewin Higgins.

15

FROM KOREA TO VIETNAM
Australian strategic policy after the Korean War

Peter Edwards

It has been commonplace to assert that the 1950s and 1960s were times when Australia became locked into the Cold War policies of the United States, leading to the costly, futile and divisive involvement in America's war in Vietnam. Let us subject that view to a closer examination.

To better understand the place of the Korean War and its aftermath in the history of Australian strategic policy, we should stand back a little to grasp the shape of the forest rather than of the individual trees. This reveals a recurring pattern. After a major turbulence in the world order, such as a world war, there is a period of vigorous strategic debate in Australia, as policy-makers seek to assess the shape of the emerging postwar world order and to develop broad policies that will place Australia to best advantage in that order. This generally involves a degree of tension between the two poles around which Australia's strategic thought has long revolved. One pole, the globalist approach, asserts that Australia is a large continent with a small population. Not only its geography but also its interests, values, ethnicity and identity dictate that it must remain closely associated with allies, especially those that Robert Menzies famously described as our 'great and powerful friends': Britain and the United

States.[1] The other pole, the regionalist approach, questions whether these distant allies have the capacity, or perhaps even the will, to support Australia's defence needs and asserts that excessive reliance on allies leads to involvement in other people's wars; it argues that Australia should take a more independent policy, concentrating on making friends and deterring potential enemies within its own region. The tension between these two approaches—the globalists who speak of alliance and the regionalists who speak of independence—has been evident since at least the mid-nineteenth century.

During the debate over the new world order, the government of the day usually seeks to develop a strategic posture that will reassure both the globalists and the regionalists, as far as possible, by demonstrating that Australia's alliances strengthen its regional relationships and vice versa. In a democracy, it is highly desirable that the new posture can be expressed in a simple and electorally appealing formula. Over the twentieth century, Australian governments generally succeeded in coming up with a posture and a formula that met these demands, a posture that lasted for roughly a generation. After this time, once there was any major war or transformation of the world order, the old strategic posture would be regarded as obsolete or discredited, and the search for a new one would begin. This cycle can be identified on four occasions, coinciding roughly with the four quarters of the twentieth century.

The process of resolving the global and regional imperatives usually leads to a strategic posture that takes, at its core, a triangular form. At one corner is Australia, at the second is Australia's major ally, or alliance structure, and at the third is what Australia's policy-makers perceive to be the most significant actual or potential threat, situated somewhere in the Asia-Pacific region. Today, for example, many strategic pundits are devoting their attention to the Australia–US–China triangle. It displays some remarkable similarities to, as well as some highly important contrasts with, the triangle formed by Australia, Britain and Japan that preoccupied Australian attention for the first four decades of the twentieth century. This approach has become the standard way in which Australians have thought about their strategic challenges.

---

1   R. Menzies, 'Election speeches', 1949, Museum of Australian Democracy at Old Parliament House, electionspeeches.moadoph.gov.au/speeches/1949-robert-menzies.

15. FROM KOREA TO VIETNAM

During the 1920s and 1930s Australia's strategic posture was known as the Singapore strategy: the concept that the development of a British naval base at Singapore would deter, and if necessary defeat, any southward thrust by the Japanese against British and Australian interests. This strategic approach was regional, in that it focused on the threat of Japanese expansionism in the Asia Pacific, and it was also an alliance policy, relying heavily on Britain's capacity and will to act in the region. Thus it was essentially triangular. The spectacular failure of this strategy, culminating in the fall of Singapore on 15 February 1942, was not only 'the worst disaster and greatest capitulation in British history', as Winston Churchill famously described it, but also a catastrophe for Australia's national strategic policy. For the next three and a half years Australia was heavily involved in what was, in fact, one world war, but one that has often been discussed almost as if it were two separate wars: the one fought in Europe alongside, and some would say for, Britain; and the other in the Pacific, allegedly more in Australia's immediate national interests, fighting alongside the United States against the empire of Japan.

After 1945, Australian strategic policy-makers entered a new period of debate as they sought to assess the nature of the strategic challenges in the postwar world order and the appropriate response for Australia. Once again, the central quandary was whether to take a global-alliance or a regional approach, or in some way to combine the two. Should Australia concentrate—as British civilian and military authorities urged—on the perceived threat of a third world war, in which the principal enemy would be the Soviet Union? If so, Australia would once again be expected to make its principal military contribution in the regions extending from the Middle East into southern Europe, covering North Africa as well as western and south-western Asia. Within this area were names that already resonated in Australian military history, including Gallipoli, Beersheba, Villers-Bretonneux, Tobruk, Greece, Crete and El Alamein. (Today we might add Iraq and even, to stretch but not break the boundaries, Afghanistan.) Alternatively, should Australia be more concerned by the numerous revolutions, rebellions and insurgencies in South-East Asia in the shadow of the 1949 victory of the Chinese Communist Party in China's civil war? While policy-makers debated these and related issues, there came a blunt reminder of the aphorism that life is what happens while we are making other plans, for a major war broke out quite unexpectedly in north-east Asia. Nevertheless, even as Australia and many other nations were engaged in combat on the Korean Peninsula, decisions were being made that would shape Australia's strategy and its military commitments for the next generation.

The strategic posture of the third quarter of the twentieth century was often encapsulated in the phrase 'forward defence'. After the Vietnam War, this posture was for some decades discredited. What were the principal elements of forward defence, and how was it influenced by the experience of the Korean War?

The first point to note was the virtually exclusive focus on South-East Asia. Because we now tend to think of this period as the lead-up to the Vietnam War, this South-East Asian focus is often taken for granted, but it was by no means as automatic as it now appears. After extensive debate and discussions, especially with British authorities, Australian policy-makers took a clear and conscious decision to focus Australia's military and diplomatic commitments on South-East Asia rather than the Mediterranean and Middle East theatre. By the late 1940s there was great turmoil in South-East Asia, prompted by the complex interaction of two great historical processes of the twentieth century. On one hand, a worldwide Cold War was developing between the communist and anti-communist blocs. On the other hand, anti-colonial nationalist movements, seeking independence from the European empires, were proving far stronger than most in the West had expected. Trying to work out what was anti-colonial nationalism and what was communist expansionism became a major preoccupation for policy-makers and planners. The turmoil in South-East Asia began even before the outbreak of the Korean War, for 1948 saw a number of revolutions and insurgencies erupt across the region, reminiscent of Europe in 1848.

From this time onwards the dominant, almost exclusive focus of Australian strategy and diplomacy was on the successive crises in the area to Australia's north. This attention was not totally exclusive, for RAAF aircraft participated in the Berlin airlift of 1948–49 and two RAAF fighter squadrons were posted to Malta in 1952–54 to support British and NATO activities. But by far the dominant concerns for Australian policy-makers were the Indonesian revolution and its protracted aftermath; the dispute over the future of West New Guinea, which was not settled until the early 1960s; the Malayan Emergency, which lasted officially from 1948 to 1960 and which saw the first commitment overseas of Australian troops in peacetime; *Konfrontasi*, the Indonesian Confrontation of the new federation of Malaysia in the early 1960s; and a succession of crises on mainland South-East Asia variously involving Vietnam, Thailand, Laos and Cambodia and culminating in the Vietnam War, which dominated the world's attention in the late 1960s and early 1970s. Today, the terms *Malaya* and *Confrontation* (or 'Borneo') now figure alongside Vietnam on memorials and in Anzac Day commemorations, but even well-informed Australians have little idea of how deeply concerned Australians were, not only by these conflicts but also by other actual and potential conflicts in the region.

The second major element of forward defence involved the alliance corner of the strategic triangle. The Australian Government in the 1950s and 1960s, especially during the long prime ministership of Robert Menzies, was absolutely determined that its armed forces would be committed only in South-East Asia and that they would operate only in close collaboration with those 'great and powerful friends'. While it was a strongly regional policy, it was also strongly an alliance policy. Self-reliance was explicitly ruled out. In 1959 the government's senior military and civilian defence advisers urged the government to move towards at least a limited degree of self-reliance, largely in reaction to the unhelpful direction of US policy on West New Guinea. The cabinet firmly rejected any such notion, reasserting that Australian forces were to be designed to operate only in South-East Asia and only in close alliance with Britain and the United States, or preferably (as in Korea) both. The Korean experience of serving in a British Commonwealth force within a wider US-led coalition established a highly attractive model.

Robert Menzies's famous reference to 'great and powerful friends' was in the plural. Although historians have been trying to correct the record on this for more than 30 years, one still hears accounts that imply that Australia turned dramatically and totally from the United Kingdom to the United States as its primary strategic partner. Australian Labor Party supporters still like to point to Curtin's famous statement of December 1941: 'Australia looks to America, free of any pangs as to our traditional links and kinship with the United Kingdom.' For their part, Liberals point to Percy Spender's skill in achieving the Australia, New Zealand, America Security Treaty (ANZUS) 60 years ago as the turning-point in Australia's strategic policy. Both these accounts tend to overlook the fact that Australian governments in the 1950s and 1960s were dedicating their efforts to keeping both the British and the Americans engaged in South-East Asia. This was the central principle governing Australian diplomacy and Australia's military commitments. The troops sent to Malaya in the 1950s fought alongside forces from Britain, New Zealand, Fiji and what was then Rhodesia (now Zimbabwe). Their engagement in the Malayan Emergency was officially only their secondary role. Their primary role was as part of the Australian contribution to what was called the British Commonwealth Far East Strategic Reserve, intended to prepare for, and hopefully to deter, a major war with China or other communist forces. Similarly, the Australian commitment to Confrontation was fought entirely in a Commonwealth context, supporting Britain and Malaysia, with no US involvement.

This was consistent with Australia's willingness to provide testing grounds for British atomic weapons at Maralinga and elsewhere in the 1950s, amid talk of a new force in world politics: the 'fourth British Empire'.[2] Australians did not want the West to have to rely solely on the United States, even though it was far and away the most powerful nation in the world. Far better if Britain's strength and place at the top table of world powers could be restored, so that—all around the world, but especially in South-East Asia—Australia could call on support from two strong allies, not just one.

For a long time in the 1950s and early 1960s, leaders in British countries, which included Australia and New Zealand, liked to think that, while Washington had enormous power and dynamism, London had greater maturity and experience in handling international crises. For many years they recalled MacArthur's imprudent advance to the Yalu and that some leading Americans had flirted with the idea of using nuclear weapons during the Korean War and again at the time of the French defeat in Indochina in 1954. More than once during the Cold War crises of the 1950s, Australia joined Britain to urge caution on Washington in crises that might lead to a major war with China. In 1956 Prime Minister Menzies was highly critical of the policies of President Eisenhower, which undermined the Anglo-French and Israeli operation in the Suez crisis. But that crisis brought home to Menzies where the centre of international power now resided. In the following year he announced that Australian weapons platforms and systems would be standardised with those of the

---

2   See W. Reynolds, *Australia's Bid for the Atomic Bomb*, Melbourne University Press, Melbourne, 2000.

United States, not those of Britain. The transfer of primary allegiance from Britain to the United States in the 1950s and 1960s was gradual, incremental and in many ways reluctant.

One manifestation of Australia's desire to maintain a strategic association with both the United Kingdom and the United States was the frequent emphasis, in statements of Australian foreign and defence policy in the late 1950s and early 1960s, on SEATO—the Southeast Asia Treaty Organization, intended to be a regional equivalent to NATO—rather than on ANZUS. SEATO included Britain and the United States, as well as other powers within and outside the region, and offered the prospect that any Australian military operations in South-East Asia would be conducted under the leadership of a multinational coalition rather than unilateral US command. Although not often expressed publicly, Australian policy-makers held what we might call a MacArthur complex, which owed much to Korea in the 1950s. On the one hand, they were frightened that the United States would withdraw from a region that figured much more strongly in Australia's priorities than in those of the United States; on the other hand they were concerned that an all-powerful American commander might act in a way that was rash and unduly provocative towards such enemies as China. Australian governments also held great hopes that, through such structures as the SEATO Planning Office in Bangkok, they would gain access to the military plans of both London and Washington. So Australia kept reasserting the importance of SEATO, even as its numerous flaws made it increasingly implausible as a vehicle for diplomatic and military collaboration.

In the early 1960s, Australian policy-makers faced what they regarded as one of the most demanding challenges to their national security policies, as the political and military situations in both Indonesia and South Vietnam deteriorated rapidly. There were, to pursue the geometric metaphor, two strategic triangles that were far from congruent. Britain sought further support in Confrontation, describing Indonesia's President Sukarno as a Hitler-like expansionist dictator, while being extremely reluctant to become involved in supporting the United States in Vietnam. At the same time, the United States was urging Australia to apply only the minimum degree of force in Confrontation in order to avoid driving Sukarno further into the hands of the Chinese, while calling for Australia's support in what the United States saw as the crucial theatre of operations, Vietnam. Caught between these conflicting pressures from its two major allies, Australia developed a strategic policy that was, as the diplomats liked to say, refined but not defined by alliance considerations. Now, those Australian diplomats with a sense of history like to look back on Australian policy during Confrontation as one of the golden periods of Australian diplomacy, an example of world's best practice in a complex international environment.[3]

Not until April 1965, with the commitment of the first battalion of combat troops to Vietnam, did Australia become substantially involved in a war other than in close association with Britain. Even that followed hard on the heels of the commitment, just three months earlier, of another battalion of infantry, as well as Special Air Service (SAS) troops, to support the British Commonwealth effort in Borneo. In 1965 and 1966, Australia had forces committed to both conflicts. We think of the controversial national service scheme under which conscripts served in Vietnam as having been introduced solely for that war; but at the time of its introduction, policy-makers had Indonesia at least as much in mind as Vietnam, and a handful of national servicemen did, in fact, serve in Borneo or New Guinea.

All this is to say that we should not assume that the point of the strategic triangle occupied by Australia's chief ally can be identified as easily as at other times before and since. This was a period in which Australia sought to have two great allies for as long as possible, ending only in the early 1970s when Britain began its withdrawal from east of Suez, leaving Australia with just one great power ally in the region. The side of the strategic triangle that represents Australia's relationship with its allies is a decidedly complex story.

The side of the strategic triangle that represents Australia's perception of its major strategic threat was also more complex than it might have seemed. Historians and commentators have often recalled the melodramatic advertisements used in 1960s elections, with menacing arrows thrusting southward from China, and concluded that Australia had an irrational and excessive fear of 'Red China', as the People's Republic of China (PRC), recognised diplomatically by Britain but not by Australia or the United States until the 1970s, was widely called. This, too, is an oversimplification. The perceived threat was that of militant, expansionist communism. For some years the Soviet Union was seen as the principal inspiration and

---

3   See, for example, G. Woodard, 'Best practice in Australia's foreign policy: "Konfrontasi" (1963–66)', *Australian Journal of Political Science*, vol. 33, issue 1, 1998, pp. 85–99.

ideological driver of this threat; only later did China come to play this role. Policy-makers found it hard to understand the ramifications of the emerging Sino-Soviet split, as well as the extent to which either Moscow or Beijing was the force behind the numerous insurgencies and rebellions in South-East Asia. Some of these issues were highly contentious at the time, and to some extent remain so. There are still, for example, serious scholars who maintain that the hand of Moscow can be detected behind the simultaneous outbreak of insurgencies across the region in 1948.[4] Although there is general consensus that Australia, and other Western powers, greatly overestimated the extent to which Hanoi was acting as a proxy for the PRC, the role of the Soviet Union and China in the Vietnam War is still a matter of debate and continuing research.[5]

Many Australians in the 1960s were more concerned by the perceived threat from Sukarno's Indonesia than by developments on the South-East Asian mainland. There was a real fear, for example, that Sukarno might expand his Confrontation of Malaysia from the Borneo territories, not only westward to the Malayan Peninsula but also eastwards to New Guinea, where there was an almost indefensible land border between Indonesia's new acquisition of the western half of the island and the Australian-governed territories in the eastern half.

During the Korean War and for more than a decade afterwards, Australian policy-makers were struggling with some unusually complex strategic challenges. Normally accustomed to seeking assurance from one great ally, they were trying to deal with two. On the face of it, this should have been a source of strength, but the divergence of views and priorities between London and Washington made this more of a problem than a reassurance. At the other corner of the strategic triangle was the difficulty in clearly identifying the nature and origins of the threat. Were there one, two or numerous actual and potential challenges? To what extent were the insurgencies throughout South-East Asia dangerous manifestations of communist expansionism, driven by Moscow or Beijing or both? Were they essentially nationalist, anti-colonial rebellions to which Australians should show sympathy and support? Was Indonesia about to fall into

---

4   This was the theme of a paper given by Professor Jonathan Haslam of Cambridge University at a conference in Singapore in April 2010.
5   Lien-Hang T. Nguyen, *Hanoi's War: An International History of the War for Peace in Vietnam*, University of North Carolina Press, Chapel Hill, NC, 2012. See also the introduction to Xiao-Bing Li and R. Peters, *Voices from the Korean War: Personal Stories of American, Korean and Chinese Soldiers*, University of Kentucky Press, Lexington, KY, 2004.

the hands of a communist party aligned closely with Beijing, or was it a potential ally in the anti-communist cause? These and related issues reached crisis point in the mid-1960s. Eventually, following a complex series of events in which timing was all-important, Confrontation ended in 1966, while the Vietnam commitment escalated until it dominated not only Australia's foreign policy and strategic thinking but also its domestic politics in the late 1960s and early 1970s.

Just as the Singapore Strategy of the 1920s and 1930s came to a spectacular end with the fall of Singapore on 15 February 1942, so forward defence ended with the fall of Saigon on 30 April 1975. For years thereafter, forward defence, and anything that could rightly or wrongly be associated with it, was identified with an ignominious defeat and was discredited. In the late 1970s and early 1980s, Australia entered another period of strategic debate, comparable with the late 1940s and 1950s. Eventually a new strategic posture was developed: again seeking to resolve the tensions between global and regional emphases; again seeking to identify and prepare for the major strategic challenge that could be foreseen; and again seeking to manage our alliance and regional relationships to meet that challenge. Another cycle in the formation of Australian strategic policy had begun.

16

CHINA AND THE KOREAS
An Australian perspective

Rowan Callick

Politicians of every stripe try to uphold one common code: do not answer hypothetical questions. Journalists are a different breed. We thrive on the what-ifs that life throws up, so I guess I have to be prepared to accept the challenge. What is going to happen in the future on the Korean Peninsula, and in Korea's relations with China? And how is that likely to affect Australia?

On 28 September 2011, the then Prime Minister Julia Gillard delivered what was to me an impressive speech about a proposed white paper concerning Australia in the Asian century—impressive in its scope, ambition and realism. She said that instead of suffering as in past decades and centuries from the tyranny of distance, Australia is now benefiting from its proximity to the new centre of global economic gravity. She went on to say:

> While so much is new, many old tensions remain—and the classical world of inter-state rivalries never really went away. With no better example than the Korean Peninsula—where a republic whose friendship Australia greatly values prospers with a free future and [yet] remains threatened by its neighbour: a rogue state which is a threat to its near neighbours, to the region as whole— and to its own captive people above all.[1]

---

1   Asia Society, 'Australia PM Julia Gillard on Australia's role in Asia', 28 September 2011, asiasociety.org/australia-pm-julia-gillard-australias-role-asia.

Thus does the Republic of Korea (ROK) continue to be defined by a negative—by its relationship to its evil twin North Korea.

When the Lowy Institute, Australia's only internationally focused think tank, conducted its annual opinion poll in 2017, its section dedicated to the Korean Peninsula was, inevitably, about war. Previous Lowy Polls have indicated that North Korean heightened brinkmanship, the sinking of the South Korean corvette *Cheonan* in 2010 and the shelling of the South Korean island of Yeonpyeong made a considerable impression on Australian public opinion.

In this context, Australians were asked by the Lowy Institute in 2017: 'If North Korea invaded South Korea', could the involvement of Australian military forces be justified? By a small margin Australians were more likely not to support Australian military forces being committed to a conflict on the Korean Peninsula in this case (48 per cent), whereas 45 per cent of respondents were in favour of sending military forces. In the event that 'China initiated a military conflict with one of its neighbours over disputed island or territories', the Lowy Institute Poll found that 58 per cent of respondents were likely to oppose Australia's use of military force.[2] The poll also indicated that approximately 65 per cent of the Australian public believe that North Korea's nuclear program is the second highest threat to 'Australia's vital interests'.[3]

Asked by the Lowy Institute about their feelings towards various countries—on a scale with 100 degrees meaning very warm, 50 degrees lukewarm and zero degrees frozen—South Korea was awarded 60 degrees, Japan 71 degrees, USA 69 degrees, United Kingdom 81 degrees and New Zealand took out the top spot with 85 degrees. Towards the bottom came North Korea with a score of 30 degrees, Russia with 50 degrees and Indonesia scoring only 55 degrees.[4]

South Korea is Australia's fourth-largest trading partner and two-way trade between 2016 and 2017 amounted to $38.7 billion, making up 5.3 per cent of all Australia's international trade.[5] The ROK is the tenth largest importer of natural gas, and Australia is among the world's biggest

---

2   A. Oliver, '2017 Lowy Institute Poll', 21 June 2017, www.lowyinstitute.org/publications/2017-lowy-institute-poll.
3   Ibid.
4   Ibid.
5   Department of Foreign Affairs and Trade, 'Republic of Korea country brief', dfat.gov.au/geo/republic-of-korea/pages/republic-of-korea-south-korea-country-brief.aspx.

suppliers of natural gas.[6] The Abbott government (2013–15) presided over the signing of the Korea–Australia Free Trade Agreement (KAFTA), which came into force in December 2014.[7] There are a considerable number of Koreans in Australia: in the 2011 census there were 74,538 South Korean-born residents and 88,973 with Korean ancestry.[8]

Alison Carroll, the founding director of Melbourne-based Asialink Arts, has said: 'An energy is coming out of Korea that we in Australia just don't know about. When we send artists there—35 in recent years—they have a great time and come back enthusing. One video artist we sent never came back at all, and now represents Korea internationally.'

My newspaper, the *Australian*, ran a story in 2011 by our Tokyo-based correspondent for Japan and Korea, Rick Wallace, about the wave of Korean cultural exports, especially pop culture, which earned the country $3.8 billion that year. Cui Jian, China's most famous rock star, the Mick Jagger of the People's Republic, is famously of Korean descent. His father was a jazz musician. Cui told me in an interview that he cannot speak Korean, but at family occasions 'we party Korean style'. Yet the Korean language is taught in fewer than 50 schools across Australia, and not a single student studying Korean in his or her final year of high school comes from a non-ethnic Korean background.

It would appear that we are aware of the Korean War—that it is not, as has been said, 'a forgotten war fought in a forgotten country'. Indeed, we appear to be ready to help fight in another Korean war should it be triggered. And that is a pretty big commitment, just about the biggest that people can make. But for the rest, well, we just do not know that much about Korea, really.

China has, effectively, grabbed most of the space available for the engagement with Asia that Julia Gillard began in 2011. That year was the Australia–Korea Year of Friendship, employing the slogan 'celebrating mateship'. I would like to say something more positive about it, but I fear that it passed almost unnoticed by Australians. In his prime ministerial days, Kevin Rudd was an exception. He was the first foreign

---

6   'The World Factbook', Central Intelligence Agency, www.cia.gov/library/publications/resources/the-world-factbook/.
7   Department of Foreign Affairs and Trade, 'Republic of Korea country brief'.
8   Department of Home Affairs, 'Community Information Summary The Republic of (South) Korea-Born', www.homeaffairs.gov.au/mca/files/2016-cis-south-korea.pdf.

leader to publicly express condemnation of the sinking of the *Cheonan*. 'The international community,' he said, 'cannot let this act pass without an appropriate response.' But, of course, pass it did. And if the 'international community', whatever that might be, did indeed make a response, I would suggest that it was probably not appropriate.

Rudd, though, developed a close relationship with President Lee Myung-bak, forging links between what Rudd saw as two middle powers in the same region. Both countries joined the G20, Canberra's global summitry vehicle of choice. During a visit to Australia, Lee signed a security framework, only South Korea's second after its US alliance. The security relationship continues to grow as both countries deploy troops to the same theatres. Five Australian defence experts were among the team that confirmed it was a North Korean torpedo that sank the *Cheonan*, although they were not available to discuss their findings with the media here. For a while it looked as if our free-trade agreement negotiations with Seoul, although they started years after those with Beijing and Tokyo, would be completed first, but it was not until after the Abbott government came to power (in 2013) that KAFTA was signed.

John Walker, the chairman of the Macquarie Group in South Korea and probably Australia's leading business champion there, described the new Korea in 2011 as 'a powerhouse of global expansion'. Its construction companies, resource corporations and others are winning contracts and acquiring businesses in all markets, particularly emerging markets. However, he went on, 'there is a minimal Aussie corporate presence in Korea', and asked whether Korea was being 'confined by Australians to the status of a geopolitical relationship'. After Prime Minister Gillard's April 2011 visit to Korea, he said that she had covered a lot of ground, made a well-received visit to the scene of the battle at Kapyong, and did her best to link, rather than separate, geopolitical stability and commercial opportunities.

South Korea is setting itself up well, becoming the world's most wired country, with a good education system and an economy that was re-created following the Asian financial crisis of the late 1990s. For once it finds itself in a fortunate location, next to both China, the world's fastest growing economy, and Japan with its cashed-up innovative corporations more eager to go abroad than stay home. This is just as well, because South Korea has only modest physical resources. It will continue to buy substantial minerals and sources of energy, especially gas, from Australia.

Mutual investment should accelerate—provided Seoul does not tip the scales too much in favour of its local favourites, as was perceived to have happened over the ANZ Bank's failed 2010 bid for the Korea Exchange Bank.

But what about events above the 38th parallel?

North Korea is a place that raises a big question mark over Julia Gillard's remark in her 2011 speech that Australians are 'no longer subjects of the "tyranny of distance"': 'Asia has turned this on its head, giving us what the *Economist* has neatly termed "the advantage of adjacency". For the first time, we are closer to the fastest growing and most economically dynamic region of the world than our competitors.' Just take the Democratic People's Republic of Korea (DPRK) for example. Nowhere could be better positioned. A 1,400-kilometre border with the world's fastest-growing economy. A 240-kilometre border with the Republic of Korea, the thrusting new industrialised middle power. A 20-kilometre border with Russia, one of the world's great sources of resources and energy. And a mere paddle across from Japan, the world's third biggest economy.

Yet North Korea is an economic and human rights wreck. It is amazing to think that more than 50 years ago it was an oasis of comparative wealth, while South Koreans were strongly advised by the United Nations to look to Kenya as a model for development. How times have changed. North Korea's absolute failure to benefit from geographic advantage is unlikely to be transformed any time soon. We have seen too many false reformist dawns to believe that after his next magical mystery train tour through some of China's most successfully modernising provinces, Kim Jong-un will start to adopt an open-door strategy.

Russian scholar and Korean studies specialist Andrei Lankov worked at The Australian National University for seven years before shifting to Kookmin University in Seoul in 2004. In his book, *The Real North Korea: Life and Politics in the Failed Stalinist Utopia*, Lankov tried his hand at prediction, something he is not shy of:

> One cannot help but get a very dire picture of an insane dictatorship whose leaders enjoy a seemingly meaningless sabre-rattling while their subjects live under the constant threat of another murderous famine … 'Capitalism from below' has brought social stratification, but the new middle class (and, of course, the rich and powerful) can now afford items which were

unheard of in Kim Il Sung's time. However, the North Korean system has one major shortcoming—it cannot be reformed. The major obstacle is the existence of the rich South, and this is what makes any attempts at a managed transformation risky or even suicidal for the current elite.[9]

But Lankov is cynical about the effect of any improvements on the lot of North Korean citizens.

At the same time, less daily economic pressure might mean more time to think, talk and socialize for the North Korean citizens—and this is not good news for the regime ... people seldom start revolutions when they are desperate.

Thus the most rational survival strategy for the DPRK government is to change nothing. They will probably succeed at this task for a while. If Kim Jong-un ... wants to stay in power he has to follow three simple rules. First, to avoid Chinese-style reforms and liberalization; second, to continue the zero-tolerance policy against dissent (anybody who dares to criticize the government should be dead or in a prison camp in no time); third, to inhibit and, whenever possible, roll back the spontaneous growth of capitalist institutions ... The greater the gap between the North and its neighbours—above all South Korea—will become, the greater the potential for a future explosion is likely to be.[10]

Lankov is seriously concerned about the North Korean endgame going violent:

Another possible endgame trigger is the outbreak of serious factional infighting within the top leadership. But it seems that North Korean leaders have internalized the dictum of Benjamin Franklin, who famously said, 'Gentlemen, if we are not hanged together we will surely be hanged separately.'

The third possible scenario of the endgame is a spontaneous outbreak of popular discontent, a local riot quickly developing into a nationwide revolutionary movement—somewhat similar to what we have seen in 2011 in the Arab world. The fourth scenario

---

9   A. Lankov, *The Real North Korea: Life and Politics in the Failed Stalinist Utopia*, Oxford University Press, New York, 2013, p. 188.
10   Ibid., pp. 189, 190.

is contagion from some unrest in China—the only country where an outbreak of civilian disobedience or riot might produce some impact on North Korea.

There are few reasons to expect a North Korean revolution to be 'velvet' … It is located in the middle of a highly developed region, while its small size and long coastline make projection of force much easier. Last but not least, it has considerable nuclear stockpiles and a large WMD arsenal which no major international player would like to see unattended.[11]

Lankov concludes:

The widespread hope that the emergence of reformist groups will finally bring about a non-nuclear, non-threatening and developing North Korea seems to be wishful thinking. There are only two possible long-term outcomes: either a unification of Korea under the auspices of Seoul or a relatively stable China-controlled satellite regime—meaning that the division of Korea will become permanent.[12]

What might this mean for Australia? Canberra has attempted, from time to time, to play a minor role in the Great Game on the peninsula. Its lack of participation in the six-party talks has limited its options. The DPRK had an embassy in Canberra from 1974 to 1975, and again from 2002 to 2008, when it closed for financial reasons. Inevitably, there were a few bizarre incidents in this period, capped by the use in 2003 of the *Pong Su*, a North Korean freighter, to smuggle about 150 kilograms of heroin into Victoria. Four men were arrested, and one drowned bringing the heroin ashore. An official of the ruling Korean Workers' Party was on board. The ship tried to escape into international waters but was boarded by Special Operations forces via helicopter, and the vessel was later scuttled—after its radio had been removed and donated to the Kurrajong Radio Museum. All quite exciting, but ultimately inconclusive.

In 2008 Australia shifted its handling of North Korean matters from our embassy in Beijing to the one in Seoul. In 2011 AusAID budgeted A$5 million for humanitarian assistance, and Australia has stopped providing humanitarian aid to the DPRK through UN agencies as of

11   Ibid., p. 197.
12   Ibid., p. 202.

late 2017.[13] More recently, the then Prime Minister Malcom Turnbull described North Korea as 'one of the world's most "cunning, sophisticated criminals"'.[14]

China, Japan and the United States comprise Australia's first, second and third export markets, respectively. Any conflict in that region risks rocking Australia's continuing Asia-driven boom. But the world has run out of solutions. Kevin Rudd, when prime minister, lamented that North Korea 'does not respond to normal international diplomatic discourse'. Turnbull has ratcheted up the rhetoric against the DPRK to such an extent that he stated, 'whether it is arms, whether it is cyber-crime, whether it is drugs they are constantly raising money to finance their nuclear program'.[15]

Hong Lei, an acquaintance of mine who was the Chinese Foreign Ministry spokesman, said in a hand-wringing way after North Korea's shelling of the island of Yeonpyeong, 'We hope that the relevant parties will contribute their share to peace and stability on the Korean Peninsula'. In 2010 US President Barack Obama's Special Representative for North Korea Policy, Stephen Bosworth, urged the international community to join the United States in calling for Pyongyang to 'cease its provocative and irresponsible actions against its neighbour'. Victor Cha, a former US national security official, said that North Korea is 'the land of lousy options' for all involved. The United States, the country that Pyongyang most wishes to provoke into dealing with it directly, and China, North Korea's sole surviving ally and chief supplier of oil and other strategic resources, both appear, in relation to the DPRK, to be running on empty—except for hope.

Rudd said in 2010, 'It's very important for China to take an increasingly assertive role with North Korea'. Rudd was not on his own there. Beijing wished to extend its influence in the region, and especially in South Korea, which was for a decade becoming increasingly enmeshed with China, where among the expatriates there are more South Koreans than any other nationality.

---

13 Department of Foreign Affairs and Trade, 'Department of Foreign Affairs and Trade Annual: Report 2011–2012', webarchive.nla.gov.au/wayback/20190210114628/https://dfat.gov.au/about-us/publications/corporate/annual-reports/annual-report-2011-2012/pdf/DFAT_AR_2011-12.pdf.
14 L. Murdoch, 'Malcolm Turnbull calls North Korea "criminals", urges Hong Kong to help', *Sydney Morning Herald*, 12 November 2017, www.smh.com.au/politics/federal/malcolm-turnbull-calls-north-korea-criminals-urges-hong-kong-to-help-20171112-gzjp85.html.
15 Ibid.

16. CHINA AND THE KOREAS

When I visited North Korea a few years ago, it was hard to see any light at the end of the tunnel, despite the occasional store set up in tent-like kiosks, selling *bric-à-brac* from China. Despite the constant reminders of the brutal war of 1950–53, and despite the continuing militarisation of the country, they seemed to be starting to feel invulnerable. An official guide said to me as we drove, almost free of traffic because of the lack of petrol, past one of the many tank traps—massive concrete pillars alongside the ill-kept freeway between the capital and the border: 'There's no need for these tank traps any more, because now we have the nuclear bomb. We're safe and we're at peace.'

It is the peace of the grave, however. The skyline of Pyongyang is dominated by the pyramid-shaped, 105-storey Ryugyong Hotel building. Its brooding presence is like that of a Mayan temple mouldering in a jungle clearing, reminding travellers of lost empires and the transience of power. At night, there was scarcely a light to be seen in this city of 3 million. Electricity was available only sporadically. As a result, no one bothered even to try to acquire fridges, but they would hang around outside their blocks of flats, some of which reached 30 storeys or more, in the hope of being able to use the lift to get home sometime soon. In the second city, Hamhung, women washed clothes by hand on the rocks alongside a river flowing in front of their apartment blocks. In Pyongyang I saw trolley buses in which everyone, including the driver, was fast asleep, like the world of the Sleeping Beauty, as they waited for power to return so they could go home or get to work. It is all the fault of the Americans, I was told. Once the Americans leave South Korea, their compatriots will celebrate their freedom by inviting the Dear Leader—or the General, as he is more widely called—to rule them too.

When I arrived on an ancient Tupolev propeller plane, they took my mobile phone and kept it in a cabinet at the airport. The guide said it would be good to keep in touch by email; he explained that he was one of the privileged few with such access—but his address was shared by a dozen others, so everyone could read each other's mail. I met groups of young Chinese tourists there who said they were visiting to see how harsh life would have been for their parents in the bad old days before Deng declared, 'To get rich is glorious'. The renminbi is widely accepted as the de facto hard currency of North Korea.

As I flew out in mid-afternoon, the airport was being closed. Ours was the final flight of the day. As soon as we touched down back in Shenyang in north-eastern China, the mobile phones begin to beep and buzz as if making up for lost time. The massive, modern Shenyang airport was bustling with flights heading in every direction, all through the night.

These two places, which only a few decades ago seemed to speak the same language, are now poles apart in so many ways. Yet the failure of China to categorically step away from its support for the rogue state of North Korea serves to underline China's own failure to step away from its all-seeing, omnipotent Party, which steers what remains essentially a command economy. It is as if the Politburo Standing Committee cannot bear to risk being perceived as betraying the sacrifice of the 28-year-old Mao Anying, Mao Zedong's eldest and most loved son, who died in Korea in 1950 from a napalm bomb dropped by a South African Air Force A-26 bomber.

In general, Australians view China more as opportunity than as threat; everyone knows how important Chinese demand has been for our economy. The 2017 Lowy Institute poll showed that the vast majority of Australians see China as more of an economic partner (79 per cent) rather than a military threat (13 per cent). Interestingly, opinion is more evenly split on the question of whether or not China is likely to present a military threat in the next 20 years.[16] Professor Alan Dupont of Sydney University says that China ultimately wants 'to push the US into the central Pacific as far as possible', and Hugh White of The Australian National University has focused on the strains of no longer having our major economic partner also our main security partner for the first time in Australia's history.

In her 2011 speech Julia Gillard said that 'we are now seeing the most profound rebalancing of global wealth and power in the period since the United States emerged as a major power in the world'.[17] She gave, as an illustration of that shift, her view that the emerging and developing world could well become a net foreign investor, while developed countries become net foreign borrowers, as early as 2025. This view has only been reinforced since then.

---

16   Oliver, '2017 Lowy Institute Poll'.
17   Asia Society, 'Australia PM Julia Gillard on Australia's role in Asia'.

The fate of the Korean Peninsula within this shift must remain open: one half heading in one direction, engaging in an increasingly effective way with its neighbours, including Australia, if it can be counted as such; the other half remaining in mountain-clad feudal isolation—the whole a kind of fable of human progress, its possibilities and its failures, in one place. Convulsive change will probably come, in Korea as in China. But I am not predicting it will come any time soon, or if so, how.

William Shakespeare would have written, if he were alive today, about this big theme, this big story, with its continuing tragedies of divided families and lost warriors. As Macbeth reaches its conclusion, our hero—or rather anti-hero—recalls being told by the witches that he will be safe 'till Birnam Wood shall come' to his castle at Dunsinane, which of course transpires. I was reminded keenly of this when being told by a senior South Korean official of an early tentative negotiating session with DPRK cadres who had come south to Seoul. The leading North Korean remarked as the talks opened that he knew that the southerners had brought most of the cars in the south to Seoul specially to create an impression. The top South Korean negotiator responded that this was true, that their ruse had been rumbled. He added, 'What's more, we dragged all the skyscrapers in the country here too'.

CONCLUSION
Korea armistice and reflections for the twenty-first century

John Blaxland

All warfare is based on deception.
Sun Tzu

Open hostilities in the Korean War ended on 27 July 1953, more than six and a half decades ago. Yet strangely enough, the armistice that was signed ending open hostilities at that time remains the poignant symbol of an incomplete conclusion—of a war that retains a distinct possibility of resuming at short notice.

This incomplete conclusion has resulted in an armistice that has at times barely even held together across the Demilitarised Zone (DMZ) on the 38th parallel. North Korea's artillery shelling of Yeonpyeong Island in 2010, the sinking of the South Korean corvette *Cheonan* in the same year and North Korea's sabre-rattling nuclear testing in 2017 and 2018 highlights that despite the 2018 and 2019 presidential summits, there is considerable unfinished business and unresolved historical grievances on the Korean Peninsula.

The names of the leaders have changed and the character of the forces arrayed against each other have evolved over time. But the United Nations Command (UNC), to which Australia actively contributed forces, remains, and the United States Forces in Korea, alongside the Republic of Korea Armed Forces, have continued to practice military drills, just in case. Indeed, Australia has been an active participant in recent years, with Vice Admiral Stuart Maher being appointed Deputy Commander of the

UNC in mid-2019. The Korean Peninsula continues to be the nexus of strategic rivalries in the highly contested region of north-east Asia, which includes Russia, China, the United States, Japan and both Koreas. The unification of the Korean Peninsula remains unlikely while North Korea continues to be supported by China and the South is supported by the United States. Moreover, north-east Asia has historically seen a significant number of Great Power clashes. From the Japanese seaborne invasions of Korea during the sixteenth century, to the Boxer Rebellion, the Russo-Japanese War of 1905 and up to the present, north-east Asia has been a highly contested theatre of great powers.

The Australian Government actively supports and advocates for the UN sanctions on North Korea spanning from restrictions on banking and trade, scientific cooperation and travel to a ban on the provision of arms or weaponry. Former Foreign Minister Julie Bishop asserted the government's conviction that UN sanctions would work when she stated in August 2017 that 'UN sanctions will have a significant impact on North Korea's economy and its ability to fund these illegal weapons programs'.[1] In the supercharged environment of deception on the Korean Peninsula, the Kim dynasty and the North Korean elite's primary objective appears to be to ensure the survival of the regime. Understanding how it came to this requires some considerable reflection on the Korean War and its legacy. This book has set out to provide some important context, particularly for Australia, as it seeks to understand the dynamics at work on the Korean Peninsula.

So what did Australia contribute to the Korean War from June 1950 to July 1953? What were the Australians doing there? How significant was their contribution? What difference did it make; what has that meant for Australia since then; and what might that mean for Australia at the end of the second decade of the twenty-first century? From a contemporary perspective, it is imperative to interrogate Australia's interests in north-east Asia and ask whether, in light of these interests, Australia would take part in a future conflict on the peninsula. In addition, what role would Australia play in a potential conflict, and does the Australian Defence Force have sufficient capabilities? This historical reflection has sought to go some way to help answer these questions.

---

1   A. Remeikis and D. Wroe, 'Julie Bishop places faith and hope in sanctions as North Korean tensions escalate', *Sydney Morning Herald*, 30 August 2017, www.smh.com.au/politics/federal/julie-bishop-places-faith-and-hope-in-sanctions-as-north-korean-tensions-escalate-20170830-gy6vhp.html.

Australians in postwar Japan

We have seen that as the Korean War broke out on 25 June 1950, the Australian-led British Commonwealth Occupation Force (BCOF), headquartered in Kure, Japan, was preparing to pack up and close down in anticipation of the completion of postwar rehabilitation and the handover from the US-led occupying forces to the people of Japan.

The BCOF presence had shrunk considerably from the 40,000-strong group that had deployed to Japan in early 1946. But the anticipated resistance to the occupation failed to materialise, and BCOF quickly shrank to a considerably smaller force—one predominantly operated by Australians. Australia remained engaged in large part to ensure that its concerns about a possible military resurgence of Japan did not materialise, to influence the postwar treaty arrangements with Japan, to encourage continued US engagement in the region and to bolster ties with its wartime ally, the United States, with whom a treaty alliance had not yet been concluded.

Australia's air force contribution

As Richard Hallion and Jack McCaffrie point out in chapters 6 and 7, respectively, Australia had a squadron of Royal Australian Air Force (RAAF) fighter aircraft still based at Iwakuni, ships of the RAN still operating in and around Japan and a battalion of infantry combat soldiers, the 3rd Battalion, Royal Australian Regiment (3RAR), as well as support elements.

Elements of the RAAF's No. 77 Squadron were quick to deploy, flying ground attack missions and bomber escorts missions from Iwakuni in support of the United States Air Force (USAF). Before long, the squadron relocated to Korea, operating from a succession of airfields providing and conducting a range of missions in support of ground forces. In Chapter 6 Hallion explains how, with the early introduction into the conflict of Soviet-sourced MiG jet aircraft in support of the North Korean forces, the Mustangs proved obsolete.

In time, the Mustangs were replaced by the Meteor—a British-sourced twin-engine jet aircraft, with considerably greater power but less manoeuvrability then the Soviet MiGs or the US F-86 Sabre aircraft used by the USAF. With Sabres in short supply and Meteors the only viable option, Hallion observes, the RAAF had to adjust the spectrum of missions it could viably undertake. Sabres would become the mainstay of the RAAF's fighter aircraft fleet once they became available after the Korean War.

The experience of working closely with the USAF and other British Commonwealth air force elements played an important role in shaping the post–Second World War RAAF into a professional and advanced air force in the jet age. One clear lesson was for the RAAF to seek to be equipped with the most advanced technology fighter aircraft that money could buy. By and large, that meant equipping the RAAF with US-sourced aircraft or at least aircraft produced by close US allies (such as Britain's Canberra bomber, first ordered in 1950, and the French Mirage fighter jets, ordered in 1960 to replace the Sabres and later F111s and F/A-18s). Indeed, that mindset has persisted in the RAAF, with the RAAF's inventory today being dominated by US-sourced aircraft and related technology.

Australia's naval contribution

For the Royal Australian Navy (RAN), the Korean War marked continuity and change. Drawing on skills and procedures for interoperability refined during the Second World War, the RAN was quick to deploy ships in support of the US-led and UN-mandated fight against the North Koreans. In doing so, the RAN maintained two warships on station throughout the war, starting with HMAS *Shoalhaven*, an Australian-built frigate launched in 1944, tasked with conducting patrols and escorting duties in the Yellow Sea alongside other British Commonwealth forces commanded by a British rear admiral. A month later, HMAS *Bataan*, an Australian-built destroyer commissioned in 1945, was involved in a naval bombardment near the site of the Inchon landings. The RAN participated alongside RN and later USN task groups in a way that consolidated the imperatives for a professional RAN to be maintained for operations alongside allies.

In Chapter 7 McCaffrie explains that change came with the establishment of the RAN Fleet Air Arm in 1948 and following the purchase of HMAS *Melbourne* and HMAS *Sydney*, both of which were light aircraft carriers. HMAS *Sydney* was received by the RAN in 1949 and deployed upon request to Korean waters in 1951, replacing Britain's HMS *Glory*, which had been on operations in Korean waters up to that point. *Sydney* operated on the more restricted waters off Korea's west coast and maintained a high tempo of operations over the four months of its deployment in late 1951 and early 1952, despite maintenance and deck crews operating at times in severely inclement conditions. It returned to Australia early in 1952, and thereafter Australia maintained two warships on station until well after the armistice was signed. In the end, some 4,500 RAN personnel served on operations in Korean waters, with five killed and six wounded, but the RAN did not again send an aircraft carrier to fight in the Korean War.

The RAN after Korea

The RAN's Fleet Air Arm would continue after the war, but there was fluctuating government enthusiasm for maintaining a strong aircraft carrier-based offensive military capability. Arguably, the air operations conducted over Korea provided an inadequate return on investment. Operational aircraft carriers are costly capabilities to maintain, and governments like to see a clear and prominent return on their investment, particularly in coalition settings. Enthusiasm ebbed as the technology involved became more complex and expensive and the national defence strategy shifted from forward defence to the defence of Australia. With a shift away from supporting fixed-wing operations far from Australian shores, the last of the two aircraft carriers, HMAS *Melbourne*, was decommissioned by 1982, leaving the RAN with no carriers from which to conduct fixed-wing operations. Ironically, it was the Falklands War in 1982 that sealed the fate of the RAN, as the aircraft carrier Australia had planned to acquire from Britain, HMS *Invincible*, was withdrawn from sale due to its proven utility and importance for the success of Britain's campaign to retake the Falkland Islands. Australia overlooked the significance of such capabilities for force projection. Indeed, I would argue, Australia is a middle power that tends to act with small power pretensions and as a result has shied away from seeking to maintain the ability to project force in such an overt way in and beyond its immediate neighbourhood.

In recent years, however, Australian governments have recognised that an island nation requires some self-reliant force projection capabilities. The East Timor crisis in 1999, in addition to other earlier crises in the Pacific, brought this message home particularly clearly. Subsequently, the RAN has commissioned HMAS *Canberra* and HMAS *Adelaide*.

These ships are categorised as Landing Helicopter Dock ships (LHDs) rather than aircraft carriers, even though their flight decks are larger than those found on HMAS *Sydney* or HMAS *Melbourne* and are in fact designed to take fixed-wing aircraft. Still, the prospect of fixed-wing aircraft operating from these new ships remains remote, although unattended fixed-wing platforms (drones) are already in the mix.

The new amphibious configuration, focused on helicopters and the ability to carry and offload stores and equipment across shorelines, supported by drones, reflects a shift in the Australian approach, which emphasises a closer integration of Australian land, air and maritime capabilities as a joint force. It is unlikely but not inconceivable that an Australian naval task group could once more deploy to zones of conflict, as was the case during the Korean War, so the RAN maintains a suite of warfighting capabilities that echo those employed during the Korean War. But it is perhaps with ground forces that the enduring parallels and the significance of the Korean War can be more clearly be seen.

Land forces in Korea

Back in June 1950, 3RAR remained the last Australian land combat force stationed with BCOF in Japan. It was an infantry unit with equipment from the Second World War and with reduced personnel, having its numbers thinned in anticipation of an imminent return to Australia. But under dynamic and forceful leadership, under Lieutenant Colonel Charles Green, 3RAR was quick to deploy and played a prominent part within the 27th British Commonwealth Brigade as part of General MacArthur's UN Command.

The contribution of one infantry battalion was a very much smaller contribution than Australia had mustered at the height of the Second World War, when Australia fielded 14 divisions. In March 1952, Australia's contribution to the Korean War expanded to include two infantry battalions and supporting elements that formed the nucleus of the 28th British Commonwealth Brigade; command of the brigade passed from British to Australian leadership. This composite brigade was part of the 1st Commonwealth Division, which included the Canadian 25th Brigade and the British 29th Brigade. The postwar Australian approach would focus on deploying smaller and more professional forces.

The significance of Australia's contribution, alongside that of Britain, Canada and New Zealand, went beyond the actual units involved. In fact, the influence of these English-speaking countries was disproportionate to their contribution, with the British Commonwealth forces able to bargain collectively with their US counterparts to gain favourable standing for the Commonwealth forces in the war.

Australian troops consolidated their professional reputation for the operations undertaken during the more fluid stages of the war in 1950 and into 1951, playing a leading role in the advance to and subsequent retreat from the Yalu River, and in consolidating the defensive line along what would eventually become the DMZ between North and South Korea. 3RAR played a leading role at the Battle of Kapyong in late April 1951, alongside the Canadian 2PPCLI and other elements of the 27th Brigade, including artillery support from the New Zealand gunners, a US armoured unit, and British command and control support, with British combat troops in reserve. As we have seen, the Battle of Kapyong was the first time the so-called 'five eyes' countries (Australia, New Zealand, Canada, the United States and United Kingdom) had operated together in the one land combat formation. It would not be their last, but it set the tone for more than half a century of close collaboration, cross-examination and sharing of experiences and burdens as part of what has come to be known as the ABCANZ partnership between the armies (and marine forces) of the five countries.

After the Battle of Kapyong, the designations shifted and Australia's two infantry battalions and supporting elements were redesignated to be part of the 28th Brigade. They fought in the Battle of Maryang San, described by the official historian of Australia's involvement, Robert O'Neill, as 'Australia's finest feat of arms in the Korean War'. The chapters that discuss this battle, especially Chapter 10 by Bob Breen and Chapter 12 by William Purves, are some of the most illuminating in the book.

Korean War legacies for Australia

Reflecting on the legacy of the Korean War for Australia, a number of points can be made. First, Australia's prompt contribution of air and land forces as well as naval assets to the US-led counter offensive under General MacArthur proved to be a significant turning point. Until then, the United States had been unwilling to engage with Australia in the formulation of a mutual security treaty. Thereafter, the United States took a different approach, welcoming the signing of the Australia, New Zealand, United States Security Treaty (ANZUS). The Australian External Affairs Minister at the time, Percy Spender, deserves credit for ensuring that Australia's contribution was made early and prominently.

Second, the experience working with the United States under a UN mandate helped to consolidate the place and standing of the United Nations at a time when the world was polarised between the so-called 'First World' aligned with the United States and the 'Second World' of communist countries as the two sought to compete and contest against each other over parts of the so-called 'Third World'. The legacy of the failed interwar League of Nations left many concerned that the United Nations would be stillborn. The Korean War demonstrated that, under the right circumstances, the United Nations could act decisively.

Third, as Peter Edwards points out in Chapter 15, Australia's participation in the Southeast Asia Treaty Organization (SEATO) from 1956 onwards and its contribution of forces to the Vietnam War from 1962 onwards were further manifestations of the mindset that was confirmed by the experience in the Korean War; that is, Australia would seek to bolster security institutions and arrangements that were linked with the United States and that helped encourage the United States to remain engaged in Australia's neighbourhood. This was widely understood by Australian government officials as being the best and most economical way of bolstering the stability and security and, in turn, the prosperity of Australia and its neighbourhood. More recently, the Australian Government has been highly supportive of the expansion and intensification of relations between the Association of South East Asian Nations and the United States during the Obama administration because it was seen as way of further embedding and consolidating US interest and engagement with east and South-East Asia. Historically, Australia has considered it beneficial to its own security when the United States is engaged and interested in the Asia-Pacific region.

Fourth, the Australian armed services, now known as the Australian Defence Force (ADF), have come to place considerable emphasis on the benefits that accrue from close engagement with their US and other close counterparts. Experience working intimately alongside others has helped to hone the ADF and to ensure access to the latest and best military technology. That has been seen as crucial for a small, boutique ADF, with niche but highly capable forces able to deploy rapidly and confidently, near or far.

That approach of emphasising interoperability has been largely maintained by successive Australian governments in recent years, with Australia seeking to make a substantive military contribution to military campaigns in Afghanistan, then Iraq, then Afghanistan again, and then Iraq again. This has been in part at least intended to burnish Australia's credentials with the United States while also mindful of the need to address transnational security concerns emanating from the Middle East that have had a spill-over effect in Australia and its neighbourhood. This engagement has come at a cost in terms of Australia's ability to engage constructively and consistently with its regional security partners nearby. The situation in the Middle East will undoubtedly continue to fester, but closer to home significant security challenges have arisen in places such as Marawi, in the Philippines, which have reminded the ADF to focus on relationships and capabilities required for security challenges closer to home.

Looking ahead

At the time of publication, there is a strange sense of *plus ça change, plus c'est la même chose* (the more things change, the more they stay the same) when it comes to the prospect of war on the Korean Peninsula. While no one expects a possible outbreak of conflict on the Korean Peninsula to resemble the nature of the Korean War from 1950 to 1953, Australians should nonetheless be mindful of the lessons from that experience and of the fact that the future is unknowable. Australia remains under obligations as a party to the UNC and the ceasefire arrangements.

In particular, Australia is one of seven countries (originally 16 in 1953) that is still committed to the UNC Military Armistice Commission, along with Canada, New Zealand, the Philippines, Thailand, the United Kingdom and the United States. Under the current Status of Forces Agreement in place with Japan, an RAAF group captain is currently assigned to the United Nations Command-Rear as the commander of the joint Yokota Air Base as part of the UNC logistics arm and Australia's Vice Admiral Stuart Maher is the UNC Deputy Commander. This is a functioning reminder of the Korean War. Australia also still maintains liaison officers with the UNC in Tokyo, an important and enduring point that 'symbols [are] important in diplomacy'.[2] Australian security scholar and former diplomat Andrew Selth has argued that the limited number of Australian personnel would 'be automatically associated' with any substantial action taken by the UNC.[3] In addition, even though 'Australia's residual connections with the UNC are largely nominal', it is difficult to conceive of a situation in which, if US troops were attacked in South Korea, that Australia, as a formal treaty ally, would not be asked to assist.[4]

President Donald Trump's summits with Kim Jong Un are not entirely unprecedented in terms of the foreign policy of the peninsula since the end of the war in 1953. Indeed, during the leadership of Kim Jong Un's father and grandfather, periods of intense brinksmanship and rivalry often de-escalated slightly at the prospect of more talks or financial/political incentives being offered by the United States. One example of this de-escalation tendency occurred with South Korean President Kim Dae-jung's adoption of the Sunshine Policy in 1998, which was intended to facilitate engagement with the DPRK through closer economic and social cooperation. North Korea even obtained two light water nuclear reactors from the United States in 1994, under the US–DPRK Agreed Framework, and received multimillion dollar assistance for dismantling a cooling tower at the Yongbyon Nuclear Scientific Research Centre. Incentives such as these were not enough to stop the DPRK from continuing to test nuclear weapons and walking out on the Fifth Round of Six Party Talks in 2009.

Australia today has become the United States' closest and most trusted ally in the Indo-Pacific region. The ties are broad, deep and strong. Australian forces are more compatible and interoperable with their US counterparts than ever before. Indeed, Australian forces have conducted military exercises in recent years alongside US and ROK counterparts. These factors combined suggest that should a conflict arise on the Korean Peninsula, the lessons of Australia's experience in Korea from more than 65 years ago might well have a particular and important resonance for its armed forces in a contemporary context.

---

2   A. Selth, 'Australia and the Republic of Korea: Still allies or just good friends?', Griffith Asia Institute, Griffith University, 2018, p. 10, www.griffith.edu.au/__data/assets/pdf_file/0023/424364/Selth-Korea-paper-final.pdf.
3   Ibid., p. 10.
4   Ibid., p. 10.

APPENDIX

Table 1: Comparative UN coalition air effort, by mission area and sorties, 1950–53

Mission area	United States		Coalition partners		Mission effort	
	USN–USMC	USAF	Air forces	Naval forces	Sorties	Percentage
Interdiction	126,874	192,581	15,359	12,500*	347,314*	29.67
Close air support	65,748	57,665	6,063	5,500*	134,976*	11.53
Counter air sorties	44,607	79,928	3,025	2,500*	130,060*	11.11
Reconnaissance	26,757	60,971	[?]	2,000*	89,728*	7.68
Maritime patrol—anti-submarine warfare	11,856	—	1,647	1,500*	15,003*	1.28
Strategic bombing	—	994	—	—	994	0.08
Cargo/troop lift	Unknown	181,659	9,0784	—	190,737*	16.29
Miscellaneous	24,852	222,078	13,848	1,000*	261,778*	22.36
Totals by component	300,694*	795,876	49,020*	25,000*	1,170,590*	(100.00)
Totals by US/coalition	1,096,570 est.		74,020*		1,170,590*	(100.00)
				Total UN coalition sorties		1,170,590*

* Estimated

Table 2: Total coalition sorties by air forces

Air Force	Sorties
United States Air Force	796,876
Royal Australian Air Force	18,872
South African Air Force	12,610
Republic of Korea Air Force	10,475*
Royal Hellenic Air Force	2,916
Royal Thai Air Force	2,500*
Royal Air Force	1,647

* Estimated

INDEX

38th parallel 16, 25, 32, 36, 51, 58, 66, 68–72, 78, 87, 88, 236, 246, 293, 301
Acheson, US Secretary of State Dean Gooderham 34, 126
ANZUS (Australia, New Zealand, United States Security Treaty) 6, 7, 14, 20, 27, 88, 95, 283, 285, 308
Apple Orchard (battle) 186
Australian Army
    1st Battalion, Royal Australian Regiment (1RAR) 168, 181, 190, 192
    2nd Battalion, Royal Australian Regiment (2RAR) 18, 90, 163, 173, 177, 178, 179, 180, 190, 203, 250–56
    3rd Battalion, Royal Australian Regiment (3RAR) 17, 18, 28, 36, 40, 73, 87, 88, 93–95, 146, 163, 168–71, 173–74, 177–79, 181, 182, 184, 186–88, 198, 205–15, 217–41, 250, 251, 257, 258, 303, 306, 307
    1st Heavy Brigade 172
Australian Army Nursing Service (AANS) 201, 263, 264, 269
Australian Government 6, 7, 16, 20, 39, 44, 95, 160, 165, 166, 167, 280, 283, 285, 291, 292, 302, 305, 306, 309

Australia, New Zealand, United States Security Treaty *see* ANZUS

B-29 (bomber) 83, 128, 129, 133, 140
Boulder City 249, 252, 254–56, 258
Boxer Rebellion 31, 302
Bridgeford, Lieutenant General William 171
Bridges, Major General Sir William Throsby 165–66
British Army
    1st Battalion Argyll and Sutherland Highlanders (the Argylls) 199, 236–37
    1st Battalion Black Watch 235, 248
    1st Battalion Duke of Wellington's Regiment (the Dukes) 241, 249
    1st Battalion Durham Light Infantry (the Durhams) 173, 250
    1st Battalion King's Own Scottish Borderers (the King's Own, or the KOSBs) 208, 209–10, 215, 217–26, 231–33, 235, 237, 239–41
    1st Battalion Middlesex Regiment (the Diehards) 236–37
    1st Battalion Royal Fusiliers 173, 250

1st Battalion Royal
  Northumberland Fusiliers
  (RNF, or the Fusiliers) 209,
  211, 213, 217, 218, 220,
  225–32, 237, 239, 250
27th British Commonwealth
  Brigade 36, 40, 41, 73, 93,
  168, 169, 170, 236, 237,
  306, 307
28th British Commonwealth
  Brigade 10, 11, 40, 163, 165,
  168, 171, 172, 173, 174, 176,
  177, 179, 181, 207, 214, 218,
  220–23, 226, 229–33, 237,
  249, 250, 306, 307
29th British Infantry Brigade 74,
  171, 173, 174, 176, 177, 209,
  237, 248, 306
1st Commonwealth Division 90,
  94, 171, 173, 233, 245–48,
  254, 256, 306
British Commonwealth General
  Hospital (BCGH) 259, 260,
  261, 267
British Commonwealth Occupation
  Force (BCOF) 146, 167, 170,
  185, 271, 303, 306
Broken Bridge (battle) 186

Canada 7, 8, 9, 13, 16, 35, 36, 157,
  307, 309
Canadian Army 9, 188
  2nd Battalion, Princess Patricia's
    Canadian Light Infantry 95,
    188, 237, 307
  25th Canadian Infantry Brigade
    8, 171, 173–74, 177,
    249, 306
Cassels, Major General James 94,
  171–72, 173, 208, 237, 242
ceasefire 12, 19, 29, 40, 45, 78, 257,
  275, 309
Chiang Kai-shek 5, 31, 69
China, *see* People's Republic of China

Chinese People's Volunteer Force
  (CPVF) 61, 64, 65–66, 68–84,
  122, 132–36, 138–39, 141
Cho Man-sik 51
Chosin 68, 122, 137, 262
Chosin Reservoir (battle) 67–68,
  122, 137
Christianity 13, 51, 53
Clark, Admiral Joseph James 137–38,
  139
Clark, General Mark 109, 110, 111,
  112, 137, 138, 139
Coad, Brigadier Basil Aubrey 40, 93,
  94, 236
Cold War 1, 4, 30, 33, 36, 62–64,
  85, 97, 109, 110, 115, 279, 282,
  284
Cooper, Sergeant Brian Charles 178,
  253–56
Cooper, Corporal Kevin Joseph 90
Corsair (aircraft) 125, 129, 130, 133,
  136, 187

Democratic People's Republic of
  Korea (DPRK) 1, 3, 9, 13, 15, 20,
  21, 22, 29, 54, 55, 58, 125, 293,
  294, 295, 296, 299, 310
Duntroon 172, 173, 184, 190, 207,
  208

Eisenhower, Dwight D. 46, 111–13,
  284

Far East Strategic Reserve 284
Farrar-Hockley, Sir Anthony 8
Ferguson, Lieutenant Colonel Ian
  Bruce 88, 169, 171
Firefly (aircraft) 120, 144–45,148,
  151–52, 155
Fusen 137

Gerke, Major Jack 207, 210, 212,
  213, 223–26
Gillard, Julia 289, 291, 292, 293, 298

Green Finger 90, 250, 252, 254
Green, Lieutenant Colonel Charles Hercules 88, 90–91, 94, 169, 171, 306
Guomindang (GMD), *see* Kuomintang (KMT)

Han River 69, 152, 153
Hassett, General Sir Francis 169, 181, 198, 206, 207–15, 220–21, 223–25, 230–33
Hill 119, *see* Boulder City
Hill 146, *see* the Hook
Hill 217 209, 211, 218, 226–32, 239
Hill 317, *see* Maryang San
Hill 355, *see* Kowang San
Hinge, the 20, 211, 213–14, 218, 226, 229, 231, 232, 239, 240, 243
HMAS *Bataan* 8, 89, 146, 168, 304
HMAS *Cerberus* 144
HMAS *Murchison* 39
HMAS *Shoalhaven* 8, 146, 147, 168, 304
HMAS *Sydney* (III) 5, 8, 13, 39, 120, 143, 144–45, 148–60, 168, 304, 306
HMAS *Tobruk* 145
HMAS *Warramunga* 147
HMNZS *Pukaki* 8
HMNZS *Tutira* 8
HMS *Amethyst* 153
HMS *Belfast* 153
HMS *Glory* 145, 148, 153, 304
HMS *Illustrious* 145
HMS *Theseus* 145
HMS *Vengeance* 159
Hook, the (battle) 19, 90, 174, 176–80, 190, 202, 205, 245–58, 275
Hungnam 122, 153

Imjin River 17, 177, 217, 223, 226, 237, 238, 245, 247, 251
Imjin River (battle) 17, 177, 217, 223, 237, 238, 245, 247
Inchon 13, 36, 57, 58, 66, 70, 122, 132, 236, 304

Jamestown Line 174, 233, 246, 258, 275
Japan 1, 22, 31, 32, 51, 64, 88, 141, 166, 241, 256, 270–71, 280, 290–93, 296, 302, 303
  forces based in 15, 33, 35, 88, 89, 109, 110, 124, 146, 147, 158, 167–78, 185, 186, 200, 259–60, 262–64, 267, 303, 306
  occupation of Korea 13, 32, 50, 51
Japanese Army 51, 80, 129, 281

Kaesong 37, 78
Kapyong (battle) 2, 7, 37, 40, 88, 94, 95, 164, 168, 169, 187, 188, 205, 212, 237, 245, 246, 258, 292, 307
Kim Il Sung 13, 32–33, 36, 38, 46, 51–54, 57, 59, 88, 132, 294
Kim Jong-un 293, 294, 310
Kim Ku 50
Korea Military Advisory Group (KMAG) 41, 56, 99–108, 110, 113, 114
Korea Strait 15
Korean Force (K Force) 5, 92, 186, 207, 264–65, 270
Korean Provisional Government (KPG) 50
Koreans Attached Commonwealth Division (KATCOM) 45
Kosong 135
Kowang San 17, 42, 174, 190, 192–93, 208, 209, 212, 217–34, 238

Kuomintang (KMT) 4, 50, 61, 63, 64, 69
Kyosen 138

Langdon, Private Keith 92, 95
Lawrence (née Crocker), Sister Betty 261–62, 264–66
League of Nations 30, 32, 47, 308

Macarthur, General Douglas 3, 26, 33, 35–37, 61, 66, 71, 77, 87, 89, 132–33, 146, 166, 167–68, 170, 171, 284, 285, 306, 307
MacDonald, Lieutenant Colonel Arthur 163, 174, 175, 182, 208, 219, 225, 232–33
Manchuria 32, 64, 121, 133, 136, 141
Mao Zedong 3, 4, 17, 31, 62–64, 66, 68, 70–73, 76, 77, 78, 80, 83, 84, 85, 122, 134, 135, 142, 298
Maryang San (battle), see Operation Commando 2, 7, 17, 18, 40, 92–93, 168, 181, 188, 205–15, 217–34, 235–44, 245, 250n1, 258, 307
McCarthy, Captain Perditta Marjorie 201, 263, 271
McGibbon, Ian 8
McNamara, Robert Strange 2
Menzies, Robert 34, 88, 279, 283, 284
Meteor F.8 jet 11, 43, 119, 125, 129, 141, 303, 304
Middle East 15, 33, 34, 43, 47, 88, 146, 160, 166, 185, 281, 282, 309
MiG 15 fighter 15, 43, 83, 119, 122–29, 133–42, 147, 303
Munsan 135, 138
Mustang, P-51 (F-51) (fighter) 42, 43, 83, 89, 125, 126, 129, 141, 168, 303

napalm 132, 137, 187, 236, 258, 298
NATO (North Atlantic Treaty Organization) 33, 35, 43, 89, 112, 147, 282, 285
New Zealand 6, 8, 19, 21, 27, 34, 35, 36, 38, 88, 146, 167, 170, 171, 173, 174, 197, 205, 212, 215, 225, 233, 238, 252, 253, 254, 256, 257, 283, 284, 290, 307, 308, 309
   16th Field Regiment, Royal New Zealand Artillery 89, 95, 197, 254
North Atlantic Treaty Organization (NATO), see NATO
North Korean People's Army (NKPA) 64, 68–76, 121, 122, 131, 132, 134, 135, 138, 139, 141, 246
North Korean People's Army Air Force (NKPAAF) 121, 124, 127, 130

O'Brien, Private Denis 92, 95
O'Daniel, Lieutenant General John 94, 171–72
O'Dowd, Major Ben 91–95
Operation Athenaeum 153
Operation Commando 188, 189, 192, 198, 207, 209, 217, 220, 224, 229, 232, 233, 246, 247
Operation Strangle 136, 150

Paik Sun-yup, General 61, 56
Pak Hon-yong 51, 53, 54
Pakchon (battle) 236
Panmunjom 37, 78, 154, 179, 251, 256, 276
Panther, F9F (aircraft) 124, 128–29
Peach, Major Stuart 25
Pears, Lieutenant Maurice Bertram 208, 210, 213, 223, 226
Pembroke, Lieutenant Arthur Thomas 208, 213

Peng Dehuai, General 64–66, 68, 70–76, 83, 85, 132–34, 136
People's Liberation Army (PLA) 14, 18, 55, 58, 61, 62, 63, 69, 73, 77, 80, 82, 122, 123
People's Liberation Army Air Force (PLAAF) 123, 127
People's Republic of China (PRC) 2, 13, 20, 22, 31, 35–37, 40, 45, 52, 58, 61–85, 138, 236, 281, 284, 286–87, 289–99, 302
Plimsoll, James 44
Purves, Second Lieutenant William 200, 219, 242–43
Pusan 106, 107, 132, 147, 186, 236
Pusan Perimeter 29, 55, 122, 130, 131
Pyongyang 53, 58, 66, 131, 132, 136, 138, 236, 297

Rankin, Squadron Leader Ronald 25
Republic of China (ROC) 31
Republic of Korea (ROK) 1, 5, 9, 10, 12, 13, 20, 21, 22, 29, 33, 45, 52, 53, 54, 55, 125, 126, 130, 139, 140, 290, 310
Republic of Korea Army 14–15, 51, 55, 56–57, 58, 65, 69–70, 73, 74, 79, 95, 97–115, 153–54
Rhee, President Syngman 32, 33, 36, 44, 50, 59, 98–101, 107, 113, 126
Ridgway, Lieutenant General Matthew 37, 69, 70, 77, 98–100, 104, 106, 107, 109, 135, 137, 141
Robertson, Lieutenant General Horace 170–71
Robertson, Sergeant Ian 91
Rowell, Lieutenant General Sir Sydney 88, 163
Royal Australian Air Force (RAAF) 5, 8, 11, 43, 119, 125, 129, 141, 144, 166, 262, 263, 282, 303, 304, 308

No. 77 Squadron 11, 33, 42–43, 89, 129, 141, 146, 168, 170, 303
Royal Australian Air Force Nursing Service (RAAFNS) 202, 260
Royal Australian Army Nursing Corps (RAANC) 260, 261, 262, 264, 265, 267, 268, 269, 271, 272
Royal Australian Navy (RAN) 5, 8, 39, 120, 143–44, 146–48, 151, 157–60, 166, 168, 303–06
20th Carrier Air Group 143, 145
805 Squadron 145, 148
808 Squadron 145, 148
817 Squadron 145, 148
Fleet Air Arm 8, 120, 143–44, 148, 159–60, 304–05
Rudd, Kevin 291–92, 296
Russo-Japanese War 32, 302

Sabre, F-86 (fighter) 43, 122, 126–28, 135, 139–40, 303–04
Samichon 18–19, 90, 177, 245–58
Samichon (battle) 18–19, 90, 177, 245–58
Saunders, Captain Reginald 91, 95
Sea Fury (aircraft) 120, 144–45, 148, 155, 158
Sea of Japan 15, 147
SEATO (Southeast Asia Treaty Organization) 181, 285, 308
Seoul 52, 53, 54, 89, 109, 152, 262, 292, 293, 295, 299
 Chinese offensive on 13, 19, 26, 33, 37, 56, 69, 78, 164, 205, 246, 258
 defence of and recapture 17, 36, 54–55, 57, 58, 68, 71, 74, 77, 129, 206
Shelton, Major Jim 209, 212, 225
Smart, Brigadier General Jacob Edward 137–38
South African Air Force 141, 298

Southeast Asia Treaty Organization, *see* SEATO
Soviet air force, *see* Voenno-Vozdushnye Sily (VVS)
Speakman, Private Bill 199
Spender, Percy 34, 42–43, 88, 95, 146, 283, 308
Spring Offensive 71–77, 85
Stalin, Joseph 31, 33, 47, 54–55, 63, 68, 71, 82, 83, 125, 126, 133, 142
Strout, Squadron Leader Graham 89

Taiwan 3, 31, 45, 46, 61, 63, 64, 67, 84
Taiwan Strait 64
Taylor, Brigadier George 207–10, 213–15, 218, 229, 233, 239
Taylor, General Maxwell 114, 181
Thompson, Major Dulcie 259, 261, 267
Triangle Hill (battle) 79
Truman, Harry S. 3, 33–37, 42, 43, 44, 46, 64, 71, 110, 111
Trump, Donald 1, 310
Turkish Brigade 69, 88, 89, 177, 249, 254

Uijongbu 74, 236
Union of Soviet Socialist Republics, *see* USSR
United Nations 4, 5, 15, 30–33, 35, 44, 47, 52, 61, 122, 123, 135, 141, 187, 246, 293, 308
United Nations Command (UNC) 35, 36, 37, 38, 40, 42, 45, 58, 150, 154, 157, 246, 247, 248, 258, 301–02, 309–10
United Nations Security Council (UNSC) 3, 13, 25, 30–33
United States Air Force (USAF) 10, 42, 57, 121–42, 147, 303, 304
United States Army
  1st Cavalry Division 65, 69
  24th Division 69, 73–74, 94
  25th Division 73–74, 249, 254
  Eighth Army 56, 69–71, 95, 98, 103–05, 107, 110–11, 114, 132–33, 135, 137, 139, 181, 208
  I Corps 65, 73–74, 76, 94, 103, 246–47
  IX Corps 73
  X Corps 58, 73–74, 114, 132–33, 247
United States Government 55, 98, 109, 110, 112
United States Marine Corps (USMC) 10, 18, 122, 126, 129–30, 133–34, 137, 138
  1st Marine Division 58, 67–68, 73, 90, 95, 177–79, 245, 247, 249
  7th Marine Regiment 90, 177, 247, 249
USN (US Navy) Task Force 77 126, 128–30, 133, 136, 139
USS *Bandoeng Strait* 150
USS *Essex* 124
USS *New Jersey* 152
USS *Rendova* 150
USS *Sicily* 130
USSR (Union of Soviet Socialist Republics) 3, 21, 43, 63

Van Fleet, Lieutenant General James A. 14, 75, 97–111, 114, 137, 139, 141
Voenno-Vozdushnye Sily (VVS) 15, 82, 121, 123, 126–29, 133, 140

Walker, Corporal Ron 253–55
Walker, General Walton Harris 107, 135
Walsh, Lieutenant Colonel Floyd Stanley 171
Washington, Sister Betty 202
Wells, Lieutenant General Henry 163, 171

West Point Military Academy 107
West, Major General Michael
    Montgomerie Alston Roberts 40,
    173, 175–76, 177, 179, 248–49,
    258
Wilton, Brigadier John 10–11, 40,
    163, 165–82, 250, 257
Wonsan 58, 132, 136, 152

Yalu River 3, 36, 65, 82, 129, 132,
    133, 135, 137, 140, 205, 236,
    284, 307
Yellow Sea 15, 31, 38, 150, 304

www.ingramcontent.com/pod-product-compliance
Lightning Source LLC
Chambersburg PA
CBHW050925240426
43668CB00021B/2433